From Deliberation to Demonstration

Political Rallies in France, 1868–1939

Paula Cossart

Translated by Clare Tame

© Paula Cossart 2013

© With the kind authorisation of the Presses Universitaires de Rennes

First published by the ECPR Press in 2013

Book cover: Jean Béraud, "Réunion publique à la salle Graffard", 1884. © Fabius Frères.

The ECPR Press is the publishing imprint of the European Consortium for Political Research (ECPR), a scholarly association, which supports and encourages the training, research and cross-national co-operation of political scientists in institutions throughout Europe and beyond.

ECPR Press
University of Essex
Wivenhoe Park
Colchester
CO4 3SQ
UK

All rights reserved. No part of this book may be reprinted or reproduced or utilised in any form or by any electronic, mechanical, or other means, now known or hereafter invented, including photocopying and recording, or in any information storage or retrieval system, without permission in writing from the publishers.

Typeset by ECPR Press

Printed and bound by Lightning Source

British Library Cataloguing in Publication Data

A catalogue record for this book is available from the British Library

ISBN: 978-1-907-301-46-9

eBook ISBN: 978-1-907-301-76-6

www.ecpr.eu/ecprpress

"The rhetoric of acknowledgments requires a paean here to spouse and child. Lacking both, I want to offer thanks to my family and friends, to whom I owe nearly all happiness in my life"
(Joshua Miller)

Among them, this book is dedicated to my mother, Claudina Cossart, and to my translator, Clare Tame. For their work, courage and indestructible support. The three of us managed to build a great and friendly team.

Paula Cossart
August 2013

Series Editors:
Dario Castiglione (University of Exeter)
Peter Kennealy (European University Institute)
Alexandra Segerberg (Stockholm University)
Peter Triantafillou (Roskilde University)

ECPR Essays:

Hans Kelsen and the Case for Democracy (ISBN: 9781907301247) Sandrine Baume

Is Democracy a Lost Cause? Paradoxes of an Imperfect Invention (ISBN: 9781907301247) Alfio Mastropaolo

Just Democracy (ISBN: 9781907301148) Philippe Van Parijs

Maestri of Political Science (ISBN: 9781907301193) Donatella Campus, Gianfranco Pasquino, and Martin Bull

Masters of Political Science (ISBN: 9780955820335) Donatella Campus, and Gianfranco Pasquino

ECPR Classics:

Beyond the Nation State: (ISBN: 9780955248870) Ernst Haas

Comparative Politics: The Problem of Equivalence (ISBN: 9781907301414) Jan W. van Deth

Citizens, Elections, Parties: Approaches to the Comparative Study of the Processes of Development (ISBN: 9780955248887) Stein Rokkan

Democracy: Political Finance and state Funding for Parties (ISBN: 9780955248801) Jack Lively

Electoral Change: Responses to Evolving Social and Attitudinal Structures in Western Countries (ISBN: 9780955820311) Mark Franklin, Thomas Mackie, and Henry Valen

Elite and Specialized Interviewing (ISBN: 9780954796679) Lewis Anthony Dexter

Identity, Competition and Electoral Availability: The Stabilisation of European Electorates 1885–1985 (ISBN: 9780955248832) Peter Mair and Stefano Bartolini

Individualism (ISBN: 9780954796662) Steven Lukes

Modern Social Policies in Britain and Sweden: From Relief to Income Maintenance (ISBN: 9781907301001) Hugh Heclo

Parties and Party Systems: A Framework for Analysis (ISBN: 9780954796617) Giovanni Sartori

Party Identification and Beyond: Representations of Voting and Party Competition (ISBN: 9780955820342) Ian Budge, Ivor Crewe, and Dennis Farlie

People, States and Fear: An Agenda for International Security Studies in the Post-Cold War Era (ISBN: 9780955248818) Barry Buzan

Political Elites: (ISBN: 9780954796600) Geraint Parry

State Formation, Parties and Democracy (ISBN: 9781907301179) Hans Daalder

Territory and Power in the UK: (ISBN: 9780955248863) James Bulpitt

The State Tradition in Western Europe: A Study of an Idea and Institution (ISBN: 9780955820359) Kenneth Dyson

Please visit www.ecpr.eu/ecprpress for up-to-date information about new publications.

Contents

List of Figures vi

Introduction 1

Returning to the History of Assemblies 19

PART I: CONSOLIDATING REPRESENTATIVE DEMOCRACY

Chapter One: The Ideal of Participation Without Action 35

Chapter Two: Public Opinion and Consensus on the Common Good 71

Chapter Three: The Assembly at the Heart of the Electoral Process 101

PART II: SETBACKS IN REPUBLICAN PEDAGOGY

Chapter Four: Making a People of Citizens 145

Chapter Five: Resistance to the Civilisation of Political Mores 177

PART III: WHEN A SHOW OF FORCE THREATENS FREEDOM OF ASSEMBLY

Chapter Six: The Political Rally as a Party Showcase 217

Chapter Seven: The Political Assembly in Danger 245

Conclusion 277

Bibliography 281

Sources 301

Index 307

List of Figures

Figure 1.1: 'The election period. A club of women. Miss Astié de Valsayre on the platform', *L'Illustration*, 23 September 1889 — 56

Figure 3.1: 'An electoral assembly in the Triat Gymnasium in Paris', *L'Illustration*, 15 May 1869 — 102

Figure 3.2: 'The elections. Electoral assembly hold on 12 November in the old quarries of Puteaux. [...] Sketch by M. Provost', *L'Illustration*, 20 November 1869 — 127

Figure 4.1: 'Paris. A public assembly in the Theatre of the Prince Imperial. According to a sketch by M. Pignard', *L'Illustration*, 13 March 1869 — 162

Figure 5.1: 'The meeting of the Ligue des Patriotes', *L'Illustration*, 1 October 1898 — 207

Figure 6.1: *L'Humanité*, 9 April 1938 (left); *Le Populaire*, 27 November 1938 (right) — 221

Figure 7.1: 'The guard on foot and on horseback dispersing taxpayers at the end of their meeting', *L'Illustration*, 4 February 1933 — 252

Figure 7.2: Camelots du Roi guaranteeing order in an assembly of the Action française (top); Jeunesses Patriotes protecting the platform during an assembly of the Ligue républicaine nationale (bottom). *L'Illustration*, 21 July 1934 — 257

Figure 7.3: 'In Paris, around the Parc des Princes, where the communist meeting is being held, the police charged the counter-demonstrators of the Parti Social Français' (top). 'In London, the police charge fascists as well as counter-demonstrators'. *L'Illustration*, 10 October 1936 — 275

Introduction

C'était hier samedi jour de paye
Et le soleil se levait sur nos fronts;
J'avais déjà vidé plus d'un' bouteille
Si bien qu'jamais j'm'avais trouvé si rond.
V'là la bourgeois' qui rapplique devant l'zingue:
"Brigand, qu'ell'dit, t'as donc lâché l'turbin!"
Oui que j'réponds, car je vais au métingue,
Au grand métingu' du Métropolitain!

Les citoyens dans un élan sublime,
Étaient venus guidés par la raison.
À la porte, on donnait vingt-cinq centimes,
Pour soutenir les grèves de Vierzon.
Bref, à part quat'municipaux qui chlinguent
Et trois sergots déguisés en pékins,
J'ai jamais vu de plus chouette métingue
Que le métingu' du Métropolitain!

Y avait Basly, le mineur indomptable,
Camélinat, *l'orgueille* du pays…
Ils sont grimpés tous deux sur un' table,
Pour mettre la question sur le tapis.
Mais tout à coup on entend du bastringue,
C'est un mouchard qui veut faire le malin,
Il est venu pour troubler le métingue,
Le grand métingu' du Métropolitain!

Moi, j'tomb' dessus, et pendant qu'il proteste,
D'un grand coup d'poing j'y renfonc' son chapeau;
Il déguerpit sans demander son reste,
En faisant signe aux quat'municipaux;
À la faveur de c'que j'étais brind'zingue
On m'a conduit jusqu'au poste voisin…
Et c'est comm'ça qu'a fini le métingue,
Le grand métingu' du Métropolitain!

Some people may still remember the words of one of Maurice Mac-Nab's most famous satirical songs. Mac-Nab was an emblematic figure at the Montmartre cabaret Le Chat Noir. The song was written in 1887 after an assembly organised at the Cirque d'Hiver by the radical party to discuss the construction of the metropolitan railway in Paris — an assembly raided by anarchists and Blanquists.[1] I recall the song here to give you a glimpse of the sort of political life I had in mind when I decided to take a look at assemblies held at the end of the nineteenth and early twentieth centuries.

How can we get individuals to participate in political life beyond the mere act of voting? Can there be a more active form of popular sovereignty without there being a risk for public order? What forms of participation would this entail? What means are there to allow other forms of democratic expression to complement the vote without the risk of competing with political representation? At the end of the nineteenth century, in reply to these questions, political assembly was the main form of participation encouraged by republicans. It was seen as the best way to get the masses to participate without undermining representative government, through the creation and expression of public opinion. This book is devoted to this aspect of the republican enterprise of defining public space. It arises from a fascination with a period of French history when little was spoken about disinterest in politics, where people did not hesitate to devote time to discussing political issues, a period when citizens thought that politics could change things.

This golden era of assemblies is quite different from the end of the twentieth century when, even during important electoral contests, the public of political meetings is basically made up of activists of the organising parties.[2] Today, gathering together in a political rally is the political activity of a minority[3] — even if the last presidential elections in France in 2012 saw a renewal of interest in electoral rallies.[4] In the period of the enquiry, the popular passion with assemblies was such that, in the big cities, attending one was a commonplace way to spend an evening, and not only during electoral campaigns. This was a period when Aristide Bruant, another famous *chansonnier* at the Chat Noir, sang: 'I go to all the meetings, I never'd miss an assembly' to the tune of 'la Carmagnole'.[5] The

---

1. Maurice Mac-Nab, 'Au grand métingu' du Métropolitain!', *Poèmes mobiles*, Paris, Atelier des Brisants, 2002, pp. 129–131.

2. For further information about the meetings held for municipal elections, see: Daniel Gaxie and Patrick Lehingue, *Enjeux municipaux. La constitution des enjeux politiques dans une élection municipale*, Paris, PUF, 1984.

3. In the 1989 European elections, only 3 per cent of electors took part in an assembly, the same percentage as for party membership. Russell J. Dalton, *Citizen Politics. Public Opinion and Political Parties in Advanced Industrial Democracies*, New York, Chatham House, Seven Bridges Press, 2002, pp. 39–43.

4. See, for instance, Paula Cossart, 'À quoi servent les meetings dans une campagne électorale?', *Mediapart*, 23 February 2012; Paula Cossart, '2012, la guerre des meetings de plein air', *Atlantico*, 15 April 2012.

5. The song is called 'Pus d'patrons'. Aristide Bruant, *Dans la Rue. Chansons et monologues*, vol. 2, Paris, A. Bruant, 1895.

meetings were then much more numerous than today, and the public filling the halls was incomparably larger. Today it is not unusual to hear the organisers of a 'school hall assembly' happy to have gathered a few hundred people; a century ago, political actors would hesitate to hold a political rally for such a limited public. To describe the first decades of the Third Republic, Michelle Perrot speaks of a 'frenzy of public assemblies', and compares it with the 'weariness [that such meetings] encounter today'.[6]

The atmosphere of meetings has also changed with the disappearance of contradictory assemblies, where political adversaries met face to face before a divided and animated public. The change was also the result of the widespread use of microphones and loudspeakers which drown out the sound of interventions, protests and interruptions from the floor. In parallel, what Jean-Jacques Courtine described as a 'rhetorical education in vocal strength which made the meeting resemble a spoken opera' became obsolete.[7] Finally, the mediatisation of political life has transformed the nature of meetings which have largely become 'televised messages' made with a view to transmitting selected extracts.[8] Starting this study, I was not stimulated by a particular interest in the type of political rallies that I had the opportunity to attend; it was more of a fascination with the spirit of the '*grand métingu*' du Métropolitain'.

Nevertheless, it is contemporary concerns that guide me in the analysis of assemblies in the past. Since the end of the 1980s observations and analyses on the crisis of representation currently affecting France and other Western democracies have multiplied.[9] Recurrent descriptions of this disaffection with voting and the decline of political commitment and union membership, contrast sharply with reports of Paris at a time when, before voting day, half the electors had attended an assembly.[10] Given my curiosity for political assemblies at the end of the nineteenth and early twentieth centuries, I wanted to have a better understanding of this massive participation in a form of political activity which, nowadays, meets with a disinterest symptomatic of the contemporary disaffection for conventional political participation in general.

---

6. Michelle Perrot, *Les ouvriers en grève. France, 1871–1890*, Paris, Mouton, 1973, vol. 2, p. 589.
7. Jean-Jacques Courtine, 'Les glissements du spectacle politique', *Esprit*, 1990, vol. 9, p. 158.
8. Yves Pourcher, '"Un homme une rose à la main". Meetings en Languedoc de 1985 à 1989', *Terrain*, 1990, vol. 15, p. 90.
9. For different perspectives, see: Pierre Rosanvallon, 'Malaise dans la représentation', in Furet, Julliard and Rosanvallon (eds), *La République du centre. La fin de l'exception française*, Paris, Calmann-Lévy, 1989, pp. 133–182; Bernard Lacroix, 'La "crise de la démocratie représentative en France". Éléments pour une discussion sociologique du problème', *Scalpel*, 1994, vol. 1, pp. 6–29; Marcel Gauchet and Philippe Raynaud, 'La République enlisée', *Le Banquet*, 1995, vol. 6, pp. 174–188.
10. 'According to the police, 170,000 Parisians (out of 350,000 registered voters) attended "meetings" during the electoral period of August 1893'. Michel Offerlé, *Un homme, une voix? Histoire du suffrage universel*, Paris, Gallimard, 1993, p. 90.

If the state of contemporary political life has stimulated my interest in the assemblies of the past and prompted my questions, it is above all because of a reflection on the possible virtues of deliberation in democracy which has developed over the last twenty years, notably in reaction to the current crisis of Western representative government. When I began my analysis, not only was there an increasing amount of research on participatory or deliberative democracy, but outside the academic sphere, there were also concrete experiences in the use of deliberative devices. What these experiences have in common is being concentrated around the proclaimed goal of intensifying or extending citizens' political participation through the collective discussion of public issues.[11] In examining assemblies held over a century before the advent of this type of research and experience, I wanted to study the republican idea that deliberation among assembled citizens could effectively complement representative democratic institutions.

In France freedom of assembly experienced three important episodes of liberalisation which correspond to the first three French Republics. It was affirmed in 1881 by the law of 30 June which is still valid today. Under the other governments, with the exception of the short experience of the Commune, this right was either inexistent or only subsisted within a very tight framework, making it a major republican demand. Each time that the need to grant citizens a right of assembly was defended by the republicans it was in the name of reinforcing the institutions of representative democracy. What justifies the fact of giving citizens the opportunity to meet together to discuss politics is the idea that popular participation in democracy extends beyond voting. The assembly – an organised and static event held in a place which is distinct from the public street, where citizens come to give and to hear speeches, and to exchange ideas – is considered the ideal way to reinforce democracy as it makes the masses participate by mixing public opinion and representation. In the last three decades of the nineteenth century freedom of assembly was presented as the best device to complement and accompany the vote. This was because the republicans believed in the virtues of deliberation. Deliberation would permit people to form a reasoned opinion taking into account the common good whilst steering individuals towards an apprenticeship of citizenship. It is impossible not to draw a parallel with the arguments put forward today in favour of deliberative democracy. Indeed, I rediscover an almost identical discourse among many public actors and in an important current of contemporary political philosophy.[12]

---

11. If there are deliberative devices which are barely participatory, and participatory procedures which are barely deliberative, the democratic forms developing today often tend to emphasise both these dimensions, making the distinction between participatory and deliberative democracy quite relative, see: Loïc Blondiaux, 'Prendre au sérieux l'idéal délibératif: un programme de recherche', *Swiss Political Science Review*, 2004, vol. 10, (4), pp. 158–169.

12. See, in particular, Julien Talpin, 'Des écoles de démocratie? Formation à la citoyenneté et démocratie participative', 2005, http://www.univ-paris8.fr/scpo/talpin.doc (accessed 6 June 2006).

Under the Third Republic, the contradictory assembly, that is, the assembly as a place for debate between participants, is regularly presented as a feature of French political life. Contemporary commentators affirm with insistence that it is not found in Britain or the United States. At first sight this is surprising since France seems to be characterised — in comparison with the Anglo-Saxon world and Northern Europe — by 'a lesser cultural attachment to the virtues of deliberation': the 'valorisation of contradictory debate' is less present in France today, even if, as Loïc Blondiaux reminds us, it had once been 'at the heart of the parliamentary ideal'.[13] The importance of deliberation for the founders of the Republic in the United States is well-known.[14] However, since the mid-nineteenth century electoral campaigns are well and truly marked by the organisation of large partisan meetings by each political group. Support is brought from outside to swell the public and people are attracted by non-political elements (concerts, food and drink, balloon trips, etc.); and the partisan press contests the numbers present at their meetings and at those of their adversaries.[15] In nineteenth-century America Richard Jensen compares the parties to armed rivals at 'monster meetings'.[16] Jon Lawrence demonstrates that for Britain until the introduction of secret voting with the 1872 Ballot Act, an electoral assembly where voting is by a show of hands, is a place of contradiction; rival candidates present their programmes to a challenging public, they submit themselves to questioning and uproar often ensues. But these assemblies progressively give way to meetings organised for a candidate.[17] In France, the contradictory assembly has long been the form of assembly closest to the republican ideal of a place where individuals gather to debate together and to learn citizenship values.

In attempting to identify the political culture of the early Third Republic, James R. Lehning affirms that republicanism has a double venture: 'the creation of institutions allowing popular participation' and 'the creation, through the transformative powers of the Republic, of the citizens who would participate in these institutions'.[18] In observing assemblies in the closing years of the Second

---

13. Loïc Blondiaux, *Le nouvel esprit de la démocratie. Actualité de la démocratie participative*, Paris, Seuil, 'République des idées', 2008, p. 43. Blondiaux is referring to J.-P. Heurtin, *L'espace public parlementaire. Essai sur les raisons du législateur*, Paris, PUF, 1999.
14. Joseph M. Bessette, *The Mild Voice of Reason. Deliberative Democracy and the American National Government*, Chicago, Chicago University Press, 1997.
15. Glenn C. Altschuler and Stuart M. Blumin, 'Limits of Political Engagement in Antebellum America. A New Look at the Golden Age of Participatory Democracy', *The Journal of American History*, 1997, vol. 84, pp. 855–885.
16. Richard Jensen, 'Armies, Admen and Crusaders. Types of Presidential Election Campaigns', *The History Teacher*, 1969, vol. 2, (2) p. 36. My thanks go to Dafnah Strauss for having provided the references for many works on this issue.
17. John Lawrence, *Electing Our Masters. The Hustings in British Politics from Hogarth to Blair*, Oxford, Oxford University Press, 2009.
18. James R. Lehning, *To Be a Citizen. The Political Culture of the Early French Third Republic*, Ithaca, Cornell University Press, 2001, p. 9.

Empire and under the Third Republic, I want to help highlight how we arrive at the definition of a legitimate public space and the delimitation of boundaries of an acceptable political conduct in a republican democracy. I also want to analyse how the republicans intended to shape the political behaviour of citizens so as to guarantee government stability. This is a question of understanding exactly how the assembly constitutes one of the elements in articulating an emerging representative democracy. In exploring the issue of public sphere in the Republic, I have focussed part of this research on the end of the Empire. First, because the political assembly took shape partly in the period 1868–1870 when a law voted on 6 June 1868, albeit not very liberal, permitted many meetings to be held. Furthermore, the republicans had already developed their discourse on the virtues of freedom of assembly under the Empire. Without closing an eye to this important period or previous experiences of assemblies, the analysis does not focus on the Commune, but on the periods when assemblies of citizens could become commonplace. I want to observe the diffusion in the society, the assimilation by political mores and the potential routinisation of this form of participation.

Promoting public opinion

The establishment of republican institutions took place alongside the development of a body of theories about the crowd, particularly influenced by social psychology. These take 'the advent of the crowd or the masses as new social subjects as a gift, and try to describe how they functioned'.[19] The important developments in crowd psychology only occurred at the end of the century, but it was 'shortly after the 1870 war that [it] appears in France'.[20] Susanna Barrows demonstrates how approaches as diverse as those of Taine, Sighele, Tarde or Le Bon resemble each other in their claim to scientific methods and in their 'nearly always terrifying' vision of the crowd. Moreover, Barrows argues that crowd psychologists were fully aware of the negative aspects of political and social conduct in France at the time. The fear of the crowd was shared by part of the political class of republicans when they came to power, and the will to define suitable modes of mass participation in public life was by no means unrelated to this concern. The convergence between fear of the crowd and the republican will to transform individuals into a People which could support the government, has already been noted, particularly by Olivier Bosc:

---

19. Pierre Rosanvallon, *Le peuple introuvable. Histoire de la représentation démocratique en France*, Paris, Gallimard, 1998, p. 109. On crowd psychology, see: Robert A. Nye, *The Origins of Crowd Psychology. Gustave Le Bon and the Crisis of Mass Democracy in the Third Republic*, London, Sage, 1975; Serge Moscovici, *L'âge des foules. Un traité historique de psychologie des masses*, Paris, Fayard, 1981; Susanna Barrows, *Distorting Mirrors: Visions of the Crowd in Late Nineteenth-century France*, New Haven, Yale University Press, 1981; Jaap Van Ginneken, *Crowds, Psychology, and Politics, 1871–1899*, Cambridge, Cambridge University Press, 1992.

20. Barrows, *Distorting Mirrors*, p. 10.

The conservatives [...] need the crowd to forget the People, whereas republicans need the People to forget the crowd. This is why in the republican programme, republican institutions, the school, the army, we find many devices to achieve the transformation of the crowd, this badly-defined group, this community related to dangerous social classes, in the People, an organic group composed of autonomous citizens capable of guaranteeing the democratic regime by its existence.[21]

The memory of revolutionary agitation, particularly the Commune, is also present. Thus the question of how to 'associate the figure of the People, without mobilising the suspect strength of the crowd',[22] arises with particular acuity.

Dominique Reynié has described the basically legislative process of circumscribing public space which, even if not limited to this period, remains characteristic of the creation of the institutions of representative democracy in the last decades of the nineteenth century.[23] What is certain is that it is the need to justify the government that acknowledged participation of the masses as necessary: it was encouraged because 'it appeared likely to provide [...] reasons to abide by the new authority'.[24] But the concern to guarantee public order also plays a role. The aim of republican mass politics was to preserve public decision-making from the excessive influence of crowds in defining the boundaries of public sphere. This largely depends on the promotion of public opinion as a 'positive element of the collectivity'.[25] Until the end of the nineteenth century, the most dangerous form of public gathering was considered to be the spontaneous gathering in a public place. Alongside a ban, what appeared necessary in order to avoid these unstructured gatherings was to grant some right of framed assembly. In Reynié's words: 'From the perspective of public order, the solution is not a summary and drastic ban. It is a ban accompanied by authorisations'.[26] This is the context where the assembly is conceived as an ideal form of collective participation of the People in public affairs. Assemblies must thus be held in a defined place and not on the public street: 'As long as the legislator will not authorise a public space *de jure*, the public place will be *de facto* the political space'. For this reason the *locus* of participation had to be shifted from public *place* to public *space,* and the nature of participation transformed from *action* to *opinion.* The two operations are linked. Citizens' assemblies must help promote this collective abstraction of 'public

---

21. Olivier Bosc, *La foule criminelle. Positivisme, politique et criminologie en Italie et en France à la fin du XIXe siècle. Scipio Sighele (1868–1913) et l'école lombrosienne*, PhD dissertation, Paris IX, 2001, p. 272.
22. Olivier Ihl, *La fête républicaine*, Paris, Gallimard, 1996, p. 17.
23. Dominique Reynié, *Le triomphe de l'opinion publique. L'espace public français du XIXe au XXe siècle*, Paris, Odile Jacob, 1998.
24. Reynié, *Le triomphe de l'opinion publique*, p. 86.
25. This expression is used by Pierre Rosanvallon to interpret the development of opinion polls. See: Rosanvallon, *Le peuple introuvable*, p. 340.
26. Here and below, Reynié, *Le triomphe de l'opinion publique*, p. 52.

opinion', and respond to the republican ideal of popular participation without jeopardising public order.[27]

For republicans in the last three decades of the nineteenth century the public opinion that should emerge from assemblies is not divided. It is naturally unified because it is based on reason, tends to the common good and avoids conflicts. Indeed, it is heir to a notion of public opinion prevailing in the eighteenth century.[28] The opposition between public opinion generated by an elite and general, popular opinion, which existed on the eve of the French Revolution, has been highlighted particularly in the wake of Habermas' seminal work.[29] 'Public opinion erected in sovereign authority, […] is necessarily stable, one, and based on reason', stresses Roger Chartier. 'It is thus the opposite of popular opinion, multiple, versatile, with its prejudices and passions'.[30] If it extends beyond the elite to all citizens, public opinion promoted by the republicans in the last three decades of the nineteenth century is certainly not the popular opinion of the previous century. Indeed, it differs because it is seen as the outcome of discussion based on reason. To depict it one can use the words employed to describe the notion of public opinion in the second half of the eighteenth century: 'rational, impersonal, unitary: […] the depoliticised image of a consensus based on reason'.[31] But the body of those who constitute this public opinion had by then expanded to take in all citizen-electors. What follows is a period of transition between public opinion as authorised opinion formed by discussion between an elite of educated citizens, and public opinion as we now understand it, and that Patrick Champagne characterises as follows:

> This direct and spontaneous opinion does not have the same features as that of the political elite, which is, in principle, the result of a specific political task. It

---

27. By republican ideal model or project I mean a body of ideas largely shared with respect to the form taken by political life and which serves as a framework of interpretation; I do not claim that the republican ideology is an entrenched system of thought or perfectly homogeneous, see: Sudhir Hazareesingh, *Intellectual Founders of the Republic. Five Studies in Nineteenth Century French Political Thought*, Oxford, Oxford University Press, 2001, pp. 1–21.

28. On the history of the concept of public opinion, see: John A. W. Gunn, 'Public Opinion' in Terence Ball, James Farr and Russell Hanson (eds), *Political Innovation and Conceptual Change*, Cambridge, Cambridge University Press, 1989, pp. 247–265; Patrick Champagne, *Faire l'opinion. Le nouveau jeu politique*, Paris, Éditions de Minuit, 1990, pp. 41–86; Loïc Blondiaux, *La fabrique de l'opinion*, Paris, Seuil, 1998; and Javier Fernández Sebastián and Joëlle Chassin (eds), *L'avènement de l'opinion publique. Europe et Amérique, XVIIe–XIXe siècles*, Paris, L'Harmattan, 2004.

29. Jürgen Habermas, *The Structural Transformation of the Public Sphere: An Inquiry into a Category of Bourgeois Society*, Cambridge, Polity [1962] 1989.

30. Roger Chartier, *Les origines culturelles de la Révolution française*, Paris, Seuil, 1990, p. 41. See also: Raymonde Monnier, *L'espace public démocratique. Essai sur l'opinion à Paris de la Révolution au Directoire*, Paris, Kimé, 1994; and Jon Cowans, *To Speak for the People. Public Opinion and the Problem of Legitimacy in the French Revolution*, New York/London, Routledge, 2001.

31. Keith Michael Baker, *Inventing the French Revolution: Essays on French Political Culture in the Eighteenth Century*, Cambridge, Cambridge University Press, 1990, p. 372.

is less a reasoned opinion achieved after considerations, than of deeply-rooted prejudices, or a borrowed opinion, barely restrained, hardly internalised, rapidly abandoned, close to what we get from ordinary chatter.[32]

A third notion of public opinion calls on republican aspirations when working to set up republican institutions, already during their earlier opposition under the Empire: a consolidated, pacific and reasonable opinion, generated by deliberation of the entire body of citizens. This is a notion close to that re-emerging among some analysts and promoters of deliberative democracy today. James Fishkin, for instance, affirms that genuine public opinion is not the outcome of the consultation of individual citizens on issues about which they are barely informed and have not had the chance to exchange ideas. Real opinion, the one that must be taken into account, would only emerge as the outcome of public deliberation.[33]

Building a People of citizens

Defining forms of political participation in the Republic is not limited to a circumscription of public sphere. It is also a question of transforming the individual, that is, the social being, into a citizen. This book hopes to contribute to a better understanding of the pedagogic enterprise of the apprenticeship in citizenship. In order to consolidate the republican government, in the last three decades of the nineteenth century, education for democracy was conceived as the necessary complement to the institutionalisation, particularly juridical, of popular participation. In the eyes of republicans, government is consolidated through the education of its citizens which the Republic can then govern: discerning and rational citizens able to produce an enlightened opinion. Several social scientists have written about the way the act of voting leads the elector to practice an 'apprenticeship of self-constraint, by which the social being becomes another (the citizen)'.[34] The assembly is also considered as a place of transformation of the individual into a citizen, a place which is perhaps as important as the polling station.

To create a People of citizens, the first step was to dissociate politics from everyday social ties. According to Michael Walzer, 'citizens come to the public sphere armed with nothing else but their arguments. All non-political goods must be left outside: weapons and wallets, titles and qualifications'.[35] In the individualist republican model, the political bond is built against ties of primary socialisation and its particularisms. Yves Déloye highlighted the tensions created by this drive to dissociate the social being from the citizen; tensions existing

---

32. Champagne, *Faire l'opinion*, pp. 64–65.
33. James Fishkin, *The Voice of the People. Public Opinion and Democracy*, New Haven, Yale University Press, 1997.
34. Yves Déloye, *Sociologie historique du politique*, Paris, La Découverte, 1997, p. 104.
35. Michael Walzer, *Spheres of Justice: A Defence of Pluralism and Equality*, New York, Basic Books, 1983, p. 345.

in particular between this secular citizenship and its main rival: the conception of political bond upheld by the catholic elite.[36] If this separation between social affiliation and citizen identification is today considered by many as a distinctive mark of citizenship in France,[37] the process of distinction should not be taken for granted. To make citizens accept this aspect of political order, republican moral entrepreneurs focused their efforts particularly on the school, where instruction to 'educate sensitivities and civic mores for political ends was developed'.[38] 'Studying "the offer" of citizenship cannot be [...] enough since this offer is only realised in the multiple uses that give it sense', wrote Michel Offerlé.[39] We must then ask how the figure of the autonomous citizen has had a tangible impact on the practical forms of the apprenticeship of politics. Stressing that the imposition of the republican notion of citizenship is not automatic means admitting competition between different notions of citizenship, but it also means stressing the concrete terms and difficulties of the citizens' apprenticeship.

Furthermore, republican civil behaviour supposes that a person learns to adopt reasoned behaviour and a moderate attitude by dissociating himself from his social background. My aim is to highlight this curious circularity. Indeed, what strikes the observer of political practices that the pedagogic republican mission wants to direct is that while civil behaviour is deemed necessary for the good use of one or another form of participation, the latter is in turn considered able to favour the apprenticeship of republican civil mores among participants. Olivier Ihl and Yves Déloye have shown how the polling station is a very regulated space, characterised by the fact that whoever enters is encouraged to 'bend to a mode of expression which valorises the notions of decency and reserve'.[40] In observing what goes on in assemblies, I want to stress the existence of places other than the polling station presumed to encourage forms of expression and behaviour in line with the civilisation of political mores. A citizen's behaviour is not learnt exclusively in school, and not only 'by heart'.[41] Neither is becoming a citizen learnt solely by repeatedly casting a vote. Ihl has shown that even the scenography of republican

---

36. Yves Déloye, *École et citoyenneté. L'individualisme républicain de Jules Ferry à Vichy*, Paris, Presses de la FNSP, 1994.

37. Jean Leca, 'Individualisme et citoyenneté', in Pierre Birnbaum and Jean Leca (eds), *Sur l'individualisme. Théories et méthodes*, Paris, Presses de la FNSP, 1991, pp. 159–209; Jean François Thuot, *La fin de la représentation et les formes contemporaines de la démocratie*, Montreal, Nota Bene, 1998, pp. 67–83.

38. Yves Déloye, 'L'apprentissage de la citoyenneté', *Cahiers français*, 1998, vol. 285, p. 76. See also Thomas L. Dynneson, *Civism. Cultivating Citizenship in European History*, New York, Peter Lang, 2001.

39. Michel Offerlé, 'La nationalisation de la citoyenneté civique en France à la fin du XIXe siècle', in Raffaele Romanelli (ed.), *How Did they Become Voters? The History of Franchise in Modern European Representation*, The Hague, Kluwer Law International, 1998, p. 38.

40. Yves Déloye and Olivier Ihl, 'Deux figures singulières de l'universel: la République et le sacré', in Marc Sadoun (ed.), *La démocratie en France*, vol. 1, Paris, Gallimard, 2000, p. 188.

41. Offerlé, 'La nationalisation de la citoyenneté civique', p. 46.

festivities 'reflects the basic statements of the republican notion of the political bond in democracy'.⁴² Yet it is also through the exercise of other, less framed, forms of participation that republicans intend to form a citizen capable of making choices for the public good, and which are encouraged as means to accompany and complement voting. Among them, the political assembly plays a key role.

This pedagogic dimension of participation relies particularly on controlling the display of emotions in the public sphere. To use Roger Chartier's expression for the eighteenth century context, the Republic must exclude the 'blind emotions of the multitude'.⁴³ When he evokes the expectations of the electoral ritual, Yves Déloye writes that 'the "good voter" is presumed to distance himself [...] from his impulses and emotions'.⁴⁴ Does this mean that republicans wanted to ban all emotion from political life so that participation relied on reason alone? Republicans called for the elimination of uncontrolled passions from the public sphere, but a role could nevertheless be attributed to 'good' emotion, that is, to controlled emotion not opposed to reason. Such an emotion could even facilitate the spread of republican ideas. The enterprise of defining public space thus envisages the establishment of a specific emotional regimen. By emotional regime I mean the 'complex of practices that establish a set of emotional norms and that sanction those who break them'.⁴⁵ For William Reddy, a new emotional regime arose in nineteenth century France, banning emotions in the public sphere by prohibiting the sentimentalist doctrines of the previous century; that is, the idea that natural feelings, necessarily shared by all, lead to public virtue and that all good political decisions are based on the sincere expression of emotions.⁴⁶ Emotion would then be conceived as being contrary to reason which is the sole legitimate motor of political action. Yet, the emotional regime that the republicans wanted to establish in the last three decades of the nineteenth century did not entirely rule out emotion in the public sphere. This had a place on various occasions in popular assemblies, where it was anticipated by organisers as a sign of loyalty to the Republic. What mattered then was that emotion was visible to all to help the success of the gathering,⁴⁷ but without any spillover.

---

42. Yves Déloye and Olivier Ihl, 'Deux figures singulières de l'universel', p. 220; Ihl, *La fête républicaine*.
43. Roger Chartier, *Les origines culturelles de la Révolution française*, Paris, Seuil, 1990, p. 52.
44. Yves Déloye, *Sociologie historique du politique*, 1997, p. 103.
45. William M. Reddy, *The Navigation of Feeling. A Framework for the History of Emotions*, New York, Cambridge University Press, 2001, p. 323.
46. In particular during the French Revolution, see also the study of 'the exaltation of tears shed in common', in: Anne Vincent-Buffault, *Histoire des larmes. XVIIIᵉ–XIXᵉ siècles*, Paris, Rivages, 1986, p. 85.
47. On the idea that one cannot deduce the existence of genuinely felt emotion from signs of emotion shown by participants in a collective ritual, and that there is no need to suppose that the emotions of participants are real to understand the efficacy of a ceremony, see: Nicolas Mariot, *Conquérir unanimement les cœurs. Usages politiques et scientifiques des rites. Le cas du voyage présidentiel en province, 1888–1998*, PhD dissertation, EHESS, 1999.

Related to the control of passions, republicans also wanted to eliminate violence from citizens' behaviour. As regards the electoral ritual we have seen that it 'tends to pose another perspective to the vindicatory rhetoric of force: that of silent adhesion by which the political mechanism of delegation is established, ritually but peaceably'[48] — deepening the discussion of Elias' thesis on the mechanisms which lead to a pacification of mores, a movement which leads social actors to gradually exhibit less violence when violence became a state monopoly.[49] We will see that when its right has been granted the republicans perceive the assembly as a way to contribute to this pacification of collective modes of political expression and thus of public space.

A co-production of forms of participation

In starting this investigation what I had in mind was the contrast between the large contradictory assemblies of the early Third Republic and the impressive partisan meetings that succeeded them on the one hand, and the political rallies of the twentieth century that no longer seemed to attract or enthuse on the other. To this I grafted the idea that one cannot attribute these changes solely to the appearance of radio and television propaganda – without claiming that it did not play a key role in the fact that 'the public assembly loses its central place in electoral mechanisms'.[50] The form of assemblies had already changed during the Third Republic. In this book I want to explore the hypothesis that it is also this evolution which explains the relative disaffection with assemblies. For this, the analysis of the definition of legitimate forms of participation and political behaviour must also take into account the way in which people play with the norms, appropriate or subvert them, and how this reception can itself engender change in the definition of what constitutes good political behaviour in a representative democracy.

Studying the republican enterprise of framing popular participation and civic education in representative democracy, seeking its ideological foundations and the forms it has taken, without examining how the opportunities for participation it intends to provide unwind in practice, would implicitly bring us to suppose that it automatically succeeds, and that the 'demopedic fervour'[51] always bears fruit. The observer places himself in some way as if he was one of these pedagogues convinced of the necessary success of such a legitimate enterprise. This perspective amounts to presuming that there was a political modernity which

---

48. Yves Déloye and Olivier Ihl, 'La civilité électorale: vote et forclusion de la violence en France', *Cultures & Conflits*, 1993, vols. 9–10, pp. 75–76.
49. Norbert Elias, *The Civilizing Process*, vol. 1, *The History of Manners*, Oxford, Blackwell, 1969 and *La Dynamique de l'Occident*, Paris, Calmann-Lévy, 1976. Claudine Haroche, 'Retenue dans les mœurs et maîtrise de la violence politique', *Cultures & Conflits*, 1993, vols. 9–10, pp. 45–59.
50. Offerlé, *Un homme, une voix*, p. 96.
51. This is an expression used by Pierre Rosanvallon for the years 1880–1900 in: *Le sacre du citoyen. Histoire du suffrage universel en France*, Paris, Gallimard, 1992, p. 470.

imposed itself progressively from above and to which citizens had to adapt. This partly developmentalist attitude rests on a belief that the force of ideas, which is much depleted, forgets that politics is also what people make of it. If it is essential to understand the precise nature of the republican conception of the role played by assemblies in supporting government, and if I dedicate to it an important part of my enquiry, this is not the only approach that I want to adopt. I also want to show how a form of participation, the assembly in particular, is a co-production between the republican concern to contain the masses and the differentiated uses of defined freedoms.

Focussing on these mechanisms prevents us from taking politicisation as a top-down process of diffusion in society, spreading from cities to rural areas. Albeit not without encountering some difficulties, but finally and inevitably – in caricaturing the position of these authors, this is the approach proposed by Eugen Weber[52] and Maurice Agulhon,[53] the latter having nevertheless replied to some of the critiques which had been levelled at him in this sense.[54] The way to conceive and to carry out politics is also produced by those who take part in it. The warning is no longer very new and relates particularly to the politicisation of rural areas.[55] Alain Corbin thus opposes the approach of the phenomena which 'drawn according to the schema of the flow, was, after all, not very attentive to reception'. For the question and the period that interests us, not to take People as 'soft wax offered for apprenticeship',[56] leads us to see that something else happens at the level of the reception, more than a mere assimilation of the practices promoted by republicans, but also more than their simple rejection.

Several authors argue that we should observe what occurs at the local level and that politicisation can only be understood by looking at it from below. Yet it is quite rare to find studies that give a thorough analysis of this sort of logic showing that reception is an active process of creation. Beyond the insistence on

---

52. Eugen Weber, *La fin des terroirs. La modernisation de la France rurale. 1870–1914*, Paris, Fayard, 1983.

53. Maurice Agulhon, *La République au village. Les populations du Var de la Révolution à la IIe République*, Paris, Plon, 1970.

54. Maurice Agulhon, 'Présentation', *La politisation des campagnes au XIXe siècle. France, Italie, Espagne, Portugal*, Rome, École française de Rome, 2000, pp. 1–11; Maurice Agulhon, '"La République au village". Quoi de neuf', *Provence historique*, 1998, vol. 194, pp. 423–433.

55. Christine Guionnet, *L'apprentissage de la politique moderne. Les élections municipales sous la Monarchie de Juillet*, Paris, L'Harmattan, 1997; Alain Garrigou, *Le vote et la vertu. Comment les Français sont devenus électeurs*, Paris, Presses de la FNSP, 1992; Caroline C. Ford, *Creating the Nation in Provincial France. Religion and Political Identity in Brittany*, Princeton NJ, Princeton University Press, 1993; Peter McPhee, *The Politics of Rural Life: Political Mobilization in the French Countryside, 1846–1852*, Oxford, Clarendon Press, 1992. See also the synthesis of Michel Offerlé on this subject: 'Capacités politiques et politisations: faire voter et voter, XIXe–XXe siècles', *Genèses*, 2007, vol. 67, pp.131–149 and vol. 68, pp.145–160.

56. Alain Corbin, 'Préface', in Édouard Lynch, *Entre la commune et la nation. Identité communautaire et pratique politique en vallée de Campan (Hautes-Pyrénées) au XIXe siècle*, Toulouse II, Archives des Hautes-Pyrénées, 1992, p. 7.

the fact that the practices of representative democracy are not assimilated as such, we must observe the changes in the forms of participation which are developed by the population itself. We cannot simply ask whether or not the republican venture of 'citizenisation', through participation in assemblies and promotion of public opinion likely to support institutions of representative democracy has succeeded. We need to understand how the uses of freedom of assembly as framed by republicans — especially through legal rules or discourses *qua* modes of assembly — have transformed the form of political gatherings. Saying that the Republic did not impose itself immediately is not just a question of noting that the process of acculturation was long and difficult. It also shows that it met with resistance, a resistance which contributed to transform the terms of popular participation.

This focus on the 'good tricks of the weak in the order established by the strong',[57] is drawn indirectly from a sociology of reception which highlighted the creativity of cultural consumers in generating meaning with the texts and images before them: their acceptance plays a role in a process of co-production.[58] While avoiding the 'naïve optimism' of authors who have been criticised for letting us believe that reception always produces public resistance,[59] research particularly from the school of cultural studies, focuses on the production of meaning in the interaction of spectators and readers with images and texts. This invites us to examine what occurs in the practice of the assembly, in order to see how its form can be influenced. The task is not an easy one, especially when working on the past and when faced with a paucity of direct testimony together with the difficulty of interpreting secondary sources. Recalling, in the case of reading, the scarcity of traces of how a work is received, Roger Chartier invites us to return to the analysis of the printed object: the material reality of texts functions as a support and a constraint for readers' acts of appropriation.[60] In much the same way I try to emphasise the mechanisms and material conditions that orient participants in a meeting hall, before observing what one can still see of the interactions during the assembly, and the modes of intervention of participants.

Such an approach supposes that we do not adopt the perspective of republican 'moral entrepreneurs', to use Howard S. Becker's term, to describe those who create or enforce norms. The 'prototype of the rule creator' says Becker 'is the crusading reformer'.[61] This sort of reformer considers any resistance to his plan as

---

57. Michel De Certeau, *L'invention du quotidien. 1. Arts de faire*, Paris, Gallimard, 1990, p. 65.
58. Cécile Méadel and Serge Proulx, 'Usagers en chiffres, usagers en actes', in Serge Proulx (ed.), *Accusé de réception. Le téléspectateur construit par les sciences sociales*, Québec, Presses Universitaires de Laval, Paris, L'Harmattan, 1998, p. 91. On the term 'co-production' for the political life of the period examined, see: Michel Offerlé, 'Périmètres du politique et co-production de la radicalité à la fin du XIXe siècle', in Annie Collovald and Brigitte Gaïti (eds), *La démocratie aux extrêmes. Sur la radicalisation politique*, Paris, La Dispute, 2006, pp. 247–268.
59. Daniel Dayan, 'Les mystères de la réception', *Le Débat*, 1992, vol. 71, pp. 146–162.
60. Roger Chartier, *Au bord de la falaise. L'histoire entre certitudes et incertitudes*, Paris, A. Michel, 1998, pp. 255–268.
61. Howard S. Becker, *Outsiders. Studies in the Sociology of Deviance*, New York, The Free Press, 1963, p. 147.

an evil afflicting democracy, but one which will tend to disappear with progress. What republicans consider deviant behaviour is the result of the way in which the norm is defined in a given historical moment. In her study of the socio-historical construction of electoral deviance, Nathalie Dompnier shows how electoral fraud 'is not primarily a legal ban or a practice in essence contrary to the good functioning of democracy', emphasising that it is 'the fruit of a social activity of definition and specification'. This type of reasoning makes us aware that if some 'bad' behaviour or 'dangerous' forms of participation seem to disappear when they are denounced less, this may also be due to a change in the political norm, progressively leading to 'changes and clarifications of the legal norm', as in the case of electoral fraud.[62]

An element in the repertoire of collective action

From the last decade of the nineteenth century the main aim of meetings was to gather together people already convinced of a shared cause in order to demonstrate its strength. The phenomenon was affirmed after the adoption of the 1901 law on associations and the successive organisation of party propaganda. The assembly shifted away from being a place of debate and became a form of collective action, in the sense of 'common action whose aim is to achieve shared ends'[63] — here I discard the definitions which oppose collective action, due to the 'social dimension' of interests defended, 'to more specifically political forms of mobilisation, such as voting or partisan commitment'.[64] In the present case, it is not pertinent to establish a clear caesura between participation and mobilisation, in the same way as between conventional and non-conventional forms of legal action.[65]

For Charles Tilly the repertoire of collective action is:

> a model where the accumulated experience of actors intersects with the strategies of authorities, in making a body of limited means of action more practical, more attractive and more frequent than many other means which could, in principle, serve the same interests.[66]

---

62. Nathalie Dompnier, *La clef des urnes. La construction socio-historique de la déviance électorale en France depuis 1848*, PhD dissertation, IEP Grenoble, Université Grenoble II, 1992, pp. 42–43.
63. Patrice Mann, *L'action collective. Mobilisation et organisation des minorités actives*, Paris, A. Colin, 1991, p. 7.
64. Richard Balme and Didier Chabanet, 'Action collective et gouvernance de l'Union européenne', in Richard Balme, Didier Chabanet and Vincent Wright (eds), *L'action collective en Europe*, Paris, Presses de Sciences Po, 2002, p. 27.
65. On the idea of a 'continuum of political participation', see: Olivier Fillieule, *Stratégies de la rue. Les manifestations en France*, Paris, Presses de Sciences Po, 1997, pp. 136–145.
66. Charles Tilly, 'Les origines du répertoire de l'action collective contemporaine en France et en Grande-Bretagne', *Vingtième Siècle*, 1984, vol. 4, (4), p. 99. On the queries and criticisms of this notion, see: Michel Offerlé, 'Retour critique sur les répertoires de l'action collective (XVIIIe–XXIe siècles)', *Politix*, 2008, vol. 81, pp. 181–202.

By replacing assemblies in the repertoire of collective action, mainly in the interwar years, I question not only the competition, but also the complementaries and possible hybridisations among the different modes of action, in particular between assembly and demonstration. This is the perspective used here to discuss the crisis of the political assembly in the 1930s. We are then dealing with a period of change in the form taken by assemblies, which indirectly led to their relative decline. Indeed, when it comes to a means of action, there are other more effective forms than assembly, occupying the street in particular. In periods of political and social agitation, Paris was no longer in a state of 'permanent meeting', to use the words of Maurice Agulhon for 1848, but in a state of permanent demonstration.[67] The competition between meeting and demonstration helps us understand that the decline of the assembly began well before the appearance of radio-television propaganda.

Without resorting to counterfactual history,[68] we can still ask whether the role of the assembly as a *locus* of debate would have been preserved had the outcome of citizens' deliberation actually reached decision makers and helped shape their choices. This is arguably the sole condition that could have made public assemblies gain by not being transformed into a means of collective action. While we invoke anew the need for places to gather in order to debate public issues, the experience of participation in assemblies under the Third Republic reminds us that it is not sufficient to recognise the legitimacy of the political word of the People, but that there also have to be effective means linking popular deliberation to public decision making: 'What is the role of deliberation if not with a view to action? […] How do we convince citizens to participate if they do not have prior assurance that their opinion will be heard?', ask Loïc Blondiaux and Yves Sintomer.[69]

Assemblies observed

What do we mean by political assemblies? The question turns out to be all the more important when the latter are designated by their contemporaries by a variety of terms, which do not always correspond to a variety in their forms. Observers who left descriptions of these events in police reports and press articles, referred to them as assemblies, meetings, gatherings or crowds. This was done without there always being a difference between the facts observed and several denominations can be used in a single text — even if we see that these terms are not all used with the same frequency depending on the period. I call a political assembly (*réunion politique*) any meeting in a given place which is organised beforehand, and preceded by a call to assemble. It must then gather together participants

---

67. Maurice Agulhon, *1848 ou l'apprentissage de la République. 1848–1852*, Paris, Seuil, 1992, p. 53.
68. On the counterfactual approach of history — 'What If History' — and the controversies it raises, see in particular: Martin Bunzl, 'Counterfactual History. A User's Guide', *American Historical Review*, 2004, vol. 109, (3), pp. 845–858.
69. Loïc Blondiaux and Yves Sintomer, 'L'impératif délibératif', *Politix*, 2002, vol. 57, p. 31.

in a place where one or more people deliver speeches. It thus excludes simple discussions among friends, diners and conversations in cafés.[70] As it must be fixed, processions, parades and demonstrations are also excluded. The speeches delivered in the assembly must be political discourses. This excludes not only lectures dealing with non-political subjects (literary, artistic, scientific issues, etc.), but also assemblies within a political group dealing with organisational problems, such as strategic and material issues. Finally, an assembly must not be held on the public street. This is the main criteria which differentiates it from the mob (*attroupement* in French law), defined as a concerted or spontaneous meeting of people on the public street, and hence likely to create disorder. I have also chosen not to set a precise threshold for the number of participants in assemblies.

On the basis of this definition we need to avoid amalgamating assembly and association, these are 'two oft-confused sisters', in the words of the legal expert Roger Arnette in his work on freedom of assembly.[71] Associations and assemblies had long been confused in French law. The 1868 law on public assemblies was 'the first since the French Revolution to clearly distinguish the "assembly" with its occasional character, from permanent "association"'.[72] Freedom of assembly suffered from this misunderstanding: the distrust caused by freedom of association pushed governments to limit it. This has jeopardised freedom of assembly in the long run. If they were confused, it was because assemblies were one of the key activities of associations, and it was difficult to imagine an association without assemblies. Associations can be considered simple assemblies repeated. But they differ from the latter in their permanent and lasting character and by affiliation, that is, the link which unites members around a common aim. The 1901 law defined associations as the 'convention by which two or more people place their knowledge or activity permanently in common in order to share the benefits'.

This study also includes meetings which are not presented as political assemblies by their organisers. These were important at the end of the Second Empire, when all means were used to get around the restrictive dispositions of the 1868 law, freeing assemblies from the need for prior authorisation only meetings, such as electoral assemblies and public meetings not dealing with political or religious subjects. Many assemblies were then organised around *a priori* non-political themes, indicated in the compulsory prior declaration, which were nothing but pretexts for delivering political speeches. At the beginning of the Third Republic legitimist masses were held where the sermons were speeches for a restoration of the monarchy and which participants did not necessarily attend in order to pray. Another way to avoid the restraints on the right to assembly was to organise meetings with the outward appearance of private assemblies, thus avoiding laws

---

70. On the café as place of political discussion, see: W. Scott Haine, *The World of the Paris Café. Sociability Among the French Working Class, 1789–1914*, Baltimore, Johns Hopkins University Press, 1996, pp. 207–233.
71. Roger Arnette, *La liberté de réunion en France. Son histoire et sa législation*, Paris, Arthur Rousseau, 1894, p. 11.
72. Raymond Huard, *La naissance du parti politique en France*, Paris, Presses de la FNSP, 1996, p. 127.

on public assemblies. This research reaches beyond assemblies recognised as public, to include private assemblies insofar as they comply with my criteria for defining a political assembly. As a particular form of private assembly, the banquet also corresponds for instance to this definition if speeches are made.

In order to discover the different uses made of freedom of assembly, and how participation takes many forms — as different from each other as from the participation suggested by republican pedagogues — the study is not limited to one political group. For the period from 1868 to the First World War, I examine assemblies organised not only by different republican groups but also by socialists, anarchists, nationalists, Boulangists, legitimists, Bonapartists, etc. For the interwar period, I focus on the assemblies of the two large leftist parties, the SFIO (*Section Française de l'Internationale Ouvrière*) and the PCF (*Parti Communiste Français*), in order to make an in-depth analysis of the way their meetings were organised and reported. But I also refer to assemblies held at the same time by other political groups, in particular the huge rallies organised by the extreme right.

One last aspect of the definition of my terrain needs to be made. In the concrete observation of the way people take part in assemblies, I focus on urban and, above all, Parisian use (Paris and its immediate suburbs). This is basically because 'Paris held an eminent position in perceptions of crowd violence'.[73] The repeated upheavals experienced by the city throughout the nineteenth century, particularly the events of June 1848 and the Commune, have helped foster an image of the capital as a 'place of revolution'.[74] If I carried out additional research — before 1914 on the region of Bouches-du-Rhône, Marseilles in particular, and for the interwar period on the region of Rhône-Alpes — my main objective remains that of relating the republican project of domesticating the crowd through participation in assemblies to the way these actually take place in Paris.

The Introductory Chapter which follows gives a short review of the history of political assemblies. Part I (Consolidating Representative Democracy) shows how the assembly lies at the heart of the republican plan of the definition of forms of participation likely to complement the vote. Part II (Setbacks in Republican Pedagogy), focuses on pedagogues' expectations of participation in debate in assemblies, their valorisation as an opportunity for individuals to undergo an apprenticeship in civic behaviour, and reveals the problems encountered by this aspect of the demopedic republican venture. Part III (When a Show of Force Threatens Freedom of Assembly), brings us to the interwar period, where we observe the use of assemblies as a form of partisan propaganda in the big cities and their conurbations. Holding huge political rallies was a way for party organisers to demonstrate their strength but led to a crisis of the political assembly in the 1930s.

---

73. James R. Lehning, *To Be a Citizen. The Political Culture of the Early French Third Republic*, Ithaca, Cornell University Press, 2001, pp. 58–59.

74. Lehning, *To Be a Citizen*, pp. 58–59. See also Christopher Prendergast, *Paris and the Nineteenth Century*, Oxford, Blackwell, 1992; David W. Harvey, *Paris, Capital of Modernity*, New York, Routledge, 2003.

Returning to the History of Assemblies

> Unfortunately this lively and crucial form of democratic political life [has] been somewhat neglected by French historians, even when examining how to renew the approaches and methods of political history.

This is what Vincent Robert wrote on the study of public assemblies at the end of the Second Empire and under the Third Republic.[1] Whatever the period examined, studies dealing with French political assemblies are rare and, in the words of Nicolas Roussellier in 2001, 'a history of public assemblies [...] still has to be written'.[2] Yet a journey through the history of the rights and practice of assemblies in France allows us to present some studies that do deal with this issue. Since it would be unproductive here to search for what was said about the 'first' assemblies, a venture that would lead us to phenomena that have little to do with our subject, we start our story with assemblies held during the French Revolution, when 'the figure of the individual elector really began to emerge'.[3] This is the period for which available works are the most numerous.

The French Revolution: from freedom of assembly to its control

Under the *ancien régime* any freedom of assembly was the outcome of a certain indulgence on the part of the authorities; consequently, the Revolution is considered as having founded the right of assembly. The number of assemblies organised by political societies increased between the summer of 1789 and the *coup d'État* on 18 *brumaire* (9 November) 1799. This was a consequence of 'a generally well-disposed legal framework which authorised a public and collective expression of opinions and political programmes for the first time'.[4] The first provision regarding this freedom was the decree of 14 December 1789 which proclaimed the right to peaceful and unarmed assembly for all active citizens. The following year, the decrees of 19–20 September and 13–19 November 1790 reaffirmed this right to assemble, on the condition that the law be observed. Finally, the Constitution of 13–14 September 1791 guaranteed citizens 'freedom to assemble peaceably and unarmed on condition that they comply with compulsory police rules'.

---

1. Vincent Robert, *Entre Réforme et Révolution. Horizons, rituels, sociabilités et souvenirs dans la France du dix-neuvième siècle*, Paris I, HDR dissertation, 2005, p. 6.
2. Nicolas Roussellier, 'La diffusion de l'éloquence en France sous la IIIe République', in Fabrice D'Almeida (ed.), *L'éloquence politique en France et en Italie de 1870 à nos jours*, Rome, École française de Rome, 2001, p. 44.
3. Pierre Rosanvallon, *Le sacre du citoyen. Histoire du suffrage universel en France*, Paris, Gallimard, 1992, p. 34.
4. Jean Boutier and Philippe Boutry (eds), *Les sociétés politiques. Atlas de la Révolution française*, vol. 6, Paris, EHESS, 1992, p. 9.

However freedom of assembly quickly became subject to measures to control and limit its exercise. The first restrictive provisions were introduced even before the adoption of the Constitution; in May 1791, the Constituent Assembly declared that 'no citizen or assembly of citizens could proclaim anything in the form of decisions, deliberations or in any other compulsory or imperative form'. Some months later, the decree of 19–22 July 1791 required the chairmen, secretaries or commissaires of clubs to report the days and places of assemblies to the municipal registry office. But it was above all the law of 29–30 September 1791 that introduced a real constraint by forbidding clubs to summon to their bar an official or a citizen, to obstruct the actions of the authorities, to publish their debates or to organise petitions. This law was accompanied by a report by Isaac Le Chapelier[5] which denounced popular societies as damaging to representative government and dangerous for the public peace, and required that their activity remain private. The societies emerged weakened from these provisions.

Yet with the victory of the Montagnards they regained unprecedented size and power, now protected by the decree of 23 July 1793. This stipulated that: 'Any authority, any individual who dares [...] to place obstacles in the way of assemblies or to use any means to dissolve popular societies, will be treated as guilty of an attack on freedom'. Clubs were invited to report disloyal citizens and to select loyal patriots competent for public office, thus becoming 'the arms of a triumphant Montagnard government'.[6] A year later, after the downfall of Robespierre on 9 *thermidor* (27 July 1794), a reaction against clubs surfaced under the Convention, with the law of 16 October 1794 that defended collective affiliations and petitions, and the closure of the Jacobin club on 14 November 1794. A law of 23 August 1795 banned and dissolved 'all assemblies known by the name of club or popular society'. Yet Isser Woloch has shown how the clubs continued to exist under the Directory, even if there are few studies dealing with their activity other than for the societies of 1789–1795, which is particularly due to a relative lack of historical sources.[7]

Many historical works have examined the subject of Jacobin clubs, yet little has been written about the assemblies they organised and how people took part in them. The most important body of research emphasises the role played by clubs in the process of politicisation of the French and advocates the use of the notion of sociability to understand this phenomenon. These studies were conducted in reaction to those describing clubs as a machine for generating unanimity, in which manipulated individuals counted very little.[8] Jean Boutier and Philippe Boutry's research team explicitly contests this theory arguing that, neither machine, nor

---

5. The Le Chapelier law of 14 June 1791 banned all association among persons in the same trade and all forms of professional alliance or union.

6. Isser Woloch, *Jacobin Legacy. The Democratic Movement Under the Directory*, Princeton NJ, Princeton University Press, 1970, pp. 7–8.

7. Woloch, *Jacobin Legacy*, p. 8. See also: Bernard Gainot, *1799, Un nouveau jacobinisme? La démocratie représentative, une alternative à Brumaire*, Paris, CTHS, 2001.

8. The machine metaphor is developed in particular by: Augustin Cochin, *Les sociétés de pensée et la démocratie moderne. Études d'histoire révolutionnaire*, Paris, Plon, 1921. It is taken up by François Furet. See, in particular: François Furet and Mona Ozouf (eds), *Dictionnaire critique de la Révolution Française*, Paris, Flammarion, 1988.

party, Jacobin societies should be understood as a movement inventing 'new and contrasting forms of democratic sociability' which constituted 'one of the basic modes of political acculturation'.[9] These works give us a better knowledge of the Jacobin associative phenomena. In particular, they have produced a precise cartography of societies, a sociology of their members, a descriptive presentation of their inner life and the study of relations between this revolutionary sociability and that of the *ancien régime*. These studies have also reawakened interest in the people taking part in club activities which the theory of the 'Jacobin machine' tends to conceal. However, they do not focus much on what actually occurred in club meetings, how those assembled, club members or the general public, took part.

There is also a great deal of research that analyses the legislative debates on club activity. These debates question the basis of the right of association which is closely linked to the right of assembly. Those which took place under the Directory in the Council of the Five Hundred (*Conseil des Cinq-Cents*) and the Council of Ancients (*Conseil des Anciens*), published as pamphlets, and widely distributed, received the most attention. Christine Peyrard notes that 'the interest of these debates, weak as regards the regulation, but with strong political content, lies in the collective reflection on the promotion of opinion and the place of intermediary bodies in representative government'.[10] The author retraces the positions of protagonists on the principle of a natural right to assemble, the question of meetings' public character and political pluralism. Raymond Huard distinguishes, among the contributions to these debates, what touches 'great principles', from questions bearing on the internal organisation of associations and rules concerning the surveillance of the activity of societies. Huard's research also shows how the memory of Jacobin clubs recurs in legislative debates throughout the nineteenth century.[11] The numerous law dissertations on freedom of assembly written between the 1880s and 1940s constitute another body of work analysing such legislative debates, and are part of our terrain. Note here that the large number of these dissertations is explained by the standardisation of the law doctorate at the end of the nineteenth century. We must see there the impact of the 1889 law which allowed a two-year exemption of military service for those holding a doctoral degree. Barristers were particularly keen to obtain more diplomas,[12] and Imbert notes that 'the number of dissertations multiplies in proportions never previously obtained'.[13] The consequence was that candidates chose subjects which were easier to deal with because already examined in other dissertations — this is precisely the case with the right of assembly.

---

9. Boutier and Boutry (eds), *Les sociétés politiques*, pp. 11–12.
10. Christine Peyrard, 'Les débats sur le droit d'association et de réunion sous le Directoire', *Annales historiques de la Révolution française*, 1994, vol. 3, p. 463.
11. Raymond Huard, *La naissance du parti politique en France*, Paris, Presses de la FNSP, pp. 35–42.
12. Jean-Louis Halpérin (ed.), *Avocats et notaires en Europe. Les professions judiciaires et juridiques dans l'histoire contemporaine*, Paris, LGDJ, 1996, p. 174.
13. Jean Imbert, 'Passé, présent et avenir du doctorat de droit en France', *Annales d'histoire des facultés de droit*, 1984, vol. 1, p. 25.

The end of the right of assembly under the Empire

Napoleon Bonaparte's *coup d'État* and the government of the Consulate mark the end of France's first liberal experience with political assemblies. Until then, from 1789 to 1799, a large part of the population had become familiar with the practice of such gatherings. But the consular and imperial constitutions are silent on the right of assembly. On first sight, although Title VII of section III of the penal code is 'Illicit Associations and Assemblies', it seems to deal with associations rather than assemblies. Article 291 of the penal code indeed stipulates that 'no *association* of more than twenty persons whose goal is to assemble daily, or on specific days, in order to deal with religious, literary, political or other issues, can be formed without government consent'. Associations and assemblies were in fact implicitly confused so as to include both under this regime of pre-emptive authorisation. The discussion of Articles 291–295 in the Conseil d'État reflects the fact that their provisions also applied to simple assemblies: thus the *rapporteur* Berlier affirms in his legal recital that 'the absolute and definitive right to assemble to examine political, religious or others affairs, […] would be incompatible with current politics'.[14]

All gatherings were thus subject to prior authorisation by the executive power, making it practically impossible to hold political assemblies. Huard concluded that 'whatever the diversity and richness of forms of association and political organisation under the Revolution, there remained very little, if anything, at the start of the Restoration.'[15] It is not surprising then that there are few studies on assemblies under the Empire: once limited to the feeble activity of secret societies, which by nature left few traces, they disappear almost completely during this period.

The censitary monarchies: tolerance and mistrust

The 1814 Constitutional Charter makes no mention of freedom of assembly. Article 14 simply stipulates that the King can take all actions necessary 'for the security of the State'. The situation thus remains under the regimen of the 1810 penal code. Activist societies, such as the *Charbonnerie* were however founded during the first years of the censitary monarchy:[16] 'Semi-political societies, semi-military plots, […] they constitute a secret armour in preparation for seizing power.'[17] This ended with the 1830 Revolution. In the four years that followed,

---

14. Marcel Le Clère, *Les réunions, manifestations et attroupements en droit français et comparé*, Paris, Impr. Petites Affiches, 1945, pp. 11–12.
15. Huard, *La naissance du parti politique en France*, p. 47.
16. Alan Spitzer, *Old Hatred and Young Hopes. The French Carbonari Against the Bourbon Restauration*, Cambridge MA, Harvard University Press, 1971; Pierre-Arnaud Lambert, *La Charbonnerie française, 1821–1823. Du secret en politique*, Lyon, Presses Universitaires de Lyon, 1995.
17. Huard, *La naissance du parti politique en France*, p. 63.

and which Agulhon describes as those of the 'awakening of democracy',[18] France enjoyed a relative freedom of expression and association. The infancy of the July Monarchy was thus marked by a strong activity of republican associations. The *Société des Amis du Peuple*, created in 1830, 'organised massive assemblies in Paris with up to several thousand militant republicans and workers'.[19] Dissolved in 1832, it was re-established in 1833 as the *Société des Droits de l'Homme et du Citoyen* in which one finds, according to Claude Nicolet, 'the memory of revolutionary societies, particularly Jacobin societies'.[20] But on 10 April 1834 a law was introduced which reinforced the weapons that could be used against freedom of association. Henceforth, even members of associations divided into sections of under twenty people incurred heavy fines and prison sentences.[21] After that date, the more radical republicans rediscovered secret societies, whilst the moderates frequented circles and cafés.[22]

There have been few studies on assemblies organised by political societies, partly due to a lack of reliable sources. This is understandable for secret societies, but even for public societies there are no extensive minutes of assemblies left, in contrast with the case of revolutionary clubs.[23] Those who worked on their activity rarely speak of meetings held and never describe exactly how these proceed. The work of Raymond Huard, however, contains some information on the assemblies of the *Société des Droits de l'Homme,* whose action was mainly propaganda, and particularly oral propaganda.[24]

---

18. Maurice Agulhon, '1830 dans l'histoire du XIXᵉ siècle', *Romantisme*, 1980, vol. 28–29, pp. 15–27.
19. Philippe Boutry, 'Des sociétés populaires de l'an II au parti républicain. Réflexions sur l'évolution des formes d'association politique dans la France du premier XIXᵉ siècle', in *Storiografia Francese ed Italiana a confronto sul fenomeno associativo durante XVIII e XIX secolo*, Turin, Fondazione Luigi Einaudi, 1990, p. 123.
20. Claude Nicolet, *L'idée républicaine en France*, Paris, Gallimard, 1982, p. 136.
21. To get around the provisions of the Penal Code, societies split into groups of less than twenty members and met sporadically.
22. Maurice Agulhon, *La République au village*, Paris, Plon, 1970 and *Le cercle dans la France bourgeoise, 1810–1848*, Paris, A. Colin, 1977.
23. Among the works on the societies of the censitary monarchy see: Ronald Aminzade, *Ballots and Baricades. Class Formation and Republican Politics in France, 1830–1871*, Princeton NJ, Princeton University Press, 1993, pp. 28–33; Jean-Claude Caron, 'La société des Amis du Peuple', *Romantisme*, 28–29, 1980, pp. 169–180; Gabriel Perreux, *Au temps des sociétés secrètes. La propagande républicaine au début de la Monarchie de Juillet (1830–1835)*, Paris, Hachette, 1931; Pamela M. Pilbeam, *Republicanism in Nineteenth Century France, 1814–1871*, London, Macmillan, 1995; Iouda Tchernoff, *Le parti républicain sous la Monarchie de Juillet. Formation et évolution de la doctrine républicaine*, Paris, A. Pedone, 1901; Philippe Vigier, *Paris pendant la Monarchie de Juillet, 1830–1848*, Paris, Hachette, 1991, pp. 23–43; Georges Weill, *Histoire du parti républicain en France (1814–1870)*, Paris, F. Alcan, 1900; and Thomas Bouchet, 'Les sociétés secrètes pendant la monarchie censitaire', in Jean-Jacques Becker and Gilles Candar (eds), *Histoire des gauches en France*, vol. 1, Paris, La Découverte, 2004, pp. 161–168.
24. Huard, *La naissance du parti politique en France*, pp. 68–73.

Meetings related to electoral activity enjoyed a relative tolerance on the part of the government. Even under the Restoration, the government recognised the legitimacy of these 'occasional meetings of selected men (the electors), with no public echo, in any case known by the authority as the organisers had to declare them'.[25] Under the July Monarchy, with the increase in the number of voters and the greater tolerance of the government, they become important. 'In Paris', wrote Huard, they 'gave rise to animated debates which were reported in the press'. In the provinces, 'the tours of republican candidates [...] gathered crowds much larger than the local electorate'.[26] One notes that during the discussion of the 1834 law, reinforcing the legislation on associations, the distinction between assemblies and associations begins to emerge, particularly because the government, in response to republican criticism, stipulated that the law did not apply to preparatory electoral assemblies.[27] In general, the administrative authorities were tolerant of this type of gathering. Christine Guionnet, observing political practices during municipal elections, focuses particularly on preparatory assemblies. In describing those held in countryside cabarets, Guionnet demonstrates that the political roles are not distinguished from daily roles: 'The announced aim is the practice of ordinary village conviviality, and not to incite the individual to adopt a political and abstract role as voter or candidate'. At the same time, towns of a certain importance hosted assemblies in whose organisation the author sees 'the conception of an important distinction between electoral activities and normal daily behaviour'.[28]

Political banquets, whose importance has been shown again recently in various works, constitute another form of assembly under censitary monarchies.[29] Vincent Robert brought to light the existence of liberal banquets overlooked by historiography, before the famous 'banquet campaign' of 1848, invented by the reformist opposition to mitigate the absence of a right to public assembly.[30] According to the author, we should then see the banquet as 'a grounds for upheaval, education and political expression of major importance for the French'. Robert proposes that banquets were then the 'sole form of public assembly tolerated, almost as funerals of political figures from the opposition were the sole form of

---

25. Huard, *La naissance du parti politique en France*, p. 49.
26. Huard, *La naissance du parti politique en France*, p. 53.
27. Huard, *La naissance du parti politique en France*, pp. 52–53; Albert Joubrel, *Du droit de réunion*, Rennes, Librairie générale Pilhon et Hommay, 1904, pp. 85–90. On 18 July 1837 a new law reforms the one of 19–22 July 1791, in making public assemblies subject to prior authorisation. But this authorisation was largely given.
28. Christine Guionnet, *L'apprentissage de la politique moderne. Les élections municipales sous la Monarchie de Juillet*, Paris, L'Harmattan, 1997, pp. 50, 69.
29. *Romantisme*, 137, 2007, 'Les banquets'.
30. See, in particular, Peter H. Amann, 'Prelude to Insurrection. The Banquet of the People', *French Historical Studies*, 1960, vol. 1, (4), pp. 436–444; André Jardin and André-Jean Tudesq, *La France des notables, 1. L'évolution générale. 1815–1848*, Paris, Seuil, 1973, pp. 245–249; Pamela M. Pilbeam, *Republicanism in Nineteenth Century France*, pp. 149–154.

street demonstration allowed'.[31] Emmanuel Fureix stresses in turn that if one can observe a certain stability in the 'exterior forms of rite' that constitute the banquet, its use does change a great deal. There are two traditional models that dominate the 1820s: the 'corporative or regional' banquet and the 'honorific' banquet. In 1830, 'the leftist banquet is transformed into an instrument of national propaganda'; we are dealing then with a first form of a 'banquet campaign'. Finally, under the July Monarchy, described by Fureix as the 'golden age' of banquets, the campaigns of 1840 and 1847 'aim at a great electoral reform with the extension of suffrage' and deepen the experience of 1830.[32]

The second experience of freedom: 1848

The government that emerged from the wave of banquets held between summer 1847 and early 1848 was characterised at the outset by a broad freedom of assembly. On 19 April 1848 the provisional government, while emphasising the need to ban weapons from gatherings, proclaimed that clubs were 'a need for the Republic, a right for citizens', and declared it was content to see 'citizens gather, in various places in the capital, to confer among themselves, on the most elevated questions of politics, on the need to give the Republic a energetic, vigorous and fruitful impulse'. During the months before the 'June days uprising', the Second Republic saw a burgeoning of assemblies organised by the clubs, which increased not only in Paris but also in the provinces. Peter Amann and Daniel Stern counted over 200 in the capital, rallying over 50,000 people.[33] On a national scale, according to Huard, hundreds of thousands of people 'invested at least temporarily in these assemblies that are a good testimony of the mass politisation which followed the revolution of February'.[34]

---

31. Robert, *Entre Réforme et Révolution*, Abstract and p. 355.
32. Emmanuel Fureix, 'Banquets et enterrements', in Jean-Jacques Becker and Gilles Candar (eds), *Histoire des gauches en France*, vol. 1, Paris, La Découverte, 2004, pp. 200–201. See also: Jacqueline Lalouette, 'Banqueter', in Vincent Duclert and Christophe Prochasson (eds), *Dictionnaire critique de la République*, Paris, Flammarion, 2002, pp. 988–993; and René Million, 'Histoire des banquets politiques', *Cahiers d'histoire sociale*, 2000, vol. 14, pp. 99–116.
33. Peter H. Amann, *Revolution and Mass Democracy. The Paris Club Movement in 1848*, Princeton NJ, Princeton University Press, 1975, p. 33; Peter H. Amann, 'The Paris Club Movement in 1848', in Roger Price (ed.), *Revolution and Reaction. 1848 and the Second French Republic*, London, Croom Helm, 1975, p. 123; Daniel Stern, *Histoire de la Révolution de 1848*, Paris, Sandré, 1850–1855, vol. 2, pp. 412–415.
34. Huard, *La naissance du parti politique en France*, p. 86.

In the words of Agulhon, Paris is a 'permanent meeting'.[35] Yet among the relatively numerous works evoking this multitude of clubs, those that tell us something about the way the organised assemblies took place are still rare. What form do these assemblies take? Where and when are they held? How long do they last? Who attends them and who speaks? How do participants behave? These are some of the many questions not dealt with in existing studies.[36] Amann nevertheless provided some precious indications, first emphasising the difficulty of finding places to assemble: 'During March and April 1848, space limitations may have been the basic constraint on the proliferation of revolutionary clubs'. Then we are informed about the frequency of club sessions: 'Enough clubs [...] confined themselves to three or four weekly sessions to permit some club activists to participate in two popular societies, though most had their hands full in keeping up with one'. Amann also reveals the generally turbulent nature of assemblies and the disagreements that could occur among the public:

> The disorder often reflects simple and real differences of political profile, interest or class, among the participants. Friction between moderates and revolutionaries, bourgeois and proletarian were common currency, particularly in the case of popular societies founded by the local middle-class notables attracting workers with their own ideas.

The author finally recalls the problem of making oneself heard in an era before microphones, in front of a gathering of several hundreds or thousands of people; a difficulty made worse by the inexperience of many speakers.[37] How did these societies establish an innovative experience? According to Huard the 1848 clubs and their assemblies reproduce, without any particularly new features, models found under the Revolution or in the *Société des Amis du Peuple*.[38] For Jean-Claude Caron the fact that 'the word club is used in 1848', rather than 'political or popular society', testifies to a 'conscious will to introduce an organisational model from across the Channel'. That is to say, an association 'composed of a membership which must be presented and admitted only after investigation'. But he adds: 'many clubs, however, function *de facto* on the model of the popular society: the public of assemblies consists of both members (or associates) and spectators'.[39]

---

35. Maurice Agulhon, *1848 ou l'apprentissage de la République. 1848–1852*, Paris, Seuil, 1992, p. 53.
36. See *inter alia*, Aminzade, *Ballots and Barricades* and John M. Merriman, *The Margins of City Life. Explorations on the French Urban Frontier, 1815–1851*, New York, Oxford University Press, 1991.
37. Amann, *Revolution and Mass Democracy*, pp. 57–71.
38. Huard, *La naissance du parti politique en France*, p. 86.
39. Jean-Claude Caron, 'Les clubs de 1848', in Jean-Jacques Becker and Gilles Candar (eds), *Histoire des gauches en France. vol. 1, L'héritage du XIXᵉ siècle*, Paris, La Découverte, p. 182.

Freedom of assembly was formally reaffirmed by the Constitution of 4 November:

> Citizens have the right to associate, to assemble peacefully and unarmed, to petition, to manifest their thoughts in the press or in other ways. The only limits to the exercise of these rights are the rights or freedom of others and public security.

This reminder of the Republic's regard for the right of assembly did not cancel the decree on clubs voted by the Assembly on 28 July.[40] It was a step forward relative to the provisions of the Penal Code and the law of 10 April 1834 which it replaced, but by introducing surveillance of club activity it was also the end of the absolute freedom that France had enjoyed since February. The legislator had once again confused assembly and association; assemblies were also affected by its provisions. The decree commanded those responsible for clubs not to 'tolerate the discussion of any proposal contrary to public order'. The Minister of the Interior, Jules Sénard, gives a very broad definition of 'public order': 'No-one can understand public order without the family and property'.[41] This first intent of regulation did not prevent several clubs from reopening in August, but they were subject to near constant legal harassment. The many trials involving clubs studied by Amann show how the zeal of public prosecutors and judges caused the decline, but not the destruction, of the club movement.[42] More radical measures were adopted after the events of 13 June 1849.

On 19 June a law was introduced which authorised the government to ban 'all public assemblies likely to endanger public safety', for a year, which was subsequently extended for two years. A police presence became systematic at irregularly held preparatory electoral assemblies — the only authorised meetings. According to John Merriman at least 110 political rallies and 74 banquets were banned between 19 June 1850 and 5 May 1851. He affirms that Napoleon III's success was largely the result of this policy of 'compression' of the left.[43] The opposition then reverted to non-political circles or secret societies.[44]

---

40. See Iouda Tchernoff, *Associations et sociétés secrètes sous la deuxième République, 1848–1851*, Paris, F. Alcan, 1905, p. 10.
41. Cited by: Michel Papaud, 'La répression durant le ministère Léon Faucher (janvier–mai 1849)', in *Société d'Histoire de la Révolution de 1848 et des Révolutions du XIXe siècle, Maintien de l'ordre et polices en France et en Europe au XIXe siècle*, Paris, Créaphis, 1987, p. 95.
42. Peter H. Amann, 'Political Justice in the Second French Republic', *The Journal of Modern History*, 1976, vol. 48, (4), pp. 87–124.
43. John M. Merriman, *The Agony of the Republic. The Repression of the Left in Revolutionary France, 1848–1851*, New Haven/London, Yale University Press, 1978, p. 56. See also: Thomas R. Forstenzer, *French Provincial Police and the Fall of the Second Republic. Social Fear and Counterrevolution*, Princeton NJ, Princeton University Press, 1981.
44. Huard, *La naissance du parti politique en France*, pp. 103–110.

From the denial of freedom of assembly to the liberal Empire

While Article 1 of the Constitution of 14 January 1852 states that it 'recognises, confirms and guarantees the great principles proclaimed in 1789, and that are the basis of French public law', one of the first acts of the government following the *coup d'État* of 2 December was to subject the right of assembly to severe regulation. On 2 April 1852 a decree replaced public assemblies under the yoke of prior authorisation, in making Article 291 and all subsequent articles of the Penal Code applicable to them, irrespective of their nature and without distinction between types of association. 'Electoral assemblies, as per the 1848 law, were not prohibited in principle; but were confused in fact with public assemblies subject to authorisation by the 1852 decree.'[45] The Supreme Court confirmed, by an order of 4 February 1860, that the new regime of public assemblies also applied to electoral assemblies.[46] Yet this decree did not affect private assemblies, which is the sole reason for which it is surprisingly more liberal than the July 1848 decree. The regulation prevented public political assemblies from being held for an extensive period of time. Freedom of assembly had not been as weak since the First Empire. Huard claims that:

> Apart from some meeting rooms or circles ignored by power, particularly in rural areas, mutual assistance societies [...] and some secret societies which escaped repression [...], the activity of political sociability [...], was [...] completely interrupted for a certain time.[47]

In the 1860s the regime moved towards greater liberalism.[48] Discrete private preparatory assemblies were held, particularly in the run-up to the 1863 legislative elections. Jules Simon recalls how '[he would enter] a shop or café through a by-way and be directed to a back-room' where people would 'speak in a low voice like conspirators ready to perform some villainous act'.[49] We have to wait until the end of the decade for a real change. In a letter of 19 January 1867 to the Minister of the Interior, Eugène Rouher, Napoleon III declared it 'necessary to regulate the right of assembly legislatively according to the limits demanded by public security'. This opened the way for a new law on 6 June 1868, depicted by the republican opposition as being too restrictive of freedom, and by the authoritarian right as being dangerous and likely to cause a return to the disorders of the clubs. It was, however, only a law of tolerance. It removed the need for authorisation — but not the declaration, to be made three days in advance by seven citizens living in the municipality — for public assemblies not discussing political or religious

---

45. Raymond Huard, *Le suffrage universel en France (1848–1946)*, Paris, Aubier, 1991, p. 75.
46. Marcel-Louis Degrenne, *Les réunions et les pouvoirs de police*, Caen, Caron & Cie, 1938, p. 42.
47. Huard, *La naissance du parti politique en France*, p. 111.
48. Roger Price, *The French Second Empire. An Anatomy of Political Power*, Cambridge, Cambridge University Press, 2001.
49. Jules Simon, *Le soir de ma journée*, Paris, Flammarion, 1901, pp. 303–305.

subjects and for electoral rallies. Without insisting here on the various conditions to which assemblies are subject — holding in a 'closed and covered' place, the obligation to end before the public closing hour, responsibilities of the *déclarants*, the owner of the room, the members of the *bureau,* etc. — we should note that an administrative or legal official was entitled to attend any assembly and dissolve it if he thought that it was dealing with issues alien to the subject indicated in the declaration or whenever it was judged likely to become unruly. Any assembly considered likely to disrupt public order could also be adjourned by the prefect or banned by the Minister of the Interior. Assemblies that were organised in the run-up to legislative elections and open exclusively for candidates and electors in the constituency could only be held during the electoral periods which excluded the five days prior to the vote. They could be held one day after the declaration rather than three as had formerly been the case.

Despite these restrictions the law led to a rush towards political assemblies, particularly in Paris, thus largely exceeding the aims of its promoters. From June 1868 to May 1870 a thousand assemblies were held.[50] Regarding non-electoral assemblies, the problem of assessing precisely when an assembly addressing so-called social issues slides in the direction of politics, soon becomes evident. These permeable boundaries allowed many political assemblies to take place. The electoral campaigns of May and June 1869 demonstrated an increase with nothing in common with those quasi-clandestine assemblies held six years earlier: 'In the nine electoral districts of the capital [...], exactly 200 [assemblies] were organised, with an audience of tens of thousands'.[51] The colossal nature of this experience leads us to think that the political assembly, which prospered later under the Republic, was partly shaped under the Empire. Philip Nord notes on electoral assemblies: 'Under the Third Republic, the *réunion électorale* acquired quasi-institutional status, but its origins were far from humdrum, anchored as they were in years of shadow boxing with a hostile imperial officialdom'.[52]

Unlike the studies of assemblies of earlier periods, which do not focus on specific elements, the sole subject of the book by Dalotel, Faure and Freiermuth, *Aux origines de la Commune*, are the assemblies of the end of the Second Empire. The aim in studying these assemblies, their geography, personnel and physiognomy, was to demonstrate that 'the Commune did not emerge from [...] circumstances created by the Franco-Prussian war of 1870, [...] but from revolutionary action, in particular the movement of public assemblies in the preceding years'.[53] To this end, the research focuses mainly on socialist and communist assemblies and what is called the 'red clubs', leaving aside other possible types of assembly, a fact recognised at the end of the study:

---

50. Alain Dalotel, Alain Faure and Jean-Claude Freiermuth, *Aux origines de la Commune. Le mouvement des réunions publiques à Paris. 1868–1870*, Paris, F. Maspero, 1980, p. 7.
51. Dalotel, Faure and Freiermuth, *Aux origines de la Commune*, p. 39.
52. Philip Nord, *The Republican Moment. Struggles for Democracy in Nineteenth Century France*, Cambridge MA, Harvard University Press, 1995, p. 195.
53. Dalotel, Faure and Freiermuth, *Aux origines de la Commune*, p. 7.

The men of 4 September, particularly the radicals, also had experience of public assemblies. A study oriented in this sense could have shown that they had also 'made their arms' in the meeting halls of the end of the Second Empire. This was not our purpose, since we put ourselves in the main perspective of assemblies, namely the revolutionary Commune which broke out in 1871. Our point of view, basically sympathetic to the revolutionaries, therefore could not, without [...] ignoring their importance, replace the radicals as resisting force to the proletarian revolution. Each to his own![54]

Club assemblies under the siege of Paris and the Commune

After the fall of the Second Empire the 1868 law fell into disuse without having been formally repealed. In Paris several clubs reopened and organised assemblies; Gustave de Molinari counted around thirty in the four and a half months before their closure by the provisional government on 22 January 1871.[55] On this date, a decree was published stipulating that: 'Clubs are suppressed until the end of the siege. The places where their meetings are held will immediately be closed.' Several open-air meetings were held, and after the armistice, electoral assemblies were convened — about which we have little information — before the clubs reappeared, as noted by Jacques Rougerie: 'They have increased since March, meeting in churches from the end of April.'[56]

The three authors of *Aux origines de la Commune*, Dalotel, Faure and Freiermuth, have been the only ones to carry out a thorough study of how public assemblies constituted a school of socialism in the final years of the Empire. Yet they are not alone in identifying a link between these assemblies and the Communard clubs. The period of analysis chosen by Robert D. Wolfe in his *The Origins of the Paris Commune. The Popular Organizations of 1868–1871* is indicative of the continuity he wants to reveal.[57] Martin Phillip Johnson's work: *The Paradise of Association. Political Culture and Popular Organizations in the Paris Commune of 1871*, is, according to the author, 'the third volume of a trilogy on popular organisations of 1868–1871' following *Aux origines de la Commune*, which focusses on the end of the Second Empire and Wolfe's work examining the siege of Paris.[58] Johnson's book was the first to study Communard meetings, although the author only devotes a few pages to them, examining the reasons for

---

54. Dalotel, Faure and Freiermuth, *Aux origines de la Commune*, p. 372.
55. Gustave De Molinari, *Les clubs rouges pendant le siège de Paris*, Paris, Garnier Frères, 1871.
56. Jacques Rougerie, *Paris insurgé. La Commune de 1871*, Paris, Gallimard, 1995, pp. 78–79.
57. Robert D. Wolfe, *The Origins of the Paris Commune. The Popular Organizations of 1868–1871*, PhD dissertation, Harvard University, 1966. See also: Roger V. Gould, *Insurgent Identities. Class, Community, and Protest in Paris from 1848 to the Commune*, Chicago, University of Chicago Press, 1995, pp. 121–152.
58. Martin Phillip Johnson, *The Paradise of Association. Political Culture and Popular Organizations in the Paris Commune of 1871*, Ann Arbor, University of Michigan Press, 1996, p. vii.

attending assemblies. The accounts of interrogation before a military tribunal suggest that many participants were motivated simply by curiosity or a desire to be entertained, whereas the mere act of attending a club meeting was 'a public political statement with a risk of retribution', stresses Johnson. The meetings organised by clubs, often held in churches, were then described as an opportunity to take part in a series of 'rituals in song and actions' which created a feeling of unity among participants.[59]

In 1875, when France consecrated its Republican Constitution, practically nothing changed in freedom of assembly as defined under the 1868 law. We must wait until 1879 for the opening of legislative debate and 30 June 1881 for the law which established a much more liberal regime than the previous system. We cannot say, however, that 'the Republic waited [until] 1879 before concerning itself with building a modern and definitive freedom of assembly.[60] Several legal proposals were submitted after 1876, but were largely unsuccessful due to the dissolution of the Chamber in June 1877. The article 1 of the 1881 law states that 'public assemblies are free' and replaces the old system of prior authorisation by a simple declaration which can be made closer to the date of the assembly. With this law, citizens' right to assemble entered a new phase. Freedom was further extended in 1901 when the law on associations suppressed Article 7 of the 1881 law banning clubs, and in 1907 when Aristide Briand abolished the compulsory prior declaration for all assemblies. They could now be held freely. The Third Republic was indeed the golden age of French political assemblies.

---

59. Johnson, *The Paradise of Association*, pp. 206–207.
60. Pierre Rosanvallon, *La démocratie inachevée. Histoire de la souveraineté du peuple en France*, Paris, Gallimard, 2000, p. 323.

Part I

Consolidating Representative Democracy

Chapter One

The Ideal of Participation Without Action

> Public assemblies are both an instrument of ruin for oppressive governments and the best guarantee of stability for those which [...] tread in truly democratic paths inspired by [public] opinion.[1]

Lawyer and journalist Émile Faure and Anatole Fontaine de Rambouillet, known for his defences during 'trials of opinion'[2] under the Second Empire, ended their study of the right of assembly by emphasising the link between democracy, public opinion and freedom of assembly. *Le peuple et la place publique*, published shortly after the vote on the 'dubious and hypocritical' law of June 1868, is a defence of the people's right to enjoy a true freedom of assembly. This freedom is indeed the only one that allows public opinion to develop and be expressed properly; that is, a public opinion that democratic governments should not consider to be a threat. On the contrary, these governments should be based on public opinion in order to set themselves apart from despotic regimes.

This position was shared by the whole body of republicans speaking on the question of the right to free assembly, when they struggled against the restraints imposed by the Empire or when they worked in order to establish the fundamental laws of the Third Republic. The existence of elections with universal suffrage is not a sufficient condition for a democratic society. Democracy and republic — the latter being conceived as necessarily democratic, the two terms were used interchangeably to indicate a representative government whose legitimacy is based on the will of the people — also imply that voting depends on an enlightened opinion and that mechanisms exist, in addition to the vote, that allow its development and expression. Discussion between the citizens at the assembly is seen as the most natural and democratic means to achieve this. In the last part of the nineteenth century, republicans saw assemblies as a form of popular participation which would consolidate representative democracy by replacing participation-action by participation-opinion.

---

1. Émile Faure and Anatole Fontaine de Rambouillet, *Le peuple et la place publique. Historique du droit de réunion*, Paris, Décembre-Alonnier, 1869, pp. 202–204.
2. These are trials against opinions deemed as illegal and expressed in the press, speeches, books, pamphlets and so forth.

Governing without fear of public opinion

> The new social configuration that emerges at the end of the century leads to a complete shift of the attention hitherto focussed on society and politics. The representative principle now faces a new reality: that of numbers.[3]

The arrival of the masses on the public scene raised the urgent question of what form should be taken by popular participation if it was not to compromise the stability of the regime. The principle of popular sovereignty was accepted, but its form had yet to be decided; as we have seen, the promotion of opinion is related to the conciliation between public order on the one hand, and the imperative of mass participation on the other.[4] Under the Second Empire, government policy limiting freedom of assembly was attacked by the republican opposition as being symptomatic of a distrust of public opinion, which the government claimed to have as support. The difference between imperial and republican politics regarding the right of assembly lies in particular in the conflict between repression and prevention. The latter was considered an open door to despotism: therefore the Republic opted for a basically repressive system.

The bond between the Republic, public opinion and freedom of assembly

The question of the role of public opinion in a government based on universal suffrage is already central under the Second Empire. This unavoidable reference to opinion is obvious in the debates on the 1868 law. The liberal reforms following the imperial letter of January 1867 to the Minister of State, Eugène Rouher, are thus presented as the outcome of listening to public opinion, that is, the proof that government is based on the will of the People. In his memoirs, Émile Ollivier, who joined the liberal Empire shortly after the vote on the law, writes that unlike 'conservatives', for whom the right of assembly 'causes [...] even more alarm than freedom of the press', the Emperor: 'as he prided himself on democracy [...] understood that this right is a truly democratic freedom'.[5] During the debates in the Legislative Body of March–May 1868, those defending the government bill insist on its democratic character: for them the bill favours the expression of the People's opinion. On 17 March, the Minister of Justice, Pierre Baroche, exclaimed:

---

3. François D'Arcy and Guy Saez, 'De la représentation', in François D'Arcy (ed.), *La représentation*, Paris, Economica, 1985, p. 16.

4. Pierre Rosanvallon, *Le sacre du citoyen. Histoire intellectuelle du suffrage universel en France*, Paris, Gallimard, 1992; *La démocratie inachevée. Histoire de la souveraineté du peuple en France*, Gallimard, Bibliothèque des histoires, 2000; *Le peuple introuvable. Histoire de la représentation démocratique en France*, Gallimard, Bibliothèque des histoires, 1998; Dominique Reynié, *Le triomphe de l'opinion publique. L'espace public français du XVIe au XXe siècle*, Paris, Odile Jacob, 1998.

5. Émile Ollivier, *L'Empire libéral. Études, récits, souvenirs*, Paris, Garnier Frères, 1905, p. 428.

It is not this Government that should be taught understanding and respect for public opinion! The sovereignty of public opinion has been defined in noble words; recognised with solemnity and confirmed by the Head of Government.[6]

This recollection of the position of the Empire with regard to public opinion comes as no surprise; the principle of popular sovereignty was one of the cornerstones of the political model of 'illiberal democracy' constituted by Napoleon III's government.[7]

A broad freedom of assembly had long been demanded by the liberal opposition particularly on behalf of the bond between citizens' rights to assemble, public opinion and democracy. This was also the way that the legislative proposal under debate was criticised by Émile Ollivier. On 14 March, Ollivier developed the idea that if the Empire was to be democratic, it had to grant a true right of assembly to its citizens: 'A democratic government without freedom of assembly is inconceivable.' For Ollivier the judgement of citizens on public issues takes shape in meetings. As a consequence: 'thanks to freedom of assembly [...] a government never ignores what takes place in a nation's soul'.[8] The republican opposition did not take up his argument or associate imperial government with democracy at all. Although the 1852 Constitution claims to: 'recognise, confirm and guarantee the great principles proclaimed in 1789', and even though the Empire preserved universal suffrage, this did not make it a democracy for the simple reason that it ignored freedom. The republican opposition thus suggested that it was indeed normal for the Empire to be wary of freedom of assembly; were people to express themselves freely, the government would be unlikely to outlive the criticism.

Under the Third Republic, the belief in the idea that the right of assembly is a natural consequence of democratic government emerges clearly in the debates on the draft laws submitted to the Chamber of Deputies. In 1878 the legal recital for the second law proposed by Alfred Naquet bears witness to this. Two years earlier, when close to radical republicans, Naquet had demanded an absolute right to assembly, but his proposal failed. Naquet affirmed that he had not changed his opinion, but realised it was not realistic if one wanted a law to be adopted rapidly. Therefore Naquet scaled down his demands by conceding to a framing of freedom —in parallel towards his evolution to Opportunism. On 30 May 1878 he affirms that the existence of a genuine right to assembly, above all in political matters, allows men to say whether or not a government is democratic. Resolutely declaring with reference to the past, that: 'the obstacles to the right of assembly are a legacy of absolute monarchy', suggesting that the Empire obstructed political debate as this would have been to the detriment of the government in 'making a chink in its actions'. Because 'silence and night are the preconditions for monarchy

---

6. *Le Moniteur Universel*, 18 March 1868, p. 408.
7. Pierre Rosanvallon, 'Les corps intermédiaires dans la démocratie', course at the Collège de France, 2002–2003, http://www.college-de-france.fr/media/pierre-rosanvallon/UPL28739_UPL25235_prosanvallon.pdf, p. 1020 (accessed 6 June 2006).
8. *Le Moniteur Universel*, 15 March 1868, p. 389.

and oligarchy, just as speech and day are the preconditions for the Republic', the republican government that is coming into being must be based on freedom of assembly. Indeed, it rests on popular sovereignty:

> If it is true that the People [...] are sovereign, that it is to the People and to the People alone that the government of the country is responsible, it is clear that citizens must have the right to meet to discuss their interests.[9]

Yet the same argument was used later on by those who continued to defend absolute freedom. During the debate leading to the law of June 1881 that started in 1879, three drafts were examined: that of Naquet in 1878; that of Louis Legrand, close to the republican Opportunists and the most conservative; and that of the Radical republican Louis Blanc, the most liberal. Blanc demanded the suppression of all laws limiting freedom of assembly and association. On 27 January 1880 Georges Perin, whose position was close to that of the radicals defended the draft, returning to the idea that freedom of assembly is directly related to republican democracy, the sole form of government which does not fear absolute freedom.

In the years following the vote on the 1881 law, this bond between the Republic and freedom of assembly made meetings a form of incarnation of the Republic itself. Thus, when there were incidents such as fights breaking out, the press associated them with the poor health of the Republic. If violence occurs during an assembly of revolutionary groups, the reactionary press interprets it as a sign of failure: the Republic's rash desire to grant freedom of assembly and its consequent inability to maintain order, and the regret for the time when this sort of liberty was not allowed. Depending on their more or less close proximity to government, the Republican newspapers affirmed either that government must react to maintain order — the risk being that otherwise the assemblies would discredit the Republic — or that disorder would not undermine the Republic — since those responsible were only marginal actors. The press which supported organisers of the 'guilty' assemblies often denounced troublemakers as government agents who had come to cause disorder and to scare the bourgeoisie who thought that they had taken refuge in the Republic, whose practices hardly differed from those of former tyrannies.

On 20 September 1885 an assembly was organised in the Palais de la Bourse by a workers' electoral committee. The selection of the *bureau*[10] in a packed room gave way to clashes between various groups of radical leftists: blanquists, collectivists and anarchists. A fight broke out among the public, chairs were thrown, and glasses and carafes prepared for the speakers were used as missiles. Two people were wounded in the midst of the general turmoil after two shots were fired. Yet the assembly was not interrupted. A relative calm returned and speeches were made. The use of a firearm in an assembly and the fact that the police did not intervene, but only checked the disorder at the exit, gave rise to much

---

9. Legal recital on the proposed law on right of assembly was presented by Naquet on 30 May 1878.
10. All assemblies set up a *bureau* to organise the speeches.

speculation in the press.[11] On 22 September the republican newspaper *Le Siècle* was concerned by the fact that the press of 'retrograde parties' would exploit this incident to the detriment of the Republic: 'They will not hesitate to exaggerate the facts and use them against the government of freedom that allowed them, and the government of the Republic under which they took place.'[12] Indeed the same day the anti-republican catholic newspaper *La Défense sociale et religieuse*, drew a lesson from the progress of this 'democratic-socialist anarchist, so-called worker's assembly': political mores had not 'softened' under republican government, but 'this so-called [softening and refreshing] government, now causes bitter irritation and over-excitement unworthy of a "great democracy"'. In addition to condemning the exploitation of events by reactionaries, the republican press stressed the risk of seeing the Republic 'dishonoured' by this 'revolver [used] as an argument in a public assembly'.[13] Two days earlier *Le Temps* recalled that 'the interest of the Republic' is at stake in the fight to prevent 'public assemblies [from being transformed] into battlefields' — *Le Temps* was then a newspaper for a 'better-off and more educated readership' with a very moderate editorial line.[14] In the press sympathetic to the organisers of the assembly the bond between freedom of assembly and democracy was also raised, but in different form: the revolver shots were fired by an *agent provocateur* working for the Opportunists in order to make it appear that the socialists condoned violence. Had the government resumed the practices of the Empire?

> We have the right to ask ourselves if we are not [...] in the presence of a government manœuvre; today the leaders appear [to be] anxious above all to keep the traditions, dear to all tyrannies, 'pure'.[15]

The bond between Republic, opinion and right of assembly was also affirmed in the analyses of many legal experts who have examined freedom of assembly as permitted under the 1881 law. The legal commentaries written shortly after the approval of the law always tend towards a reinforcement of republican political order: if the partial nature of biographical information on the legal experts cited here means that we cannot know whether this gave them any symbolic or material reward, we can nonetheless perceive them as 'the auxiliaries of republican politics'.[16] First, in the general formulas that affirm the bond between freedom

---

11. See the press dossier in APP/Ba/617/Réunion électorale au Palais de la Bourse, dimanche 20 septembre 1885 par le comité électoral ouvrier des 1er et 2e arrondissements, Fédération des travailleurs socialistes de France, Parti ouvrier, Possibilistes.
12. *Le Siècle*, 22 September 1885.
13. *Le Siècle*, 24 September 1885.
14. Gilles Feyel, *La presse en France des origines à 1944. Histoire politique et matérielle*, Paris, Ellipses, 1999, p. 139.
15. *Le Cri du Peuple*, 23 September 1885.
16. Guillaume Sacriste, *Le droit de la République (1870–1914). Légitimation(s) de l'État et construction du rôle de professeur de droit constitutionnel au début du siècle*, PhD dissertation,

of assembly and democracy: freedom of assembly is the 'natural consequence of the participation of the People in government',[17] and its 'destiny [...] is related to that of democratic government'.[18] The nature of this bond is specified by the reference to the role of opinion. In order to survive, a democratic government must rest on public opinion, which is the 'instrument of government *par excellence*'.[19] Assemblies are the key place for its expression and 'for public opinion to form in a country, citizens must be able to write freely and to assemble to discuss public issues'.[20] The difference with the writing of legal experts who, during the interwar period made a more belated weighing up of the impact of the 1881 law, is striking. The latter often reacted against the naivety of law-makers, who only wanted to see 'the intellectual' goals of assemblies and who only had in mind an 'exchange of ideas'.[21] The legal provisions were devised with this sole and specific view of what constitutes an assembly. But the 1930s' legal experts have stressed however, that assemblies could also become a dangerous 'exercise of mobilisation'.[22]

Putting and end to prevention

The republican legislature had broken with the system prevailing under the Empire. Although it took some years for the Republic to produce a new law, when adopted, this helped launch a distinctly more liberal form of government.[23] The willingness to change first appears in the law's opening affirmation. Article 1, which was added by the Senate to the text submitted by the Chamber, is very clear: 'Public assemblies are free.' In a report to the Senate of 8 February 1881 Émile Labiche, an active member of the republican left, justified this proclamation:

Paris I, 2002, p. 27. The author is in part opposed to analyses of Marie-Joëlle Redor, insisting on the contestation of republican order by legal experts: Marie-Joëlle Redor, *De L'État légal à l'État de droit. L'évolution des conceptions de la doctrine publiciste française. 1879–1914*, Aix-en-Provence, Presses Universitaires d'Aix-Marseille, Economica, 1992.

17. Jean Fournier-Poncelet, *La liberté de réunion au XXe siècle. Étude de droit public comparé*, Aix, de Barlatier, 1910, p. 24; Albert Joubrel, *Du droit de réunion*, Rennes, Librairie générale Pilhon et Hommay, 1904, p. 14.
18. Degrenne, *Les réunions et les pouvoirs de police*, p. 9.
19. Fournier-Poncelet, *La liberté de réunion au XXe siècle*, p. 76.
20. Degrenne, *Les réunions et les pouvoirs de police*, p. 213.
21. Maurice Menanteau, *Les nouveaux aspects de la liberté de réunion. Essai sur les caractères juridiques et politiques de la liberté de réunion en France*, Paris, Librairie technique et économique, 1937, pp. 85–86. See also: Marcel Le Clère, *Les réunions, manifestations et attroupements en droit français et comparé*, Paris, Impr. Petites Affiches, 1945, pp. 5–7, 16.
22. Le Clère, *Les réunions*, p. 14.
23. In addition to the error on the date of the 1868 law, we disagree with the affirmation that 'the Naquet law, promulgated on 30 June 1881, regulating the right of assembly, was not much more liberal than the law of 25 March 1868 that it replaced'. See: Jean-Marc Berlière, *Le monde des polices en France. XIXe–XXe siècles*, Brussels, Complexe, 1996, p. 116.

It was useful that this statement dominated all the provisions that follow, not only in order to constitute an unquestionable theoretical affirmation, but also to serve as an interpretative rule for the administration and the judiciary.

If the hallmark of the 1881 law was the desire to put an end to the despotism prevailing under the Empire, this was above all when it did away with most of the preventive measures whose purpose was to avoid potential offences from taking place, rather than applying repressive measures *post factum*. As with freedom of the press, it 'grants a freedom defined by limits beyond which legal action is triggered'.[24] Safeguarding public order was primarily the competence of the judicial rather than administrative or police authorities. It is this judicial sanction that those who intend to break the law should fear.

The choice of a repressive system had already been promoted under the Empire by the republicans fighting for freedom. The liberal press returned to this regularly and preventive measures were also denounced in the National Assembly during the debate on the 1868 law. This was the case, for example, during the discussion of the Article giving prefects the right to adjourn assemblies, and the Minister of the Interior the right to prohibit any of them considered dangerous. On 13 March 1868, Jules Simon, one of the most popular speakers in the republican group, attacks this as 'despotism *in personam*', exclaiming: 'what do we call the right to adjourn, the right to ban, in French? It is called despotic government'.[25] We find the same argument against preventive measures under the Republic. In the legal recital for his legislative proposal on 31 May 1878, Naquet rejects the idea that an assembly can be pre-emptively banned, by a prefect, a Minister or a Head of State:

> Naturally [...] the government could always break up and contest an assembly that degenerates into insurrection; but there is a veritable chasm between the repression of an offence or crime and measures to prevent crimes or offences. The preventive system is the basis of authoritarian governments; the repressive system is the basis of all liberal systems.[26]

When the debate on the two drafts still in competition opened on 24 January 1880, that of the commission presented by Naquet, and that of the government — those of Louis Blanc and Louis Legrand already been excluded — the government draft did contain some preventive measures, but the system finally adopted was basically repressive.

The main provision in this sense is Article 1 of the law. After establishing the principle of freedom of assembly, it goes on to reject prior authorisation required by the 1868 legislation on assemblies dealing with political or religious subjects. This was suppressed in all cases and replaced by a simple declaration which allowed the police to be informed that an assembly was to be held. The

---

24. Reynié, *Le triomphe de l'opinion publique*, p. 220.
25. *Le Moniteur Universel*, 14 March 1868, p. 384.
26. *Journal Officiel*, 11 June 1878, p. 6,543.

obligatory character of the declaration was later suppressed in the Briand Law of 28 March 1907. This was in order to settle the problems linked to the church's refusal to subscribe to the annual declaration for cultural assemblies stipulated in the 1905 law on the separation of church and state. Thus, all traces of prevention disappeared from the statute book.

Article 2 of the law stipulates that the declaration must specify the place, day and time of the assembly, and the names, social rank and residence of the *déclarants*. There must be at least two *déclarants*, one of whom must be domiciled in the town where the assembly will take place. The liberalisation is clear relative to imperial law, which demands that the declaration be 'signed by seven people domiciled in the town where it is to take place'. In 1881, as in 1868, the *déclarants* must have full civil and political rights. The principal disagreement between government and the commission on the content of the declaration concerns Article 4. The commission considered that in order to avoid any temptation towards prevention, the declaration should be limited to specifying the form of the assembly without specifying its agenda. The government wanted the subject of the assembly to be specified, without departing on this point from the 1868 law. Naquet opposed this firmly on 27 January 1880 while defending the commission's draft, by stressing that such a provision had been included under the Empire, in which political and religious assemblies were subject to prior authorisation: 'Given the nature of [the 1868 law], this provision imposed itself'. If citizens were granted the right to assemble to discuss all issues as the Republic wished, this remnant of imperial prevention would have to be removed. 'If I have the right to discuss everything, why do you want to impose the obligation to specify my subject [...]?'[27] When it was finally elected, Article 4 only mentioned the form of the assembly: 'the declaration will stipulate whether the subject of the assembly is a conference, a public discussion, or an electoral meeting'.

The rejection of prevention is also evident in the suppression of the right for the authorities to ban or adjourn an assembly. In its initial plan, however, the government provided for this possibility: 'In the case of impending trouble, the heads of police, prefects and vice-prefects can adjourn public assemblies in their care by referring immediately to the Minister of the Interior.' Charles Lepère, Minister of the Interior and very active in the debate, defended this article on 29 January 1880, with specific reference to the worker's insurrection of June 1848:

> Suppose, for example, within the population of Paris a [...] public mood as it was on the eve of 24 June 1848, a state of extreme over-excitement; suppose that, in this situation, authority, which is aware of this state of mind, receives fifty declarations of assemblies to be held at various points, assemblies organised by agitators speculating on the over-excitement of the population; and tell me if you do not find that there is a very great danger, [a] very considerable, imminent threat, a great public peril, and if you think that the government [...] should not be armed so as not to remain powerless in the face

---

27. *Journal Officiel*, 28 January 1880, p. 226.

of sedition organised under its eyes and by these riot regiments, [...], forming in various parts of the city and all joining the headquarters of the insurrection?[28]

The article was voted in its first sitting, but rejected by the Chamber in the second. Thus, the power to authorise, adjourn or prohibit, which Jules Simon saw as an expression of arbitrary power under the Empire, did not figure in the final version of the 1881 law. The same applies in cases of imminent risk to public order where disorder cannot be prevented by prior banning of an assembly: only in this way can despotism be avoided. The authorities could neither adjourn assemblies nor prohibit them, and after 1907 they did not even have to be informed.

In Article 9 the law nevertheless stipulates that 'an administrative or judicial *fonctionnaire* can be delegated to attend the assembly', by the prefect of police in Paris and by the prefect, vice-prefect or mayor in the *départements*. However, their powers were considerably reduced in relation to those attributed with the 1868 law. Under the Empire, the delegated official could dissolve an assembly 'if the *bureau*, once warned, allows discussion of questions alien to the object of the assembly' or 'if the assembly becomes unruly'. In practice this power led to a great many dissolutions. In the 1881 law, the right to dissolve was limited to two cases. It could not be exercised by an official representing authority 'unless called for by the *bureau*, or if crashes and physical assaults occur'. Thus the main role of an official was basically repressive, and meant drawing up a record of potential crimes committed at the meeting in order to transmit this to the judicial authorities.

The government and the commission diverge on this point. Their plans agree on the principle of the potential presence of an official, but differ as to the nature of his powers. The government plan conserves the opportunity for the official to dissolve the assembly: 'if, after three warnings, the *bureau* allows issues alien to the subject specified in the declaration to be discussed, or allows a person who commits an offense according to the laws, to speak' — an option rejected by the commission — but also 'if the assembly ignores the authority of the chairman, or becomes unruly' — which the commission accepts. With the exception of the opportunity to dissolve a meeting on the grounds that the *bureau* allows issues other than those indicated in the declaration — logically rejected since it did not cite the object of the assembly — the government draft was accepted by the chamber. If Article 9 of the 1881 law was in the last instance more liberal, it was a consequence of the intervention of the Senate.

The question of powers granted to mayors and the head of police in Paris was another key aspect of the law which testified to the shift from a heavy preventive regime to a repressive regime. It concerned the most ambiguous point of the law — an ambiguity that in the 1930s gave rise to interpretations which altered the spirit of the law. Article 9 of the 1881 law stipulated that: 'there are no changes

---

28. *Journal Officiel*, 30 January 1880, p. 1026. It was particularly the failure to make the Chamber adopt some preventive provisions contained in the government draft which led to Lepère's resignation from the Ministry of the Interior. See: Adolphe Robert and Gaston Cougny, *Dictionnaire des parlementaires français de 1789 à 1889*, Paris, Bourloton, 1889–1891, vol. 4, p. 106.

with regard to the provisions of Article 3 of the law of 16–24 August 1790, Article 9 of the law of 19–22 July 1791 and Articles 9 and 15 of the law of 18 July 1837'. Three years later, the law of 5 April 1884 on the organisation of municipalities replaced the first and third of these elements. From then on the policing powers of mayors were governed by the laws of July 1791 and April 1884. The first made the municipal police responsible for 'maintaining normal order and the peace' and gave them the power to issue orders on matters falling within their competence. Furthermore, 'with regard to those places where everyone is freely admitted, such as cafés, cabarets, shops and so forth, police officers can always enter to check for disorder or breaches of regulations'. The law of 5 April 1884 gave mayors: 'powers to suppress attacks on the public peace such as [...] uproar flaring up in places of public gathering' and 'keeping good order in places where there are large gatherings of people'.[29] Thus the mayor had the power to regulate assemblies. In particular, he could break up any assembly considered likely to disturb the peace. But what about his preventive powers? Could a municipal order be taken pre-emptively to ban an assembly considered a threat to public order?

The answer of the legal experts who expressed their opinions after the vote on the 1881 law was negative. Recalling the general powers of the police authorities does not mean recognising preventive powers for mayors. In 1881 the lawyer Charles Constant wrote that: 'a mayor's power is purely repressive, and not preventive; this is a right of surveillance and not of banning'.[30] Thus, the adoption of the 1884 law did not change anything. Commenting on the issue, Léon Morgand also recognised only repressive powers of mayors with regard to assemblies.[31] In 1894, Roger Arnette wrote that the powers of municipal magistrates would 'always be repressive and never preventive'.[32] Thus, until the early twentieth century the juridical commentaries on the law of assembly affirmed that the municipal authorities could not exercise preventive municipal orders. The same position is found in the *repertoire* of legal rulings.[33]

In the first decades of the twentieth century another interpretation of the 1881 law emerged and in 1913, Louis Gervais wrote:

> One accepts that mayors and prefects, whom the law makes responsible for preventing attacks on the public peace, have the right to ban public assemblies organised with a goal openly contrary to law or good behaviour.[34]

---

29. Roger Arnette, *La liberté de réunion en France. Son histoire et sa législation*, Paris, Arthur Rousseau, 1894, p. 168.
30. Charles Constant, *Code des réunions publiques, des réunions électorales et des réunions privées. Commentaire pratique de la loi du 30 juin 1881 à l'usage des préfets, sous-préfets, maires, juges de paix, ainsi que des organisateurs de réunions publiques ou privées*, Paris, A. Durand et Pedone-Lauriel, 1881, p. 73.
31. Léon Morgand, *La Loi municipale, commentaire de la loi du 5 avril 1884 sur l'organisation et les attributions des conseils municipaux*, Paris, Berger-Levrault, vol. 2, 1885, pp. 36–39, 49–50.
32. Arnette, *La liberté de réunion en France*, pp. 172–173.
33. *Répertoire Becquet*, 1907, 'réunion', p. 9; *Répertoire Dalloz*, 43, 'réunion', p. 462.
34. Louis Gervais, *Du droit de réunion en France et en Angleterre*, Montpellier, Impr. De Firmin et Montane, 1913, p. 64.

Yet, premature and isolated recognition of preventive powers testifies to a new interpretation of the law and we see significant consequences of this development in the 1930s. In the meantime, over the decades, the 1881 law established a regimen of freedom without precedent in reducing preventive measures to a minimum. Since the latter were perceived as an open door to the despotic use of power over assemblies and a sign that the authorities distrusted the People, they were unthinkable under a republican government founded on public opinion. This idea prevailed when the 1881 law was adopted and remained valid for a long time. Police and administration only intervened to suppress breaches of the peace.

The most natural and democratic way to frame public opinion

The legislators therefore did not adopt Naquet's proposal, made in 1876 and taken up by Blanc in 1878, for an absolute freedom of assembly. Indeed the dominant idea was that such meetings should be regulated by law so that they constituted an ideal place to develop public opinion and a pillar of representative democracy. The significance given to the normative framing of assemblies can be ascribed to the fact that the new government '[treated] the legal norm as a supreme instrument of social regulation'.[35] Nonetheless, the question of framing freedom of assembly was as sensitive under the Republic as it had been under the Empire. It would be banal to affirm that the right to meet is a natural right, and a need inherent in man's very nature. Then how can we justify legislating on it?

Legislating on a natural right?

Before and after the adoption of the 1868 law, the right of assembly was defended by the liberal opposition to the Empire with reference to its natural character. 'Human nature' condemns limitations placed on 'the ability to assemble to discuss interests of the city and the nation together', wrote Charles Limousin, editor of *Le Siècle*, and the lawyer André Rousselle in 1869.[36] In the same year Émile Faure and Anatole Fontaine de Rambouillet affirmed that human nature demands that men be able to assemble freely because 'man is primarily a social being'.[37] Thus, freedom to assemble cannot be conditional; it is the expression of a natural due and must be considered an inviolable right. This notion of right of assembly was also discussed in the debates in the National Assembly. Garnier-Pagès of the democratic opposition contested the draft law on 12 March 1868, referring to the history of the right of assembly to show that it was 'indeed the right to live in society'.[38]

---

35. François Beaudenon, *Entre ordre et liberté. Le combat républicain contre l'anarchisme. 1880–1900*, MA dissertation, Grenoble, IEP, 1997, pp. 57, 101.
36. André Rousselle and Charles Limousin, *Manuel des réunions publiques non politiques, publiques électorales, électorales privées*, Paris, A. Le Chevalier, 1869, p. 1.
37. Faure and Fontaine de Rambouillet, *Le peuple et la place publique*, p. i.
38. *Le Moniteur universel*, 13 March 1868, p. 376.

There were two responses among the supporters of the government policy. The first was a straight denial that it constituted a natural right. This was the position of the Minister of the Interior, Ernest Pinard, who on 18 March stated:

> This right of assembly is a relative right, a conditional right, a civil right, a right that depends on the temperament, behaviour, character of peoples, and not an inviolable, inalienable, natural right.[39]

This means that it is feasible and necessary to safeguard public order and to set rules to limit its exercise. The second response was a defence of the right of assembly *qua* natural right, but that did not rule out its regulation so as to maintain order. The recognition of the natural character of a right does not automatically imply establishing a regime of absolute freedom. This was the position of Louis Eugène Peyrusse, the law's *rapporteur* who affirmed on 14 March: 'In a properly organised society [...], all natural powers, are subject to limitations and restrictions demanded by public interest'. That is, even if the right to assemble is a natural right, because men are imperfect it must nonetheless be regulated. Leaving them to assemble freely would mean endangering public order: 'Unlimited freedom in politics [...] is a dream, a generous dream, but clearly a dream.'[40] The argument was echoed in the conservative press by Henry-Marie Martin: 'Freedom is a relative thing measured by the condition of each people'.[41]

Although the Assembly did not opt for absolute freedom in 1881, the idea that the right of assembly is inherent to human nature was not absent from legislative debates under the Republic. Interestingly, we find it in the introduction to the report presented by Naquet on behalf of the commission responsible for examining the drafts on 15 July 1879:

> Sirs, public assemblies are as old as human society itself. Ever since men created society, they have felt the need to group together, to assemble, to associate in order to consult each other on their common interests.[42]

The legal recital of the government plan, presented by the Minister of the Interior, Lepère, on 11 December 1879, referred to 'the natural right of citizens to assemble' as though it were self-evident.[43] However, with the exception of the argument advocating the suppression of all legislation demanded by Louis Blanc, insistence on the idea of man's natural right to assemble was less marked under the Republic than when those who eventually developed the law were in opposition to the imperial government.

The justification for the restrictions placed on this natural right by both the government spokesman and the spokesman for the commission echoed that used

---

39. *Le Moniteur universel*, 19 March 1868, p. 414.
40. *Le Moniteur universel*, 15 March 1868, p. 388.
41. *Le Constitutionnel*, 6 September 1868.
42. *Journal Officiel*, 18 August 1879, p. 8,566.
43. *Journal Officiel*, 4 January 1880, p. 74.

in 1868 by Peyrusse the *rapporteur* of the imperial law. On 24 January 1880 Naquet replied on behalf of the commission on the issue of absolute freedom in Blanc's plan, arguing that this would only be possible when 'people's manners [were] profoundly changed', and 'the spirit of freedom' developed — which in particular implied that the Republic was accepted by all. Only then could all rules framing the right of assembly be removed. The granting of immediate absolute freedom to the people might endanger 'public order',[44] and the desire to preserve it was thus legitimate grounds for framing a natural right.

Above all Naquet affirmed that it was to protect freedom itself that a law should specify the conditions in which men could assemble: 'want[ing] to completely eliminate all laws that govern the matter, […] it would not safeguard freedom sufficiently'.[45] There must also be laws to protect freedoms. A similar justification was made by the Minister of the Interior on 13 May: 'For a discussion to be free, so that citizens can truly enjoy the right of assembly […], it must, above all, be order that reigns', also making reference to 'the state of our mores'.[46]

Here we find a basic principle of republican thought on issues of organisation of popular participation in politics. That is, as long as citizens do not acquire republican mores, it is necessary that laws protect not so much public peace as freedom itself. The law's provisions are also a way to frame participation so as to apprentice the People in these new mores. A similar reasoning is used by legal experts. In a speech made in 1880 during a meeting for incoming junior lawyers, Germain Cumenge, lawyer and doctor in law, affirms the 'natural basis' of the right of assembly, while rejecting the idea that legislation would be 'humiliating for citizens'. Establishing a law meant protecting a right; this would be particularly important in France where passions 'run high', parties are 'many' and where men have a 'propensity to oppose each other'.[47] The absence of laws could only be justified by political mores devoid of passion and divisions.

If legislators and legal experts recognise that it is in human nature to assemble in order to discuss, they agree to admit that when the Republic is founded, the right of assembly has to be regulated. The fact that the Republicans 'refuse to accept the mere abolition of all the restrictive legal texts', leads Pierre Rosanvallon to affirm that 'their approach to the question of public assemblies remained characterised by their unwillingness to accept a fully democratic philosophy of public space'.[48] The restrictions on freedom in the 1881 law may be, above all, an indicator of an idea

---

44. *Journal Officiel*, 25 January 1880, p. 760.
45. *Journal Officiel*, 25 January 1880, p. 760.
46. *Journal Officiel*, 14 May 1880, p. 5,220.
47. Germain Cumenge, *Dissertation sur le droit de réunion lue à la séance solennelle de rentrée des avocats stagiaires le 5 décembre 1880*, Toulouse, Douladoure-Privat, 1881, pp. 4, 46–48. See also: Louis Puibaraud, *La législation sur le droit de réunion en France. Extrait de la Revue générale d'administration*, Paris, Berger-Levrault et Cie, 1880.
48. Pierre Rosanvallon, *La démocratie inachevée. Histoire de la souveraineté du peuple en France*, Gallimard, Bibliothèque des histoires, 2000, pp. 323–324.

of popular participation taking the form of a pacified public opinion, which must emerge through the framed use of the right of assembly; that is, a 'holistic ideal of opinion' centred on the 'common good'.[49]

Competition with the press

A month before the vote on the law of 6 June 1868 and a month after that on the law of 30 June 1881, the government legislated on freedom of the press, on 11 May 1868 and July 1881 respectively. The joint formulation of the laws concerning those two modes of expression of opinion — press and assemblies — encourages us to analyse the way in which they are mutually understood and can be compared. Dominique Reynié argues that they are both part of the same process of circumscription of public space. As with the right of assembly, freedom of the press accorded in 1881: 'appears less important *per se*, than for its ability to contain the city and the crowd'.[50] However, according to the author the two freedoms are not regarded in the same way because from the perspective of public order freedom of assembly has always generated more mistrust than freedom of the press. On the one hand, we have a freedom that can be used by a great number of people, which implies collective participation, and that can threaten to spill-over onto the street. On the other hand, we have a freedom whose use is limited to a small number of people, which only implies an abstract collectivity of readers, and does not threaten to confuse the public highway with the public sphere when expressing opinions. Thus, in a more obvious way than the assembly 'the press is a public space compatible with public order'.[51]

When the Republic was established, the legal guarantee of a real right of assembly was more sensitive. It was a mode of participation in public life considered by many as particularly democratic in comparison to that of the press. Even if the two cleavages intersect, the contrast between a presumed elitist and a democratic mode of formation of opinion must not be confused with an opposition between a so-called elitist vision and a so-called democratic vision of the place that opinion in general should occupy in a democracy. On one hand, there is competition between two conceptions of the way in which public opinion is constituted. On the other hand, there is competition between two assessments of the influence that public opinion must have on government choices. Competition between a democratic opinion formed by direct contact with citizens and an aristocratic or bourgeois opinion formed in the exchange of ideas at a distance did not start at the end of the nineteenth century. In the words of Roger Chartier:

---

49. Javier Fernández Sébastián, 'L'avènement de l'opinion publique et le problème de la représentation politique (France, Espagne, Royaume-Uni)', in Javier Fernández Sebastián and Joëlle Chassin (eds), *L'avènement de l'opinion publique. Europe et Amérique, XVIIe–XIXe siècles*, Paris, L'Harmattan, 2004, p. 248.
50. Reynié, *Le triomphe de l'opinion publique*, p. 14.
51. Reynié, *Le triomphe de l'opinion publique*, p. 310.

Before 1889, there are two contrasting ways of constitution of this sovereign authority, [public opinion as an independent court, infallible, imperative] [...]. The one, intellectual and critical (i.e. the exchange of ideas from a distance allowed by circulation of writings). The other, collective and amalgamating, thinks of it as the result of deliberation together and practices of political sociability (i.e. the production of a consensus starting from physically proven experience of unity). [...] The Revolution perpetuated these two ways of conceiving the public. One that, used the reference to the antique city, recognises it as the result of citizens gathering around a living voice, inspired by urgency. One that, faithful to intellectually enlightened people, identifies it with the diffuse society of readers who, without mingling, develop, in their specificity, the same idea of the *res publica*.[52]

As already pointed out, *Le peuple et la place publique*, stresses commitment to freedom of assembly. In their book, Faure and Fontaine de Rambouillet reject the idea of limiting the 'violent need to communicate thought with others' to the sole use of the press. For them, 'it is too easy to see that the written matter, in spite of its progress, is not within the reach of all. And then, it is only an indirect way to communicate thought'.[53] I will return to the difference between the press and the assembly which lies in the fact that there is something in the mere act of gathering together to deliberate that has little to do with what occurs in a dispersed community in Chapter 2. The distinction that occupies me here concerns the quality of those who can devote themselves to the constitution of public opinion.

Contrary to what Dalotel, Faure and Freiermuth write,[54] the defence of the right of assembly was certainly not neglected by the republican opposition to the Empire to the sole benefit of the 'bourgeois' freedom of the press. The right of assembly was vital for republicans, but the argument that freedom of assembly is more important than freedom of the press because it is open to all met with little consensus. It is logically not mentioned in newspapers, and is almost absent from legislative debate under both the Empire and the Republic. The rarity of this type of argument reveals the particular attachment of republicans to freedom of the press. The bond between democracy and the right of assembly is highlighted by speakers in legislative assemblies. This bond is epitomised by Émile Ollivier on 14 March 1868 defending the idea of the right of assembly before the Legislative Body as a 'veritable popular right', comparing it directly with freedom of the press. This is 'an aristocratic right' for which one needs 'material capital, money', but also 'intellectual capital, acquired instruction'. The right of assembly, he says:

---

52. Roger Chartier, 'Opinion publique et propagande en France', in *L'image de la Révolution française. Communications présentées lors du Congrès mondial pour le bicentenaire de la Révolution, Sorbonne, Paris, 6–12 juillet 1989*, Paris, Pergamon, 1990, p. 2,350.
53. Faure and Fontaine de Rambouillet, *Le peuple et la place publique*, pp. vi–vii.
54. Alain Dalotel, Alain Faure and Jean-Claude Freiermuth, *Aux origines de la Commune. Le mouvement des réunions publiques à Paris. 1868–1870*, Paris, F. Maspero, 1980, p. 22.

Is the right of the People, the right of the poor man, the means by which the humblest can take part in public life, as we, educated people, do it through freedom of the press.[55]

Under the Second Empire competition between the press and assemblies as privileged vehicles of opinion revolved around the accounts of meetings appearing in the press, particularly the meetings of the extreme left, which were the most numerous. Journalists were often accused by organisers of downgrading assemblies, distorting speakers' remarks, and depicting what occurred in a rather derogatory way. 'It is', announce the authors of a brochure containing reports of socialist and communist assemblies,[56] 'in order to put an end, once and for all, to invectives and insults with which Messrs. Journalists every day overwhelm public assemblies in Paris, that we are publishing the present account of popular sessions'. Tension was high from the first public assemblies after the adoption of the 1868 law.

There is nothing surprising in the fact that the attitude of the pro-government conservative press was denounced by the participants in gatherings of the extreme left. The reports that these newspapers reproduce are very disparaging about their progress and are quick to report any violence, verbal or physical, real or imagined. The assemblies referred to are above all non-electoral public assemblies organised by the socialists, who profited from the vagueness of the law to publicise the study of economic and social issues on their agenda. Thus, 'public assemblies' became the classic title of articles, or an entire section of these newspapers. On 27 January 1869 Henri Baudrillard, who specialised in attacks on assemblies, wrote in *Le Constitutionnel* that 'it is the duty of the press to indicate these excesses for which Paris is the favourite theatre'. According to a report commissioned in 1875 by the Ministry of the Interior on the 'practice of the law of 6 June 1868', and based on the collection of police minutes, the administration recognised this role of the press by transmitting its reports to them:

> From January 1869 the administration helped by stenographers the police commissioners delegated in the most important assemblies. [...] The typewritten reports were passed by the police prefect to the newspaper *Le Pays* which incorporated them, commented on them, in a way which was not always impartial.[57]

The disapproval aroused by these attacks on public assemblies by the pro-government press came from the tribunes of the meetings as well as from journalists in the liberal press. Indeed, the latter regularly defended the fledgling exercise of the right of assembly by showing that these were minor incidents exaggerated

---

55. *Le Moniteur Universel*, 15 March 1868, p. 389.
56. *Les orateurs des réunions publiques de Paris en 1869. Compte rendu des séances publiques. Publié par Louis-Albert avec le concours d'une société de citoyens communistes et socialistes habitués des assemblées populaires*, Paris, Plataut, 1869.
57. APP/Ba/1520. *Le Pays* is one of the important publications of the imperialist press.

by the official press, brandishing the 'red spectre' to scare provincial readers and egging them on to vote for the imperialists. According to *Le Siècle*, the moderate liberal bourgeoisie newspaper:

> The worker population in Paris is portrayed to the provinces as a bunch of communists, bloodthirsty clubists, immoral, perverse beings, burning to sate their most hideous appetites on *honest folk*.[58]

The liberal press was, however, also criticised by the organisers of assemblies. Its overall position is to denounce the obstacles to their free exercise, deplore the increase of preventive suspensions of assemblies, condemn the legal actions against speakers, and stress that public order was never really threatened by assemblies. Yet the very same liberal press sometimes expressed regret for 'excessive language' — an expression used several times by various newspapers — a criticism of the ideas of some speakers, generally described as not serious, and lamenting the attitude of participants when they did not allow everybody that wanted to speak to do so. This was the position of a series of liberal newspapers, analysed for the period running from June 1868 to June 1869,[59] with variations in the more or less mocking way of reporting these 'excesses'. The position of journalists is, however, always to say that these are minor evils that will pass with the free exercise of the right to assembly.

Journalists working for *Le Siècle* that were often attacked in meetings, protested particularly against the fact that 'democratic newspapers' such as theirs, were presented as the enemies of assemblies instead of the contrary, their defenders. Talking about Parisian assemblies, the journalist and professor of history, Léon Plée, wrote: 'We defended them in principle, and we have only disapproved of some details. Some allowed violent language and sometimes these violent words are against us.'[60] In January 1869, the antipathy of the liberal press for such meetings was denounced by the chairman of a public assembly. On 20 January Charles Limousin, co-author of the aforementioned *Manuel des réunions publiques* and editor of *Le Siècle*, responded with an article entitled 'The Press and Meetings'. It presented the reproaches issued by the worker speaker, who would have 'claimed that journalists being privileged, monopolists, take umbrage at free forums [...] because they threaten their position'. The journalist considered this to be an ungrateful attitude towards a newspaper that had fought unceasingly for freedom: 'Let them show in *Le Siècle* a sole attack or even an insinuation against the right of assembly!'

The division between assemblies and the press did not disappear under the Republic. The fact that the pro-government press demonstrated more moderation towards its political opponents did not change things very much. The debate on the role of journalists in a revolutionary meeting of 'unemployed workers' organised

---

58. *Le Siècle*, 12 February 1867.
59. *Le Siècle, La Presse, Le Temps, Le Réveil, Le Journal des Débats*, etc.
60. *Le Siècle*, 8 February 1869.

in the Lévis meeting room on 23 November 1884, testifies to this.[61] According to police and press reports the public at the assembly, a few thousand people, was made up of anarchists, socialists of various types, unemployed workers not known as militants, and 'curious onlookers', that is to say, people unknown to the police or press and who did not correspond to their image of revolutionary activists or impoverished workers. During the assembly, the agitation does not seem to have been above the normal level for this type of event. There were many interruptions, and the noise was difficult to control, but a dispute set a section of participants against the police officers posted at the exit, one of whom was pursued by a group. The entire press reported the event and few newspapers present the assembly as a calm gathering of poverty-stricken workers come to hear speakers rightly expressing their distress and anguish. Most describe the speeches as heated and likely to incite the public to violence. According to *Le Temps*: 'We see citizens used in anarchist assemblies on the platform […]. All with the same cry: "Death to the bourgeois! Death to the sated!" […] The room proclaimed.'[62]

When a trial opened in January 1885 against some organisers and speakers, it was not only these press reports that were cited by the prosecution. Journalists were also called on to testify on what was heard and transcribed.[63] The 'provocations to crimes and offences' committed in public assemblies can indeed be punished by virtue of chapter IV of 1881 law on freedom of the press, 'Crimes and offences committed by way of the press or by any other means of publication'.[64] However this required proof that the speeches uttered really had this character. A report by the district commissioner where the assembly took place informed the head of police that they had, in accordance with orders, 'sought some honourable persons in [his] neighbourhood who had attended […] the public assembly at the Lévis meeting room and had heard the provocation and incitement of the speakers'. These were mainly tradesmen. But, the commissioner added '[to ignore] if these persons want to say what they heard to the investigating judge', and specified that '[he has not] seen them in order to avoid anything that could be taken for moral pressure'. Faced with these difficulties, the court made recourse to witnesses easier to identify, that is, journalists. Casabianca, of the republican daily *L'Evénement*, who had signed an article on the assembly, refused to testify on the grounds that 'it was against his profession'. However the prosecution stressed that 'journalists [are] like other men and that since they take part in assemblies, there is no professional secret which prevents them from reporting what occurs'. Casabianca justified the refusal by saying that 'he had not attended the assembly in person and consequently did not want to take responsibility for the article that he had signed'. Another journalist summoned after publishing an article in *Le Temps*, refused to testify,

---

61. APP/Ba/1522/Meeting du 23 novembre 1884, salle Lévis.
62. *La Temps*, 24 November 1884.
63. See police reports in: APP/Ba/1522/Meeting du 23 novembre 1884, salle Lévis.
64. Polydore Fabreguettes, *Traité des infractions de la parole de l'écriture et de la presse*, Paris, A. Chevalier-Marescq, 1884, vol. 1, pp. 14–21, 269–281.

this time because his article was written in collaboration with another journalist: 'I do not believe I am authorised', he said, 'to speak of facts whose telling is not mine alone.'

The organisers and speakers of the assembly were critical of the position taken by the press. From the moment the first reports appeared, the commission organising the gathering in the Lévis meeting room sent a letter to the editor-in-chief of the republican newspaper *La Bataille* to 'protest against the malicious reports and lies published by most newspapers'; this protest and the corrections were both published on 26 November 1884. An assembly was immediately organised by anarchists on 29 November, concerning the attitude of journalists. The press in general was accused of ill-will towards assemblies. During the trial mentioned, the defendants denounced the voluntarily misleading nature of press reports. In response to accusations by the prosecution, supported by press excerpts, one participant in the meeting replied: 'Everything I said was distorted.' Another criticised the inaccuracy of the reports and the malice of journalists: 'Everything in the newspaper accounts is a lie.' Thus, in the first decades of the Third Republic we still find a tension between organisers and participants in worker, socialist and anarchist meetings, and a press generally considered bourgeois and keen to conserve the monopoly of expression of opinion, in defiance of the true People.

The question of access of all to assemblies

Ideally, in the absence of barriers limiting their access to a particular category of people, public assemblies should have the advantage over the press of opening up to all. Once declared that public assemblies are free, there has to be guarantee that they are free for all and that the right to meet is truly democratic. However the 1881 and 1868 laws demand that *déclarants* in a public assembly be in full possession of 'their civil and political rights' (Article. 2), excluding women, who cannot organise public assemblies without the assistance of male *déclarants*. This question, all the more important because women only contribute to a minor degree to the expression of opinion by the press, was of little interest to legislators. Regarding the Third Republic, it was only on 31 March 1881 that the Chamber was persuaded to discuss this subject, thanks to the deputy Alfred Talandier who, as 'part of the *avant-garde* of the republican party, [supports] uncompromising politics against Gambettist opportunism'.[65] When it came to voting on Article 2 of the draft law, once returned to the Chamber after its adoption with amendments by the Senate, Talandier proposed an amendment removing the words 'and political', but keeping the condition of possession of civil rights. Thus, women would be entitled to organise assemblies. But the discussion was soon interrupted. In his capacity of *rapporteur*, Naquet admitted the relevance of this suppression, but invoked an urgency to vote for the law in order to avoid having to submit a revised draft to the Senate. Talandier proposed to withdraw the amendment and to transform it later into a legislative proposal. In the last instance it was not adopted.

---

65. Robert and Cougny, *Dictionnaire des parlementaires français*, vol. 5, p. 355.

Women could not be *déclarants*. This restriction disappeared in 1907 with the suppression of the prior declaration, but another restriction in the 1868 and 1881 laws still limited women's participation in electoral assemblies, where the public was narrowed down to adult male voters.

Yet taking part in political assemblies has been an important way for women to become involved in the public arena. Women were as present on the platforms as in the audience at assemblies during the Revolution and in 1848. However each time they were forced to abandon this move beyond the private sphere. After the vote on the 1868 law, women were once again present in meetings. The agenda of public assemblies frequently addressed 'social questions' and issues concerning women directly: the right to work, divorce, education, etc. Many women attended such assemblies. For example, they constituted a fifth of the public in assemblies dealing with women's right to work.[66] Some observers welcomed their presence. On several occasions the liberal newspaper *Le Siècle* expressed admiration for the quality of speeches made by women. On 19 July 1868, Louis Jourdan, one of its main political editors, praised the performance of the feminist and socialist Paule Minck, who had defended the political rights of women in many conferences.[67] On 20 August, Charles Limousin affirmed that the talent of a lesser known woman speaker, Mademoiselle Breuil, who spoke on the day before at Wauxhall, was *per se* a response 'to those who argue women's inability'; 'she responded showing herself to be capable'. Taking part in assemblies was thus a way to defend women's involvement in politics by illustrating how they can contribute to the public debate as well as men.

But reactions are far from always being positive. Gustave de Molinari, one of the great figures of economic liberalism and opposition journalist, wrote in the *Journal des Débats* on 21 August 1868 regarding the public assemblies of Wauxhall: 'The tedious discussion on *women's work* ended amid scenes of disorder which reminded us of the stormy sessions of the notorious *women's club* on Boulevard Bonne-Nouvelle in 1848'.[68]

The remarks about women taking part in public life are frequently harsh, especially concerning women speakers who are criticised or mocked. They are regularly denigrated in the press as speakers 'in petticoats', and accused of being 'less womanly' on account of their 'violence'. The remarks in the Orleanist weekly *Le Journal de Paris* are particularly aggressive:

> Sometimes, an emancipated woman addresses the platform with a martial air. The popular whirlpool has always brought to the surface, amid other debris, some degeneration of the *beau sexe*. What these ladies say is usually very daring; one gets an idea, if one considers what boldness needs someone who

---

66. Dalotel, Faure and Freiermuth, *Aux origines de la Commune*, p. 126.
67. *Dictionnaire biographique du mouvement ouvrier français. Le Maitron, 3. 1871–1914*, CD Rom, Éditions de l'Atelier.
68. Reprinted in Gustave de Molinari, *Le mouvement socialiste et les réunions publiques avant la révolution du 4 septembre 1870*, Paris, Garnier Frères, 1872, p. 34.

The Ideal of Participation Without Action | 55

has found enough courage to stray so far from the domestic hearth. These viragos have confused ideas about some very arduous issues affecting the organisation of society; it is to these women that we owe the most vehement diatribes against marriage and the current institution of the family. They also have theories on the upbringing of children that [would] terrify mothers.[69]

During the first years of the Third Republic, men's regard for women's participation in assemblies did not really change, mainly because it was associated with periods of revolutionary turmoil. In the words of Alain Garrigou: 'Between the pandemonium and the riot, women's participation evokes the spectre of the revolutionary crowd and its involvement of men, women and children alike'.[70] Even if mockery appears less frequently, it is still alive, especially in the conservative press: '[She] pleases me less as a speaker than as a woman', wrote a journalist of *Le Figaro* on 3 August 1881 about the woman speaker of a Gambettist assembly, her rebuking 'vinegary little voice'.[71] The comments on the voices of women speakers are a classic theme of criticism levelled at women's participation. Jokes abound, particularly when women organise their own assemblies to claim their participation in political life. Thus, in September 1889 after an assembly at which the Secretary of the League of Socialist Women, Marie-Rose Astié de Valsayre, spoke, the Catholic daily ran the title: 'Women's Assemblies' and reported '1,200 women citizens crowded together, in the Jeune France room, in Clignancourt, of all ages and mixed beauty and babbled.'[72] In the same vein 'A Women's Club', ran the title of *L'Illustration*, with engravings (see Figure 1.1): 'Some women citizens of advanced opinions have agreed to give the electoral period the comic note that it seemed to lack'.[73]

Women's participation does not really seem to be important in the republican press. When *Le Temps* minimises the importance of socialist or communist assemblies, journalists often stress that their public includes many women. For example it was reported that at a socialist assembly in Fourmies: 'The theatre room was packed [...]; 700–800 people; but more than half were women, girls, and children attracted by the free entertainment.'[74] The aim of the journalist here was also to anticipate election results and, since women did not have the right to vote, their presence indicated that this assembly was in no way threatening, they were a symbol of the trifling importance of the theories expressed. Women's opinons have as little significance as children's. In any case, their participation in assemblies is not considered a necessary democratic condition. The emerging republican public space is largely masculine, leaves little room for the word of

---

69. *Le Journal de Paris*, 28 January 1869.
70. Alain Garrigou, *Histoire sociale du suffrage universel en France, 1848–2000*, Paris, Seuil, 2002, p. 272.
71. *Le Figaro*, 3 August 1881.
72. *La Croix*, 21 September 1889.
73. *L'Illustration*, 23 September 1889.
74. *Le Temps*, 29 April 1892.

Figure 1.1: 'The election period. A club of women. Miss Astié de Valsayre on the platform', L'Illustration, 23 September 1889

the female public and is not, in this respect, very different from those of previous periods.

Another democratic barrier to the right of assembly, very different from the marginalisation of women, is the shortage and cost of hiring meeting rooms. Rent often had to be paid and a citizen wanting to organise a public assembly could be *de facto* denied his right due to a lack of the necessary means. Sometimes participants are charged entry to offset the cost of rent. But here too, particularly when the right of entry is compulsory, charging a fee undermines the democratic nature of freedom of assembly and did not go uncriticised; for example, an article on an electoral assembly in 1876 states that:

> Yesterday voters in the 18th *arrondissement* met [...] in the room of *cirque Fernando*. [...] At the door [...], wooden boxes, where each person arriving was 'held' to contribute 25 centimes for the cost of rent. In other assemblies, we noted that the subscription was purely optional. This strict price appeared to us to be anti-democratic.[75]

Dalotel, Faure and Freiermuth have shown that the question of meeting rooms was a real problem regarding assemblies at the end of the Empire. People met a

---

75. APP/Ba/571: Élections législatives, 20 février et 6 mars 1876. 16e à 20e arr. et banlieue: *L'Écho*, 15 February 1876.

lot in dance halls (Wauxhall, Alcazar d'Italie, Salle Lévis, Folies-Belleville, etc.), but also in cafés, concerts, wine merchant shops, theatres and circuses. Entry to assemblies was regularly subject to a financial contribution, and the authors estimate that the organisers very probably had often 'to make up the amount of entry money within their collecting box': 'public assemblies were [...] without doubt a non-negligible source of democratic sponsorship'.[76] The reticence or refusal of owners to rent rooms to one or other political group, on the grounds of their convictions or pressure, is another element undermining the democratic nature of assemblies. The problem of meeting rooms is intensified during electoral periods, when the number of assemblies reaches a maximum and the stakes are particularly high: 'Money and influence gave government [candidates] many resources'.[77] Plans to buy or build independent rooms end in failure, largely due to lack of money.

The situation is not much better at the beginning of the Third Republic. The question of the availability of meeting rooms is not raised during the debates on the 1881 law. In the following years it is on the initiative of socialist deputies that several legislative proposals are filed including the free provision of meeting rooms. In 1889, in the legal recital for a 'proposal of law tending to guarantee freedom of electoral assemblies', presented particularly by Jules Guesde, the lack of rooms and the fact that their 'hostile or intimidated' owners refuse to rent to some candidates, is considered as the 'annulation of the right of assembly'. In 1906 the recital for a proposed law on 'the democratic organisation of universal suffrage' stipulated that 'everywhere where it has the right, the electorate should [also] have the material means to assemble'.[78]

The situation almost improved during the discussion of the 1907 law eliminating the previous declaration. As already noted, it is the desire to appease the tensions resulting from the church's refusal to subscribe to the declaration stipulated under the 1905 law that is largely behind the draft law of the Clemenceau government on 22 January 1907 — made after the submission of a legislative proposal along these lines. Although this is not its primary purpose, it nonetheless modifies the 1881 law rendering it more liberal. On 29 January, Aristide Briand, Minister for Education and Religions, recalled that: 'The government brings you a bill which will extend the benefit of the freedoms enjoyed in matters of public assembly to all citizens.'[79] Several deputies on the extreme left denounce the fact that this 'law of circumstance' only benefits the church, which has its own cultural buildings, while the public has a great problem finding places to assemble freely. During the debate, interruptions from the extreme left suggested requisitioning the churches for the benefit of all citizens. These deputies submit several articles and amendments obliging mayors to provide meeting places for citizens, but all of their attempts

---

76. Dalotel, Faure and Freiermuth, *Aux origines de la Commune*, pp. 47–48.
77. Dalotel, Faure and Freiermuth, *Aux origines de la Commune*, p. 50.
78. Annexe 594, session extraordinaire, 21 décembre 1906, *Journal Officiel. Documents Parlementaires. Chambre*, pp. 317–318.
79. *Journal Officiel*, 30 January 1907, p. 245.

fail. If the assembly is promoted in order to favour the expression of an opinion of all citizens, and if the legislation indeed goes in that direction, there are some obstacles which date to the establishment of the Republic, between this ideal and its accomplishment. We start to see objections raised against the republican notion of public space and the supposed role of citizens' meetings.

The meeting room as an ideal public space

In an attempt to ensure that assemblies would be an effective way to develop opinion rather than the cause of disorder, the republicans try to exclude the public highway as a *locus* for holding them; political participation is to be circumscribed in a specific domain set apart from the street.[80] This is why the meeting, enshrined by law, is an instrument to avoid participation through action. In Chapter 2 we will see how the concept of opinion unified around the public good also reveals a concern to avoid action: the one which would follow the division of public opinion in parties putting pressure on the elected authorities, or even supplanting them — the threat then weighs less on public order than on the principle of representation. The distrust of political participation 'on the street', had long been superimposed by a rejection of assemblies *qua* intermediary homogeneous bodies — the two were related since, as Samuel Hayat stressed: 'the street protest' was also rejected insofar as it was 'seen as only representing special groups'.[81]

Off the street!

Article 3 of the 1868 law stipulates that 'an assembly can only be held in a closed and covered locale'. Article 6 of the 1881 law requires that 'assemblies cannot be held on the public highway'. The desire to avoid gatherings from spilling over onto the street is always significant and a real change does exist between imperial and republican legislation regarding this definition of places of assembly. It is thus excessive to sum up, as Reynié did, that the will of republican legislators was to 'create a reserved place, set apart, open the door of a locale, let the crowd enter, then reclose the door', and to 'make [a political activity] invisible to the population'.[82] Public republican space is not characterised by this 'dissimulation of ordinary politics';[83] imperial public space was. Nonetheless both agree on the need to exclude the street as a *locus* for crowd gatherings.

During the debate on the 1868 law and in its commentaries in the press, the liberal opposition criticised the limitation of the type of meeting rooms authorised for assemblies: they rebuked the need for them to be closed less than the obligation for them to be covered. Freedom of assembly on the public highway is not

---

80. Reynié, *Le triomphe de l'opinion publique*.
81. Samuel Hayat, 'La République, la rue et l'urne', *Pouvoirs*, 2006, vol. 116, p. 34.
82. Reynié, *Le triomphe de l'opinion publique*, pp. 154–155.
83. Hayat, 'La République', pp. 154–155.

demanded, although it is specified that it would not be dangerous — the British and American examples are proposed to demonstrate that such assemblies can take place without risk to the public peace. On 16 March 1868, Eugène Pelletan, of the democratic opposition, addressed the Legislative Body during the debate on Article 3 and evoked the British example of outdoor assemblies specifying that the restriction of assembling in a closed meeting place would be acceptable. This did not mean, however, that the meeting place must be covered. The government wanted to introduce the idea of 'covering' in the law in order to create an additional obstacle to the exercise of right of assembly. In small municipalities, it would be difficult to find a location meeting these criteria, as stressed by Jules Favre, another key opponent of the government, during the same discussion.[84] Pelletan also expresses concern regarding the obscure nature of the notion of 'covered place':

> I suppose [...] that one wants to draw a tent above a courtyard to avoid the indirect rays of the sun, that, by their presence, would constitute a crime; will this place appear to you to be legally covered and therefore innocent?

On the same day, Jean-Baptiste Josseau, member of the committee responsible for drafting the law, insisted above all on the need to assure that the assembly be set apart from the street so as to 'avoid the serious risks of tumult and disorder'. Meetings should not be held 'where the crowd can group, gather and expand'. Josseau's definition of covered place is relatively broad: 'When a place is covered, little matters the nature of the covering'. 'A meeting place covered with simple canvas is a covered place in the legal sense.'[85] Once the law was adopted, its terms continued to be an object of debate. Legal experts defended the provisions on the nature of place of assembly somewhat restrictively. For Henri Ameline, auditor to the Conseil d'État and lawyer to the imperial court: 'the locale should be *closed* and *covered* in this sense that the ears and the eyes of those who are not admitted can see and hear nothing of what is happening'.[86] The legal expert Georges Dubois also insists that the setting must '[prevent] seeing and hearing clearly what is happening inside'.[87] More than simply preventing spill-over into the street, the law is thus seen to impose isolation on the assemblies.

The police attempt to prevent groups forming on the public highway, especially at the end of assemblies. Subsequently the liberal press insist on the excessive character of police deployment. During the electoral assemblies of May 1869, Alfred Gaulier, future radical deputy of the Third Republic, ironically notes in *Le*

---

84. Robert and Cougny, *Dictionnaire des parlementaires français*, vol. 2, pp. 616–620.
85. For the citations of Eugène Pelletan, Jules Favre and Jean-Baptiste Josseau see: *Le Moniteur Universel*, 17 March 1868, p. 399.
86. Henri Ameline, 'Commentaire de la loi de 1868 sur les réunions politiques', *Revue pratique de droit français*, 1868, p. 377.
87. Georges Dubois, *Commentaire théorique et pratique de la loi du 6 June 1868 sur les réunions publiques*, Paris, Imprimerie et Librairie Générale de Jurisprudence, 1869, pp. 118–119.

Temps that if a crowd forms, the police are as culpable as the disturbers:

> Then let policemen gather, all alone, as yesterday evening on Boulevard Sébastopol. Towards eleven o'clock we noted that there was *at least*, one policeman for every three promenaders, and of these three promenaders, at least two were attracted by the presence of the policemen, grouped in gloomy groups at street corners. This is a singular way to reassure, one must admit, but an almost infallible way to create gatherings.[88]

The law did not prevent groups forming on the streets, if only because one had to queue up to enter the meeting room, and participants did not disperse immediately after the meeting. The liberal newspaper *La Liberté* points out that at an assembly at the Folies-Bergère, despite the presence of 'forty massed policemen' in front of the entrance, and 'several police officers coming and going', 'the street around the assembly is crowded'.[89] There remain other forms of meeting that take place in Paris, particularly during the electoral campaign of May 1869. *Le Moniteur Universel* — formerly the official journal of the Empire — reported on 16 May: 'Yesterday there were again some gatherings in Paris, besides the throng crowding at the doors of the public assembly rooms.'[90] 'Demonstrations' took place in various points of the capital. These troubles initially arose around the assembly organised by Émile Ollivier on 12 May in Châtelet, against the radical republican, Désiré Bancel.[91] During these events, the police prefect in Paris issued an ordinance stating that in order to repress spill-over from assemblies into the street they were willing to resort to the June 1848 law on mobs.

At the start of the Third Republic the desire to prevent gatherings from spilling onto the streets remains strong. The 1881 law requires that assemblies should not be held on the public highway. The government and the commission drafts are identical on this issue. In its initial draft however, the government uses the term 'location' instead of 'place' in contrast to the commission. This, stresses Naquet on 27 January 1880, lets us 'assume that there will be a return to previous legal provisions'.[92] In the end the word 'place' is kept in both drafts, no longer demanding that the assembly be held in a closed room, and allowing meetings outdoors on the condition that the public highway is respected. This is a long way from the imperial attempt to confine assemblies to 'closed and covered' places. The draft submitted by Blanc calls for absolute freedom, and thus contains no bar on the street as a place of assembly. On 24 January 1880, Blanc criticised this provision, with reference to the British example.[93] Naquet replies on 26 January,

---

88. *Le Temps*, 17 May 1869.
89. *La Liberté*, 30 April 1869.
90. *Le Moniteur Universel*, 16 May 1869.
91. Dalotel, Faure and Freiermuth, *Aux origines de la Commune*, p. 39; Robert and Cougny, *Dictionnaire des parlementaires français*, vol. 1, pp. 149–150.
92. *Journal Officiel*, 28 January 1880, p. 930.
93. *Journal Officiel*, 25 January 1880, p. 758.

but without resorting to the argument that one must be wary of the spill-over of the crowd. If assemblies cannot be held on the public highway, this is in particular, he ensures, in order to avoid 'blocking the traffic' and 'commercial transactions in the markets'. In particular, 'parties [which are] enemies of the Republic', might organise false republican assemblies in the market places to cause discontent among the population and:

> The day after [...], dropping their masks and resuming their monarchist character, [they would] say to rural populations: the Republic? Here it is! This is a government that cannot keep order.

Naquet adds to this rather surprising development that it is inexact to say that assemblies in public places can be held freely in England where there are also 'texts of formal law that prohibit [them]'. The system here is in effect to leave it up to the people 'affected by the obstacles caused for the movement of traffic' to lodge a complaint themselves against the organisers of the assembly. If this system can function in a country where people have acquired the habit of freedom, in France it would be a 'nest of trials'.[94]

During the debate on the 1907 law, the socialists asserted the right of citizens to gather together on the street. The counter-plan defended on 29 January by Henri Ghesquière, deputy for the *Parti Ouvrier Français*, contained the following article: 'Assemblies can be held on the public highway on the condition that they do not block the traffic.' Three arguments are used in its support: first, the idea that such a right exists in England, Belgium and the Netherlands, three monarchies which seem to fear freedom of assembly less than French republicans; second, the fact that the government already tolerates such assemblies on the street; finally, there is the reference to religious processions which are held freely in public places.[95] The same day, Clemenceau replied on behalf of the government, stressing first that it was unrealistic to hold an assembly on the public highway without blocking the traffic: 'This is much like planning to take a bath without getting wet.'[96] Clemenceau went on to note that assemblies already benefited from a degree of leeway with the idea that the situation promotes freedom. To legislate would be to accept the arbitrary power of the mayor who could block an assembly depending on his own political preferences — the reasoning of the President of the Conseil d'État is obscure since in the absence of legislation authorising assemblies on the public highway, arbitrary municipal power already exists. Clemenceau also refers to the immaturity of French behaviour, moving away from Naquet's argument in 1880. The argument no longer regards only freedom of circulation and commerce or the risk of disorder, provoked to discredit the Republic, rather Clemenceau is referring to the violence in assemblies and on the streets that is developing. Subsequently Ghesquière and his co-signatories withdrew the counter-draft. The

---

94. *Journal Officiel*, 27 January 1907, pp. 867–868.
95. *Journal Officiel*, 30 January 1907, pp. 248–249.
96. For this citation and the following ones, see: *Journal Officiel*, 30 January 1907, pp. 249–250.

right to organise assemblies on the public highway was claimed the next day in the form of an additional article by three socialist deputies, Aldy, Willm and Ghesquière. The arguments and counter-arguments are broadly the same as before, except when Aldy relies on Clemenceau's confused reference to the idea that mayors must not be responsible for authorising assemblies on the public highway. He emphasised that this power already existed since it had been recognised several times that mayors could authorise assemblies on the street. Nonetheless the amendment was not adopted. Under the Republic, the prospect of assembling on the public highway always met with resistance. The fear of the crowd and its potential to spill-over onto the street continued to be an issue, even if not used directly as an argument in the legislative debate. Despite this, republicans had no wish to confine participants in assemblies to a strictly segregated place.

An outlet delegitimising action

On 20 May 1869, Auguste Vacquerie wrote for *Le Rappel*:

> Among free peoples, there is a permanent right of assembly. Citizens can always meet, consult each other, act together, give their opinion, propose, advise, blame. This is a daily evaporation of passions and discontent. Meetings are safety valves against explosions.[97]

The main difference between republican and imperial perceptions of the boundary between an assembly room and the public highway is that, for republicans, both under the Empire and at the start of the Republic, the assembly is considered an outlet where opinions can be expressed, as long as what is said does not constitute a direct incitement to violent action and remains within the framework of the assembly. Thus the assembly room constitutes a materialisation of an ideal public space. From this perspective, no speech is truly dangerous, insofar as it is uttered within the framework of the assembly and provided that its words do not become actions. The corollary to this perception of assembly is that disorder outside is seen as less tolerable because citizens have already been granted a place to express their discontent. Danielle Tartakowsky notes:

> What is the function and, above all, the legitimacy of the demonstration when universal suffrage and the democratic laws of the 1880s constitute a legal framework in which each man can 'manifest his thought' and be heard?[98]

If one cannot affirm that participation is 'locked' by the republican legislator and thus 'invisible', it is relevant to consider that there is a solid political objective to encourage the expression of opinions in the framework of assemblies, to prevent the masses from intervening in political life through street action. Faced with

---

97. *Le Rappel*, 20 May 1869.
98. Danielle Tartakowsky, 'La manifestation comme mort de la révolte', *Révolte et société*, vol. II, Paris, Publications de la Sorbonne, 1989, p. 240.

socialist and anarchist assemblies causing disorder on the public highway in the first decade after the adoption of the 1881 law, the position of the republican press, testified to the idea of assembly as a 'safety valve' to avoid the fury of passions.

The republican press is generally unanimous in affirming that there is nothing to fear from violent speech. Nonetheless, some did complain that this sort of speech stripped the assembly of its proper role of providing room for reasoned debate. However it was not considered dangerous, insofar as such speech was confined to the setting of the meeting room. Little concern should be given to the increase of speeches announcing the approach of a revolution. This position was all the more important because the reactionary press systematically exploited verbal violence to highlight the Republic's presumed inability to guarantee order. On 10 August 1881 the Orleanist daily *Le Soleil* evokes: 'the most brutal and most savage declarations of war on society' uttered by 'the fanatics who are listened to and applauded in the electoral clubs of radical and jacobin Paris', the journalist Gayet de Cesena warns his readers against any tendency to be complacent:

> Society is still strongly enough organised to withstand these attacks of speech, [...] but it would be wrong to despise them. Behind the obscure minority of socialist revolutionaries crying 'long live the Commune', in public assemblies where demagogy holds court, there is an army of evil whose soldiers are always ready to pass to action in the hour of crisis.[99]

For the monarchist press the violent discourse represents a real threat to public order, and the prelude to impending action. Far from relativising the importance of the speeches made in revolutionary assemblies, the monarchist press insists on the dramatic nature of the situation. Responsibility for this is laid at the door of the Republic.

On the contrary, the republican press wanted to demonstrate that the speeches in socialist and anarchist assemblies, even those considered more violent, do not imply any real risk. The Republic is strong enough to remain intact because it rests on the opinion of the People; popular judgement would be clear with respect to the excess characterising of the speeches of extremist groups. In the years following the adoption of the 1881 law, journalists from *Le Temps* stressed the contrast between the violence of speakers' discourses on the podium of assemblies and the calm of participants in the room:[100] 'Fortunately, the time is past when the madness declaimed could cause [...] contagion and win the weakened spirit of an entire people'.[101] Several articles show that the revolutionary and anarchist ideas are not echoed. The speeches uttered are considered as nothing but a collection of

---

99. *Le Soleil*, 10 August 1881.
100. Paula Cossart, 'Un peuple sage ou indiscipliné? La construction par *Le Temps* d'un cadre interprétatif de la participation aux réunions politiques des années 1860 à 1910', *Revue d'histoire du XIXe siècle*, 2003, vol. 26–27, pp. 173–200.
101. *Le Temps*, 18 October 1881.

'nonsense',[102] 'foolishness',[103] or 'madness';[104] expressions repeated in the articles on assemblies of the extreme left. Participants are presented as being aware that when they take part in assemblies they do not necessarily subscribe to all the messages that are disseminated.

The newspaper depicts participants in 'revolutionary' assemblies as a public of 'curious onlookers'. After having reported on an assembly, the journalist concluded: 'The spectacle [...], offered nothing new [...]. They will need to find [something] better next time if they want to keep the curiosity of this particular public of revolutionary meetings in suspense'.[105] Journalists repeat the need to attract the public to anarchist meetings through a figure that people come to see. Following an assembly in the Lévis meeting room when the anarchist speaker Louise Michel was late arriving a journalist described an 'angry public': 'They paid, they want to see'. When she finally appeared 'the curiosity of the public [was] satisfied'.[106] This is proof that many regarded these assemblies as a spectacle and that the speeches were not taken seriously by participants. There was a lot of laughter. An article evoking an anarchist assembly affirmed that a speaker 'caused hilarity among the 250 people whom he addressed',[107] and three days later, about a socialist assembly, '[here] there are only people enjoying themselves'.[108] *Le Temps* gave its readers the impression that the participants only came for the fun to be had.

However the amusement could not last. Even if speakers increased the ferocity of their words in order to continue capturing participants' attention, the latter still ended up getting bored. If a room is not packed, if assemblies are less frequent, journalists point it out immediately as a sign of popular fatigue in the face of wild theories:

> It is interesting to note the increasingly growing discredit into which demagogic public assemblies [have fallen]. These assemblies [...] are now quite rare, and for the good reason that they no longer enjoy success. [...] Workers are weary of the declarations of the same old speakers, where they instinctively see a vacuum.[109]

The same sort of remark is made when a meeting room empties during an assembly. On 4 October 1884 a journalist wrote that violent language 'ends by causing a certain weariness of assemblies',[110] so that people leave the assembly before the end.

---

102. *Le Temps*, 11 November 1881.
103. *Le Temps*, 23 October 1881.
104. *Le Temps*, 1 November 1881.
105. *Le Temps*, 11 November 1881.
106. *Le Temps*, 4 September 1882.
107. *Le Temps*, 29 November 1883.
108. *Le Temps*, 2 December 1883.
109. *Le Temps*, 14 September 1884.
110. *Le Temps*, 4 October 1884.

This equanimity regarding the influence of speeches made by the extreme left in assemblies is accompanied by the accusation that they spill out onto the street. When an aforementioned meeting of 'unemployed workers' ended with fights in the street, *L'Evènement* reported it as 'a stupid and monstrous fact'.[111] The events were considered particularly blameworthy because in liberalising the right of assembly the Republic had already given citizens a place where they could express themselves. In contrast to the Empire, republican legislation authorised almost any kind of speech to be made in meetings. For this reason, it is considered to be particularly unacceptable that disorder should continue onto the street, especially when leaving assemblies. *L'Evènement* is clear on this point:

> Precisely because they have exercised the right to vociferate at their ease against infamous capital and the abominable bourgeoisie, and even to evoke the benevolent and glorious Commune, nothing excuses them from having fallen on the poor guardians of the peace and from having stunned them, uttering savage cries.

Republican newspapers promoted a limitation of citizens' participation to legitimate forms, excluding action. Some days later, after another chaotic assembly, *Le Siècle* evoked 'this proper and legitimate agitation to which [they] have the right to resort to make their wishes and needs known to Parliament', this 'agitation' that could be realised 'by public assemblies, the press, by petitions'.[112] *Le Temps* even affirmed that assemblies then had less 'utility' as a place of 'discussion of public affairs' than as an 'outlet for political passions'.[113] Yet, crucially, the conviction remained that this was only temporary, and that citizens would learn to make good use of assemblies.

The presence of the police around assemblies, and the dispersion of groups once they end — a sign that the Republic opposes any expression that stretches out onto the street — is consequently defended by pro-government republican newspapers. Police intervention to prevent an 'outdoor meeting' in front of the *Opéra* in February 1885 and the fact that the police were seen to be 'resolved to ensure that the law on street demonstrations is respected', was welcomed by *Le XIXe siècle*.[114] At the start of the Republic, the nature of speeches made in assemblies was less important than keeping participation in assemblies within the domain of discourse — while under the Empire, the content of speeches was one of the main reasons for suspending assemblies. It was considered especially important to prevent action, particularly street action. There is a place for legitimate participation, which is the assembly, and thus there is no room for the use of violence on the public highway, as summarised by a journalist from *Le Siècle*: 'We will let them say everything in

---

111. *L'Evènement*, 25 November 1884.
112. *Le Siècle*, 1 December 1884.
113. *Le Temps*, 20 October 1881.
114. *Le XIXe siècle*, 11 February 1885.

their assemblies, but they can do nothing on the street'.[115] That is, one can speak of almost everything, but tolerance stops when participation leaves the domain of discussion and the expression of opinions. In 1903, the legal expert Edouard-René Lefebvre stated that: 'This then, it seems, is the spirit of the 1881 law. All political or social theories have the right to appear, provided they do not lead to violence'.[116]

Presenting the notion of assembly as a place of participation which delegitimises violent action on the street completes the analyses of the vote as a privileged means of pacified political expression. For Yves Déloye and Olivier Ihl:

> The rejection of violence as a form of political action means having to create special 'neutralising' spaces able to counter the threat of social contact. The implementation of electoral activity occupies a decisive role in this respect. […] The political participation expected of the citizen can be summed up as a specific activity: whereby members of the Nation take part collectively in the selection of leaders and indirectly in the formation of public policies. In so doing the vote becomes the legitimate, if not exclusive, form of citizen participation.[117]

Beyond the vote, the political assembly is seen as a legitimate *locus* of political participation, and one which rules out street protest and violent action as modes of expression.

Keeping surveillance: public and private assemblies

The 1868 and 1881 laws only deal with public assemblies. Private assemblies avoid the regulation and are moreover protected by the inviolability of domicile, by the 'right of each citizen to only receive those he wants in his home'.[118] If a representative of authority wants to enter a private assembly, the organiser can deny him access, invoking Article 184 of the Penal Code. As a consequence, it is more difficult to know exactly what is said or done there than in a public assembly. Surveillance, however, is not impossible, since even if government or police agents cannot attend in this capacity, informers can. Nonetheless, to send informers the authorities must be notified of a planned private assembly, and this is only possible if the latter is not organised with sufficient discretion. Thus we see that 'the publicity of the assemblies is of great legal and practical importance. The extent of police powers must depend on the qualification of the assembly as "public" or "private"'.[119]

---

115. *Le Siècle*, 25 November 1884.
116. Edouard-René Lefebvre, *Le droit de réunion*, Paris, Impr. H. Bouillant, 1903, p. 81.
117. Yves Déloye and Olivier Ihl, 'La civilité électorale: vote et forclusion de la violence en France', *Cultures & Conflits*, 1993, pp. 75, 85.
118. Marcel-Louis Degrenne, *Les réunions et les pouvoirs de police*, Caen, Caron & Cie, 1938, p. 70.
119. Maurice Menanteau, *Les nouveaux aspects de la liberté de réunion. Essai sur les caractères juridiques et politiques de la liberté de réunion en France*, Paris, Librairie technique et économique, 1937, p. 121.

The notion of private assembly is not easy to define. Firstly because it changed in the course of the nineteenth century, when it expanded into a political content: 'The private assembly gradually moved beyond the circle of family and friends, [...], cultural life or business. It crossed the boundaries of private life', writes the legal expert Maurice Menanteau in 1937. Menanteau has in mind assemblies organised by trade unions and political parties, which can be referred to as private assemblies, but at which the public is not united by a personal bond.[120] The private assembly moves beyond the framework of private life, and is, as the author notes, set in motion before the arrival of parties and trade unions. An assembly could indeed be organised to discuss questions concerning public subjects, to gather people together who had no other bond than that of having been invited, but still be deemed 'private'. The confusion arises from the extension of the notion of 'privacy'. This is all the more important because the 1868 and 1881 laws did not stipulate the character of publicity for an assembly, leaving the question to the judgement of the courts. Judges were frequently called on to rule as many public assemblies disguised themselves as private assemblies in order to avoid the formalities of the law, particularly under the Empire.

The place of gathering as a distinguishing criteria is generally rejected by legal experts. 'A private assembly can [...] be held in a public place, and a public assembly in a private place', notes Ameline in 1868.[121] This idea persists under the Third Republic and in 1938 Marcel-Louis Degrenne writes in the same vein:

> A public assembly can take place in a private home. [...] On the other hand, a private assembly can be held in a place usually open to the public (dance hall, café etc.). Doctrine and legal precedent agree on this point.[122]

Thus, if the principle of place is not relevant, an assembly held outdoors or in a room that allows what is said inside to be heard outside, cannot be considered private.[123]

The number of assistants is another possible distinctive feature of a private assembly. Under the Empire, before the adoption of the 1868 law, the republicans organised private assemblies especially prior to elections. They tried to preserve this right during the debate in the National Body, by rejecting the criteria of the number of assistants as a defining feature of a private assembly. On 14 March Eugène Pelletan states: 'All private assemblies, irrespective of the number of people taking part, [...] enjoy full freedom under the present government'.[124] Doctrine and legal precedents were mixed on this point. Several Supreme Court decisions and various legal commentaries made it a criterion to be taken into account when deciding on the nature of an assembly where this is ambiguous

---

120. Menanteau, *Les nouveaux aspects de la liberté de réunion*, pp. 32–33.
121. Ameline, 'Commentaire de la loi de 1868', p. 368.
122. Degrenne, *Les réunions et les pouvoirs de police*, pp. 79–80.
123. See, for example, Arnette, *La liberté de réunion en France*, p. 130.
124. *Le Moniteur Universel*, 15 March 1868, p. 389.

under both the Empire and the Republic. Yet most agree that this is not sufficient. Joubrel summed up the position in 1904:

> We must [...] recognise that the larger the assembly, the more difficult it is to observe all the necessary conditions for a private assembly. Nevertheless, jurisprudence must beware of taking the high number of assistants as sufficient proof of an assembly being public. There may be serious presumption in favour of publicising the assembly; but this sole fact does not give the judge sufficient proof to decide in this sense.[125]

The nature of the bond between the people present is a delicate issue covering two problems: the bond between the invitees, and the bond of each invitee with the organiser of the assembly. Regarding the first, it is not normally recognised as a valuable criterion *per se*, once again this is more of a sign likely to arouse the mistrust of the judge. Dubois wrote in 1869: 'In general, a private assembly only includes people who know each other personally, or who have a common interest in business, study or pleasure which leads to an exchange of opinions or solutions'. Adding that 'however, the assembly can conserve a private character, although the assistants do not know each other', he still goes on to state that in order for such an assembly to remain private, the assistants must be 'summoned by name and personally known to the organiser of the assembly'.[126] The question of relations between organisers and invitees is not dealt with by many legal experts; but is still no less controversial: under the Second Empire, whereas the republicans affirm that an assembly held by invitation in a private location is private, jurisprudence also tends to take into account the nature of relations between organisers and invitees.

The most consensual criterion is the means of admission, the criterion of invitation. Here one leaves the domain of presumption for that of evidence.

> One point beyond doubt is that the private assembly is where not everyone is admitted at random [...]. Indeed, according to the interpretation of the Supreme Court and the opinion of most authors, a private assembly is where only persons holding a personal individual invitation, issued by the organiser, can take part.[127]

This basic criterion is prioritised under both the Empire and the Republic, while the other criteria remain secondary. This supposes not only that invitations were made, but also that admission to the room was effectively subject to possessing an invitation.

The legal limbo around the distinction between public and private encourages attempts by some organisers to make public assemblies pass as private, so as to avoid declaring them in order to circumvent the regulation. This continued under the Republic, but was above all recurrent under the Empire where, even after

---

125. Joubrel, *Du droit de réunion*, p. 119.
126. Dubois, *Commentaire théorique et pratique*, p. 60.
127. Joubrel, *Du droit de réunion*, p. 120.

the vote on the 1868 law, the regulation of public assemblies remained strictly binding. A debate on this subject opened around trials held in 1868, especially the Lacy-Guillon and Larcy trials, both prosecuted for wanting to hold a public electoral assembly less than five days before the legislative vote — the law rules that they be held 'until the fifth day before that set for opening the polls'. The defence argued that it was not a public assembly and that the organiser was thus in the right.

During the trial of the *légitimiste* Baron de Larcy, the accused invoked two criteria to distinguish public assembly from private assembly. The first was that no-one could enter without an invitation. The second was the assurance that no-one could hear what was said from outside.[128] But the criteria at the origin of the trial were broader. When the commissioner banned the assembly they gave three reasons for its illegality: its goal; the number of people attending; and their social ranking. Although the debate revolves primarily around knowing whether or not invitations were delivered to everyone, the reasons for banning the assembly clearly testify to a tendency to confuse political assembly with public assembly. Articles in the liberal press emphasise that it is this blurred criteria distinguishing the one from the other that allow the arbitrary exercise of the law: 'The assembly is private if one just plays whist, or performs a bourgeois comedy. [Assemblies] become public when one talks politics. Such is jurisprudence'.[129]

Under the Republic, if the assembly is perceived as the place where all opinions must be expressed, it is also regarded as necessary that they be made in broad daylight. The government has nothing to fear from the free diffusion of revolutionary or monarchist opinions, but if opinions are allowed to thrive in the dark they may become more important. Expressed publicly, they end up disappearing — I will return to this belief in the virtues of promoting public deliberation in order to eradicate extremist ideas in the next chapter. The assembly must also allow the government to know these ideas, and to measure their reception: 'There is no question of [public power] losing sight of what is being done in this domain'.[130] For these two reasons, public assemblies are valued in relation to private assemblies. With reference to two 'revolutionary' assemblies', where one ended in a public vote for 'the indictment of the Republic', *La Semaine Populaire*, supplement of the Gambettist newspaper *La Petite République* published:

> During elections we have seen, and we will see again before the return of the Chambers, exploits of this absolutely revolutionary type. But they have no more effect than *légitimistes* masses and banquets. [...] Order has nothing to fear when agents of disorder denounce themselves.[131]

---

128. An account of the hearing in the criminal court of Alais is republished in: *Le Temps*, 11–12 September 1868. See also: Robert and Cougny, *Dictionnaire des parlementaires français*, vol. 3, pp. 592–593.
129. *Le Temps*, 21 February 1870.
130. Reynié, *Le triomphe de l'opinion publique*, p. 154.
131. *La Semaine Populaire*, 9 October 1881.

The republican preference for public assembly is also based on the fact that private assemblies are more likely to unite individuals supporting the same cause or the same candidate. That is, people who share the same ideas, and are thus perceived as unlikely to promote the development of a public opinion unified around a shared notion of the common good. This type of assembly can intensify the division of society into different parties. The republican plan to transform popular participation rests on a special conception of public opinion: one that would be pacified and unified.

Chapter Two

Public Opinion and Consensus on the Common Good

> Are you afraid of the assembly of men to the point that you think that every time they gather it will be falsehood, and not the truth, that will prevail? For my part, I place my trust in the truth [...]; this is what is successful in the long run; there is no sophism, nor passion, nor anger that can resist in the face of the cold and severe language of truth.[1]

Jules Simon addressed the Legislative Body of the Second Empire on 13 March 1868 to defend freedom of assembly against government restrictions. His principle idea was that the assembly of citizens, far from being a factor of social division or likely to exacerbate unfounded passions was, on the contrary, one of the best ways to eliminate extreme positions by confronting them directly with 'the greatest force in the world, that of reason'.[2] In the foundation of the republican concept of assembly, seen as a way to develop a public opinion concerned with the common good and to protect against divisions likely to destabilise representative democracy, there was an asserted faith in individual reason, 'promoted as the sole guide of social and political action'[3] and an often expressed conviction that it would inevitably gain the upper hand in any debate.

Under the Empire the conception of assemblies as a vector of social harmony was largely shared by the republicans who pleaded for a real freedom of assembly. We find it again at the beginning of the Third Republic with the adoption of the 1881 Law on assemblies and during the early days of its application. For the republicans, the opinion created by assemblies was the outcome of a discussion based on reason where participants set aside their personal interests, tending instead towards the common good. The idea that differences of opinion were normal and legitimate has long been rejected by republicans.[4] From then on, the outcome sought by assemblies was an opinion on which there was consensus on what constitutes the general interest. Rational discussion allows men to go beyond

---

1. Jules Simon, 'Les réunions publiques', extract from *Journal Officiel*, 10 August 1868, Paris, Degorce-Cadot, 1869.
2. *Le Moniteur Universel*, 14 March 1868, p. 384.
3. Yves Déloye, 'Idée républicaine et citoyenneté. L'expérience française (1870–1945)', in Jean-Michel Lecomte and Jean-Pierre Sylvestre (eds), *Culture républicaine, citoyenneté et lien social*, Dijon, CRDP de Bourgogne, 1997, p. 69.
4. Raymond Huard, *La naissance du parti politique en France*, Paris, Presses de Sciences Po, 1996, p. 154.

ideology, which is perceived negatively, in order to reach a form of consensus successfully, or at least a compromise, on what is good for society as a whole. It is thus deemed necessary to prevent assemblies from grouping people around a specific idea, where the aim is not to discuss, but to gather strength, to promote this idea, and to put pressure on those in government. This type of assembly intervenes between citizens and their representatives, whereas only the latter are considered responsible for decision-making and must not be influenced by any intermediary group.

The virtues of deliberation: an opinion assembled

Compared with the opinions being generated by the press, the valorisation of the opinion emanating from assemblies is realised above all through a discourse on the virtues of direct debate among citizens. The fact that many people gather together in the same place to defend differing ideas should tend to exclude extreme ideas and those that only represent the interest of the particular group to which a speaker belongs. This would favour ideas based on reason and aspiring to the common good. The opinions of citizens are thus modified as a consequence of an exchange of ideas. From this viewpoint, what emerges at the end of an assembly is not the simple aggregation of the individual opinions of participants who enter the room. I have already suggested the similarity of this conception of the assembly with the discourse on deliberative democracy as a new ideal political system, developed in the last twenty years, particularly in Anglo-Saxon political philosophy. Influenced by Habermas and Rawls,[5] several authors stress the beneficial effects of participation on collective discussions organised to address public policy decisions. This parallel invites us to reflect on the novelty of the role and virtues currently accorded to popular deliberation.[6] Indeed, today's fashion for deliberation appears to keep its historical precedents in the dark. If there is specificity in what is proposed and experimented today, connecting the present to the past still provides useful clarification for contemporary questions, as well as for those of the last three decades of the nineteenth century.

---

5. See, in particular: Jürgen Habermas, *Between Facts and Norms: Contributions to a Discourse Theory of Law and Democracy*, Cambridge MA, MIT Press, 1998; John Rawls, *Justice as Fairness: A Restatement*, Cambridge MA, Harvard University Press, 2001.

6. Paula Cossart, 'Lecture critique: Historiciser les expériences délibératives. L'éducation civique par la discussion aux États-Unis (années 1820 – années 1830)', *Revue française de science politique*, 2010, vol. 60, (1), pp. 136–141; Paula Cossart, Julien Talpin and William Keith, 'Comparer les pratiques délibératives à travers les époques: une aberration historique?', *Participations*, 2012, vol. 2, (3), pp. 5–47.

Letting truth triumph

On 31 May 1878 in the recital for his proposed law on the right of assembly,[7] Alfred Naquet declared:

> I have confidence in the superiority of our ideas, in the strength of the truth that triumphs, and I have no fear for the Republic of free discussion.

The discourse on the benefits of deliberation among citizens gathered together, and on the force of reason that reveals the truth through free discussion, was ready to burst onto the scene at the outset of the Third Republic. This discourse was fundamental for the creation of the 1881 Law, but it was developed even more under the Second Empire. Indeed, the republican opposition was then faced with a rather different notion of the possible effects of freedom of assembly to discuss public affairs, that of the imperial government. The Empire considered assemblies where political questions could be addressed as inherently dangerous, convinced as it was that they tended to exacerbate extreme ideas. This justified the fact that political assemblies, with the exception of those held for elections, remained bound by prior authorisation. Men, ran the argument, are not naturally inclined to use reason. On the contrary, they will continue to be dominated by their passions and to follow the most fanatical among them. The speakers defending the government's plan made this clear to the Legislative Body. On 13 March 1878, Jean-Baptiste Josseau, a member of the commission for the draft of the law on assemblies, refused to consider the idea of meetings to discuss politics:

> As regards political matters, allowing these to be dealt within public assemblies in our present epoch, and without taking into account the experience acquired, the agitation that they have produced, the uprisings that they have caused in an era not yet far removed from our own, is it prudent? Is it possible? For my part, I do not think so. [...] The right of assembly in political matters [...] has always been considered, allow me to say this, an instrument of revolution![8]

Government spokesmen perceived assemblies where political questions were dealt with as a place where 'evil passions [...] stir up in the lower regions of society', and where 'the worst passions', 'the tumultuous passions' — taking the expressions used on 13 March by the Minister of State, Eugène Rouher — would inevitably be exacerbated. For Rouher, thinking that 'in public assemblies the influence of sovereign reason will always [prevail over] tumultuous passions', means being 'profoundly naive'.[9] If opinions change in an assembly, this is not in favour of ideas based on reason — which in this context are the synonym for moderate, not to say conservative, ideas — but in the direction of passions, largely understood in the sense of revolutionary ideas. Léon Bienvenu, man of letters,

---

7. *Journal Officiel*, 11 June 1878, p. 6,543.
8. *Le Moniteur Universel*, 14 March 1878, p. 382.
9. *Le Moniteur Universel*, 14 March 1878, p. 385.

journalist and author of critical and satirical works on the imperial world caricatured these references to passions which destabilise any system authorising political assemblies several days later. The article, in his series 'Manual of Literature and Official Eloquence for the Use of Civil Servants and Candidates of All Ranks', was published in *Le Charivari*.[10] In a section entitled 'A Deputy's Discourse against the Right of Assembly', Bienvenu recalls that 'a discourse against the right of assembly must be very ardent', and that 'the emphasis and the choice of words must express the most full-blooded indignation against "*the revolutionary hydra*" and "*evil passions*"'. He then proposes a discourse of a deputy arguing against the right of assembly in the form of a parody peppered with expressions such as 'revolutionary passions', 'hydra of anarchy' and 'anarchic passions'.

I opened this chapter with a quotation from the speech made by Jules Simon on 13 March 1868. The republican statesman and philosopher spoke out against the 'deceit', 'unreasonable will', 'exaggerations', 'sophisms', 'passions', and 'anger' of a few 'dissenters', 'agitators', 'the unruly', and 'the less judicious', in favour of the 'truth' of the 'wiser', the 'force' of 'reason', and the 'voice of common sense'. For Simon, it is always the latter that will emerge victorious from free assembly. Even if 'the most able speakers take the upper hand', this will not last when faced with a language inspired by reason to which assembled citizens '[will listen] better'. Imperial government insisted that assemblies of men tended to exacerbate passions and to radicalise positions. The republicans replied to this with an optimistic faith in the superiority of the force of reason in debate. Denouncing the endless agitation of the 'red ghost' by the Empire, they argued that what actually predominates in a free discussion held in an assembly is not passion. On the condition that one allows the discussion to develop freely it will be the best arguments, that is, those based on reason, which triumph. The similarity with the Habermasian 'ideal speech situation', a 'situation of free discussion, unlimited in duration, constrained only by the consensus which would be attained by the "force of better argument"' is striking.[11] There is relative agreement among theorists of deliberative democracy about the idea that democratic debate favours such an exchange of arguments. 'Whatever forms [deliberative democracy] takes it must refer to the ideal of public reason, to the requirement that legitimate decisions are those that "everyone could accept" or at least "not reasonably reject"'.[12] This 'ideal of public reason' was already the grounds for the legitimacy of freedom of assembly among the republican opponents of the Second Empire.

After the adoption of the 1868 law, the republican discourse on the virtues of deliberation in citizens' assemblies continued to develop culminating when the barriers to freedom of discussion were fortified in January 1869. In other

---

10. *Le Charivari*, 17 March 1878.

11. James Fishkin, *Democracy and Deliberation. New Directions for Democratic Reform*, New Haven CT, Yale University Press, 1991, p. 36.

12. James Bohman, 'The Coming of Age of Deliberative Democracy', *The Journal of Political Philosophy*, 1998, vol. 6, (4), pp. 401–402.

words, a relative tolerance only lasted until the end of 1868, after which time one finds many assemblies dissolved, speakers and chairmen put on trial,[13] and ministerial memoranda called for a strict application of the law. The letter of 16 February 1869 from Adolphe Forcade, Minister of the Interior, to the police prefect reflects the spirit guiding this new government policy, triggered by the fear of the dangers of completely free discussion.[14] Forcade invites the prefect to order the civil servants supervising assemblies to dissolve them if they deal with issues outside of their declared purpose: 'there is a certain degree of violence in the ideas and language that [it is the] duty [of governments] to contain or repress when it occurs in public'. According to Forcade, the aim of government should be to 'make [freedom of assembly] penetrate morals by diverting passionate debate and dangerous theories, and returning to discussions which help prepare legitimate progress and serve the real interests of the country'. Republicans responded to this hushing-up with articles in the press, by publishing works about freedom of assembly, in speeches addressed to the Legislative Body, and during trials. Their discourse distinguishes between what would, in a free discussion, issue from 'error', 'excess' or 'eccentricities', on the one hand, and from 'reason', or 'common sense', on the other. Once again there is the affirmation of the inevitable victory of the latter over the former. Charles Delescluze editor-in-chief of the republican newspaper *Le Réveil* stated:

> On the platform, before 1,000–2,000 men from all backgrounds, with their own consciences and their own reason, if more daring theories are not always hidden, they collapse in the face of contradiction which, in the last instance, always awards the victory to general good sense.[15]

For this reason debate in assemblies should be left to have free rein, without preventing certain questions from being addressed, and without an impatient police commissioner eager to break up the gathering. This idea was defended by Edmond de Pressensé, a pastor critical of imperial politics. In 1871 he was elected deputy to the Assembly for the electoral district of la Seine where he stood as a candidate 'of republican and, above all, anti-Bonapartist, faith'.[16] In 1869 he published *Les réunions publiques à Paris et les élections prochaines*, particularly

---

13. ADP/D3U9/34/Jugements de la Cour d'Appel de Paris. The most active speakers in socialist and communist assemblies were accused of 'attacking the rights of the family' (arrêt no. 2797), 'offence against morality' and 'offence to public and religious morals' (arrêt no. 2797), '[exciting] citizens to contempt or hatred' (arrêt no. 2796), 'attacks on the right to property' (arrêt no. 2983), 'verbal offences against state magistrates on duty' (arrêt no. 2925), etc.
14. Reproduced in Auguste Vitu, *Les réunions publiques à Paris, 1868–1869*, Paris, Éditions Dentu, 1869, pp. 93–95. On this pamphlet, see: Alain Dalotel, Alain Faure and Jean-Claude Freiermuth, *Aux origines de la Commune. Le mouvement des réunions publiques à Paris. 1868–1870*, Paris, F. Maspero, 1980, pp. 36–37.
15. *Le Réveil*, 9 January 1869.
16. Adolphe Robert and Gaston Cougny, *Dictionnaire des parlementaires français de 1789 à 1889*, Paris, Bourloton, 1889–1891, vol. 5, p. 44.

in response to an anonymous pamphlet published by Auguste Vitu which was very critical of the first public assemblies in Paris. Without denying that not all political assemblies are characterised by the moderate nature of opinions expressed, Pressensé lays responsibility on the fact that the law, and the way it was applied after some months, prevented deliberation from taking place properly. Using the example of an assembly where the republican economist Henri Cernuschi invited the public to fight 'the favourite ideas of Proudhonian socialism', he wrote: 'I am convinced that if freedom of discussion were [...] preserved, reason would take the upper hand and the foolish exaggerations would soon become "old rope"'.[17] By refusing to allow free assemblies the government not only prevented 'erroneous ideas' from being defeated by concrete arguments in the free play of deliberation, but also reinforced the 'wrong ideas', making martyrs of those who professed them. In August 1869, Jules Simon addressed the Legislative Body to reprimand the government for having followed its initial tolerance with harmful severity, at a time when 'the practice of assemblies began to emerge and with it the practice of public speaking'. For Simon, by preventing 'erroneous ideas' from being discussed, the government simply reinforced them. Had free discussion been maintained it would have proven to be the most effective weapon against error.

> Believe me, there is no other weapon against error than that of reasoning. There are doctrines which displease you: how does one overcome this? [...] By going where [people] teach them and discussing them without fear. [...] By repression, you only triumph over a man, and the error, which was nothing, becomes something when, by your action, he who professed it has become a martyr. [...] No sirs, there is no repression against the crimes of thought, there is nothing but the proof, nothing but the fight, there is no other force against error than the truth.[18]

In the Habermasian 'ideal speech situation' a rationally motivated consensus is sought after, one that cannot be rationally refuted. 'Democratic legitimacy lies in the agreement of individuals with the capacity for rationality, placed in a relation of inter-subjectivity and eager to reach a consensus by means of discussion.'[19] Not all theorists of deliberative democracy agree on the prospect of achieving this consensus in the real world. Some even consider it dangerous to insist on going beyond pluralism,[20] insofar as consensus may be a synonym for oppression.[21]

---

17. Edmond de Pressensé, *Les réunions publiques à Paris et les élections prochaines*, Paris, Librairie Meyrueis et Librairie Le Chevalier, 1869, p. 11.

18. Jules Simon, *Les réunions publiques. Extrait du Journal Officiel du 10 Août 1868*, Paris, Degorce-Cadot, 1869.

19. Loïc Blondiaux, 'La délibération, norme de l'action publique contemporaine?', *La Revue Projet*, CERAS, 2001, vol. 268, http://www.ceras-projet.org/index.php?id=1884 (accessed 6 June 2006).

20. On the disagreement on this question of consensus and pluralism, see: Amy Gutman and Dennis F. Thompson, *Why Deliberative Democracy?*, Princeton NJ, Princeton University Press, 2004, pp. 26–29.

21. Ian Shapiro, 'Optimal Deliberation?', *The Journal of Political Philosophy*, 2002, vol. 10, (2), 2, p. 199.

Nevertheless, most works accept, at least implicitly, that in discussion, 'citizens and their representatives, going beyond mere self-interest and limited points of view, reflect on the general interest or on their common good',[22] so that 'deliberative exchange is [...] assumed to produce a commonly shared sense, step-by-step'.[23] This means we can define a general interest as a consequence of the public use of reason. At the end of the nineteenth-century republican discourse on the virtues of citizens' deliberation in assembly was characterised by this search for the common good, implying a rejection of ideology which only reflected particularistic interests. Beyond the harmful differences of opinion in parties, there will be a necessary and possible alliance around the general interest. This notion of general interest is closer to the idea of a 'search for consensus' through the 'dialectic surpassing [particularistic interests]', than to that of a 'consensual sum of particular interests'.[24] Rosanvallon reminds us that 'political rationalism à la française is based on the conviction that the general interest embodies the "truth" of society, and thus cannot be deduced from particular interests'.[25]

This 'rationalist definition of democracy'[26] largely consists of a rejection of opinions deemed to be extreme, such as those of 'revolutionaries', socialists or anarchists and, in the early days of the Republic, anyone advocating a return of the monarchy. These are all debarred on behalf of a rationally motivated consensus which can only be achieved by demonstrating the meaningless nature of such theories. A key aspect of the discourse developed concerning the virtues of deliberation developed at that moment. 'Is it that the silence of death imposed on France, after 2 December, prevented the various schools of socialism from recruiting followers?', asked Rousselle and Limousin, before going on to state:

> With freedom, [...] in broad daylight, the pure theories, the musings, the utopias will disappear crushed by their impotence; the doctrines which contain a grain of truth [...] will be purified in the battle, will move closer together, and perhaps will end up by merging in a common aspiration for justice through freedom.[27]

Socialist ideas developed in assemblies were often presented as illusions in which only 'followers' could believe, and not as ideas that could be defended by enlightened citizens through the use of reason.

---

22. James Bohman, *Public Deliberation. Pluralism, Complexity, and Democracy*, Cambridge MA, MIT Press, 1996, p. 5.
23. Yannis Papadopoulos, 'Délibération et action publique', *Swiss Political Science Review*, 2004, vol. 10, (4), p. 148.
24. François Rangeon, *L'idéologie de l'intérêt général*, Paris, Economica, 1986, pp. 8–9.
25. Pierre Rosanvallon, *Le sacre du citoyen. L'histoire intellectuelle du suffrage universel en France*, Paris, Gallimard, 2001, p. 597.
26. Pierre Rosanvallon, 'Les élites françaises, la démocratie et l'État. Entretien avec Pierre Rosanvallon', *Esprit*, 1997, vol. 236, p. 62.
27. André Rousselle and Charles Limousin, *Manuel des réunions publiques non politiques, publiques électorales, électorales privées*, Paris, A. Le Chevalier, 1869, p. 108.

Outside election times the public assembly under the Empire rapidly became the quasi-monopoly of the socialists, after some months when it was also used by the liberal opposition. By late 1868, the differences which emerge in the non-electoral public assemblies are no longer between liberals and socialists. The new cleavage is between mutualists on the one hand, and collectivists and communists on the other. In his study of popular organisations for the period 1868–1871, Robert D. Wolfe notes that 'it required approximately six months for the public meetings in Paris to assume an overtly socialist character'.[28] Wolfe stresses that 'the socialists always occupied a larger place in the public meetings of the Empire than their actual influence would have warranted', particularly because of the exclusion of politics, under the 1868 law, from the subjects that can be discussed: 'While the republican opposition was forbidden to press its political demands, a communist could advocate a complete social revolution [...]'.[29] The presence of republicans becomes increasingly rare in public assemblies, with the exception of electoral and often contradictory assemblies known as *réunions contradictoires*. The latter remain more composite and in the campaign for the May 1869 legislative elections, we find 'moderate and radical republicans, at the front of the platform and receiving the greatest applause'.[30] It is only after March 1870 that the liberal opposition returns for some months to the practice of non-electoral public assemblies.[31]

When the government increases its attack on freedom of assembly as of January 1869, the discourse on the virtues of public deliberation permits republicans facing socialist-dominated assemblies to stay close to those defending freedom. They do this by condemning governmental repression whilst distinguishing themselves from the organisers and speakers of the assemblies under attack. Freedom of assembly is never criticised in the republican press. Journalists claimed that the problem of assemblies was that free deliberation was impossible, not only due to the intolerance of those dominating them, but also because the law prevented political issues from being addressed. Furthermore repressive measures, such as breaking up assemblies, prevented debates from taking place properly, hindering opposition to and criticism of socialist ideas. The journalist Léon Plée condemned the fact that a memorandum from the Minister of the Interior encouraged the dissolution of assemblies.[32] Plée argued that this was all the more regrettable since deliberation had begun to bear fruit in the service of truth:

---

28. Robert D. Wolfe, *The Origins of the Paris Commune. The Popular Organizations of 1868–1871*, PhD dissertation, Harvard University, 1966, p. 44.
29. Wolfe, *The Origins of the Paris Commune*, p. 43.
30. Dalotel, Faure and Freiermuth, *Aux origines de la Commune*, p. 39.
31. Wolfe, *The Origins of the Paris Commune*, p. 73.
32. *Le Siècle*, 20 February 1869.

When the reformers of assemblies presented themselves with their radical plans, it was enough for an auditor questioning them about their means to make them step down from the pedestal. [...] Everyone noted that eccentricities decreased; verbal abuse was tempered.

It is not freedom of assembly that is criticised, but the fact that deliberation, which could reveal socialist errors, cannot take place.

The exclusion of revolutionary ideas in the name of common sense continued under the Republic. The pro-government republican newspaper *Le Journal des Débats*, thus evokes the 'insanities recited by the collectivists and other revolutionaries'. In an editorial it states that there was no need to see any danger in revolutionary ideas because 'under a regimen of freedom, public common sense always regains its rights' and 'reasonable opinions' triumph.[33] We can measure how deeply anti-democratic such a discourse on the virtues of deliberation may be. The conviction that agreement must be reached on a general, or at least consensual interest, may disqualify protest and confrontation, particularly when an idea is expressed passionately, and far from the moderate presentation of rational arguments called for by the deliberative model. The potentially conservative connotations of deliberation have been highlighted by Lynn M. Sanders, who emphasises the dangers for democracy in the deliberative procedure; that is, the idea that all democratic discussion must be rational, moderate and non-egoistical, and that its implicit aim should be to develop a relative consensus around the general interest.[34]

Today, with the participatory and deliberative injunction, we are witnessing a 'serious change in the way of justifying representative government': 'the common good [is no longer] the monopoly of professional politicians and can be co-produced with citizens'.[35] At first glance, it may seem surprising that the discourse on the virtues of deliberation could be developed by republicans at the end of the nineteenth century. Indeed, their primary aim was to consolidate representative democracy and to prevent anything which might threaten it. In fact, partly entrusting citizens with their assemblies is by no means a question of involving citizens in decision-making. It simply means promoting the creation of a public opinion oriented to the common good. Thus, the model of representative government is in no way refuted, freedom and autonomy of public opinion being one of its characteristic dimensions.[36] It is never a question of establishing concrete ways to trace the outcome of deliberation in assemblies up to the level of government. On the contrary, the republican press contains criticism of assemblies

---

33. *Le Journal des Débats*, 11 August 1881.
34. Lynn M. Sanders, 'Against Deliberation', *Political Theory*, 1997, vol. 25, (3), pp. 347–376.
35. Julien Talpin, 'Des écoles de démocratie: formation à la citoyenneté et démocratie participative', 2005, http://www.univ-paris8.fr/scpo/talpin.doc, p. 3 (accessed 6 June 2006).
36. Bernard Manin, *The Principles of Representative Government*, Cambridge, Cambridge University Press, 1995.

that parody the parliament or courts, the sole legitimate *loci* of decision-making. The idea that it would be necessary to link citizens' deliberation in assemblies with the parliamentary initiative was later defended, but by socialist parliamentarians, and in vain. In 1906, a bill to establish 'the democratic organisation of universal suffrage' was presented by several socialist deputies calling for a state of 'continuous popular deliberation', without which 'universal suffrage, popular sovereignty, are nothing but empty words without any real content'. Voters would be divided into sections and would meet to examine public issues and their deliberations would be relayed to the municipal and general councils and to the legislative chambers.[37]

It is interesting to note that legal experts also insist on the difference between citizens' political meetings and the decision-making assemblies. Thus, in 1894 when Roger Arnette began the historical part of his dissertation on freedom of assembly, he distinguished between the assemblies of his research and those with a public decision-making role:

> It is above all important to avoid [...] the undoubtedly natural, but nonetheless unacceptable, confusion, between meetings as we understand them today, and assemblies that [...] have exercised by any right (legislative, administrative or judicial), a part of public power: the mere fact that they take binding decisions will be the sign by which we will recognise them, and, consequently, ignore them as alien to our subject.[38]

Other legal experts sketch a genealogy of assemblies including distant ancestors such as the assemblies of the Athenian *agora* or the Roman *comitia*. Nevertheless, they note in general that these assemblies have a legislative or administrative role, and that this is not the case for the citizens' assemblies existing at the time of their studies.

Does the fact that the republican plan at the end of the nineteenth century did not include the will to involve citizens' gatherings directly in decision-making make it really different from the contemporary theories of deliberation?

> At the heart of the deliberative conception of democracy is the view that collective decision-making is to proceed deliberatively — by citizens advancing proposals and defending them with considerations that others, who are themselves free and equal, can acknowledge as reasons.[39]

---

37. Annexe no. 594, session extraordinaire, 21 décembre 1906, *Journal Officiel. Documents Parlementaires. Chambre*, pp. 317–318.
38. Roger Arnette, *La liberté de réunion en France. Son histoire et sa législation*, Paris, Arthur Rousseau, 1894, pp. 27–28.
39. Joshua Cohen and Charles Sabel, 'Directly-Deliberative Polyarchy', *European Law Journal*, 1997, vol. 3, (4), p. 327. Habermas argues, however, that it is more the formation of public opinion which is at the centre of the reflections on deliberation; see: *Between Facts and Norms*, p. 307.

Nevertheless, some authors show that the objective of the main current in participatory and deliberative devices is not a real sharing of decision-making and that 'almost all of them have a consultative character'.[40] The assemblies conceived by the republicans in the nineteenth century did not even mention this consultative character explicitly. But the consultative role of the contemporary procedures has also been questioned. Decision-makers take little account of what is generated by deliberation in assemblies. As far back as 1981, Barry Checkoway drew up a balance sheet of the use of public hearings in the United States and concluded that:

> There is little research evidence to indicate that hearings have influence on agency decisions. On the contrary, evidence indicates that agency officials may either give cursory consideration to or ignore altogether certain views expressed in hearings.[41]

This analysis is not unique and is also found for many other mechanisms. Some still stress that participatory and deliberative cases have other important roles;[42] but among the latter many are managerial objectives of conflict-management, rather than a form of genuine democratic enrichment.[43]

The French regard for contradictory debates in assembly

As late as 1943, Vincent Auriol, whilst completely engaged in drawing the portrait of a Republic regenerated by large organised parties, nevertheless continued to praise the organisation of public assemblies which should reproduce the form of a parliamentary debate and put the champions of the two main parties face to face.[44]

Nicolas Roussellier remarks that for Vincent Auriol, 'the deliberative assembly seemed an indispensable complement to political life, more than the meetings where we only find followers of the same organisation'. The author goes on to state that:

---

40. Loïc Blondiaux, 'Prendre au sérieux l'idéal délibératif : un programme de recherche', *Swiss Political Science Review*, 2004, vol. 10, (4), p. 159.
41. Barry Checkoway, 'The Politics of Public Hearings', *Journal of Applied Behavioral Science*, 1981, vol. 17, (4), pp. 569–570.
42. See, for example: Brian Adams, 'Public Meetings and the Democratic Process', *Public Administration Review*, 2004, vol. 64, (1), pp. 46–52.
43. I refer to the presentation of the functionalist perspective of deliberation which leads us to think that 'on the pretext of reinforcing democratic citizenship, the authority would [...] find new ruses', in: Loïc Blondiaux, 'La délibération, norme de l'action publique contemporaine?', p. 4.
44. Here and below: Nicolas Roussellier, 'Deux formes de représentation politique: le citoyen et l'individu', in Marc Sadoun (ed.), *La démocratie en France*, Paris, Gallimard, 2000, vol. 1, p. 266.

Electoral campaigns were long characterised by a multiplicity of public assemblies organised as 'contradictory assemblies' during the course of which two or more candidates would face one another under the presidency of a '*bureau*' which had to guarantee the *ad hoc* rules of debate and in the presence of a public seldom committed beforehand to one or other duellist.

For a long time the contradictory assembly was effectively the dominant form of political assembly in France. It was particularly important during elections, when it was an opportunity for direct confrontation between candidates (see Chapter 3). Regarding electoral campaigns at the end of the nineteenth century, Huard stresses that the public assembly was 'almost inevitably contradictory'.[45] Yet this form of assembly could not be reduced to the sole confrontation of candidates before a public gathering. At the time meetings where speakers from the organising group accept the contradiction, irrespective of whether it is made by one or many speakers on the platform or by the public, are also called contradictory assemblies. It is nevertheless true that the contradictory form remains active for longer in the case of electoral campaigns, while it becomes rarer for other types of assemblies from the early twentieth century onwards.

Meanwhile, and particularly in the first decades of the Third Republic, the contradictory assembly was a feature of French political life, in comparison with Britain or the United States, as already mentioned in the introduction of this book. The commentators at the time stressed that the dedication to deliberation in assembly was a typically French phenomenon. In *La campagne électorale de 1869*, Étienne Masseras, former editor-in-chief of the *Courrier des États-Unis*, emphasises the contrast between the use of assemblies in France and in English-speaking countries:

> Last year again, talking about a meeting that ended up in a brawl, London newspapers stated that in principle a public assembly could only take place if there is full conformity of opinions between speakers and audience, and among the audience itself. This principle became a maxim in the United States where no-one would dream of calling a meeting without having first settled the smallest details, chosen speakers of a given political colour, and above all prepared an audience [which is] both homogeneous and compliant.

In France, by contrast, people of different political opinions are gathered together in the same room, on the same platform and the same floor. This is what 'the two peoples that we can call the veterans of the right of assembly would declare impossible, [but] France comes to give them an unexpected spectacle', writes Masseras, adding:

> Not only did candidates have to explain themselves before a mixed public, unknown to each other and which often changes, but they had to reply to a thousand questions put to them unexpectedly by the audience. Better still: we

---

45. Raymond Huard, *Le suffrage universel en France (1848–1946)*, Paris, Aubier, 1991, p. 283.

have seen rivals, political opponents, side-by-side before electors whose votes they were soliciting simultaneously, developing in turn, in the same meeting, diametrically opposed professions of faith [...].[46]

Stressing the difference between the English or American and French use of freedom of assembly appears, here, to pay credit to the quality of political life in France with its direct confrontation of ideas.

The fact that the contradictory assembly was the usual form of assembly in France was evoked for a long time. But starting from the late 1880s it was also criticised'. Contradictory assemblies could be the cause of disorder, disturbance and violence, which rarely occurred in assemblies in Britain and the United States. This critical discourse unfolded in the republican press, alongside the depletion of public assemblies to the benefit of private assemblies in the republican camp. A journalist of *Le Temps* opined that the 'assemblies called contradictory [...] cannot but engender the disorder and oppression of one part of the assembled by the other', giving the example of countries where 'the parties [have] their own, independent assemblies'.[47] *Le Petit Parisien* reported that: 'In England, [...] as in Switzerland and the United States a meeting never gathers together people of different opinions. [...] A contradictory meeting always ends up in a brawl'.[48] Faced with the increase of disorder in their midst, the fact that assemblies give rise to a direct confrontation between political opponents begins to lose its positive implications. The deliberative assembly is nonetheless the configuration closest to the original republican ideal as a place where citizens can gather together to debate and where public opinion takes shape.

What form do these exchanges in assemblies take? Stressing that debates in assemblies took place 'with direct reference to the parliamentary model', Roussellier insists on 'the formation of a *bureau* and selection of a chairman responsible for maintaining calm and order stipulated by law'.[49] In a contradictory assembly, the members of the *bureau* indeed find themselves responsible for permitting the proper procedures of debate by ensuring that different speeches can be heard. The *bureau* should consist of at least three people, a chairman and two assistants, chosen previously by those who signed the declaration or who are elected by the participants. Under the Republic, if other attributions are conferred on it, the existence of a *bureau* indicates above all that the assembly is seen as a place of contradictory debate. This is particularly evident from the discussions in the Chamber of Deputies before the adoption of the 1907 law which suppressed the need to declare in advance that an assembly was to be held.

---

46. Étienne Masseras, *La campagne électorale de 1869*, Paris, A. Lacroix, Verboeckhover et Cie, 1969, pp. 14–15.
47. *Le Temps*, 31 October 1888.
48. *Le Petit Parisien*, 2 August 1887.
49. Nicolas Roussellier, 'La diffusion de l'éloquence en France sous la IIIe République', in Fabrice D'Almeida (ed.), *L'éloquence politique en France et en Italie de 1870 à nos jours*, Rome, École française de Rome, 2001, p. 45.

The proposed law submitted on 15 January 1907, before the government presented its plan, included the abrogation of Article 8 of the 1881 law according to which 'each assembly must have a *bureau*'. This measure is described as nothing other than the enlargement of what is already granted to religious assemblies. The idea is not taken up in the government plan submitted to the Chamber, precisely because the political assembly is in general considered to be a debate gathering people of different opinions. The legal recital of 22 January ended with the idea that 'the designation of a *bureau* [...] is not a formality prejudicial to the right of assembly'. We are reminded that 'this is [...] typical of deliberative gatherings to entrust the direction of their debates and the maintenance of order in their ranks to a *bureau* of their choice'. The *bureau* can be suppressed in cases of religious assemblies, precisely because these stand out due to the fact that 'contradiction is not allowed'. On the contrary, 'ordinary assemblies generally imply a discussion and hence call for the nomination of a *bureau*'. In its report of 24 January the commission responsible for examining the government draft law and the draft law previously submitted, reminds us again that:

> In what concerns public electoral or other assemblies, where deliberative debates call for indispensable direction, [the] commission, in agreement with the Government, thought that one cannot, without the risk of compromising the proper exercise of the right of assembly, suppress the formality of the nomination of a *bureau*.[50]

If the assembly is a place of debate under the Republic, its organisation is therefore recognised as indispensable in order to avoid the sort of disorder caused by an unregulated confrontation of contrasting opinions.

The legislative terms of 1881 on the role of the *bureau* link up with those of 1868 on three points: it must 'maintain order' in the meeting; 'prevent any violation of the laws'; and control the speeches made. According to the 1868 law, which stipulates that 'the special and appointed object of the assembly' must be specified in the declaration, '*bureau* members must not tolerate any discussion of questions foreign to the [declared] subject of the assembly'. The 1881 law specifies that the *bureau* is responsible for 'prohibit[ing] all discourse against public order and public morals, or containing provocation to any act which qualifies as a crime or offense'. The fact that in a contradictory assembly the *bureau* must guarantee effective freedom of discussion, allow speakers to speak, and permit questions from the audience, is based on the fact that it is also responsible for 'conserving the nature of the assembly specified in the declaration'. The law simply rules that 'the declaration will proclaim whether the form of the assembly is a lecture, a public discussion, or [...] an electoral assembly', without raising the question of whether or not it is contradictory. However, the interpretation found in the legal commentaries is that the *bureau* must maintain the contradictory nature of any meeting announced as such. '*Bureau* members ensure that the nature of the

---

50. The legal recital and the report are reproduced at: http://www.eglise-etat.org/loi280307.html

assembly, as per the declaration, and the convocation or posters, is respected', writes Degrenne. He goes on to specify that in the same way 'a conference announced as contradictory must really be [contradictory]', that 'opponents must have the chance to reply freely to speakers', and that if 'the *bureau* can regulate and also limit the speaking time of each, [...] each must be able to make remarks that he considers relevant'.[51] The legal experts agree on how difficult it is for the *bureau* to do its job with only 'moral means' at its disposal.[52] In the 1881 *Code des réunions publiques*, Charles Constant wrote that *bureau* members 'must above all use moral authority granted them by their mandate [...] to maintain the regulation and dignity of discussions by the exhortations and remonstrance addressed to those who interrupt, restore calm by means of calls to order'.[53] If these means are insufficient, and if the *bureau* fails to direct the assembly, it must dismiss the meeting. The assembly becomes illegal if it does not.

In contradictory assemblies, or those declared as such, the chairman frequently says a few words to the effect that all opinions will be heard. In 1889, at a public electoral assembly in Paris, 'the chairman reminded [participants] that the assembly was contradictory and that all opinions must be respected at the platform'.[54] In a rather different style, in 1893 at an anarchist assembly in Marseilles, 'the chairman declared that the assembly was absolutely free and that those who wished to speak had only to do so'.[55] The chairman often insisted on the neutral stance of the *bureau*, whose role was to guarantee that all positions could be defended, irrespective of the opinions of its members. At a public electoral assembly in Aubagne in 1906, the chairman 'thanks the audience for the trust bestowed on him in electing him to the chairmanship of this assembly, and declares that the discussion will be conducted with the greatest impartiality and engages the public to listen to speakers calmly'.[56] Occasionally a chairman may not be content with this type of declaration and specifies the limits of the contradiction. A police officer attending a public assembly organised in Paris in 1885 by a Bonapartist electoral committee reported that:

---

51. Marcel-Louis Degrenne, *Les réunions et les pouvoirs de police*, Caen, Caron & Cie, 1938, p. 205.
52. Albert Joubrel, *Du droit de réunion*, Rennes, Librairie générale Pilhon et Hommay, 1904, pp. 72–73, 149; Edouard-René Lefebvre, *Le droit de réunion*, Paris, Impr. H. Bouillant, 1903.
53. Charles Constant, *Code des réunions publiques, des réunions électorales et des réunions privées. Commentaire pratique de la loi du 30 juin 1881 à l'usage des préfets, sous-préfets, maires, juges de paix, ainsi que des organisateurs de réunions publiques ou privées*, Paris, A. Durand et Pedone-Lauriel, 1881, p. 60.
54. APP/Ba/1462/1889/Élections diverses. Réunions. 7e arr.: Rapport, préfecture de Police, 2e brigade de recherches, cabinet, 1er *bureau*, 31 août 1889.
55. AD BDR/1M/866/Réunions publiques, associations, 1893: Rapport du commissaire de police au commissaire central, 12e arr., 9 août 1893.
56. AD BDR/1M/876/Partis et mouvements politiques. Réunions, 1906–1910. Réunions Associations, 1906: Rapport du commissaire de police au préfet des Bouches-du-Rhône, Aubagne, 29 août 1906.

[The chairman] declared that he would allow all serious and reasoned opponents wanting to discuss the issues dealt with by the speakers, to do so; [but added that] he would use all his power to oppose any disturbers in the pay of reactionary parties causing disorder in the assembly.[57]

In 1907 at a royalist assembly in Marseilles, the chairman declared that:

The deliberation will be [...] open and all those who wish to put questions to the speaker may do so on condition that these do not go beyond the question and above all so as not to loose time in idle talk.[58]

These may be simple declarations of intent not necessarily followed by effects, but their recurrence reveals the position that the chairmen of these assemblies want to adopt.

In a context where public discussion is valued, the contradictory assembly is considered the most legitimate form of political meeting. The organisation of a contradictory assembly, or the participation in an assembly organised by political opponents to expose different opinions, is a way to show how the prospect of criticism in no way weakens the ideas of those confronted with it. The private assembly is the form which deviates the most directly from this type of assembly as a place of debate. When an assembly is private, it is taken as given that for the organisers the meeting room is like being 'at home', so that it is legitimate for them to refuse to be challenged. Since we assume that all those present have been invited, the fact of their being there is taken as a sign of an agreement with the ideas of the speakers. If there are interruptions despite this, they are delegitimised by the private nature of the assembly. In 1880, the chairman of a catholic legitimist assembly at the Élysée Montmartre, which was private but attended by 1,200 people, reacted to an interruption by a man belonging to a republican group who had got into the hall, by reminding him that 'as the assembly is private, no-one has the right to interrupt'. In order not to appear anxious about contradiction, the speaker nevertheless added that 'as catholics are supporters of freedom, the interrupter could express himself after the meeting'.[59] In these private assemblies speakers sometimes thanked the public for their support, thus indicating that they were correct in supposing that all of the participants agreed with them. During the same legitimist assembly, at which it was evident that not everyone did agree, one speaker declared: 'I thank you, and I congratulate you for coming here in a crowd, to protest against the odious attacks made on religion and freedom by our governors.'[60] Police observers also describe the private assembly as a place where the audience cannot express disagreement with the speakers. A 1884 report on a

---

57. APP/Ba/62/Comités bonapartistes, 1874–1886: Rapport police municipale, 2e brigade de recherches, 11 août 1885.
58. AD BDR/1M/876/Partis et mouvements politiques. Réunions, 1906–1910. Réunions, Associations, 1907: Rapport du commissaire spécial, 24 décembre 1907.
59. APP/Ba/403/Menées légitimistes, 1880: Rapport de l'inspecteur principal, police municipale, 1e brigade de recherches, 11 août 1880.
60. APP/Ba/403/Menées légitimistes, 1880: Rapport de l'inspecteur principal, police municipale, 1e brigade de recherches, 12 août 1880.

private legitimist assembly held in Paris notes: 'The assembly was private, it was impossible to challenge the speakers'.[61]

In this period, those who do not organise contradictory assemblies are denounced as cowards. Rather than risk being challenged by the audience many preferred to 'teach the people a lesson', as observed by political editor Louis Jourdan, reporting on a non-contradictory conference given by Émile Ollivier.[62] Rather than confront their ideas with those of their opponents, in sharing the platform they prefer to preserve them carefully in the shelter of the contestation. This type of criticism is even more frequent thirty years later, when the clash between Dreyfusards and anti-Dreyfusards comes to a head, giving way to the organisation of a great many huge rallies by the two sides. The Dreyfusards criticise the fact that their opponents only hold closed assemblies where deliberation is ruled out. The Dreyfusard journalist Lucien Victor-Meunier wrote with regards to an assembly of the *Ligue des Patriotes*:

> We, when we go to tell the People what we have in our hearts we open the doors wide to let everyone in. Yesterday, we were only allowed in to hear M. Déroulède on presentation of a letter of invitation; it was a private assembly with all its discretion, safe among supporters of the same idea.[63]

Accusations are particularly acute when the organisers of an assembly, despite having chosen not to authorise contradiction, are unable to make their speakers heard. A well-known example is the electoral assembly held for Gambetta on 16 August 1881, in a hangar in rue Saint-Blaise, in the heart of the Charonne quarter of Belleville. The assembly was by invitation but ended up being largely open due to bad organisation, with a crowd of 5,000–10,000 people. The 'champion of Belleville' was unable to make himself heard due to loud heckling. As soon as the *bureau* was named the first shouts and whistles could be heard, challenging the choices made. The chairman invited Gambetta to speak, but his voice could not be heard above the noise of the crowd. He insists, calls for respect of republican democracy but the heckling of obstructionists grows. Gambetta becomes angry, raps the table with a cane and raises his voice: 'Silence you bawlers! Silence you loudmouths! Silence to those who have neither decency nor conscience!'. The uproar continued but before leaving the room Gambetta utters one last warning:

> Do you know what you are? Do you know? [...] You are drunken slaves and, therefore irresponsible. I have only one thing, one single thing to add, and it is this: on 21 August, the vote of true and loyal citizens will avenge me of this infamy. [...] As for you, the day after the vote, you will return, you handful of loudmouths, to your old habits. But, know ye that I will know how to find you even at the bottom of your lairs.[64]

---

61. APP/Ba/405/Menées légitimistes, 1884: Rapport du 28 juillet 1884.
62. *Le Siècle*, 14 May 1868.
63. *Le Siècle*, 26 September 1898.
64. See: *Les grands orateurs républicains. Gambetta*, Monaco, Hemera, 1949–1950, pp. 198–200 (Preface and comments by Gérard Bourdin).

These final threats received many comments. The day after, the entire press reported on the event, and many insisted that Gambetta should not have refused the contradiction in order to ensure the acclamations of a selected public in a private assembly. Clemenceau's radical republican newspaper stated:

> Yesterday an event of unquestionable importance took place at Belleville. Monsieur Gambetta, who had convened 6,000 electors in a private meeting, was forced to renounce his speech. [...] This took place in a meeting where the invitees had been hand-picked and where one could only enter by means of a special invitation. This is what makes the event particularly significant. M. Gambetta had declined a public and contradictory debate. He had chosen his audience, and the latter has declared itself against him. We never approve of impediments to free speech, yet we cannot help remarking that if something was by nature to justify them, this is the oratorical system adopted by M. Gambetta. The Belleville deputy issued this claim to deliver a monologue and carefully avoided any discussion. The electors of the 20th *arrondissement* clearly wanted to protest against a procedure that made cheap use of the dignity of universal suffrage.[65]

The choice of organising a non-contradictory assembly can be interpreted as an act of cowardice. And despite of this choice, being unable to make oneself heard and not receiving applause are interpreted as an evident sign of popular rejection.

The organisation of falsely contradictory assemblies also testifies to the fact that the only legitimate form of gathering is where debate is possible. Above all, it is a cliché when assemblies are announced as contradictory but in the last instance do not allow political opponents to speak freely. Without giving the impression of a fear of debate, and while trying to give the impression that the participants had chosen their side, debate is avoided in practice. The obstruction against contradictors is not always a strategy on the part of the organisers. It may simply be due to the presence of a group which is not expected. It may, however, be organised in advance. This is affirmed by a police observer at a public assembly in Paris organised by the *Ligue royaliste populaire* in 1883. At the start of the meeting, the chairman guaranteed freedom of the platform: 'The chairman declared that the assembly was contradictory and that he would allow all those requesting to speak to do so; he called on the audience to be calm and to listen to the speakers, whatever party they belonged to.' However the author of the report then states that 'the royalists have recruited around fifty individuals, without any clear profession, whose task is to applaud speakers of their party and to prevent its opponents from addressing the assembly'.[66] Nevertheless the practice was still rare in the early 1880s and only really developed at the end of the century. Sometimes the chairman or a speaker calls for contradiction, insisting on his willingness to

---

65. *La Justice*, 17 August 1881.
66. APP/Ba/405/Menées légitimistes: Rapport, police municipale, 2e brigade de recherches, 17 mars 1883.

reply to criticism, all the while knowing that no-one present will contest his ideas, but conscious that it is always a good idea for a speaker to stress his inclination to accept contradiction. This is in much the same way what happened in the many assemblies in Marseilles at which the militant anarchist Henri Dhorr (real name Lucien Weil) took part in February–March 1898. In one of them: 'despite the insistence of the speaker', 'no challenger [asked] to speak'.[67] At the beginning of another, Dhorr specified that 'Sr Cassan member of the *Parti ouvrier de Paris* on his way to Marseilles had promised to come to the assembly to refute his arguments, but that he had received a letter informing him that [Cassan] could not attend due to an accident'.[68] Sometimes the contradictor actually plays an agreed role. The commissioner reporting on an assembly where Dhorr responded to a challenger, who had put several questions from the floor, said that 'he appeared to be more the speaker's accomplice'. Even if the questions were not sympathetic, the speaker still appeared to have no problem in replying and the alleged contradictor ended by declaring himself: 'satisfied with the explanations given'.[69]

The contradictory assembly corresponds only imperfectly to the described ideal of deliberation as a free discussion where participants listen to each other's arguments. It is no less important to note that the most legitimate form of political assembly at the end of the nineteenth century the gathering where individuals with different opinions came to weigh their discourse directly against that of others. The role of the contradictory assembly was so essential that a refusal to organise this sort of meeting, or not attending one when invited to do so, was seen as an act of cowardice. Some were even willing to simulate the call for contradiction. Therefore under the Third Republic, the assembly was not a gathering of individuals sharing the same opinion. On the contrary, it had long tended 'towards a verbal dispute', as the legal expert Maurice Menanteau recalled in 1937: 'placed [...] under [the banner] of an exchange of ideas and verbal debate', assemblies were then 'gatherings for discussion'.[70]

Assemblies as potential intermediaries between the citizen and the State?

Throughout the nineteenth century France was characterised by a 'political culture of generality', to use Pierre Rosanvallon's expression, inherited from the Revolution. This was basically a rejection of intermediary bodies in so far as these tend to 'compete with the legal expression of the general will' and try to usurp the

---

67. AD BDR/1M/869/Réunions publiques, 1898, janvier–avril: Rapport du commissaire de police au commissaire central, 17 février 1898.

68. AD BDR/1M/869/Réunions publiques, 1898, janvier–avril: Rapport du commissaire de police au commissaire central, 24 février 1898.

69. AD BDR/1M/869/Réunions publiques, 1898, janvier–avril: Rapport du commissaire de police au commissaire central, 6 mars 1898.

70. Maurice Menanteau, *Les nouveaux aspects de la liberté de réunion. Essai sur les caractères juridiques et politiques de la liberté de réunion en France*, Paris, Librairie technique et économique, 1937, pp. 25–34.

role of the representative organs of government, taking away their 'monopoly of collective expression'. Furthermore, they also 'bias [the] mode of formation' of this general will and prevent the outcome of citizens' deliberation from being the common good.[71] Yet, 'beginning in 1880 under governments led by [the moderate] opportunist republicans, political associations began to expand freely even while the legal restrictions remained firmly in place'.[72] In this period we are dealing with a 'republican tolerance' of associations — particularly for those which are not a threat to the 'established powers'.[73] Three laws testify to a change in the status of associations: the law on the creation of professional syndicates of 21 March 1884;[74] the law on the creation of mutual aid societies of 1 April 1898; and the law giving a legal framework to associations of 1 July 1901. Jean-François Merlet describes the change taking place since the 1880s as a 'Copernican revolution'.[75] Rosanvallon is more restrained and refers to a 'certain tilting in the years 1880–1900',[76] not a 'negation of the French model', which simply 'inflected'.[77]

At this point I will not retrace the history of the long reluctance of republicans *vis-à-vis* associations, or that of the progressive recognition of a need for them in certain domains. This has already been done. Beyond the already-cited research, several works on the history of associations were published, or republished, on the centenary of the 1901 law.[78] We can also refer to the many works published on the subject in the early twentieth century,[79] in particular to the many law dissertations defended after the adoption of the 1901 law.[80] The fact remains that we cannot

---

71. Pierre Rosanvallon, *Le modèle politique français. La société civile contre le jacobinisme de 1789 à nos jours*, Paris, Seuil, 2006, p. 14. See also, Jean-François Thuot, *La fin de la représentation et les formes contemporaines de la démocratie*, Montreal, Nota Bene, 1998, pp. 80–81.

72. Raymond Huard, 'Political Association in Nineteenth Century France. Legislation and Practice', in Nancy G. Bermeo and Philip G. Nord (eds), *Civil Society Before Democracy. Lessons from Nineteenth-Century Europe*, Lanham, Rowman & Littlefield, 2000, p. 146.

73. Bruno Benoît, 'Réflexion sur le phénomène associatif', *Cahier Millénaire3*, 2002, vol. 1, (26), p. 15.

74. Denis Barbet, 'Retour sur la loi de 1884. La production des frontières du syndical et du politique', *Genèses*, 1991, vol. 3, (3), pp. 5–30.

75. Jean-François Merlet, *Une grande loi de la Troisième République. La loi du 1er juillet 1901*, Paris, LGDJ, 2001, p. 8.

76. Rosanvallon, 'Les corps intermédiaires', p. 1,016.

77. Rosanvallon, *Le modèle politique français*, p. 18.

78. Claire Andrieu, Gilles Le Béguec and Danielle Tartakowsky (eds), *Associations et champ politique. La loi de 1901 à l'épreuve du siècle*, Paris, Publications de la Sorbonne, 2001; Jean-François Merlet, *Une grande loi de la Troisième République. La loi du 1er juillet 1901*, Paris, LGDJ, 2001; Jean-Claude Bardout, *L'histoire étonnante de la loi 1901. Le droit d'association en France avant et après Waldeck-Rousseau*, Lyon, Juris-Service, 2000.

79. Paul Nourrisson, *Histoire de la liberté d'association en France depuis 1789*, Paris, Sirey, 1920; Edouard Clunet, *Les associations au point de vue historique et juridique*, Paris, Marchal et Billard, 1909.

80. See, in particular: Claude Couprie, *L'association déclarée d'après la loi de 1901*, Paris, Impr. de H. Jouve, 1905; A. de Faget de Casteljau, *Histoire du droit d'association de 1789 à 1901*, Paris, A. Rousseau, 1905; Adolphe Pichon, *Des caractères distinctifs des associations soumises à la loi du 1er juillet 1901*, Paris, H. Jouve, 1905.

understand how the assembly is perceived as constituting, under certain conditions, an ideal mode of participation in a representative democracy, without placing this study in the context of the republican distrust of associationism. In spite of the progressive re-evaluation of the role of associations as of the 1880s, the republican ideal of popular participation without action must be paralleled with the insistence on the need to distinguish them from assemblies.

'To assemble means the desire to shed light on issues and to reflect together; to associate, [...] to work together, to weigh itself up and to act.' This excerpt from a speech made by Etienne Hervé, deputy and defender of ministerial policy, on the debate of the 10 April 1834 law on associations, sums up what had long been seen as the basic difference between assembly and association — on the one hand, discourse, thought and opinion, and on the other, action.[81] The idea was proposed in similar forms by legal experts after Hervé's wake. In 1893, Maurice Hauriou defined the assembly as 'a group of men that forms momentarily in order to reflect together', and specified that 'it differs from the association which presupposes men grouped in a permanent way in order to act in common'. He adds that it is 'with good reason' that the State fears that associations would 'be harmful'. He nevertheless considers that the State has an interest in recognising associations '[pursuing] the aims of the general interest' or 'establishments of public utility'.[82] Until the end of the nineteenth century, the position of moderate republicans in power — unlike the radicals who defend freedom of association — differs from the concept formulated by Hervé only in terms of the consequences that are drawn from it. The assembly is not a threat to representative democracy on condition that it does not solely assemble people of the same opinion, *a fortiori* people belonging to the same association. The association, on the other hand, is still seen as a threat dividing people according to group interests. In political matters, association would thus prevent from reaching a peaceful outcome of citizens' deliberation. It can distance citizens from the pursuit of the general interest, and can compete with governmental institutions.

The memory of political clubs as a foil

> We have taken clubs when they appeared in France and have carefully observed the role they have played. From the beginning, we have seen them cause trouble, bring regular government to a halt, encroach on the rights of national representation, and, their power growing with their audacity, they throw the country into the path of violence and bloodshed.

---

81. Speech cited by Naquet on 15 July 1879 in his report presented to the Chamber on behalf of the commission examining the proposed law on the right of assembly, see: *Journal Officiel*, 18 August 1879, p. 8,568.
82. Maurice Hauriou, *Précis de droit administratif contenant le droit public and le droit administratif*, Paris, L. Larose et Forcel, 1893, pp. 151–152, 157–160.

The concluding argument of Alphonse Jouet's dissertation, *Des clubs*, is clear: 'Do we have peace? Let us keep it! [...] One should profit from the lessons of history, and not reinstate the clubs!'[83] The experience of the past, the memory of what had occurred during the Revolution and of what was repeated in 1848 and later in the Paris Commune, only convinced the legislator not to re-establish the freedom of clubs. The fact that times had changed, and that France was no longer in a period of revolutionary agitation, altered nothing. For the author, and for a number of his contemporaries, the clubs remained a danger for public institutions.

Legal experts writing at the end of the nineteenth century and early twentieth century, criticise clubs not so much for having been a factor of agitation which upset the established order, but for having behaved as elected institutions, or for having exerted pressure on the latter. The experience during the Revolution was by far the most widely invoked comparison. Legal experts assert that assemblies combined with association in the clubs — presented as a hybrid monster, 'a curious mix of association and assemblies'[84] — would have allowed some to direct the decisions of the legitimately constituted authorities, undermining representative government. In 1883, René Petit evoked the '[intervention] of societies without a mandate [...] in the competences of the constituted powers'.[85] In 1938, Marcel-Louis Degrenne denounced the fact that under the Revolution 'associations, invoked popular sovereignty, going as far as giving orders counter to those of the public and legally constituted authorities'.[86]

The case of the 1848 clubs seems to be considered less important. When they are mentioned, it is generally to affirm that they were behind the insurrection of 15 May — when rebels attempted a *coup de force* taking up arms against the Assembly in an attempt to form a revolutionary government — and that it was following these events that the authorities decided to take action against the clubs. These were designated as supporters of disorder rather than as bodies with any real influence on public powers. The 1848 clubs tried to exert as much influence as those under the Revolution by 'setting themselves up as little parliaments'.[87] However in so doing they did not manage to lay down the law, but only 'claim[ed] precedence over the others [parliaments]'.[88] Their main feature was to have been 'centres of agitation'.[89]

It is more surprising that the place taken by clubs under the Paris Commune passed almost unnoticed. Indeed, 'the clubs viewed themselves, in varying degrees,

---

83. Alphonse Jouet, *Des clubs*, Paris, A. Giard, H. Jouve, 1891, pp. 331–332.
84. Jean Fournier-Poncelet, *La liberté de réunion au XXe siècle. Étude de droit public comparé*, Université d'Aix-Marseille, Typographie et lithographie Barlatier, 1910, p. 52.
85. René Petit, *Du droit de réunion*, Paris, A. Cotillon, 1883, p. 26.
86. Degrenne, *Les réunions et les pouvoirs de police*, p. 23.
87. Michel Baffrey, *Le droit de réunion en Angleterre et en France*, Paris, Les Presses Modernes, 1937, p. 126.
88. Baffrey, *Le droit de réunion en Angleterre et en France*, p. 126.
89. Henri Nucé de Lamothe, *La liberté de réunion en France*, Toulouse, Impr. Sebille, 1911, p. 42.

as intermediaries between the Commune and the citizenry'. Highlighting the different roles that these have held, Eugene W. Schulkind selects: 'to participate in the drafting of measures to be presented to the Commune for deliberation and subsequent action; [to] aid in the administration of the *arrondissements* and the application of the Commune's decisions'.[90] The communard clubs were thus a potential example of how to cross the boundary between places of debate and organs of action trying to influence the constituted authorities and to usurp a part of their normal functions. Yet, legal experts seem to behave as if the Commune, clearly still too near, had never existed. In a dissertation on the clubs, Alphonse Jouet evokes 'the horrors of the Commune', without specifying what he means by this,[91] and Menanteau speaks of 'disorders of the Commune', without being more explicit.[92] Thus the memory of Jacobin clubs is triggered more than the clubs of 1848 or 1871.

Under the Empire the memory of the revolutionary period is also seized on by legislators as a way to justify the restrictions placed on freedom of assembly. There is ample reference to this in March 1868 by those in favour of keeping political assemblies under the regimen of prior authorisation. The clubs are presented as the inevitable consequence of the freedom of assembly to discuss politics. On 13 March, Jean-Baptiste Josseau, a member of the commission that had drafted the bill, made an amalgam of the political assembly and the club. This was taken up by all those defending the exclusion of politics from the subjects authorised for discussion in assemblies: 'do not bring back this revolutionary instrument! Letting political assemblies go free and unchecked means restoring the right to clubs'.[93] On the same day, the Minister of State, Rouher argues that the outcome of assemblies discussing political issues is the clubs, declaring: 'the absolute right of assembly, this is the restoration of clubs'.[94] During the same session the law's *rapporteur,* Louis Eugène Peyrusse, wanted to forestall the criticism of those that might have denied any link between political public assemblies and clubs on the grounds that the clubs were related to the associations phenomenon rather than that of assemblies:

> Public assemblies dealing with political or social matters [....] are nothing more than clubs. Ah! I know what you will say; clubs, this is affiliation, this is association. [...] But we need to get to the bottom of things and the truth of the facts. Do you know how the clubs were formed? After 1789, the clubs followed the public assemblies. Some representatives met up together earlier. They called on the public. This is the origin of clubs. Clubs sprung up from public assemblies. Assemblies are the origin of clubs.[95]

---

90. Eugene W. Schulkind, 'The Activity of Popular Organizations During the Paris Commune of 1871', *French Historical Studies*, 1960, vol. 1, (4), pp. 400–401.
91. Jouet, *Des clubs*, p. 307.
92. Menanteau, *Les nouveaux aspects de la liberté de réunion*, p. 14.
93. *Le Moniteur Universel*, 14 March 1868, p. 382.
94. *Le Moniteur Universel*, 14 March 1868, p. 385.
95. *Le Moniteur Universel*, 14 March 1868, p. 388.

Jacobin clubs were blamed in particular, which explains why they were the most developed reference in the arguments of the speakers close to the government. These clubs had competed with the public powers and tried to 'impose their own will on deliberative official assemblies', constituting in Josseau's words 'a State within the State'.[96] The clubs of 1848 are reported as having been dangerous factors of disorder, and their evocation joins that of the 'red spectre', of the revolutionary passion generated by political assemblies. Under the Empire, the memory of clubs, particularly Jacobin clubs, was a scarecrow used to justify the refusal to extend freedom of assembly to political assemblies. This is all done in the name of rejecting intermediary bodies competing with the legitimate authority of the organs of the state.

The first point in the reply of opposition deputies is based on the need to distinguish between assembly and association. On 13 March Jules Simon denounced the confusion made by government speakers in order to reject the demand for freedom of political assembly:

> In this law which only involves the right of assembly, as soon as you argue, as soon as you try to justify your refusal, your restrictions, you are not talking about the right of assembly, you are talking about the right of association, which is something else.[97]

Given the frequently repeated declaration that the legislative debate only concerned assemblies, the opposition made little reference to the role of associations. Yet Jules Simon specified favour for the freedom to set them up, and that associations only became dangerous when transformed into 'rivals of the regular powers of the State'.[98] Moreover: 'in his famous "Belleville programme" (15 May 1869) Gambetta demanded "the abrogation of Article 291 of the Penal Code" and "the full and complete freedom of association"', and 'at the same time, Ferry, candidate in the electoral district of the *rive gauche*, was no less categorical'.[99]

Assembly and association: separation and overlapping

According to Jean Rivero and Hugues Moutouh:

> Of all collective freedoms, freedom of assembly is [...] the least incompatible with the individualism of 1789. Thus, it is not surprising [...] that it was the first freedom to receive legal status under the law of 30 June 1881.[100]

---

96. *Le Moniteur Universel*, 14 March 1868, p. 382.
97. *Le Moniteur Universel*, 14 March 1868, p. 384.
98. *Le Moniteur Universel*, 14 March 1868, p. 384.
99. Jean-Pierre Machelon, 'La liberté d'association sous la IIIe République. Le temps du refus (1871–1901)', in Claire Andrieu, Gilles Le Béguec and Danielle Tartakowsky (eds), *Associations et champ politique*, p. 144.
100. Jean Rivero and Hugues Moutouh, *Libertés publiques*, Paris, PUF, 2003, vol. 2, pp. 241, 253–254.

Conversely, in the case of associations, they note that the 'individualist tradition of 1789' joins 'the fear that the actions of political groups inspired the authorities, aggravated by the memory of the excesses of the clubs during the Revolution', and leads to the maintenance of Article 291 of the Penal Code. We have seen that the freedom of assembly granted in 1881 was related to the need to ensure the stability of representative government by the formation of public opinion, and should not take the form of action. 'True to the tradition of an individualist democracy [the promoters of the 1881 law] conceived assemblies as an instrument of thought, an opportunity offered to a limited number of individuals to exchange ideas', writes Georges Burdeau.[101] For this reason it was necessary to agree on a right to assembly that distinguished the association:

> Long confused with associations, because at the close of the eighteenth century the revolutionary clubs had spontaneously assumed a hybrid form, public assemblies have since acquired a precise definition. The result is the granting of a protective legal regimen.[102]

The removal of restrictions on the right of assembly at the beginning of the Third Republic took place precisely by dissociating the two types of gathering. The terms of Article 7 of the 1881 law ('clubs remain banned') should not be interpreted as an indication of persisting confusion in the spirit of the republican legislator between assembly and association, as suggested recently by legal theorists describing the evolution of the French regimen of public freedoms.[103] The debates prior to the adoption of the law show that the government and the commission promoting the draft law were, on the contrary, attached to the distinction of these modes of grouping. In his counter-plan Louis Blanc demands full freedom of association and of assembly, to which the commission and government replied that the two had to be considered separately.

On 24 January 1880 Blanc recognises the dissimilarities between the two types of meeting declaring:

> I admit that there are differences between association and assembly. I recognise that the second lacks the permanent character typical of the first; I recognise that members of an association are bound by a principle of solidarity, excluding the accidental and transitory character of a simple assembly.

Nevertheless, he believes that the one could not be considered without the other, and thus that we cannot legislate on the one without legislating on the other: firstly, because what provides distinction between the assembly and the association is less important than what they have in common. Freedom of assembly and association

---

101. Georges Burdeau, *Les libertés publiques*, Paris, LGDJ, 1972, p. 217.
102. Jean Morange, *Droits de l'homme and libertés publiques*, Paris, PUF, 2000, p. 247.
103. See, in particular: Arlette Heymann-Doat and Gwénaele Calvès, *Libertés publiques et droits de l'homme*, Paris, LGDJ, 2005, p. 49.

meet the same need in man: the search in the collectivity for what he cannot find in isolation, and to resist the oppression with the force which comes from placing feelings in common, from bringing thoughts closer, from the harmony of efforts.

The second reason is that the right of assembly, just as the right of association, only expresses true utility with the existence of the other.

Without freedom to associate, citizens would loose the more lucid intellectual and moral benefits that the right to assembly brings, and, on the other hand, how difficult would it be [for citizens] to associate if the freedom of assembly would have been refused?

As a token of the relation between these two rights the speaker invokes the fact that previous governments dealt with them in the same way.[104]

However through its *rapporteur*, Naquet, who spoke the same day, the commission defended what it considered to be a constructive separation. A true right of association cannot be granted, they argue, without there being a parallel right of assembly, but a true freedom of assembly can exist even without freedom of association:

I consider [...] that the right of assembly is inevitably implied in the right of association as the less is contained in the more; but just as the more is not implied in the less, I consider that the right of association is not necessarily implied in the right of assembly.

The second argument stresses that confusing the two rights does not benefit freedom of assembly. The latter is often sacrificed in warnings against the risks of association.[105] Dominique Reynié insists on the artificial nature of the split between association and assembly that the republican legislator tries to create or consolidate. He speaks of a 'duality so obviously against nature', going as far as to say that 'there are two words for the same social reality'. According to him, their dissociation can only be explained by the strategy of defining what constitutes legitimate public space: 'the fear of losing control of public freedoms is the only reason to maintain this fragmentation.'[106] But we have already seen that, assembly and association are, on the contrary, two very different forms of meeting.

The separation of association and assembly is largely established through the law.[107] Legal experts supported the separation of the two, hitherto confused, forms of participation. We are dealing, they say, with a 'distinction [...] of the greatest importance'.[108] They claim that the club which was to be outlawed absolutely, is a

---

104. *Journal Officiel*, 25 January 1880, p. 756.
105. *Journal Officiel*, 25 January 1880, p. 759.
106. Dominique Reynié, *Le triomphe de l'opinion publique. L'espace public français du XVIe au XXe siècle*, Paris, Odile Jacob, 1998, pp. 53, 155–156.
107. Reynié, *Le triomphe de l'opinion publique*, p. 158.
108. René Petit, *Du droit de réunion*, Paris, A. Cotillon, 1883, p. 72.

hybrid mix of association and assembly; that is, an association whose basic activity is to organise assemblies. Many of the experts note that the link between the two forms of gathering is the expression of man's natural inclination to group together with fellow men. They all consider that the natural consequence of association is nearly always the assembly. They also stress unanimously, with Naquet, that the opposite is not true; that is, that assembly can dispense with the association. They argue that two features of association allow us to distinguish it from the simple assembly: affiliation, but also and above all permanence, or at least regularity. Fortunately, they also note, these criteria are recognised by the legislator, who no longer makes the mistake of confusing the two forms of gathering. In 1894, Roger Arnette expressed his satisfaction: 'The debates before the vote on the current law [...] have shown that no member of parliament, not even enemies of the draft law, refused to recognise the basic distinction between assembly and association'.[109]

In the legislative debates, arguments based on the dangers of association are used to justify the fact that the Chamber dealt primarily with the right of assembly. Naquet insists that it is necessary to come to a rapid agreement on freedom of association stating on 26 January 1880: 'I do not want to appear to combat a right that I accept'.[110] However the speaker also indicates that there are concerns in both the government and the Chamber regarding the right of association, and that the commission cannot ignore this. In Naquet's opinion, if the commission chooses to present a plan regarding the two rights, it would be difficult for it to be adopted. This will in turn delay the much-awaited liberalisation of the right of assembly. The latter, notes Naquet on 24 January, 'from the political viewpoint [...] surpasses the right of association'.[111] A series of reservations *vis-à-vis* association emerge when the relevance of Article 7 of the draft law is debated. The Article is initially conceived in a form on which the commission agrees with government — which is the initiator: 'All public regular assemblies whose aim is to deal with political issues are prohibited. Yet this ban does not apply to lectures.' This version is criticised by several speakers, and the Article was finally adopted on 29 January in a different form: 'clubs remain banned'. The initiative for this new formulation is taken by the Minister of the Interior, Charles Lepère. In the meanwhile the commission rallies the opinion of those who judged the article to be useless because it was related to the right of association. The way in which this article is maintained demonstrates the persisting fear of an association which regularly organises assemblies and adopts resolutions — irrespective of whether or not it is known by the term 'club'. The risk anticipated is that it may compete with the legitimate institutions. Alexandre Ribot, of a republican, albeit conservative opinion, was alone in making a direct and extenuated appeal on 26 January, to the memory of clubs, pointing out the danger they had represented in the past to the

---

109. Arnette, *La liberté de réunion en France*, p. 22.
110. *Journal Officiel*, 27 January 1880, p. 869.
111. *Journal Officiel*, 25 January 1880, p. 760.

state assemblies that were subjected to their will.[112] Naquet's position was rather that even without personal faith that 'democracy, freedom and the Republic [would be] lost if the clubs were re-established', others did have that belief: 'timid people who approach the Republic with sincerity and honesty, but who are not convinced, as we are, of the harmless nature of the greatest freedom'. On 27 January he declared that allowing clubs could 'harm the solidity of our republican institutions'.[113] The objection made by the government was different. On 29 January, Lepère declared that 'deliberative associations', those regular assemblies headed by 'a committee of associated members' which 'take deliberative forms', may have constituted 'a special danger'.[114] It is pointed out, with regards to the debate, that assemblies adopt resolutions which imitate the form of resolutions that only the organs of the state can take, and that they tend to impose on the latter.

If the reason given during debates for treating the two rights independently indicates a certain caution in the republican camp as regards freedom of association, this comes from the resolve to combat religious congregations, as is well-known.[115] The rejection of a freedom that can allow congregations to develop occurs several times as a way to justify the distinct nature of allowing freedom of assembly or freedom of association. Without tracing here the positions taken on this issue, we notice that congregations are mentioned in particular by Madier de Monjau, who opposes Louis Blanc in stressing that the suppression of Article 291 of the Penal Code would leave the Republic defenceless to deal with them. Madier de Monjau also stood at the extreme left of the republican group, but his anti-clericalism surpassed the defence of political freedom. For Blanc, the question of congregations could be separated from that of associations: 'The dimensions deemed of concern to association in general' are focussed on the question of congregations.[116] The battle against congregations should thus be understood as a struggle against religious institutions and as an element in the process of separating Church from State. Yet it is also a critique tending to 'absorb and [...] weaken [...] intermediary bodies', where by intermediary bodies we mean long-term gatherings of individuals with particular shared interests and liable to intervene between citizenry and State. In the words of Pierre Rosanvallon: 'by anathematising congregations, the republicans [...] overlap the resolution of a historical question on the conduct of a political combat identified with anti-clericalism'.[117]

---

112. *Journal Officiel*, 27 January 1880, p. 875.

113. *Journal Officiel*, 28 January 1880, p. 935.

114. *Journal Officiel*, 30 January 1880, p. 1,020.

115. Jacqueline Lalouette and Jean-Pierre Machelon (eds), *Les congrégations hors la loi? Autour de la loi du 1er juillet 1901*, Paris, Letouzey & Ané, 2002; Jacqueline Lalouette, *La séparation des Églises et de l'État. Genèse and développement d'une idée, 1789–1905*, Paris, Seuil, 2005; Christian Sorrel, *La République contre les congrégations. Histoire d'une passion française (1899–1904)*, Paris, Cerf, 2003.

116. For this quotation and the one that follows, see Rosanvallon, *Le modèle politique français*, pp. 321–322.

117. Rosanvallon, *Le modèle politique français*, p. 323.

We have stressed the existence of a relative acceptance of associations under the Third Republic. This is the case, in particular, from the time when the opportunists came to power in the wake of Mac-Mahon's resignation, that made Maurice Agulhon write: 'the date of 1880 is certainly more important than [that of] 1901'.[118] Associations did not wait for the 1901 law before coming into being. Republican tolerance allowed them to develop despite punitive legislation as 'the 1880s were characterised by a genuine expansion of associative life, particularly at the local level'.[119] The fact that among the many draft laws submitted before 1901 two were made in the name of government, is another sign of a move towards accepting associations.[120] 'In 1901, the parliamentarian who wanted to study the right of association [...] was faced with [...] thirty-three draft laws since 1871', wrote Edouard Clunet in 1909.[121] But should we really consider that 'with the onset of the Third Republic, the ban on association is no longer in the air?'[122] Tolerance can also be seen as the source of an arbitrary regimen, where government does not generally apply Article 291 of the Penal Code, except when it feels threatened by its political enemies. The term used by Paul Nourrisson to describe this period in his *Histoire de la liberté d'association* was 'arbitrary'.[123] Georges Burdeau writes that 'in 1899 all the leagues (*ligue des patriotes, ligue des droits de l'homme, ligue antisémite*, etc.) went to court for violating Article 291', indicating that the republican government was 'free to use the arms in its possession or not, allowed the establishment of an arbitrary government'.[124]

The 1901 law does not testify fully to a republican recognition of the value of intermediary groupings; it is not the sign that 'individualism has had its day'.[125] Jacques Ion emphasises the 'existence of a significant problem basically connected with a hostility to the revival of anything which looks like intermediary bodies' in the debates prior to the 1884 law on trade unions and the 1901 law.[126] Similarly Pierre Rosanvallon analyses the underlying reasons of the process which led the

---

118. Maurice Agulhon, 'Associations and histoire sociale', *Revue de l'économie sociale*, 1988, vol. 14, p. 39.
119. Gilles Le Béguec, 'Le moment 1901', in Andrieu, Gilles Le Béguec and Tartakowsky (eds), *Associations et champ politique*, p. 68.
120. Paul Nourrisson, *Histoire de la liberté d'association en France depuis 1789*, Paris, Sirey, 1920, vol. 2, p. 159.
121. Edouard Clunet, *Les associations au point de vue historique and juridique*, Paris, Marchal et Billard, 1909, p. 291.
122. Elie Alfandari, 'La liberté d'association', in Rémy Cabrillac, Marie-Anne Frison-Roche and Thierry Revet (eds), *Libertés and droits fondamentaux*, Paris, Dalloz, 2005, p. 403.
123. Paul Nourrisson, *Histoire de la liberté d'association en France*, vol. 2, p. 261.
124. Burdeau, *Les libertés publiques*, p. 191.
125. Nourrisson, *Histoire de la liberté d'association en France*, vol. 1, p. 30.
126. Jacques Ion, *La fin des militants?*, Paris, Éditions de l'Atelier, 1997, pp. 23–24. See also: Martine Barthélemy, *Associations. Un nouvel âge de la participation?*, Paris, Presses de Sciences Po, 2000, pp. 48–57.

republicans to disassociate the association from the congregation. On one hand, there is a symbolic and 'demonised vision' of the congregation as 'the association of bodies in its most radical and most unacceptable dimension, that of a total and irreversible absorption of individuals in a sole entity'. On the other, we find an 'enchanted portrayal' of association as a 'contract where individuals remain absolutely sovereign'.[127] If the 1901 law breaks with over a century's rejection of association, this is not recognised as a 'social institution playing a role in the formation of the public good'.[128]

In facilitating the progressive birth of large political parties, the 1901 law gave rise to renewed debate among legal experts, a debate which seemed obsolete, on the dangers of confusing assembly and association. In 1937 Menanteau wrote that 'the moment of equilibrium reached in 1881 had to be brief', and observed that again 'instantaneous and permanent forms of human grouping benefit from the same liberal statute'; 'the two sorts of phenomena thus tend to interpenetrate, and merge'. This concern is based on the formation of parties as organisers of public assemblies. The new type of association could threaten representation insofar as it diverts the assembly from its role as a *locus* of expression and exchange of ideas and transforms it into a means of exerting political pressure. In 1937 Michel Baffrey declared:

> Parties [...] replace the clubs of the Revolution; they sponsor their own candidates and push [people] to vote for them. They discuss the line of conduct to be followed by government; so that France is directed in accordance with the aims pursued by this party, regardless of the real interests of the country. Groups, parties, trade unions influence the State's directive core itself. They amount to a new flourishing of clubs in a slightly different guise, yet the results are identical and just as harmful.[129]

The terms of the 1881 law were adapted to a form of gathering whose aim was the exchange of ideas among a relatively limited number of people, rather than to large meetings of people belonging to the same party.

---

127. Rosanvallon, *Le modèle politique français*, pp. 326–327.
128. Rosanvallon, *Le modèle politique français*, p. 337.
129. Baffrey, *Le droit de réunion en Angleterre et en France*, pp. 115–116.

Chapter Three

The Assembly at the Heart of the Electoral Process

> Electoral assembly: a gathering of people who come to hear one or more candidates during an electoral campaign, also called an electoral meeting. [It is] used less to convince than to keep up the morale of the candidate and his constituents, socialised in this way.[1]

A little more than a century after the adoption of the law of 30 June 1881, Paul Bacot's definition of an electoral assembly in his *Dictionnaire du vote* would have surprised those who had defended its worth for the Republic at the end of the nineteenth century. Their perception of the electoral assembly was very different. They placed it at the core of building up participation on which government could base its legitimacy, and believed in its efficacy as a tool for suffrage, no longer on the basis of personal bonds between voters and candidates, but on mutual agreement of their ideas. Electoral assemblies were not destined to maintain the enthusiasm of activists already sure of their choice. They should have a direct impact on the opinion of voters who attend and their role is to keep them informed. If the vote is not the outcome of an enlightened choice, then elections are a mere disguise for an authoritarian regime: the Second Empire is a case in point. The republicans thus assert that the assembly allows them to guide and help prepare the process of voting, improving the quality of representation.

Assemblies are most numerous and most frequent during electoral campaigns. This is obvious under the Empire since the 1868 law favoured them. It kept public political assemblies under the regimen of prior authorisation, but at the same time it partially liberalised assemblies held in preparation for legislative elections, which only required a prior declaration, albeit accompanied by a series of restrictive rulings. From then on electoral campaigns are marked by the organisation of a large number of assemblies. According to Étienne Masseras, an observer of the electoral struggle that began on 4 May 1869 for the renewal of the Legislative Body, 'during the 15 or 20 days which the law prescribed for public electoral assemblies, more than 200 were held in Paris, and probably 2,000–3,000 in all of France.'[2] There are not only a lot of assemblies, but they also attract an enormous

---

1. Paul Bacot, *Dictionnaire du vote. Élections et délibérations*, Lyon, Presses Universitaires de Lyon, 1994, p. 157.
2. Étienne Masseras, *La campagne électorale de 1869*, Paris, A. Lacroix, Verboeckhover et Cie, 1969, p. 12.

Figure 3.1: 'An electoral assembly in the Triat Gymnasium in Paris', L'Illustration, 15 May 1869

number of people. An engraving in *L'Illustration* of 15 May 1869 depicts an electoral assembly in the Triat gymnasium in Paris, where the audience is so large that many of them are literally clinging to the ropes hanging from the ceiling (see Figure 3.1). The accompanying article reports that 'private and public assemblies have been organised by all sides. We find them literally everywhere, and no-one wants to be left out of the movement'.[3] According to a police report, at the end of an assembly in Paris in February 1876, they could hear 'the *bureau* assistants saying on leaving that public assemblies should be organised every day to ensure that voters' zeal did not cool down before polling day'.[4] The sheer number of electoral assemblies is no less striking at the onset of the Third Republic and the audiences are equally massive, regularly running to thousands in Paris.

What binds the Republic so closely to assemblies is the latter's ability to put an end to the blind nature of the vote. Assemblies allow enlightened voters to

---

3. *L'Illustration*, 15 May 1869.
4. APP/Ba/574/Réunions privées et publiques, 15e arr.: Rapport police municipale, service des garnis, cabinet, 1er *bureau*, réunion salle de bal, 35 rue Frémicourt, 3 février 1876. As regards assemblies, the 1876 election campaign does not allow us to see that the state of siege is still in force. This was lifted by the new majority on its arrival in Parliament.

establish contact with candidates, to compare and evaluate their programmes, and to act together to assess the merits of each. The Republic portrays the consecration of universal suffrage as the 'holy ark, definitive and key principle of legitimation'.[5] Yet republicans are still suspicious of this universal, and easily manipulable, suffrage. It needs to be republicanised in order to create rational citizens capable of making a choice unconditioned by social ties. This republicanisation rests on the belief that 'the expression of the vote [does not acquire] an incontestable legitimacy unless [exercised] in conditions of recognised freedom'.[6] In other words, voters must have the means to enlighten themselves autonomously, and there must be free competition among aspiring deputies.

During the debate in the Chamber of January 1879, Naquet suggests that the electoral assembly should 'replace the personal solicitations and door-to-door canvassing for votes, advantageously and honourably'.[7] Indeed, did it not lead to the 'destructuring and marginalisation of a form of domination' typical of the early Republic, that of the notables?[8] The notables could withdraw towards alternative forms of assembly in order to campaign. Yet the public electoral assembly still had advantages for 'the political entrepreneur in search of voters'.[9] Its use could be linked with the emergence of a new body of republican political personnel which stressed public opinion as a legitimating principle and based electoral campaigns on an organisation: that of committees.[10]

The electoral assembly also helped government predict the disturbance that elections were likely to cause. In an era when men feared unpleasant surprises from the polls whilst touting the merits of universal suffrage, the observation of assemblies before polling day helped to predict electoral outcomes. Government still distrusted the People who they suspected of being unreliable, and sought a way to gauge the spirit of voters, a concern certainly not confined to the Third Republic.

> Since the mid-eighteenth century there have been many historical examples attesting, on the part of political authorities, irrespective of the nature of the government or the 'political formulae' on which they base their authority, a desire of knowledge or even of measure of public opinion.[11]

---

5. Pierre Rosanvallon, *Le sacre du citoyen. Histoire intellectuelle du suffrage universel en France*, Paris, Gallimard, 1992, p. 450.
6. Raymond Huard, *Le suffrage universel en France (1848–1946)*, Paris, Aubier, 1991, p. 129.
7. *Annales de la Chambre des députés*, 1879, vol. 1, appendix no. 1092, p. 190.
8. Alain Guillemin, 'Aristocrates, propriétaires et diplômés. La lutte pour le pouvoir local dans le département de la Manche 1830–1875', *Actes de la Recherche en Sciences Sociales*, 1982, vol. 42, p. 59.
9. Dominique Reynié, *Le triomphe de l'opinion publique. L'espace public français du XVIe au XXe siècle*, Paris, Odile Jacob, 1998, pp. 152–153.
10. Alain Garrigou, *Histoire sociale du suffrage universel en France, 1848–2000*, Paris, Seuil, 2002, p. 300.
11. Loïc Blondiaux, *La fabrique de l'opinion. Une histoire sociale des sondages*, Paris, Seuil, 1998, pp. 51–52.

This desire for knowledge about public opinion becomes particularly intense when universal suffrage is combined with freedom of electoral campaigns and free elections.

The guarantee of a just vote

> Because its legitimacy is based on the expression of political opinion, the Republic must be careful [...] to establish the moral conditions that guarantee the justice and impartiality of that opinion.

Yves Déloye illustrates how the Third Republic strives to achieve this objective 'to educate the individual in critical reason thus making him able to conduct his own destiny', in particular by educating him.[12] A reform of the electoral campaign was deemed necessary to ensure the reasoned character of citizens' choices. Before casting their vote electors must be able to inform themselves, to learn through mutual discussion and by meeting candidates. Candidates must adjust to the rules of free competition based on their electoral programmes. Things also had to change on the electoral scene.

Enlightening universal suffrage

There is a clear link between the Republic, the dignity of universal suffrage and electoral assemblies in the republican discourse from the early years of the Third Republic. It is largely reflected in the comments made during public assemblies held in February 1876 in Paris by the republican committees for the legislative elections. Members of the *bureau* and candidates insist on the idea that they are essential if electors are to make an enlightened choice, the only one worthy of the Republic. This was because both the merits of candidates and the criticisms made against them could be debated, and also because this was where citizens chose the best candidate to stand against the Republic's opponents. The assessor of an electoral assembly stated that:

> We come to assemblies with highly commendable, respectable, intentions, those of enlightening our faith as electors, and to judge candidates' abilities, to choose the most worthy, the one who may best endeavour to safeguard our interests and allow our convictions to triumph.[13]

Participants are reminded of the importance of their duty in attending this type of assembly. The organiser of an electoral assembly in Montreuil declares: 'In these grave circumstances, we have a serious duty to fulfil, and I congratulate

---

12. Yves Deloye, 'Idée républicaine et citoyenneté. L'expérience française (1870–1945)', in Jean-Michel Lecomte and Jean-Pierre Sylvestre (eds), *Culture républicaine, citoyenneté et lien social*, Dijon, CRDP de Bourgogne, 1997, p. 69.
13. APP/Ba/574/Réunions privées et publiques, 13e arr., salle de bal du Casino d'Italie, av. de Choisy, 198: '13e arrondissement. Réunion du Casino d'Italie', *L'Évènement*, 16 février 1876.

you on coming to consult with us on the line of conduct that we must follow for success'.[14] An election under conditions of universal suffrage must be considered seriously by the true republican, and its preparation in assemblies must be careful and commendable: 'Citizens, universal suffrage is a great thing', says Deschanel[15] at an assembly with three candidates facing each other in Colombes, before concluding that 'electoral assemblies need not be cliques'.[16] Participants are likened to a sovereign People, and assemblies become the incarnation of republican democracy.

Allowing men to enlighten others and organise electoral campaigns through meetings is an essential justification for the liberalisation of the right of assembly. On 31 May 1878, Naquet's legal recital for a proposed law affirmed that this right was 'not disputable [...] in a society based on universal suffrage', and declared: 'obliging [citizens] to decide blindly, at random', is 'the most atrocious political misinterpretation that politicians could commit'.[17] Arguments linking the vote to freedom of electoral assembly were extremely frequent during legislative debates. The electoral assembly was the preferred form of political assembly for republicans. The law provides that only 'voters of the electoral district, candidates, members of the two chambers and the agent of each candidate' can attend, and that they can only be held during electoral periods. However, it reduces the obligatory interval between the declaration and the assembly holding to two hours, rather than twenty-four for other public assemblies, and allows them to follow the declaration immediately in the case of a second ballot. Legal experts also agree on the interest of assemblies to enlighten voters. From the first page of his *Code des réunions publiques* of 1881, Charles Constant describes freedom of assembly as 'necessary in a democracy that has universal suffrage as the basis of its constitution'.[18]

Eugène Delattre a lawyer and supporter of Gambetta at the end of the Empire, published his *Devoirs du suffrage universel* in 1863, demonstrating how the latter only makes sense alongside freedom of assembly. Delattre, wrote that 'citizens who do not meet or consult together, cannot be properly informed about the best choice to make, are not fit to be voters, and are culpable with respect to those who do their duty honourably', since 'whoever says elect says choose, who says choose says know, study, compare and judge'.[19] The republican discourse claims that

---

14. APP/Ba/577/Charenton, Rue de Montreuil: Rapport 'Céran', Charenton, 5 février 1876.
15. This is probably Émile Deschanel, elected republican deputy in 1876. See Adolphe Robert and Gaston Cougny, *Dictionnaire des parlementaires français de 1789 à 1889*, vol. 2 Paris, Bourloton, 1889–1891, p. 350.
16. APP/Ba/577/Colombes, salle de bal, rue St-Denis: Rapport 'Jouve', Paris, 12 février 1876.
17. *Journal Officiel*, 11 June 1878, p. 6,543.
18. Charles Constant, *Code des réunions publiques, des réunions électorales et des réunions privées. Commentaire pratique de la loi du 30 June 1881 à l'usage des préfets, sous-préfets, Maires, juges de paix, ainsi que des organisateurs de réunions publiques ou privées*, Paris, A. Durand et Pedone-Lauriel, 1881, p. 5.
19. Eugène Delattre, *Devoirs du suffrage universel*, Paris, Pagnerre, 1863, pp. 92, 96.

universal suffrage made the development of freedom of assembly indispensable under the Empire, as a counterweight to manipulated voting. Articles in *Le Temps* in 1863 already mentioned embryonic assemblies where liberal candidates were presented. From then on the newspaper defended electoral assemblies as a vital complement to the right to vote, attacked measures preventing them, and denounced their dissolution. *Le Temps* criticised the denial of a vital need of the voter wishing to do his duty by making an enlightened choice. Henri Brisson commented on the trial of 'the thirteen' which directly concerned freedom of political assembly. This was the case concerning thirteen men who were prosecuted for the crime of illegal association which, according to the law, could only be committed by an association of at least twenty-one people. The journalist recalls that: 'universal suffrage implies [...] free choice, reasoned elections, an enlightened vote, all things that in turn imply deliberation, discussion, meeting':

> As universal suffrage is sovereign and determines the fate of the nation, we cannot allow this formidable faculty be exercised blindly. Hence this spontaneity of citizens to gather together, to assemble and to associate to prepare for the various elections.[20]

Free discussion in assemblies is thus indispensable for an elector to exercise his duty. On the basis of these justifications, *Le Temps* struggles against the obstacles to exercising freedom of electoral assembly. Journalists first focus on defending private assemblies. On 17 March 1864, the lawyer Charles Floquet, who later became a deputy, remembered in this perspective the inviolability of domicile, in protesting against the new move to weaken the right of assembly with the dissolution of privately-held assemblies by voters individually convened by the master of the house to discuss the coming election. The newspaper also denounces the increase, as of 1869, in the number of assemblies disbanded by the police commissioner present on the pretext that speakers may address a question outside the object of the assembly. Examples of such dissolutions abound in the pages of *Le Temps*, which presents them as illegal. Albert Gigot recalled that if the law permitted police to disband an electoral assembly when it became rowdy: 'it is more difficult to understand how [its] disbanding [...] can be declared on the grounds that the *bureau*, once warned, would allow the discussion of questions alien to the object of the assembly'. Indeed, 'the object of electoral debate is to discuss candidatures; from this perspective all questions can be debated'.[21] In fact the commissioner dissolved assemblies when discussion was detrimental to the government.

The republican discourse linking the truth of suffrage and citizens' meetings was thus partly constructed in response to restrictions on the freedom of assembly. During the last years of the Empire electoral assemblies began to take on a new form nonetheless, a form which was maintained under the Republic. As of 1863

---

20. *Le Temps*, 27 July 1864.
21. *Le Temps*, 10 May 1869.

the opposition manages to organise some private electoral assemblies. The 1868 law really brings them to life, so that even those declared public are free from prior authorisation. Their exercise remains limited insofar as they only concern the elections of deputies, must end by the fifth day before the election, and apply all of the aforementioned restrictions on freedom of a public non-political assembly. The 1869 elections, however, revealed a radical change in the form of electoral campaigns that brought about the adoption of the 1868 law: '[they] were quite unlike anything since 1848, especially in Paris, with crowds on the streets and in public meetings and newspapers attacking the government in often violent terms'.[22] Several researchers emphasise the existence of elements of continuity between the campaigns of the liberal Empire and those of the Republic.[23] Was the latter simply a slightly more liberal version of its predecessor?

There are two dominant perceptions of the role of these assemblies under the Empire and the Republic, of the form that they should take, and the place that they should occupy. Under the Empire, a move towards freedom of electoral assembly mainly meant conceding to increasingly urgent claims on the part of the political opposition. 'We went *up to* the right of assembly in legislative elections', declared the councillor of state and government commissioner, Chassaigne-Goyon, to the Legislative Body on 17 March 1868.[24] If the Empire granted a freedom in matters of electoral assembly, albeit limited, it was because it was not considered to be as dangerous as the more general freedom of political assembly. Electoral assemblies were only held on specific and fixed occasions, and were never close together. In this way political issues were not continually being discussed by citizens. When retracing the debates before the adoption of the 1868 law the legal expert, and follower of imperial politics, Georges Dubois, remarked that the majority of the senate commission had emphasised that:

> No assimilation is possible between political assemblies which are in some way permanent, that can be held at any time, maintaining as many trouble spots, continuously developing elements of dissolution, and meetings which can only take place at fixed and rare periods [...] and for a special purpose.[25]

During the discussion on the draft law, the refusal to let the political debate develop emerged during deliberation on the extension of freedom of electoral assembly to elections other than the legislative ones. An amendment proposing its extension to elections for the general council and the *conseil d'arrondissement* met with opposition from the defenders of the draft law. Peyrusse, the law's *rapporteur*, wanted to avoid increasing the opportunities for assemblies to deviate

---

22. Roger Price, *The French Second Empire. An Anatomy of Political Power*, Cambridge, Cambridge University Press, 2001, p. 269.
23. *See* for instance: Huard, *Le suffrage universel en France*, p. 86.
24. *Le Moniteur Universel*, 18 March 1868, p. 407.
25. Georges Dubois, *Commentaire théorique et pratique de la loi du 6 juin 1868 sur les réunions publiques*, Paris, Imprimerie et Librairie Générale de Jurisprudence, 1869, pp. 161–162.

on political questions, and explicitly stated in 1867: 'Why trouble the public peace, maintain a permanent state of agitation, create unwelcome divisions, by means of repeated assemblies that would persist almost uninterruptedly [...]?'[26] In addition, the government refused to accept changes in the type of councillors it elected. Chassaigne-Goyon's comments on 17 March 1868 illustrate this well:

> We want [...] general councils to be composed, as they are today, of the most important and most respected men in the country. [...] There is no evidence [that the administration] would find more enlightened councillors in the candidates who would be produced by public assemblies. In our opinion, the people who speak most are not always the wisest, in the same way that boasters are not always the bravest men.[27]

Moreover, pro-government speakers insist on the key innovation already represented by the newly granted right of electoral assembly. One of the ways that the opposition reacts is to say that freedom of electoral assembly has already been recognised under earlier governments, even the least liberal of them.[28] However the law's promoters argue that there is a difference between electoral assemblies in times of limited suffrage and those held under universal suffrage. On 14 March 1868 Peyrusse declared:

> We have said that under the regimen of limited suffrage voters had the right to assemble during the electoral period. But don't we all know what these assemblies in electoral colleges with an average of 200 or 300 voters were? And today we all know that the electoral districts include an average of 35,000 voters. It is sufficient to note this difference?[29]

The 1868 law and the debate preceding it do not signify an imperial recognition of the need to enlighten all suffrage, nor the idea that a vote only makes sense if preceded by free debate among informed voters, or that even candidatures must be the target of deliberation among them. On the contrary, these ideas mark the republican philosophy and practice of freedom of electoral assembly under the Third Republic.

The principal locus of competition between electoral candidates

As an observer in the 1869 electoral campaign, Étienne Masseras notes two important changes: freedom of the press and freedom of assembly, which together constitute 'a novelty in our political history'.[30] Starting from these first elections

---

26. *Le Moniteur Universel*, 30 June 1867, cited in Dubois, *Commentaire théorique et pratique*, p. 163.
27. *Le Moniteur Universel*, 18 March 1868, p. 407.
28. Louis-Antoine Garnier-Pagès, member of the democratic opposition, uses the word in this sense on 12 March: *Le Moniteur Universel*, 13 March 1868, p. 376.
29. *Le Moniteur Universel*, 15 March 1868, p. 388.
30. Masseras, *La campagne électorale de 1869*, p. 10.

under universal suffrage and albeit limited freedom of electoral assemblies, the campaigns take on a new form, characterised by intensified competition between candidates. This means an increased organisation of generally deliberative assemblies where candidates defend their programmes before voters.

> With the arrival of the masses in the electoral game, [the configuration of enlarged political markets] implies new relations between the elected and electors. In cities it is characterised by a more vigorous competition and a professionalisation of canvassing practices. [...] This is the birth of mass competition, both more autonomous and more professional.[31]

Electoral assemblies are a central element in the process. 'It is of the highest importance', declared an eyewitness of the 1869 electoral campaign in le Doubs, doctor in law and lawyer opposed to the official candidate, 'that voters can reason among themselves on the choice of the deputy who appears to merit such an elevated mission of faith'. He added: 'It is no less vital to achieve this that voters be in direct contact with candidates wishing to become representatives'.[32] Candidates had to be present at electoral assemblies. Thus it was not simply a question of allowing voters to exchange ideas about their merits. The rare preparatory assemblies for elections where no candidate was present met with little success. The liberal daily *La Liberté* reported: 'Low turnout yesterday at the Folies-Belleville; though we are at the end of elections. We must attribute this lukewarm response on the part of voters to the absence of candidates [...]'.[33] When there was no candidate, participants often demonstrated their discontent in voting a motion. In 1893, in Marseilles, the public at a public electoral assembly decided to disperse due to the absence of any candidates. However before doing so it adopted a resolution on the proposal of the chairman, 'reprimanding candidates'. The session closed to the cry of: '*Vive la République. À bas les candidats*'.[34] Participants in assemblies were also disappointed when only one candidate took part, much preferring a contradictory assembly. For example, at a public assembly organised in Ivry in 1885 by the *Parti ouvrier socialiste révolutionnaire* and announced as contradictory, only one candidate was present. At the end of the session: 'a serious reprimand [...] was voted addressed to organisers of assemblies, who announce speakers on their posters who they know cannot be present'.[35] Police and press observers also report that the public is larger when the assembly is contradictory.

Assemblies are generally organised by a committee sponsoring a candidate, who then invites its competitors. In the press and police reports, these assemblies

---

31. Olivier Ihl, *Le vote*, Paris, Montchrestien, 2000, pp. 79–80.
32. Louis Bouvard, *Les réunions électorales à Besançon et à Pontarlier et les candidats à la députation par un électeur de la 1ère circonscription du Doubs*, Besançon, Impr. J. Roblot, 1869, p. 4.
33. *La Liberté*, 19 May 1869.
34. AD BDR/1M/866/Réunions publiques, associations, 1893: Rapport du commissaire de police au commissaire central, 19e arr., 14 août 1893.
35. APP/Ba/614/Élections de 1885. Réunions, 8 janvier au 31 août: Rapport '22', 16 août 1885.

are often referred to as 'the assembly of the [name of candidate] committee', and each committee tends to monopolise a particular location. There are exceptions, albeit rare, such as an assembly held in Paris in February 1876 where one of the declarants announced to 400 people that 'neither he nor his friends had intended to set up a committee, which meant that the assembly was absolutely free and its aim was none other than the presentation of different candidates'.[36] When several assemblies took place simultaneously, candidates preferred to attend those organised by their own committees. On 19 February 1876, two candidates excused their absence by letter at an important assembly of around 2,000 people, organised by the committee supporting a third candidate. They justified this absence on the grounds that each of them had to take part in an assembly organised by 'the committee sponsoring his [own] candidacy'[37]— where they would have the greatest chance of support. It is significant that a candidate who came to debate with his opponents in an assembly not organised by him or his committee would often start a speech by stating that he knew he was unlikely to receive much support. Yet the stake remained real and the result was not always a foregone conclusion.

Committees usually organise several successive assemblies, especially in the big cities, held each evening, sometimes with several on the same evening, and almost at the same time. Thus, candidates are not only compared when they are present before the same assembly. Their performances were also compared in several assemblies at the same time or close together. The general debate consisted of what was said in the entire series of meetings. For example, many newspapers compare Gambetta's speech at the chaotic August 1881 assembly in rue Saint-Blaise in Belleville, and the assembly held the same day in Montmartre by Clemenceau. The newspaper founded by Clemenceau, commented on the two assemblies:

> [M. Clemenceau's resolved and fine discourse given [...] at the cirque Fernando to 3,000 Montmartre voters] had the strange fortune to be given at the same time as that in Belleville. This is the moment when the former deputy of Belleville and Montmartre was tearing up the 1869 programme in front of a selected audience [...] that M. Clemenceau affirmed with more energy than ever 'the pact of Paris with the Republic'.[38]

Another consequence of the increase in electoral assemblies is that they only make sense when taken in series. Thus only the first assemblies dealt with the presentation of programmes and subsequent assemblies dealt with questions and debate. At the start of the electoral campaign assemblies were announced as

---

36. APP/Ba/571/Élections générales. Réunions publiques. Renseignements généraux. 2e arr., salle Frascatti, 17 rue Vivienne: Rapport de M. Brissaud, officier de paix, cabinet, 1er *bureau*, police municipale, 2e brigade de recherches, 13 février 1876.

37. APP/Ba/571/1er arr., salle de la Redoute, rue J.-J. Rousseau: Rapport, police municipale, service des garnis, cabinet, 1er *bureau*, 19 février 1876.

38. *La Justice*, 16 August 1881.

intending 'to hear the profession of political faith' of one or more candidates.[39] However there was a rapid development of assemblies where candidates declared that they would not make a profession of faith, having done so earlier: 'my profession of faith is known, I developed it in various assemblies and I believe it is unnecessary to restate it', declared Thorel, republican candidate in an assembly of 600 people in Paris on 14 February 1876.[40] Sometimes even the chairman of the assembly gave this orientation to candidates before they spoke. In February 1876 a report on a 2,500-strong assembly in the Redoute meeting room declared: 'The chairman announced that it was pointless [...] for candidates to renew their profession of faith, which everyone knows'.[41]

Here we get a glimpse of one of the key aspects of these assemblies: the same public would attend several different meetings. Only in this way could a speaker deduce that his programme was already known for the simple reason that he had presented it on previous occasions. Participation at meetings was massive, and involved up to half the Parisian electorate. In addition, this huge public circulated between one assembly and another. Police reports describe the arrival of many people during an assembly who had come from another one. The author of the account of an assembly held on 11 February 1876 at the Frascatti meeting room in Paris, of an initial group of around a hundred people, notes:

> At 8.30 p.m. many people arrived from the assembly in the Théâtre Molière. [The candidates] M. Brelay and Loiseau-Pinson left for this assembly, followed by a large part of new arrivals. Others remained so that at 9.00 p.m. there were around 250 people in the room.[42]

Attending an assembly was not an isolated activity reserved for a limited number of activists, and it was not something done just once or sporadically. Candidates increased the number of platforms they spoke from by attending several different assemblies in the same evening, common practice from the 1869 elections onwards. Wilfrid de Fonvielle, one of the most active editors at *La Liberté*, described a 'discussion [which had collapsed] due to the lack of speakers', who had left for another assembly. Sometimes, they were taken by delegates arriving from another meeting.[43] During the evening of 14 February 1876, two electoral assemblies were organised at the same time in two rooms in the 2nd *arrondissement*. When the assembly opened in the Frascatti meeting room, several voters noted the absence

---

39. AD BDR/1M/865/Partis et mouvements politiques. Réunions et associations, 1885: Rapport du commissaire central au préfet, Marseille, 26 janvier 1885.
40. APP/Ba/571/Élections générales. Renseignements généraux. 2e arr. Réunions publiques. Salle Frascatti, 17 rue Vivienne: Rapport de M. Brissaud, officier de paix, cabinet 1er *bureau*, police municipale, 2e brigade de recherches, 15 février 1876.
41. APP/Ba/571/1er arr., salle de la Redoute, rue J.-J. Rousseau: Rapport police municipale, service des garnis, cabinet, 1er *bureau*, 15 février 1876.
42. APP/Ba/571/2e arr., salle Frascatti, 17 rue Vivienne: Rapport de M. Tchuinger, officier de paix, police municipale, 2e arr., 11 février 1876.
43. *La Liberté*, 10 septembre 1869.

of a candidate and went to look for him in the Molière meeting room. Later in the evening 'a delegate of the assembly in the Molière room, came to look for the candidate'.[44] The number of assemblies increased along with the movement of candidates from one assembly to another.

This system could allow skilled candidates to adapt their speeches and their bearing depending on the public before them. This is illustrated by a failure in the assemblies of 1876 in rue Vivienne, with a rather bourgeois public, and in the Théâtre Molière, with a mainly working-class public. The republican candidate, Thorel, tried to win the sympathy of both gatherings, first presenting himself decorated with a *Légion d'honneur* rosette in his buttonhole, wisely removing it for the second. When this tactic was discovered — not very surprisingly, given the movement of voters between different meetings — participants accused him publicly, but not in his presence, during a huge assembly of 2,000 people in rue Vivienne. A supporter tried to defend him by explaining that 'M. Thorel removed his decoration out of modesty and because he did not want people to believe that he used this symbol to win voters' confidence'. However this was all in vain, the author of the report remarked that 'he cannot say more, he is booed everywhere'.[45] Candidates were criticised for more than just their change of image, for example altering their programme in line with the different public before them. A typical attack against a competing candidate was made by one of the delegates of the radical republican Désiré Barodet's committee: 'M. Loiseau took part in two public assemblies. At the first, he was tender rose, at the second, he was red, and then he disappeared. Today, you see him absolutely red'. To this the 'accused' replied that he had 'never changed opinion' and had 'always been a republican'.[46] Barodet was one of the main defenders of the 'imperative mandate', particularly with the proposal that the Chamber 'collect and publish all electoral programmes on which new deputies had been elected in a book'.[47] It is thus not surprising that the strategic changes of programmes were condemned by Barodet's committee.

The principal stake for a candidate in assemblies is to win the votes of the electors on the day of the ballot. However they also try to obtain immediate support, and to have their candidacy approved by a vote of confidence, the closing ordeal of some of the assemblies. Early in the electoral period several candidates could be admitted by the same assembly, but in most cases only one candidate was supported. The assembly regularly accepted this candidate unanimously, or almost

---

44. APP/Ba/571/Élections générales. Renseignements généraux. 2e arr. Réunions publiques salle Frascatti, 17 rue Vivienne: Rapport de M. Brissaud, officier de paix, police municipale, 2e brigade de recherches, cabinet, 1er *bureau*, 15 février 1876.

45. APP/Ba/571/Rapport de M. Lombard, officier de paix, police municipale, 4e brigade des recherches, cabinet, 1er *bureau*, 13 février 1876.

46. APP/Ba/572/Élections générales, 4e arr. Réunions privées et publiques. Salle Rivoli, 104 rue St-Antoine: Rapport de M. Brissaud, officier de paix, police municipale, 2e brigade de recherches, 17 février 1876.

47. Daniel Mollenhauer, 'À la recherche de la "vraie République". Quelques jalons pour une histoire du radicalisme des débuts de la Troisième République', *Revue Historique*, 1998, vol. 607, pp. 608–609.

unanimously: it had then been prepared by the winner's committee. The test was often repeated in successive assemblies. For example, on 6 February 1876, Pierre-Joseph-Henri Marmottan, municipal councillor and republican candidate for the moderate left, attended a public assembly in Paris, and was: 'unanimously proclaimed republican candidate for the 16th *arrondissement*'.[48] Three days later, at a new assembly, the chairman declared: 'Citizens, at the last meeting, you accepted the candidacy of citizen Marmottan, here present. The aim of this assembly is to confirm this candidature'. This was put to the vote and 'accepted unanimously less one vote'.[49] Counter-examinations were sometimes organised following the first vote, but usually merely confirmed it. In a public assembly of October 1889, organised by the committee supporting Edmond Turquet, an ex-opportunist deputy who had rallied to Boulangism, a first 'resolution acclaiming this candidature is put to the vote and adopted by near unanimity'. A counter-examination was decided, but only 'a dozen hands were raised' in favour of the radical republican and anti-Boulangist candidate, Yves Guyot.[50]

Unanimity or quasi-unanimity is often obtained, particularly due to efficient organisation by the committee sponsoring the candidate whose name is put to the vote and whose followers partly filled the room. Police observers also suggest that in some cases a participant 'dare not raise his hand' in favour of a candidate who he knows is in a minority.[51] Sometimes, the chairman of the assembly even declares that the candidature of the person they support is unanimously approved by those present, even when this is not the case. If this is done too clumsily, the manœuvre leads to protest. In 1893 at a public assembly in Marseilles a vote of confidence motion was passed by seven votes out of around forty participants, in favour of Camille Vaulbert, the socialist candidate competing with three other socialists — Vaubert finally came last in the elections.[52] The chairman wanted to '[add] to the minutes that the motion had been passed *unanimously*', but a participant immediately raised an objection.[53] Moreover, Michel Offerlé has noted how in socialist assemblies in Paris 'the vote [on] motions [...] is often made in almost empty rooms'.[54]

---

48. APP/Ba/575/Réunions privées et publiques, 16e arr., 106 av. du Roi de Rome: Rapport du commissaire de police du quartier de la Muette et d'Auteuil, cabinet, 1er *bureau*, préfecture de Police, 6 février 1876.
49. APP/Ba/575/Rapport de M. Brissaud, officier de paix, cabinet, 1er *bureau*, police municipale, 2e brigade de recherches, 9 février 1876.
50. APP/Ba/1462/1889, Élections diverses. Réunions. 1er arr.: Rapport, préfecture de Police, 1ère brigade de recherches, cabinet, 1er *bureau*, 2 octobre 1889.
51. APP/Ba/575/Réunions privées et publiques, 17e arr.: Rapport, préfecture de Police, police municipale, service des garnis, cabinet, 1er *bureau*, Paris, 3 février 1876.
52. *Dictionnaire biographique du mouvement ouvrier français. Le Maitron 3, 1871–1914*, CD Rom, Éditions de l'Atelier.
53. AD BDR/1M/866/Réunions publiques, associations, 1893: Rapport du commissaire de police au commissaire central, 19e arr., 10 août 1893.
54. Michel Offerlé, *Les socialistes et Paris, 1881–1900, des communards aux conseillers municipaux*, PhD dissertation, Paris I, 1979, p. 449.

When a candidate does not appear to have the firm support of any assembly, he sometimes withdraws in favour of a candidate of the same political colour who enjoys more outright success. There were in fact many candidates defending similar or identical programmes, partly because the same candidate could present himself in many electoral districts. This was until, following the Boulangist movement, the law of 17 July 1889 banned multiple candidatures to the deputyship and made the declaration of candidacy compulsory. A candidate would often stand down even during an assembly and candidates who insisted on standing for election when the assemblies seemed to show that they were no longer the most popular could be reprimanded. A police report of February 1876 on a motion passed in Paris on a subsequently annulled assembly states:

> A person of a certain age said that M. Robinet had promised to withdraw in favour of the candidate with more votes than him in the public assemblies. He added that the candidacy of M. Denfert had been acclaimed at the last meeting but that Sr. Robinet had not kept his word since he persisted in standing as candidate.[55]

These two candidates were republicans. In the end, Robinet withdrew his candidacy in favour of Denfert-Rochereau, who was elected. Reproaches against candidates who insisted on presenting themselves despite their unpopularity in assemblies were heard in meetings held after the first ballot. The chairman of a public assembly of 1,500 people on 25 February 1876 in the Folies Bobino meeting room affirms that:

> If we did not have a definitive vote, it is not our fault, but that of the candidates who had to withdraw when they had given their word to withdraw as soon as public assemblies had made their choice.[56]

Thus, the public plays an important role at electoral assemblies. At the start of the Third Republic, it is often seen as more positive than that of other assemblies, as if it symbolised the 'People of citizens' coming to debate public issues. This can be related to the fact that after the 1868 and 1881 laws entry to these assemblies is reserved for voters in the district. This ruling, however, is not always applied. There was a liberal development of this point of view between the elections of the Second Empire and the Republic. In 1869, the officer present reminded the audience that only voters resident in the district could take part in assemblies and therefore asked everyone else to leave the hall. This occurred for instance in an assembly in Aubagne in May 1869, after which three people left the room.[57] In the

---

55. APP/Ba/573/Réunions privées et publiques, 6e arr., gymnase Pascaud: Rapport de M. Brissaud, officier de paix, cabinet, 1er bureau, police municipale, 2e brigade de recherches, 14 février 1876.

56. APP/Ba/574/Réunions privées et publiques, 14e arr., salle des Folies Bobino, rue de la Gaîté: Rapport de M. Brissaud, officier de paix, cabinet, 1er bureau, police municipale, 2e brigade de recherches, 26 février 1876.

57. AD BDR/1M/637/Second Empire. Opinion publique. Partis, mouvements politiques: Rapport du maire d'Aubagne au préfet, 9 mai 1869.

1876 elections in Paris it seemed that voters' documents were still being regularly checked at the door, as stated in police reports.[58] Despite this, the law was often broken. Police observers note that people were initially checked on entry, but that this requirement was soon abandoned: 'voter's documents were only checked at the beginning, before the crowd broke through and invaded the room'.[59] The reports sometimes state that 'checks were not strict',[60] or even that 'entrants were not asked for a document proving that they lived in the *arrondissement*'.[61] This negligence was repeated in subsequent elections. Police reports often reveal the presence of women and children which means that entry was not limited exclusively to voters. It is also possible that some electoral assemblies may have been declared simple public political assemblies, thus avoiding the limitation of participants.

Beyond the fact that they pronounce their opinion on the possible motions of support, it is above all through their questions to candidates that participants in assemblies express their central role. The public is not always satisfied with merely hearing monologues delivered by candidates on the platform, candidates also have to reply to voters' questions, particularly because the programmes were only presented in the first assemblies. Those candidating themselves as deputies are faced with a range of questions. These focus on the candidate's past, particularly any previous standpoints on a range of key issues, and how they have served the community. Such questions tend to privilege candidates who already hold an electoral mandate — municipal councillors, retiring deputies — although some of their votes can then be blamed by the public. The questions also dealt with the candidate's attitude on the electoral campaign. Did he fully accept the programme drawn up by the committee? Why did he not proclaim his profession of faith? Would he stand down for another candidate at a second ballot? Of course, the candidate was often asked what he would do if elected. This type of question often touches specific points, particularly the choices that the candidate intends to make once elected. Sometimes the public lets the candidate reply at length, but he may also be frequently interrupted during his explanation by another question or by a critique. Unfortunately press and police accounts do not generally inquire into the identity of those asking questions, who are referred to with vague expressions such as: 'an assistant asked…', 'a voter challenged him…', 'a voice asked him…', 'someone enquired…', etc.

---

58. APP/Ba/571/Élections générales. Réunions privées et publiques. Renseignements généraux: Rapport 'Jacquot', Paris, 21 mars 1876; APP/Ba/571/1ᵉʳ arr., réunions publiques, salle de la Redoute: Rapport, police municipale, service des garnis, cabinet, 1ᵉʳ *bureau*, 7 février 1876.
59. APP/Ba/571/2e arr. Réunions publiques, salle Molière: Rapport de M. Brissaud, officier de paix, cabinet 1ᵉʳ *bureau*, police municipale, 2e brigade de recherches, 4 février 1876.
60. APP/Ba/571/2e arr. Réunions publiques, salle Molière: Rapport de M. Brissaud, officier de paix, cabinet 1ᵉʳ *bureau*, police municipale, 2e brigade de recherches, 6 février 1876.
61. APP/Ba/575/Réunions privées et publiques, 16e arr., av. du roi de Rome: Rapport de M. Brissaud, officier de paix, cabinet, 1ᵉʳ *bureau*, police municipale, 2e brigade de recherches, 9 février 1876.

In an assembly in February 1876 in the Redoute meeting room, with over 400 people and several candidates, a voter made the following suggestion:

> Citizens, I will ask the candidate who is elected to think, when arriving in the Chamber, about the working class; I ask him to kindly study a question that could protect the worker when he reaches old age. Since we put up with all sorts of taxes, could we not add another to require us to manage our well-being ourselves; an apprentice could pay 0.50 Fr. a month; a worker 2 Fr.; it would be a compulsory mutual aid society, and would save many people from poverty; I don't know if my idea is a good one; in any case, we can study it.[62]

Participants' proposals may not always have been as developed as this one, but they generally were not satisfied just to ask questions. Candidates were sometimes given advice or instructions, guidance that the public expected to be respected. Several assemblies testify to the great temptation to apply the imperative mandate at the end of the nineteenth century, and which the candidate is sometimes asked to accept.[63] According to Rosanvallon, the imperative mandate with 'the wind in its sails' in the last years of the Second Empire,[64] was still defended by many in the first decades of the Republic, even if 'from Jules Ferry to Jules Grévy, the founding fathers never ceased [...] justifying the independence of representatives'.[65] Yet the radical republicans still recognised the value of a mandate linking them directly to their voters. In addition to making this sort of commitment before the election, I should mention the practice of holding assemblies to demand an account of the mandate. It became 'settled firmly in the radical milieu from the 1876 elections onwards and which appears to be an important element of radical identity'.[66] The pre-election meetings show that a candidate may have been expected, if not to accept an imperative mandate, at least to give a promise of loyalty to his voters, symbolised by the public who supported him in assemblies. 'With public assemblies voters can make their opinions and their way of seeing things known to their representative. The latter can also find indications on the line of conduct to follow', declared the republican Charles Loiseau, before presenting himself to the public of an assembly in Paris in February 1876.[67]

---

62. APP/Ba/571/Élections générales, 1ᵉʳ arr. Réunions publiques. Salle de la Redoute: Rapport, police municipale, service des garnis, cabinet, 1ᵉʳ *bureau*, 7 février 1876.
63. See, for example, AD BDR/1M/865/Partis et mouvements politiques. Réunions et associations, 1885: Rapport du commissaire central au préfet, 10 septembre 1885 (réunion publique électorale, rue des trois mages); AD BDR/1M/870/Partis et mouvements politiques. Réunions publiques, 1898–1899: Rapport du commissaire de police au commissaire central, 30 avril 1898 (réunion publique électorale, bar 'Nicolas' au Canet).
64. Rosanvallon, *La démocratie inachevée. Histoire de la souveraineté du peuple en France*, Gallimard, Bibliothèque des histoires, 2000, p. 256.
65. Rosanvallon, *La démocratie inachevée*, pp. 260–261.
66. Mollenhauer, 'À la recherche de la "vraie République"', p. 607.
67. APP/Ba/572/Élections générales. 4e arr. Réunions privées. Salle Rivoli, 104 rue St-Antoine: Rapport de M. Brissaud, officier de paix, police municipale, 2e brigade de recherches, 17 février 1876.

The unequal resources of candidates in public assemblies

The organisation of a series of electoral assemblies must be placed alongside the republican ambition of organising elections under universal suffrage which differed from those held under the Empire, and which can then really become the basis of the legitimacy of power in the Republic. Assemblies intensified competition between candidates through their direct evaluation by voters, allowing the latter to make a real choice when casting their vote. The electoral assembly, considered by many as a quasi-obligatory step for a candidate to take, contributed to the success of those willing to take the risk to present themselves and succeed in making themselves heard and acclaimed. This was clearly to the detriment of candidates unsure about including the assemblies in their repertoire of vote-winning techniques — either because they were reticent about using this mode of electoral mobilisation, or because they did not have sufficient means to do so.

The adaptation of the notables?

The development of electoral assemblies took place in the more general context of a renewal of the political class in the last part of the nineteenth century and early twentieth century; that is, a social renewal as the candidates' social origin changed, and a political renewal as the numbers of republicans elected increased. Jean Estèbe insists on the 'democratisation of recruitment' of the executive between 1871 and 1914, making a direct parallel between this change in the social recruitment of ministers and the 'focal points of political history'.[68] Mattéi Dogan refers to parliamentary representation as a 'silent revolution' evident between 1871 and 1919.[69]

> The first rupture introduced by the parliamentary personnel of the Third Republic is the progressive disappearance of status groups, which, since the Empire, had filled political functions, be they the nobility or senior functionaries or more generally those referred to as 'notables'.[70]

Even though the change was neither complete nor drastic – insofar as 'the time of social change must [...] be considered in the longer-term of politics'[71] – the social origin of deputies changed during this period. Alain Garrigou insists on the

---

68. Jean Estèbe, *Les ministres de la République. 1871–1914*, Paris, FNSP, 1982, pp. 24–25.
69. Mattéi Doggan, 'Les filières de la carrière politique en France', *Revue française de sociologie*, 1967, vol. 8, (4), pp. 468–469. For an analysis of the decline of nobility in Parliament see: Jean Bécarud, 'Noblesse et représentation parlementaire. Députés nobles de 1871 à 1968', *Revue française de science politique*, 1973, vol. 23, (5), pp. 972–993.
70. Christophe Charle, 'Les parlementaires. Avant-garde ou arrière-garde d'une société en mouvement?', in Jean-Marie Mayeur, Jean-Pierre Chaline and Alain Corbin (eds), *Les parlementaires de la Troisième République*, Paris, Publications de la Sorbonne, 2003, p. 45.
71. Michel Offerlé, 'Professions et profession politique', in Michel Offerlé (ed.), *La profession politique. 19e–20e siècle*, Paris, Belin, 1999, p. 12.

role played by political entrepreneurs in this relegation of notables, particularly: 'the republican contenders [who] could not accept that the elections depend on a social authority which they possessed less of'.[72] According to Max Weber's ideal-typical definition, a notable is whoever enjoys an economic situation which allows him to hold political functions without being paid to do so; and whoever enjoys social esteem and converts it into a position of political power.[73] The political entrepreneurs compete with the notables by placing themselves on the ground of public opinion: 'Socially divested, they had to compensate their handicap through political work. They must campaign'.[74] Indeed, for Garrigou, 'the "end of the notables"[75] meant first of all downgrading a way to generate votes'; 'the old methods, which consisted of using one's fortune to be elected, to win the votes of dependent groups, possibly to enframe them very rigidly, were largely abandoned'.[76] There are two related phenomena: first, the decline of the notables maintaining a candidate-elector link based on the social authority and the increase of political entrepreneurs creating a basically political relation with voters; second, the intensification of democratic electoral competition.

Yet this mutation does not mean the complete suppression of French notables unable to adapt to mass electoral competition. First, there is no clear-cut separation between the era of the notables and the era characterised by the victory of the 'new strata'.[77] Moreover, we must moderate the idea that the institution of representative democracy would mean defeat for the notables and victory for professional politicians. According to Julien Fretel and Rémi Lefebvre, what occurred was instead a 'hybridation between the notables and professional politicians', a 'reciprocal acculturation', where the former took on a part of the habitual practices of the latter.[78] On one hand, authors have shown that 'entrepreneurs appropriate the behaviour of notables'.[79] On the other hand, the notables themselves are not 'indifferent to the specialisation of [political activity]'.[80] Taking the career of Baron Armand de Mackau as an example, Éric Phélippeau reveals the 'gradual

---

72. Garrigou, *Histoire sociale du suffrage universel en France*, pp. 291–292.
73. On the problems posed by the too diverse or too broad use of the term, see: Julien Fretel, 'Le parti comme fabrique de notables. Réflexions sur les pratiques notabiliaires des élus de l'UDF', *Politix*, 2004, vol. 17, (65), pp. 45–46.
74. Garrigou, *Histoire sociale du suffrage universel en France*, p. 299.
75. Daniel Halévy, *La fin des notables*, Paris, Grasset, 1930.
76. Garrigou, *Histoire sociale du suffrage universel en France*, pp. 316–317.
77. Christophe Charle, *Les élites de la République. 1881–1900*, Paris, Fayard, 1987, p. 71.
78. Julien Fretel and Rémi Lefebvre, 'Retour sur un lieu commun historiographique. La faiblesse des partis politiques en France', *Journées AFSP* Science politique/Histoire, 2004, http://www.afsp.msh-paris.fr/activite/diversafsp/ collhistscpo04/hist04fretel.pdf, p. 39 (accessed 6 June 2006).
79. See for example: Rémi Lefebvre, '"Le conseil des buveurs de bière" de Roubaix (1892–1902). Subversion et apprentissage des règles du jeu institutionnel', *Politix*, 2001, vol. 14, (53), p. 90.
80. Jean Joana, *Pratiques politiques des députés français au XIXe siècle. Du dilettante au spécialiste*, Paris, L'Harmattan, 1999, p. 9.

deployment of [a] specialised task of winning votes'.[81] Notables were thus sometimes willing to convert to the rationalisation of political work.

The Second Empire was burdened with the 'return *en force*' of the notables. Their power had been restored by administration through the system of official candidates, but the last years of the Empire marked 'the end of [their] golden age'.[82] Electoral assemblies played a role in this decline starting in the last months of the Empire insofar as the increase in the number of assemblies helped those contesting the system of official candidates, whose position had been undermined by the new freedoms agreed in 1868. Assemblies benefited opposition candidates and more generally those who 'were aware of the need to enter into contact [...] with those to whom they must appeal for votes'.[83] The system of official candidates still existed at the time of the 1869 legislative elections, and Christophe Voilliot and Éric Phélippeau show that it had not completely disappeared in the early Third Republic, but was rather euphemistically referred to as '*candidatures officieuses*'.[84] The end of the Empire was nonetheless characterised by an upheaval in the way electoral campaigns were conducted.

The change was first felt before the liberalisation of assemblies and the press. An article in the liberal newspaper *La Presse* on 20 August 1868 evoked the election of Jules Grévy in April 1868 as deputy for Jura standing against the official candidate. The article states that 'the time when we could rely on the zeal of the government and its agents for the success of an election, is definitively over'.[85] Henceforth 'it is at the price of a close and almost permanent communication with electors sharing his opinion, that a candidate [...] can succeed': the author of the article defends the freedom of electoral assembly. Yet it was above all the 1869 elections that marked the break: 'the liberalisation of 1868 allowed republicans, for the first time, in the 1869 elections, to mount a sustained ideological and electoral offensive against the government and the notables who supported it'.[86] The increase in electoral assemblies was to the detriment of government candidates, who faced the public criticism of their opponents. As a contemporary observer of this campaign, Masseras claimed that 'the boiling up of ideas began well before the excitement of public assemblies'. They nonetheless played an important role:

---

81. Éric Phélippeau, *Le baron de Mackau en politique. Contribution à l'étude de la professionnalisation politique*, PhD dissertation, Paris X, 1996, p. 522.

82. Pierre Goujon, *Le vigneron citoyen. Mâconnais et Chalonnais, 1848–1914*, Paris, CTHS, 1993, p. 259.

83. Patrick Lagoueyte, *Candidature officielle et pratiques électorales sous le deuxième Empire (1852–1870)*, PhD dissertation, Paris I, 1990, p. 1129.

84. Phélippeau, *Le baron de Mackau en politique*, p. 217; Christophe Voilliot, *La candidature officielle. Une pratique d'État de la Restauration à la Troisième République*, Rennes, PUR, 2005, p. 11.

85. *La Presse*, 20 August 1868.

86. Roger Price, *The French Second Empire. An Anatomy of Political Power*, Cambridge, Cambridge University Press, 2001, p. 352.

On this completely new ground [of electoral assemblies], the advantage had to be for the bold. They cast themselves headlong, thwarting all the combinations of tactics which had reigned until now in elections, with their enthusiasm. Those with experience of politics were still waiting to draw up their artillery, when their opponents were already in position. When they recovered from their initial surprise, it was too late. Many of them did not really understand the decisive effect of contact established by public assemblies between a candidate and his voters until after the results; they persisted with their former propaganda up to the end. Thus, more than one of them paid with his defeat on the day of the ballot, for not having guessed the revolution that was taking place in our mores and political strategies in sufficient time.[87]

Electoral assemblies were, at least in the big cities, a new threat for the notables who were used to being easily elected in the first round, especially as a consequence of government patronage.

Before this escalation of competition and the weakening of the certainty of being easily elected, some official candidates did adapt their way of campaigning, sometimes with government support, particularly by turning towards assemblies. 'A number of candidates', notes Patrick Lagoueyte, 'still lead a campaign of notables; but their strategy appeared ever more *passéiste* and dooms them imperceptibly to failure'.[88] Official candidates who decided to campaign did not choose the large contradictory assemblies. Many seem to have avoided popular neighbourhoods in Paris and its suburbs altogether. In his memoirs, Jules Simon recounts that '[his competitor M. Lachaud] only took risks in niches favourable to his candidature'. Indeed, 'in the suburbs, [Simon] had a free field. His competitor did not follow him. These were popular assemblies'.[89] The Empire candidates preferred small-scale private assemblies. In the case of Bas-Languedoc, Huard writes that they 'draw together men of similar social position in small receptions, very different from the public assemblies of republicans, but in order to encourage the zeal of conservatives in small market towns'.[90]

Official candidates also resort to assemblies when they have easier access than their competitors in opposition, agricultural shows being a case in point. Phélippeau has shown that if '[their] activities are [most often] described as being without any partisan intent', they are still a sort of 'electoral machine' for the great notables.[91] The agricultural shows appear to have been widely used by the

---

87. Masseras, *La campagne électorale de 1869*, pp. 16–18.
88. Lagoueyte, *Candidature officielle et pratiques électorales sous le deuxième Empire (1852–1870)*, p. 1,129.
89. Jules Simon, *Le soir de ma journée*, Paris, Flammarion, 1901, pp. 306–307.
90. Raymond Huard, *Le mouvement républicain en Bas-Languedoc, 1848–1881*, FNSP, Paris, 1982, pp. 235–236.
91. Éric Phélippeau, *L'invention de la politique moderne. Mackau, l'Orne et la République*, Paris, Belin, 2002, pp. 146–162. The political use of agricultural shows is not limited to official candidates or to this period. See: Yann Lagadec, 'Quelles élites pour le progrès agricole au XIXe

administration to promote government candidates, but not without stirring up the criticism of the opposition. According to *La Presse*:

> This year agricultural shows are definitely [...] one of the key aids for the success of official candidates; the banquets that follow these assemblies are helped, encouraged and patronised by government.[92]

These shows were a particular form of assembly in a rural context, where the official candidate could attend without running the risk of having to face a republican contender in a public contradictory assembly. The point was to show that a candidate did not refuse direct contact with citizens at meetings, and that he recognised the importance of holding assemblies of electors, but without having to worry about being booed in a popular assembly.

The period of silence imposed on the electoral campaign during the five days before the vote was also used by Empire-sponsored candidates to hold assemblies to which the administration closed an eye, and even helped to organise. Many deputies were already worried about this question during the debates on the 1868 law: did the electoral five-day silence apply to all candidates? On 17 March 1868 Louis-Joseph Buffet asked in the name of the *Tiers parti* (a group of deputies who rejected the authoritarian Empire while refusing to be part of a systematic opposition): 'The administration will be allowed to use its discretionary power [in electoral assemblies], to authorise them to the benefit of one candidate, and to provoke some where other candidates might be attacked [...]?'[93] The Lord Chancellor, Pinard, delivered a categorical 'no' the very same day:

> We respond negatively, because we believe that the law does not allow us to do so, and leaves government no choice in this regard. [...] During this period we do not have the right to authorise an assembly, let alone for candidates of one political colour or another.[94]

In May 1869, however, official or semi-official candidates profited from the days of silence imposed on the opposition to hold assemblies — some never having appeared in public assemblies during the electoral period. In what can be considered as particular forms of electoral assemblies, and to counter-balance the new activity of their opponents, government candidates sought to establish contact with their electors. This type of practice was loudly criticised in the liberal press. The journalist and writer Edmond Texier denounced the organisation of

---

siècle? L'exemple des comices agricoles bretons', in Frédérique Pitou (ed.), *Elites et notables de l'Ouest. XVI*ᵉ*–XX*ᵉ *siècle. Entre conservatisme et modernité*, Rennes, PUR, 2003, pp. 105–120; Maurice Mathieu, 'Un enjeu dans les luttes politiques dans la Vienne. Les comices et les sociétés agricoles. Vers 1880, début du XXᵉ siècle', *Bulletin de la Société des antiquaires de l'ouest et des musées de Poitiers*, 1984, vol. 2, pp. 457–484.

92. *La Presse*, 27 August 1868.
93. *Le Moniteur Universel*, 18 March 1868, p. 407.
94. *Le Moniteur Universel*, 18 March 1868, p. 408.

assemblies by, or for, pro-Empire candidates: 'The assemblies, even when private, are prohibited for the opposition, but freedom is granted on this point to semi-official candidates'.[95] He cites the example of the contest between Jules Simon and Lachaud:

> M. Lachaud had never spoke as much as since the silence imposed on his competitor, M. Jules Simon. The assemblies of M. Lachaud are held in the sub-prefecture of Saint-Denis, and, in the various communes of the district, in the homes of friends. [...] In all these assemblies organised by the administration M. Lachaud persists in declaring that he is not the official candidate.

Another possible motive for a candidate refusing to step down in public electoral assemblies is to declare their candidature after the authorised period has expired. Opposition journalists referred to these as the inglorious 'last-minute candidates', for example in *La Presse* a journalist talks of individuals who openly refused 'public debate and contradiction' of their ideas, and who thus 'failed in the main obligation of the public man, to have contact with his fellow-citizens, and present his thoughts and actions for open discussion of those in whose honour we aspire to become the loyal representative'.[96]

Under the Third Republic the growth of public electoral assemblies described here did not affect all candidates in the same way. First, the most conservative of them risked having no success at all in popular assemblies. Then there were many who considered that, particularly on account of their social position, the cost of 'descending'[97] in assemblies soliciting the support of their social inferiors was too high.[98] The account is striking for the many legitimist candidates, even if it is less marked in regions where 'monarchist entrepreneurs' made an effort in matters of 'political organisation'.[99] Generally speaking, the legitimists: 'adapt unwillingly to the obligations of universal suffrage'.[100] In the first years of the Republic police reports on the 'legitimist intrigues' confirm the reluctance of some royalist candidates to attend public assemblies. A report of January 1876 states that if some

---

95. *Le Siècle*, 21 May 1868.
96. *La Presse*, 21 May 1869.
97. Count de Falloux, a member of the legitimist right, used this expression to describe attending a meeting of voters to 'develop [his] political theme by attaching [...] local issues that could interest [his] listeners'. See: Alfred De Falloux, *Mémoires d'un royaliste*, Paris, Perrin & Cie, 1888, p. 409.
98. On the threat of statutory forefeiture, see: Éric Phélippeau, 'Sociogenèse de la profession politique', in Alain Garrigou and Bernard Lacroix (eds), *Norbert Elias, la politique et l'histoire*, Paris, La Découverte, 1997, pp. 249–250.
99. Philippe Secondy, 'Royalisme et innovations partisanes. Les "blancs du Midi" à la fin du XIXe siècle', *Revue française de science politique*, 2003, vol. 53, (1), p. 99.
100. Vincent Petit, *Légitimisme et catholicisme au début de la Troisième République, 1871–1883. L'exemple du département du Doubs*, PhD dissertation, Université de Franche-Comté, 1993, p. 158. See also Steven D. Kale, *Legitimism and the Reconstruction of French Society. 1852–1883*, Baton Rouge, Louisiana State University Press, 1992, pp. 330–335.

legitimists 'speak out for oral propaganda, that is, for direct contact with voters, [...] most of these gentlemen refuse to exercise it'. Its author adds that, moreover, the legitimists were 'reluctant to use agents for this task who, according to their expression, were not worth their pay'.[101] This does not mean that they remain strangers to all propaganda via assemblies, there are possible adaptive strategies for candidates faced with the action of republican political entrepreneurs which reduces their influence, and who cannot, or do not want, to compete on the same ground.

In the 1870s and until the early 1880s it was quite common that the sermon would take the form of a campaign speech during masses. In February 1876, Count Eugène de Germiny was the hope of the clerical right and his candidacy was 'strongly supported by all the clerics of Faubourg Saint-Germain', wrote the author of a police report on a mass attended by 'around 200 people belonging exclusively to the male sex, the largest part of whom had a title or at least a "de" in front of their name'. The author also noted that:

> Père Matignon first made an address where, after having recommended his prayers for the good outcome of the elections, [called on] his audience to work actively in favour of candidates who declared a desire to defend the catholic religion and the charitable societies that support it.[102]

In much the same way an 1877 report asserts that:

> This week there will be almost daily prayers and sermons in all the parishes and religious communities for 'good elections'. [...] Never, say the promoters of these clerical demonstrations, has the church been exposed to greater danger, and these coming elections can mean the triumph or crushing of the catholic religion.[103]

Those attending the masses were close to the legitimists and the public was sometimes controlled by the stewards of legitimist committees responsible for security.[104] These 'religious ceremonies', organised 'to obtain good elections', to echo the discourse of the Mariste superior in rue de Vaugirard transcribed in an 1877 report, were a sort of private electoral assembly.[105] They were not the sole expression of the key character of the link between catholic actions on behalf of legitimist candidates.[106] Stéphane Rials has shown that if 'the clericalisation of royalism was a source of weakness on the whole', this changed after 1870.

---

101. APP/Ba/401/Menées légitimistes, 1876: Rapport, Paris, 24 janvier 1876, n.s. The great majority of reports on the activity of the legitimists are unsigned reports by infiltrators (n.s).
102. APP/Ba/401/Rapport, Paris, 14 février 1876, n.s.
103. APP/Ba/402/Menées légitimistes, 1877: Rapport, Paris, 8 octobre 1877, n.s.
104. See, for example, APP/Ba/401/Menées légitimistes, 1876: Rapport, Paris, 27 septembre 1876, n.s.
105. APP/Ba/402/Menées légitimistes, 1877: Rapport, Paris, 4 octobre 1877, n.s.
106. Reports on catholic electoral propaganda in favour of legitimist candidates, particularly lectures, are preserved in: AN/F7/12481/Action électorale catholique, 1895–1904.

In fact 'the new political situation allowed the royalisation of immense clerical batallions'.[107] In the many pro-royalist assemblies organised by catholic circles the public was made up basically of their members, often active in the electoral struggle for the legitimists. At the opening of a royalist assembly organised in 1885 in the catholic circle of Marseilles in which 400 of its members took part, the chairman '[thanked them] warmly [...] for the assistance they have given to royalist candidates during the election period'.[108] The bond with the defense of the catholic religion allows legitimist candidates to find forms of assemblies conducive to their ideas. The author of a report of February 1880 wrote that:

> Without the support of the clergy, legitimists would be reduced to expressing their regrets for the past, their bad humour with the present and their despair for the future in some drawing room without there being an explosion of these feelings that could have any echo once they step outside their mansions.[109]

Indeed, most meetings between voters and royalist candidates or those defending their candidature were made in private, and sometimes small assemblies made up of voters won over beforehand. They often took the form of lectures with a single speaker, who repeated an identical speech in various locations or *arrondissements* in Paris.[110] The banquet was a form of private assembly which they resorted to with enthusiasm. 'The royalists' stated a 1880 police report 'have got a taste for banquets', and added:

> They said yesterday that it was the *piquette* [cheap wine] of banquets that overthrew two governments and that they should substitute lectures with banquets. Moreover, the speeches at banquets astounded better than lectures because there was more enthusiasm.[111]

An 1882 report stated that 'it was banquets that confirmed the legimists'.[112] In the early 1880s, the legitimists continued to prefer private assemblies, but some of them opted for a type of assembly open to a larger public. 'The death of M. Gambetta raises everyone's expectations. The legitimist party ventures to give quasi-public assemblies, which it had never dared do before', writes the author of a synthetic report entitled *Les menées légitimistes* in 1884, about the period

---

107. Stéphane Rials, *Révolution et contre-révolution au XIXe siècle*, Paris, Albatros, 1987, p. 203.
108. AD BDR/1M/865/Partis et mouvements politiques. Réunions et associations 1885–1892/1885: Rapport du commissaire spécial au préfet des Bouches-du-Rhône, s.d.
109. APP/Ba/403/Menées légitimistes, 1880: Rapport, Paris, 17 février 1880, n.s.
110. See, for example, AN/F7/12431/Agissements royalistes. Renseignements de toute nature concernant leur activité: Rapport 'd'un correspondant', Paris, 9 décembre 1901.
111. APP/Ba/403/Menées légitimistes, 1880: Rapport, cabinet, préfecture de Police, 1er *bureau*, Paris, 12 octobre 1880.
112. AN/F7/12431/Agissements royalistes. Renseignements généraux. Campagne de banquets royalistes. Prétendu réveil de l'esprit monarchique. Moyens d'action, 1882–1883: Rapport, ministère de l'Intérieur, direction des renseignements généraux, Paris, 1882.

beginning on 1 January 1883.[113] A Parisian report of 1882 states that 'the legitimist party will organise a public assembly a week in each *arrondissement*'.[114] When the experience is attempted it frequently turns out badly for its organisers with speakers hardly able to make themselves heard. Legitimist candidates are willing to risk public assemblies, albeit rarely, because in an election period they certainly have far more legitimacy than private assemblies. Candidates not presenting themselves are accused of cowardice and of avoiding their duty. If they do not attend open meetings, it is assumed that they fear the People represented there.

The need for organisational support

Concerning the end of the Second Empire and the first decades of the Third Republic, Raymond Huard wrote that 'private assemblies were mainly organised by conservative candidates who did not want to enter the electoral fray any more than their supporters' and that: 'public assemblies were far more difficult'.[115] Public electoral assemblies were largely deserted by the official or semi-official candidates under the Empire, just as by the royalist candidates in the years 1870–1880. This did not prevent them from resorting to other, less legitimate, types of assembly. They were aware of the fact that 'after having been a concession, leading a campaign had become the norm', and that 'they had to surrender to this when the activity of "election entrepreneurs" spread and overflowed'.[116] In addition to the observation of intolerance of participants in big assemblies *vis-à-vis* those defending conservative opinions, we still need to understand what makes the electoral public assembly favour some candidates, and what makes organisational support absolutely necessary.

First of all, a specific form of eloquence is required in public assemblies, which some master better than others.[117] Above all, it is not easy to make oneself heard. There are no loudspeakers to amplify the voices of the candidates.[118] At the time assemblies gathered together hundreds, sometimes thousands, of often

---

113. APP/Ba/405/Menées légitimistes, 1883–1888: Rapport général de synthèse 'Les menées légitimistes', Paris, préfecture de Police, cabinet, s.d. (probably 1884).
114. APP/Ba/404/Menées légitimistes, 1882: Rapport '36', 20 décembre 1882.
115. Huard, *Le suffrage universel en France*, p. 282.
116. Garrigou, *Histoire sociale du suffrage universel en France*, p. 312.
117. The examples are mainly taken from assemblies in Paris in February 1876, for which sources abound.
118. These only started to appear in the second half of the 1920s and were used in the assemblies of the 1930s — even if the first forms of loud-speaker were invented at the turn of the century, it was in 1925 that the Americans Chester W. Rice and Edward Washburn Kellogg launched the first which would become a commercial success. See: B. Schmerber, 'Histoire du son', http://b.schmerber.9online.fr/theorie2/histoire.htm (accessed 6 June 2006); S. E. Schoenherr, 'Loudspeaker History', http://history.acusd.edu/gen/recording/loudspeaker.html (accessed 6 June 2006); M. Bellis, 'The History of Loudspeakers — Speakers', http://inventors.about.com/library/inventors/blloudspeaker.htm (accessed 6 June 2006).

noisy people in meeting rooms which frequently had very bad acoustics. It was not unusual for journalists or police observers to mention in their accounts how difficult it was to hear ('one can only hear a confused buzzing and a repeated ringing of the bell'),[119] and that they only understood part of what was being said ('that's all I could hear from the last place in the gangway').[120] On 12 November 1869, in a very large electoral assembly in the old quarry of Puteaux (see Figure 3.2) a rather original system was installed but without much success, according to *L'Illustration*: 'citizens-echos' were chosen, 'placed every ten metres', and 'had to repeat the announcements from the *bureau*'. The article specified that if the voice of Emmanuel Arago 'rolls strangely in the galleries', in comparison his 'competitors' have had a hard 'job being heard'.[121]

The advantage of having a powerful voice was often stressed by observers: 'it is only thanks to his energy and tone of voice that he can [...] express his ideas';[122] just as a weak voice is a handicap: 'his voice is weak [...] he seems to be short of breath and a great deal of this is needed for a substantial speech'.[123] Eloquence in a public assembly must be 'seen from a distance', to describe it in the critical terms used in 1870 by the republican Deschanel, founder of the lectures of the *rue de la Paix*, place of opposition to the Empire:

> What is commonly called eloquence is to true eloquence what the decorator is to the art of Raphaël, Rubens, Van Dyck, Rembrandt and Velázquez. It is painted in large brush strokes; it is big and made to be seen from far away, in artificial light. Close up, it is horrible. The heavy guns of eloquence have their use in meetings, in electoral battles. [...] This eloquence knows nothing of nuances, and it would not know how to allow them: from far away nuances cannot be seen.[124]

The emphatic character of the eloquence of speakers coming to be heard was denounced by the candidates who preferred private assemblies. In Paris on 16 February 1878 a private assembly of ninety-five people was organised in support of the moderate republican candidate Arrault, against the radical candidate Clemenceau, who was eventually the overwhelming winner of the election.[125] Arrault spoke as soon as the session opened: 'Sirs, [...] I will not give you a grand speech', and a little later, he added: 'I do not want to give a high-flown speech as

---

119. APP/Ba/576/Réunions privées et publiques, 20e arr.: 'Réunions électorales. 20e arrondissement. Salle des Pannoyaux', *Paris-Journal*, 16 février 1876.

120. AD BDR/1M/792/Partis, mouvements politiques, 1870–1873: Rapport du commissaire de police au préfet, Tarascon, 8 octobre 1872.

121. *L'Illustration*, 20 November 1869.

122. APP/Ba/571/1er arr. Réunions privées et publiques: Rapport de Tenaille, commissaire de police du quartier du Palais-Royal, cabinet, 1er *bureau*, préfecture de Police, 13 février 1876.

123. APP/Ba/573/Réunions privées et publiques, 9e arr., salle des Folies-Montholon, rue Rochechouart: Rapport '4', 6 février 1876.

124. Émile Deschanel, *Les conférences à Paris et en Province*, Paris, Librairie Pagnerre, 1870, p. 55.

125. Robert and Cougny, *Dictionnaire des parlementaires français*, vol. 2, p. 127.

Figure 3.2: 'The elections. Electoral assembly hold on 12 November in the old quarries of Puteaux. [...] Sketch by M. Provost', L'Illustration, 20 November 1869

do some of our intransigents'. When a voter asked him: 'Why do you not come to the public assemblies that take place in the *arrondissement*?' he replied: 'I have not yet lost all personal dignity to the point of attending assemblies where people inveigh against you!'[126] But the power of an eloquence adapted to large-scale public assemblies was well perceived by candidates. In the aforementioned memoirs, Jules Simon says of competitor and government candidate Charles Lachaud:

> It is very hard to beat the man, he has a loud voice, bold gestures, and he beats his chest, he has physical powers that I do not possess; it is not very great eloquence, but it is very big eloquence: it has its effect.[127]

It is difficult to present oneself to electors in a large assembly, particularly if it is contradictory, without a good mastery of public speaking. Each time a candidate stammers or makes a mistake in French which is noticed by the audience, the room becomes noisy and he can no longer be heard. In a 2,000-strong assembly in the Redoute meeting room in February 1876, 'a new candidate, presented himself as sieur Parlongue, calling himself a radical republican. At one point he

---

126. APP/Ba/576/Réunions privées et publiques, 18e arr., 290 rue Marcadet: Rapport de M. Brissaud, officier de paix, cabinet, 1ᵉʳ *bureau*, police municipale, 2e brigade de recherches, 16 février 1876.

127. Simon, *Le soir de ma journée*, p. 306.

said: '*Je suis été*'. Tumult ensued, with cries from all sides of: 'Enough!'[128] The same month, in front of 800 people, the councillor general for la Seine, Emile Villeneuve, had a similar experience in Neuilly: 'At a certain point in his speech, he expresses himself badly (murmurs start in the room), he wants to continue, but the tumult became so great that the chairman, unable to re-establish order, adjourned the session'.[129] Candidates with problems expressing themselves could beg the indulgence of their audience, and point out that they were 'not an orator',[130] it is usually in vain.

The intolerance of the public calls for a certain eloquence which favours candidates accustomed to this type of public speaking, and also tends to rule out 'candidates without a sufficient militant backing to put together a decent claque'.[131] The authors of police reports never fail to find 'claqueurs' in the electoral assemblies. In an account of an assembly held in Paris in August 1889 to deal with the selection of candidates to the legislative elections, we learn that the discourses were: 'frequently applauded by a "claque" carefully disposed in the centre of the room'.[132] Must we speak of 'sufficient militant backing' or sufficient budget? Although the claque is mostly recruited from among true followers, the latter are nevertheless often recompensed in money or drink. In 1876, in Paris, François Cantagrel the elected deputy of the 13th *arrondissement* after Louis Blanc stood down[133] was accused by the members of an opposing committee, of '[giving] money to his followers to applaud him',[134] and of '[settling] the cost of anything consumed'.[135] Apart from the anecdote, the question of campaign costs must be taken into account for understanding the inequalities faced by candidates in public assemblies and the factors that rendered it necessary to create organisations supporting them.

---

128. APP/Ba/571/Réunions publiques, 1er arr., salle de la Redoute: Rapport de M. Lombard, officier de paix, préfecture de Police, police municipale, 4e brigade de recherches, 7 février 1876.

129. APP/Ba/577/Neuilly, salle Legrand: Rapport de M. Lombard, officier de paix, préfecture de Police, police municipale, 4e brigade de recherches, 29 février 1876.

130. See, for example, APP/Ba/571/Réunions publiques, 1er arr., salle de la Redoute: Rapport, police municipale, service des garnis, cabinet, 1er *bureau*, 7 février 1876; APP/Ba/571/ Réunions publiques, 1er arr., salle de la Redoute: Rapport, police municipale, service des garnis, cabinet, 1er *bureau*, 15 février 1876.

131. Michel Offerlé, *Un homme, une voix ? Histoire du suffrage universel*, Paris, Gallimard, 1993, p. 90.

132. APP/Ba/1462/1889. Élections diverses. Réunions. 7e arr.: Rapport, préfecture de Police, 2e brigade de recherches, cabinet, 1er *bureau*, 31 août 1889.

133. Arlette Schweitz, *Les parlementaires sous la Troisième République. II. Dictionnaire biographique*, Paris, Publications de la Sorbonne, 2001, pp. 127–128.

134. APP/Ba/574/Réunions privées et publiques, 13e arr., salle de la Belle Moissonneuse, 31 rue Nationale: Rapport, préfecture de Police, police municipale, service des garnis, cabinet, 1er *bureau*, 23 mars 1876.

135. APP/Ba/574/Rapport, préfecture de Police, police municipale, service des garnis, cabinet, 1er *bureau*, 19 avril 1876.

First of all, there was the cost of the meeting room. To cover this, participants were often asked to make a contribution on entry or, less frequently, when leaving. The measure was unpopular and the donation was often voluntary. However, the fact that there were people at the entrance with the double task of checking voters' documents and receiving contributions suggests that it was difficult to enter without paying anything. As a result the 'democratic obolus', as it was ironically called by the Bonapartist newspaper *Le Gaulois* on 5 February 1876, was paid regularly although the sum was rarely fixed. Even if the collection is sometimes negligible, the assembly organisers may still be in pocket. This income helped cover the cost of renting meeting rooms for other assemblies. A report on an assembly in Paris of 1876 specifies that:

> There were 1,300 entries for the income, which then rose to 325 Fr. The cost of the room is 150 Fr., perhaps 200 with the extra costs. There were 175 Fr. left at the end. This making a sum of around 400 Fr. for the organisers; who are indeed in debt for around the same sum for prior costs with the Sax meeting room.[136]

Sometimes there are the additional costs of lighting and heating, and the cost of potential damage by the audience. These are settled after the assembly, once the extent of the damage costs is known. A bill sent to Jules Ferry in June 1869 by the owners of the Pascaud gymnasium stipulated that besides 'renting the room [...] for two electoral assemblies' and the furnishings for the assembly ('carpet and platform'), Ferry should also reimburse 25 Fr. for 'a number of damaged armchairs, chairs, benches and broken window panes'.[137] The owners of meeting rooms even asked candidates for a deposit as a precaution. In January 1889, when the electoral struggle between General Boulanger and the republican candidate Jacques began in Paris, a police report noted: 'The Boulangist committees wanted to rent the Mille Colonnes hall [...] for assemblies; the owner asked 100 Fr. to cover possible damage, a condition that they did not accept'.[138] In addition to the costs linked to the meeting room, there were other costs including advertising the assembly by billposting. For the Ferry campaign in 1869 there was the cost of 500 posters which he regularly had printed and put up for each assembly.[139] Beyond the organisational tasks of advertising the assembly, finding a room, getting a claque together, and

---

136. APP/Ba/573/Réunions privées et publiques, 9e arr., salle des Folies-Montholon, rue Rochechouart: Rapport '4', 6 février 1876.

137. BM Saint-Dié/Fonds public: Facture au nom de M. Ferry des 'gymnases du Luxembourg et du Marais dirigés par M. & Mme Pascaud', Paris, 17 juin 1869. My thanks go to Michel Offerlé for having provided a copy of this bill and other documents from the same *fonds* cited here. Source: Eric Badonnel, '*Une politique expérimentale*'. *L'action politique et l'opinion publique chez Jules Ferry. Une approche locale de ses pratiques électorales*, DEA sciences sociales, ENS-EHESS, 2004.

138. APP/Ba/628/Élections 1889. 14e arr.: Rapport sur la situation électorale, commissariat de police du quartier de Montparnasse, 11 janvier 1889.

139. BM Saint-Dié/Fonds public: Facture au nom de M. Ferry de 'La Parisienne. Compagnie d'affichage et d'annonces. L. Albert & Cie, 21 rue Bergère, Paris', Paris, 31 mai 1869.

so forth, these costs made it essential for the candidate wishing to launch this type of campaign to organise an electoral committee. For Charles Benoist, the 'rising star of the moderate right'[140] at this end of nineteenth century, it was 'an essential part of the electoral mechanism'. Benoist wrote about the Paris 1898 campaign, that 'committees are necessary', that 'it is "in the order", perhaps "in the nature" of elections' to have them.[141] Committee members sometimes made a financial donation to the campaign of whoever they wanted to see elected. A letter sent on 20 March 1878 to members of the committee supporting Ferry's candidacy in the canton of Raon l'Étape, explained why expenditure had outstripped income and launched 'a new appeal to the committee's devotion to the Republican cause'.[142] Then there is the account of the republican journalist Caubet of the campaign organised for the radical republican candidate Bancel, who was standing against Émile Ollivier in the 3rd electoral district of la Seine in 1869. François-Eugène Cléray, who had been 'part of the blanquist nucleus' since 1864,[143] provided substantial funding, in particular for hiring the Châtelet Theatre. Caubet writes that: 'a large part of the money [...] paid in advance was never returned', but that Cléray was happy to 'accept this sacrifice very nobly [...] with the satisfaction of being of use to the republican cause'.[144] According to Pierre Goujon, writing about the first two decades of the Third Republic:

> If the candidature of a single person, on his own individual initiative persists, [this candidature] is no longer adapted to political life, and we see the reappearance of the committees that worked under the Second Republic; committees that the republicans are the first to [...] organise and [...] make widespread.[145]

Through the parallel between committees and electoral assemblies, we observe the tension noted by Rosanvallon between a valuation of committees capable of democratising elections concretely, by 'controlling the elected', 'allow[ing] the election to take the form of a contract', and the idea that they actually '[can] limit [popular sovereignty] *procedurally*' by proposing candidates to voters and promoting their pre-selection.[146] Studying the origins of the modern party, François Miquet-Marty recalls the new techniques of electoral mobilisation at the start of the Third Republic:

---

140. Jean-Pierre Machelon, 'La liberté d'association sous la IIIe République. Le temps du refus (1871–1901)', in Clare Andrieu, Gilles Le Béguec and Danielle Tartakowsky (eds), *Associations et champ politique. La loi de 1901 à l'épreuve du siècle*, Paris, Publications de la Sorbonne, 2001, p. 142.

141. Charles Benoist, *Souvenirs*, vol. 3, Paris, Plon, 1934, p. 8.

142. BM Saint-Dié/Fonds public.

143. *Dictionnaire biographique du mouvement ouvrier français, Le Maitron 2, 1864–1871*, CD Rom, Éditions de l'Atelier.

144. Jean-Marie-Lazare Caubet, *Souvenirs (1860–1869)*, Paris, Léopold Cerf, 1893, p. 43.

145. Pierre Goujon, *Le vigneron citoyen. Mâconnais et Chalonnais, 1848–1914*, Paris, CTHS, 1993, p. 289.

146. Rosanvallon, *La démocratie inachevée*, pp. 272–273.

The most frequent practice [...] was to create temporary committees explicitly responsible for mobilisation, generally set up after private assemblies or conferences where candidates were nominated.[147]

The committees created in private assemblies among friends and acquaintances were accused of being illegitimate if they did not demand, and obtain, the validation of their mandate in a public meeting. In the first public electoral assembly held in the 13th *arrondissement* of Paris during the February 1876 campaign, the republican Wilfrid de Fonvielle, spoke out against 'a committee [...] convened in a private assembly and not in a public, and sovereign, assembly'; a committee that had already put forward Louis Blanc as candidate. De Fonvielle argued that a new committee should be presented, chosen among the participants, in a public assembly, and who would be in a position to propose a truly democratic candidate. This was supported by several speakers. Louis Combes, municipal councillor and part of the republican opposition to the Empire,[148] held that:

> The committee was null and void, because it was not the outcome of a public meeting, and as so far there had only been private assemblies in the *arrondissement*, [...] the members appointed by these assemblies should retire before the vote of the assembled electors.

In the last instance a new committee was designated.[149] The accusations of illegitimacy made against independently formed committees were particularly strong when it was a question of socialist candidatures. In Marseilles the convenor of an assembly in February 1898 protested against the creation of 'an independent socialist committee [...] outside all public assembly'.[150]

Committees created in private assemblies before the start of the electoral period found it difficult to continue when public assemblies began to organise themselves. An 1876 police report asserts: 'with the start of the electoral period, the authorisation of public assemblies must suppress private assemblies. It is even certain that the committees chosen by private assemblies will disappear and be replaced by public assemblies'.[151] This replacement was not systematic however. A vote in a public assembly may maintain a committee convened in a private assembly. Thus, on 1 February 1876, a public assembly: 'confirms [...] in its

---

147. François Miquet-Marty, *Aux origines du parti politique moderne. Les groupes sociaux à l'épreuve du formalisme démocratique, France, 1848–1914*, PhD dissertation EHESS, 1997, pp. 38–39.
148. E. Franceschini, 'Combes (Jean-Louis)', in Jean-Charles Roman D'Amat (ed.), *Dictionnaire de biographie française*, Paris, Letouzey & Ané, vol. 9, 1993, pp. 367–368.
149. APP/Ba/574/Réunions privées et publiques, 13e arr., salle de bal du Casino d'Italie, 198 av. de Choisy: Rapport, préfecture de Police, police municipale, service des garnis, cabinet, 1er *bureau*, 3 février 1876.
150. AD BDR/1M/869/Réunions publiques, 1898, janvier–avril: Rapport du commissaire du 3e arr., 1er février 1898.
151. APP/Ba/573/Élections générales. Réunions privées, 11e arr., 129 rue de la Roquette: Rapport, 30 janvier 1876.

powers' a committee formed beforehand in a private assembly and supporting the republican candidate of the extreme left, Lockroy [Etienne Auguste Edouard Simon]. The chairman of the assembly Quentin, also a committee member and candidate in another electoral district of la Seine, opened the session expressing a desire to 'make known how the committee had been set up and what it had done':

> He said that he and some of his friends [were] concerned, with good reason, about having to provide the 17th *arrondissement* with deputies in perfect communion of ideas and feelings with voters [...], thought they could not do better than to convene a committee which would prepare the process of elections congenial to democracy beforehand.

Yet Quentin specifies that if 'the committee was thus convened of its own initiative, undoubtedly usurping powers', it was only in waiting for public assemblies: 'it has always intended to account for these powers to voters who would be called on to judge them and then reject or confirm the vote'. He then explains the reasons that induced the committee to support Lockroy. Finally, although a person in the audience reminded the platform 'that they should not impose candidates, but discuss them', the assembly '[ratified] the committee's actions' and maintained its functions.[152] It was often considered necessary to validate a committee's mandate in a public assembly as a token of its democratic character and as a condition of solid legitimacy. In 1885, at an assembly of radical groups in the suburbs of Paris, the mayor of Les Lilas affirmed 'that it [is] useful that the committee members were elected in public assembly, because 'they would have much more authority'.[153] The legitimacy of committees became more problematic when they remained entrenched after the elections.[154] Their preparatory electoral activity was sometimes criticised insofar as it usurped a part of the public's freedom of choice in pre-selecting candidates, mostly when the committees were convened beyond the control of public assemblies. But the criticism becomes much more vigorous when they 'install themselves in permanent structures'.[155]

Projecting election results

In the last three decades of the nineteenth century, political assemblies were seen as a possible mainstay for the emerging representative democracy. As we have seen, under certain conditions it helped create a public space where opinion, which complements and accompanies the vote, replaces action. The attitude towards

---

152. APP/Ba/575/Réunions privées et publiques, 17e arr., salle du bal, 133 av. de Clichy: Rapport, préfecture de Police, police municipale, service des garnis, cabinet, 1ᵉʳ *bureau*, 1 février 1876.

153. APP/Ba/614/Élections de 1885. Réunions du 8 janvier au 31 août 1885: Rapport, préfecture de Police, police municipale, 2e brigade de recherches, cabinet, 1ᵉʳ *bureau*, 7 juin 1885.

154. According to Pierre Goujon, committees 'tend to become permanent and be structured' in: Pierre Goujon, *Le vigneron citoyen. Mâconnais et Chalonnais, 1848–1914*, Paris, CTHS, 1993, p. 291.

155. Rosanvallon, *La démocratie inachevée*, p. 273.

public opinion of those who then worked to stabilise the system first took the form of mentoring work to ensure that it would be well adapted to guarantee sound support for representation. This concern with the control of public opinion not only had an impact on the way the latter was formed, but also assumed the form of a desire for knowledge, and attempt to quantify, particularly when citizens elected their representatives. Indeed assemblies are also observed in order to produce electoral forecasts. Conclusions about electoral outcomes based on the observation of meetings generate another conception of public opinion: the ideal of an opinion unified around the common good gives way to taking its divisions into account.

A prefiguration of election polls

Relations between participants and police were less conflictual than under the Empire in the 1876 electoral assemblies in Paris, even if they were then under the regimen of the 1868 law.[156] The police officer present sometimes noted in his report that he had even been well received: 'I must point out the goodwill with which I have been welcomed by the members of the *bureau* and the organisers of the assembly', wrote the police chief for the district of Arts-et-Métiers.[157] Some candidates maintained good relations with the commissioner, and the one from the neighbourhood of La Muette and Auteuil wrote of a moderate republican candidate that 'on leaving the session, M. Marmottan, approached me and holding out his hand, obviously without thinking about his entourage, said: "I believe, Monsieur police commissioner, that I have not gone too far and that I was not excessive in my language"'.[158] The commissioner, however, was also there to prevent disorder and anti-government speeches. Several reports mention warnings made to the *bureau* when the words uttered were judged offensive to the government — we will see that with the advent of increasingly frequent violence in assemblies, electoral or otherwise, tensions between police and participants tended to become animated. Yet the role of the police officer in maintaining order and supervising speeches was already combined with the task of observation, assemblies being considered the key locus of expression of the electors' opinion before the vote.

Before the establishment of 'the quasi-monopoly of the expression of public opinion by opinion polls in western democracies',[159] other ways of projecting

---

156. Alain Dalotel, Alain Faure and Jean-Claude Freiermuth, *Aux origines de la Commune. Le mouvement des réunions publiques à Paris. 1868–1870*, Paris, F. Maspero, 1980, pp. 128–136.

157. APP/Ba/572/Élections générales. Réunions publiques, 3e arr., rue des Fontaines du Temple, salle Chavagnat: Rapport, préfecture de Police, 3e arr., commissaire de police, 9 février 1876.

158. APP/Ba/575/Réunions privées et publiques, 16e arr., 106 av. du Roi de Rome: Rapport, préfecture de Police, commissaire de police, cabinet, 1er *bureau*, 6 février 1876.

159. Loïc Blondiaux, *La fabrique de l'opinion. Une histoire sociale des sondages*, Paris, Seuil, 1998, p. 9. On the genesis of electoral opinion polls, see also: Susan Herbst, 'On the Disappearance of Groups. 19th and Early 20th Century Conceptions of Public Opinion', in Theodore L. Glasser and Charles T. Salmon (eds), *Public Opinion and the Communication of Consent*, New York, The Guiford Press, 1995, pp. 89–104; and: Susan Herbst, 'Election Polling in Historical Perspective',

election results were used, including the observation of assemblies. This was one of the reasons for police surveillance at the meetings under the Republic. Susan Herbst has shown that the numbers thronging to electoral meetings in the United States was the object of sustained attention in the nineteenth century, particularly on the part of the press, since it was thought to reflect the state of public opinion. A large public is the sign announcing a candidate's victory. This gave rise to frequent disagreements between newspapers over the estimates of the numbers taking part. These diminished in the early twentieth century, with the erosion of the belief in the predictive power of the numerical weight of crowds of assemblies. First because 'in the decades following the First World War [...], it had become increasingly clear that crowds could be the results of the activity of campaign strategists; and also because of the 'growing popularity of polls".[160]

In the first decades of the Republic, it was not only the size of assemblies that concerned observers, journalists and police, since the greater part were contradictory and thus attracted supporters of different candidates. It has already been mentioned that this was not the case in the United States in the same period. Nevertheless, observers thought they were able to deduce the expected electoral outcome from monitoring meetings. Forecasts were often given at the end of reports. For example in 1876: 'I believe it will go to a ballot',[161] or 'the result of this session is that Deschanel has a better chance of success than his competitor, Ch. Quentin'.[162]

The concern with forecasting becomes more animated when electoral predictions are likely to alarm the government. This was the case during the electoral struggle in Paris in January 1889, with Boulanger vs. Édouard Jacques, republican and president of the general council of la Seine, perceived as the pinnacle of the Boulangist campaign.[163] Although Boulanger won in the end, the police observers trying to predict results often thought Jacques would be the winner. It is possible that they were trying to express their own personal desire to their superiors, rather than trying to provide a reliable prediction. A member of the commissariat in the La Chapelle district reported:

> Yesterday, an important anti-Boulangist assembly was held [...] and the name of Jacques was acclaimed. Thus, there is room to hope [...] that the candidature of Jacques will muster the most votes in my neighbourhood'.[164]

---

in Paul J. Lavrakas, Peter V. Miller and Michael W. Traugott (eds), *Presidential Polls and the News Media*, Boulder, Westview, 1995, pp. 23–33.

160. Susan Herbst, *Numbered Voices. How Opinion Polling Has Shaped American Politics*, Chicago, Chicago University Press, 1993, pp. 143–144.

161. APP/Ba/577/Asnières, 3 rue de la Station, théâtre d'Asnières: Rapport '26', 10 février 1876.

162. APP/Ba/577/Courbevoie, 3 quai de Seine: Rapport 'Jouve', 9 février 1876.

163. Bruce Fulton, 'The Boulanger Affair Revisited. The Preservation of The Third Republic', *French Historical Studies*, 1991, vol. 17, (2), p. 311; Patrick H. Hutton, 'Popular Boulangism and the Advent of Mass Politics in France, 1886–1890', *Journal of Contemporary History*, 1976, vol. 11, (1), p. 86.

164. APP/Ba/628/Élections 1889, 17e arr.: Rapport sur la situation électorale, commissariat de police, quartier de La Chapelle, 19 janvier 1889.

Police observers were not alone in trying to forecast the outcome of the struggle between the two candidates starting from the observation of public assemblies. Journalists also got involved in this type of exercise. On 26 January 1889 *Le Journal des Débats*, which had declared that it supported neither Boulanger nor Jacques, stated: 'In Paris, if we judge by public assemblies, it is always M. Jacques who holds the ropes'.[165] Then the following day: 'If [...] it was counting on the result of public assemblies, M. Jacques should have a solid majority, at least in Paris'.[166] However on 26 January a journalist also noted that caution was necessary because the public of assemblies was not representative of the electorate in general: it 'only represents a minimal part of the electorate [...] including above all freemasons and *possibilistes*'.[167]

The fact that police informers often said they lacked the means to forecast electoral winners without assemblies organised in their district is an indication of the belief that voters' opinions could be evaluated in public assemblies. This is reinforced by the admission that assemblies have an impact on voters. In the run-up to the January 1889 elections the author of a report on the districts of La Muette and Porte Dauphine notes: 'until now the population [...] has not held any assembly and we still cannot estimate the chances that one or other candidate has to become deputy'.[168] Without 'popular' assemblies it would be impossible to know who may be elected. Another report states that:

> No assembly is yet planned in the Bonne-Nouvelle district to examine the different candidates present. Thus, public opinion has not had the chance to express itself, and it would be difficult to forecast the result on 27 January at this moment.[169]

The evaluations are sometimes accompanied by an attempt to relate opinions to the voters' social class. Report writers on electoral assemblies regularly devote a few sentences to a sketch of sociological analysis of participants, largely based on their way of dressing. The worker is known by his 'smock'[170] and is 'dressed for work'.[171] Members of the well-to-do classes are recognisable because they are 'dressed very formally',[172] and '[their] bearing and clothes reveal a prominent social position

---

165. *Le Journal des Débats*, 26 January 1889.
166. *Le Journal des Débats*, 27 January 1889.
167. *Le Journal des Débats*, 26 January 1889.
168. APP/Ba/628/Élections 1889, 16e arr.: Rapport sur la situation électorale, commissariat de police, 8 janvier 1889.
169. APP/Ba/628/2e arr.: Rapport sur la situation électorale, commissariat de police, 9 janvier 1889.
170. See, for example: APP/Ba/571/Courbevoie, 3 quai de Seine: Rapport 'Jouve', 9 février 1876.
171. See, for example: APP/Ba/577/Élections générales, 3e arr. Réunions privées et publiques. 7 rue des Fontaines: Rapport, préfecture de Police, police municipale, service des garnis, cabinet, 1er *bureau*, 5 février 1876.
172. APP/Ba/577/17e arr., 7 av. de Clichy, salons Lathuile: Rapport de M. Brissaud, officier de paix, cabinet, 1er *bureau*, police municipale, 2e brigade de recherches, 6 janvier 1876.

and a large fortune'.[173] Apart from inferences drawn from clothing, the observers may know voters living in this neighbourhood, especially among the bourgeois traders, who they mention as acquaintances 'in the district'.[174] Occasionally authors of reports, not content with establishing this sort of classification, also try to correlate social status with audience opinion. This occurred from the time of the struggle between the supporters of Edouard-Camille Bonnet-Duverdier, republican intransigent,[175] and those of Eugène Spuller, republican opportunist supported by Gambetta in 1876 in the 3rd *arrondissement*.[176] The reports insist on the idea that the Chavagnat meeting room where the Bonnet-Duverdier committee organised public and often contradictory assemblies, but where the committee ensured the maximum support, generally attracted a working-class audience. The Molière meeting room, where assemblies organised by the committee supporting Spuller were normally held, would generally attract tradesmen.[177] The same type of opposition was stressed by police observers for the 18th *arrondissement* where the radical republican candidate, Clemenceau, faced the more conservative Arrault. They suggest that the working-class population favoured Clemenceau and generally attended his assemblies, which were almost always public. By contrast Arrault enjoyed the support of the wealthy bourgeoisie, who made up a large part of the audience of his assemblies, which were more frequently private than the opposition's. A telegram from a police informer reported that: '400 people, all of them notables', attended Arrault's assembly.[178] At the time of the January 1889 elections where Jacques stood against Boulanger, police reports not only tried to predict the results of the vote, but also to analyse them in terms of social groupings: 'The bourgeois element generally appears to favour the candidature of General Boulanger', declared the author of a report on two assemblies of the evening.[179]

These forecasts are not made by just any informer, there is a specialisation on the part of observers. Susan Herbst demonstrates this for the American press in the nineteenth century when newspapers sent reporters to follow meetings, and the results were published in a special column.[180] In much the same way in France, even if articles on assemblies were often unsigned or simply initialled, it is the same

---

173. APP/Ba/573/Réunions privées et publiques, 8e arr., rue d'Anjou, St-Honoré: Rapport de M. Brissaud, officier de paix, cabinet, 1er *bureau*, police municipale, 2e brigade de recherches, 13 février 1876.

174. See, for example: APP/Ba/574/Réunions privées et publiques, 13e arr., salle de bal du Casino d'Italie, 198 av. de Choisy: Rapport du commissaire de police, quartiers de Maison Blanche et Croulebarbe, cabinet, 1er *bureau*, 3 février 1876.

175. Robert and Cougny, *Dictionnaire des parlementaires français*, vol. 1, pp. 391–392.

176. Schweitz, *Les parlementaires sous la Troisième République*, pp. 546–548.

177. APP/Ba/572/Élections générales 1876. Réunions privées et publiques, 3e arr.

178. APP/Ba/576/Réunions privées et publiques, 18e arr., 'Vendanges de Bourgogne', 22 rue de Jessaint: Dépêche télégraphique 'Hamon' au chef de la police municipale, 13 février 1876.

179. APP/Ba/628/Élections 1889, 16e arr.: Rapport, commissariat de police, quartier d'Auteuil, 23 janvier 1889.

180. Herbst, *Numbered Voices*, p. 75.

names that appear regularly. Sometimes a journalist specified that he had followed several assemblies.[181] During electoral campaigns, a rubric normally groups together all the accounts under 'electoral assemblies', 'assemblies', 'electoral chronicle', etc. The articles in these columns are basically descriptive but rarely without comments, whereas more openly political editorials are generally placed separately, for example on the first page if the assembly is considered sufficiently important. The specialisation of journalists is parallel to that of police observers. Michel Offerlé describes police overseeing municipal electoral assemblies organised by the socialists between 1881 and 1900 as '"quasi-specialists" of the worker movement who "cover" one or even two assemblies a day in electoral periods',[182] and qualifies the police commissioners of the period more generally as 'experts in public opinion'.[183] Some names crop up frequently among authors of reports, if it is a question of policemen (in 1876, in Paris, those of M. Brissaud, M. Hamon, M. Lombard, M. Dresch, etc.), or of informal indicators (also in 1876 in Paris, Chaisson, Raffin, Jacquot, etc.).[184] One of the consequences of this specialisation is the routinisation of the surveillance of assemblies and report writing. Besides a certain invariability in the way reports are structured, authors also tend to formulate their reports in the same way. These sometimes suggest the weariness of the observer, tired of hearing the same speakers repeating the same speeches, the same questions and the same replies. Offerlé stresses 'the use of repetitive formulae' in police notes and 'the brevity of some transcriptions'.[185] This succinct style is sometimes pushed too far. The author of an 1876 report transcribing a candidate's speech writes simply: 'His speech was not interesting thereafter; his profession of faith is identical to that of his opponent'.[186] Sometimes, the content of a speech is not even mentioned. At the end of the report on an assembly in support of Louis Blanc in 1876, the police simply wrote: 'After other worthless interventions by various speakers, the chairman recommended that [...]'.[187] This specialisation and routinisation of work reverting regularly to the same agents favoured the building up of a 'practical knowledge of forecasting'.[188]

---

181. See, for example: H.C., 'IXe arrondissement, salle de Folies-Montholon', *Le Gaulois*, 8 February 1876.

182. Michel Offerlé, *Les socialistes et Paris, 1881–1900, des communards aux conseillers municipaux*, PhD dissertation, Paris I, 1979, p. 10.

183. Michel Offerlé, 'De l'histoire électorale à la socio-histoire des électeurs', *Romantisme*, 2007, vol. 135, p. 64.

184. On the distinctions between types of police see: Jean-Marc Berlière, *Le monde des polices en France. XIXe–XXe siècles*, Brussels, Complexe, 1996, pp. 15–39.

185. Offerlé, *Les socialistes*, p. 10.

186. APP/Ba/572/Élections générales, 3e arr., réunions privées et publiques, 7 rue des Fontaines: Rapport, préfecture de Police, police municipale, service des garnis, cabinet, 1er bureau, 6 février 1876.

187. APP/Ba/572/5e arr., Vieux Chêne, 69 rue Mouffetard: Rapport, préfecture de Police, police municipale, service des garnis, cabinet, 1er bureau, 10 février 1876.

188. Éric Phélippeau, 'Conjonctures électorales et conjectures préfectorales. Le vote et la formation d'un savoir politico-administratif', *Scalpel*, 1994, vol.1, p. 57.

From police observation to political forecasting

Researchers have argued that administrative or police reports should be considered not only as sources of information, but also as objects in their own right. Pierre Karila-Cohen insists on the dissimilarity between administrative reports, and 'traditional police accounts'. The former are more complex than the latter, and give more room for in-depth analysis of the political situation; 'not [content] with stating facts or listing events'.[189] It is still possible and necessary to observe how the police reports analyse the reality facing them and the way they recount it. If I use reports as a vital source of information on the way assemblies are conducted, it is also important to take into account the way in which assemblies are analysed in the reports. In particular, we must examine how observers of assemblies evaluate the public approval of a given candidate. Since electoral assemblies are generally public and contradictory, this cannot simply be a question of counting heads. Certainly, there are also private electoral assemblies, but in general their reports do not contain forecasts of future polls, with the exception of cases where assemblies are declared private, but where there are so many invitations that the difference from a public assembly is ridiculous. Normally, forecasts are based on the observation of public assemblies which are considered to be more representative of the electorate than their private equivalents. As we have seen, observers wait for the start of the electoral campaign before making their first projections.

Estimations are not based merely on the progress of electoral assemblies *per se*. They are also inferred from what is said before the assembly, when participants queue in the street waiting to enter the meeting room. Some formulations appear in many different reports, and are the same when dealing with the same author or very similar when authors are different. For example, for the February 1876 Paris elections, reports specify the number of people waiting at the door around half an hour before it opens — often at around 100–200 people. The observers note that participants are naturally talking about the elections among themselves: 'Candidates' chances were discussed';[190] 'the conversations revolve around the

---

189. Pierre Karila-Cohen, '*L'État des esprits*'. *L'administration et l'observation de l'opinion départementale en France sous la monarchie constitutionnelle (1814–1848)*, PhD dissertation, Paris I, 2003, p. 17. This concept of reports as objects, notes Karila-Cohen, is used in other works. See, for instance those of Marie-Noëlle Bourguet, Alain Corbin or Éric Phélippeau: Marie-Noëlle Bourguet, *Déchiffrer la France: la statistique départementale à l'époque contemporaine*, Paris, Edition des Archives contemporaines, 1989; Alain Corbin, *Le monde retrouvé de Louis-François Pinagot: sur les traces d'un inconnu, 1798–1876*, Paris, Flammarion, 2002; Eric Phelippeau, 'La fabrication administrative des opinions politiques: votes, déclarations de candidature et verdict des préfets (1852–1914)', *Revue française de science politique*, 1993, vol. 43, (4), pp. 587–612.

190. APP/Ba/572/Élections générales, 3e arr., réunions privées et publiques. Salle Molière, rue St-Martin: Rapport, préfecture de Police, police municipale, service des garnis, cabinet, 1ᵉʳ *bureau*, 17 février 1876.

elections';[191] 'It dealt with the candidacy of [...]'.[192] Report writers often point out the relative agreement among those taking part in such discussions: 'there is general agreement that [...]';[193] 'the major part felt that [...] was the only candidate with a good chance of being elected'.[194] Indeed, were this not the case, the authors could not draw conclusions about voters' states of mind likely to apply to an entire electoral district. The police also take what is said on leaving assemblies as an indication of voter opinion. A report of February 1876 on a public assembly in Asnières states that on leaving:

> Those for Deschanel think him a good speaker; those for Quentin welcome his political ideas. In short, I believe there will be a second ballot as long as ideas are as much divided in the other communes.[195]

Analysis of these conversations, before or after an assembly, does not always lead to general conclusions regarding the projected outcome. Yet the simple fact that the opinions of the public are reported and that moreover the absence of divisions among participants is generally stressed, suggests that the belief that one can indeed detect an indicator of opinion in assemblies is fairly widespread.

With regards to the observation of assemblies, forecasts can be based on the votes made at the end in support of one or another candidate. They allow the observer to count the supporters of each candidate in a mixed audience. These votes, however, did not always take place, and police observers did not generally seem to take their results as a direct expression of the distribution of voters' opinions. Sometimes they are also freely interpreted and taken as an indication of a candidate's popularity, or as the simple expression of the fact that the assembly had been prepared beforehand by his supporters. The two approaches may even come from the same pen. This was the case for the 'electoral situation' of January 1889 based on two public electoral assemblies held in the evening and achieved by a vote on the candidatures of two contestants, Jacques and Boulanger. The commissioner wrote about the first of these two assemblies:

> Sr. Martin, keen to know the opinion of the audience, has invited those supporting M. Jacques to identify themselves. Some hands went up. The Boulangists were subjected to the same test and a large part of the audience raised their hands.

---

191. APP/Ba/571/2e arr., réunions publiques. Salle Molière: Rapport de M. Brissaud, officier de paix, cabinet 1er *bureau*, police municipale, 2e brigade de recherches, 6 février 1876.

192. APP/Ba/572/Élections générales, 3e arr., réunions privées et publiques, 7 rue des Fontaines: Rapport, préfecture de Police, police municipale, service des garnis, cabinet, 1er *bureau*, 16 février 1876.

193. APP/Ba/572/Salle Molière, rue St-Martin: Rapport, préfecture de Police, police municipale, service des garnis, cabinet, 1er *bureau*, 19 février 1876.

194. APP/Ba/574/Réunions privées et publiques, 15e arr., salle Ragache: Rapport, préfecture de Police, police municipale, service des garnis, cabinet, 1er *bureau*, 15 février 1876.

195. APP/Ba/577/Asnières, 3 rue de la Station, théâtre d'Asnières: Rapport '26', 10 février 1876.

The report writer concluded that 'there is no doubt, it was a Boulangist' assembly. On the second assembly he wrote that: 'a resolution in favour of M. Jacques was voted almost unanimously' and specified that 'the second assembly was as large as the first'. The overall evaluation of the author was that: 'I am, in any case, justified in believing that M. Jacques will prevail over his contestant in the district of Pont de Flandre'.[196]

The public responses to the speeches delivered by the candidates also help guide observers when sounding the opinion of the assembled voters. Reports mention who is the most acclaimed candidate, generally with a mix of shouts and applause. This sort of interjection is mentioned throughout reports whenever it interrupts passages of speeches or is directed to the speaker at the end of the assembly. The police also try to reach a general conclusion at the end of the report. This is the case, for example, for the surveillance of the assemblies presented by the police as a sign of Blanc's probable success in 1876: 'All in all, the candidature of M. Louis Blanc was acclaimed with cheering and applause';[197] 'After all, Blanc's candidacy was acclaimed by around 200 people'.[198] Sometimes, the observer does not stop at the mention of the applause received by a candidate, and goes on to give a description of their style. The 'warm' and 'enthusiastic' nature of applause for a candidate is thus emphasised to predict the probability of their success in the elections. In 1885, a public assembly was organised in La Ciotat to hear conservative candidates, but the only one present was M. Guigou whose 'line of attack', wrote a police observer, 'is to criticise all government action'. After Guigou's first speech — there is no mention of whether or not he was applauded — Camille Pelletan, candidate in the radical list in Bouches-du-Rhône, enters the room and mounts the platform. When Pelletan leaves the platform, the reporter notes that it is 'in the midst of warm applause, showing how the monarchist party was for ever doomed in La Ciotat'.[199] By contrast, when a reporter wants to minimise the applause received by a candidate, he stresses that it is lukewarm: 'As the meeting was made up almost entirely of Boulangists, speakers were naturally applauded; but the applause was subdued and lacked enthusiasm', runs an 1889 account of a Parisian assembly at the Pascaud gymnasium.[200]

Interruptions of all sorts come from the floor and are another indicator that catches reporters' attention. Noise was the norm in assemblies, and sometimes

---

196. APP/Ba/628/Élections 1889, 19e arr.: Rapport sur la situation électorale, commissariat de police, quartier du Pont-de-Flandre, 20 janvier 1889.

197. APP/Ba/572/Élections générales. Réunions publiques. 5e arr., Vieux Chêne, 69 rue Mouffetard: Rapport, préfecture de Police, police municipale, service des garnis, cabinet, 1er *bureau*, 10 février 1876.

198. APP/Ba/573/Réunions privées et publiques, 7e arr., 163 rue de l'Université: Rapport, préfecture de Police, police municipale, service des garnis, cabinet, 1er *bureau*, 11 février 1876.

199. AD BDR/1M/865/Partis et mouvements politiques. Réunions et associations. 1885: Rapport du commissaire de police au préfet, La Ciotat, 3 septembre 1885.

200. APP/Ba/1462/1889. Élections diverses. Réunions. 6e arr.: Rapport, préfecture de Police, 2e brigade de recherches, cabinet, 1er *bureau*, 5 octobre 1889.

reached a level where a candidate had difficulty ending his speech. A police officer may have deduced that the candidate had little chance of being elected. If this treatment was reserved for all candidates the assembly would be described as 'stormy' and no conclusions would be drawn. If a speech is heard and the assembly is calm, the observer may instead infer that the candidate knows how to 'catch voter attention'.[201] At a public assembly in Marseilles in 1898 a reporter noted that the 'moderate republican programme' of a candidate was heard 'in the most perfect calm'.[202] This type of interpretation becomes progressively rarer with the growth of obstructive practices at the end of the century, which, as we shall see, tends to become systematic and to encourage candidates to attend only assemblies where entry is controlled in order to avoid the presence of activists supporting an opponent.

Observing how prefects carried out the task of forecasting electoral results from 1852 to 1914, Éric Phélippeau emphasises that we need to take account of the specific nature of their position:

> The precision or imprecision is related to the fact that it is an occasion for the prefect to make the most of himself before his hierarchical authority and [...] as a consequence this says at least as much about the art of making the most of oneself as about the art of evaluation.[203]

Police reports on assemblies are not immune to this phenomenon. Their authors are tempted to minimise any sign that may displease the government. First, observers want to demonstrate that they are doing their job well and that the public order is not at risk in the assemblies where they are present. Wherever possible the *modus operandi* of the police is to highlight the calm which had characterised the progress of the assembly (for example: 'there wasn't the least disorder, the least agitation'),[204] or what occurs on the way out ('everyone in the assembly left perfectly calmly').[205] However this emphasis on the order maintained does not directly influence how observers exercise their predictive expertise in electoral matters. If the forecasts that can be drawn from an assembly are likely to indicate opposition to government, police observers may stress that the public is unrepresentative, but this is rather unusual. Let me take the example of two reports

---

201. APP/Ba/575/Réunions privées et publiques, 17e arr., salon de l'Etoile, 41 av. de Wagram: Rapport, préfecture de Police, police municipale, service des garnis, cabinet, 1er *bureau*, 2 février 1876.

202. AD BDR/1M/870/Partis et mouvements politiques. Réunions publiques 1898–1899: Rapport du commissaire de police du 6e arr. au commissaire central, 30 avril 1898.

203. Phélippeau, 'Conjonctures électorales', p. 62. See also Pierre Karila-Cohen, '*L'État des esprits'. L'administration et l'observation de l'opinion départementale en France sous la monarchie constitutionnelle (1814–1848)*, PhD dissertation, Paris I, 2003, pp. 538–549.

204. APP/Ba/577/Clichy, 37 route de la révolte, Saint-Ouen: Rapport, commissariat de police, cabinet, 1er *bureau*, 9 février 1876.

205. AD BDR/1M/866/Réunions publiques, associations, 1893: Rapport du commissaire de police au commissaire central, Marseille, 19e arr., 12 août 1893.

by the same commissioner to the prefect of Bouches-du-Rhône in 1885. In Salon on 22 March, a royalist assembly — we do not know whether it was public or not — went ahead peacefully. The report states that 'the speaker heaped responsibility on the Republic and government for all France's ills'. The 1,200-strong assembly could have been a worrying indication of the opinions of the city's electorate, but the commissioner specified that 'there is reason to believe that at least 400 are from the commune of Pellissanne, known for its links with the reactionary party, and whose voters went to Salon', and more generally a certain number of 'legitimist voters' outside the commune who had made the journey for the assembly. 'As for the city of Salon, where there are 2,000 voters, all good republicans, standing firm with the government, we can rest assured that this propaganda left them completely cold'.[206] On 23 September several republican candidates presented their programme at an assembly in Tarascon with only 200 people present. In the second report the same commissioner softens the negative inferences that can be drawn from this meagre public, claiming again that this was not representative of the population at large:

> The reluctance shown by voters in attending this public assembly could well make us suppose, if one did not know the spirit of the population, that the democratic party has lost much in this canton capital [...]; however, this is not exactly true, since we know that even if there are many monarchists in the city, the republicans are still in a majority, and the result of the vote will prove it quite adequately.[207]

With the exception of these few cases where their representativeness is challenged, participants in assemblies are generally considered an incarnation of the electorate. Firstly, because candidates must present themselves at citizens' meetings, and because of the legitimate nature of the decisions taken by them when the assembly is public. Secondly, because all electoral forecasts made by the police or the press are based on the observation of these assemblies.

---

206. AD BDR/1M/865/Partis et mouvements politiques. Réunions et associations. 1885: Rapport du commissaire spécial au préfet, Tarascon, 24 mars 1885.
207. AD BDR/1M/865/Partis et mouvements politiques. Réunions et associations. 1885: Rapport du commissaire spécial au préfet, Tarascon, 23 septembre 1885.

Part II
Setbacks in Republican Pedagogy

Chapter Four

Making a People of Citizens

At first, assemblies were held with a certain sense of decency: we had to take off our hats; but then they were *democratised*, and in the month of September, one could attend keeping one's hat on, and sometimes we could also smoke. The tone of speakers had changed as had the way of dressing.[1]

These are the words of the original copy of *Observations sur la pratique de la loi du 6 juin 1868*, the report of September 1875 on the 'impact of the 1868 law on public assemblies'. It is signed by Fontaine, one of the heads of the municipal police in Paris, and commissioned by the police prefect, Renault.[2] In the second copy of the same report, almost identical to the first, both handwritten, the word 'democratised' has been replaced with 'demoralised'.[3] There is no way of knowing whether or not the change is intentional. It may simply be the result of a moment's distraction, understandable given the hundreds of pages to be copied word for word. Yet, linking the *democratisation* of assemblies and their *demoralisation* is peculiar when we know that the aim of the report is to demonstrate that:

As it stands, the law of 6 June 1868 is impossible to practice and by reshaping it, we would vainly seek to make anything else than the most powerful and most dangerous weapon to be left in the hands of the People.[4]

This conclusion that popular meetings are places where men inevitably behave badly is constantly reflected in the way that assemblies are reported in the closing years of the Empire. The republican concept of freedom of assembly is precisely the opposite. The potential of the deliberative ideal in the republican discourse at the end of the nineteenth century makes the assembly an opportunity for men to become citizens. In 1869 Émile Faure and Anatole Fontaine de Rambouillet, lawyers critical of the 1868 imperial legislation, already referred to, considered freedom of assembly to debate political issues as one of the 'conditions of the People's greatness'.[5] Freedom of assembly focuses on public issues, and helps distance men from their particularistic interests. Above all by taking part in debates where reason-based arguments are the main way to persuade, men learn to control

---

1. The italics are the author's emphasis.
2. APP/Ba/1520.
3. BHVP/Na/155. There are other differences, but they are rare and trivial.
4. Texts are cited as found in the report kept in the Archives of the préfecture de Police.
5. Émile Faure and Anatole Fontaine de Rambouillet, *Le peuple et la place publique. Historique du droit de réunion*, Paris, Décembre-Alonnier, 1869, p. 204.

their attitudes and emotions, true to the rules of republican civility essential for the smooth progress of assemblies. In this way our allegedly virtuous voter is expected: 'to adapt to a mode of political expression consisting of decency and reserve'.[6] We find something of this in today's debate on deliberative democracy with its ability to 'renew citizenship'.[7] First, because deliberating on political issues allows those taking part to preserve or create a taste for political life. Second because deliberative democracy would constitute a potential 'school of democracy'[8] where men could become citizens through apprenticeship in a reasoned debate on public issues. This didactic 'expectation' of democratic debate is 'one of the *leitmotivs* of the literature on deliberation'.[9]

As a *locus* of civic apprenticeship the assembly should generate a virtuous circle: taking part in debate in assemblies makes men better citizens, and better citizens are more capable of taking part judiciously in debate in assemblies. This was the argument long used by republicans faced with the disorder, intolerance and violent language in assemblies at the end of the nineteenth century. The formative role of the assembly was thus emphasised not only as a place to observe whether the standards stipulated for civic behaviour have a real effect in practice. For republicans the political assembly was also an opportunity to learn how to behave as a citizen, rather than simply learning how to apply norms and values acquired elsewhere. This discourse became difficult to maintain from the early 1890s. Certainly, the 'demopedic fervour' of the republicans 'lasted for over twenty years, from the 1880s to the 1900s';[10] but the role assigned to political assemblies in this process of 'citizens' education' had a briefer existence.

It is first a question of exploring the reform of popular mores through the practice of free assemblies. Republican comments on assemblies held under the Empire and the first years of the Republic focus on the civic immaturity of the People. The criticism of immaturity allows them 'to bridge the gap between voting and expected behaviour',[11] but also between the practice of assemblies and the valorisation of deliberation in citizens' meetings. The noise, interruptions, disorder and expression of extreme opinions are not necessarily denied. They

---

6. Yves Déloye, 'Des incidents électoraux. Éléments pour une autre histoire du suffrage électoral', in Mathias Bernard, Phillipe Bourdin and Jean-Claude Caron (eds), *L'incident électoral de la Révolution française à la Ve République*, Clermont-Ferrand, Presses Universitaires Blaise Pascal, 2002, p. 30.

7. Bruce Ackerman and James Fishkin, 'Deliberation Day', in James Fishkin and Peter Laslett (eds), *Debating Deliberative Democracy*, Oxford, Blackwell, 2003, p. 9.

8. On this question, see for example: Julien Talpin, 'Jouer les bons citoyens. Les effets contrastés de l'engagement au sein de dispositifs participatifs', *Politix*, 2006, vol. 19, (75), pp. 13–31.

9. Loïc Blondiaux, 'Démocratie participative et démocratie délibérative. Une lecture critique', University of Quebec, Montreal, November 2004, http://www.chaire-mcd.ca/publications/conferences/Blondiaux-confl-November-2004.pdf, p. 14 (accessed 6 June 2006).

10. Pierre Rosanvallon, *Le sacre du citoyen. Histoire du suffrage universel en France*, Paris, Gallimard, 1992, p. 470.

11. Rosanvallon, *Le sacre du citoyen*, p. 460.

are however, seen as a lack of maturity among men whose nature is sound, but who have suffered from being bullied for expressing their opinions. If behaviour in the early assemblies was not perfect, there was no need for alarm, since men could learn. Raymond Huard revealed the existence of these distinct images of the People in nineteenth-century republican thought 'that inspired by an explicit or diffuse Rousseauism of a basically virtuous People [...] which thus detains in some way the political truth', and he adds:

> In some respects [republican leaders] share the idea of a deviant People, but do not attribute the cause of this deviance to a basic inaptitude. Bad institutions, a past of wretchedness and subjection, and insufficient instruction alone are to blame. This suggests the idea that the specific nature of popular behaviour proceeds from this interim stage which will be outdated in the future Republic thanks to educating the People and to social transformations under republican government. But there is no doubt that republican institutions will help consolidate what is best in the People, its primitive virtues hitherto stifled or distorted.[12]

When it comes to the link between the act of voting and the apprenticeship in civic wisdom, Yves Déloye stresses that: '"the good voter" is supposed to distance himself not only from his particular interests, but also from his impulses and emotions'. The 'self-discipline of citizens' means how far citizens are capable of 'moderating behaviour', particularly by controlling passions.[13] This mastering of extreme emotions is a key element in the republican mission to 'make politics enter the age of reason'.[14] This does not mean, however, that emotions are banned from the public sphere. They have their place on condition that they take a form compatible with the dignity expected of citizens.

Discovering freedom and reforming mores

During legislative debates on freedom of assembly the reference to political mores was as important for those who distrusted this right as for those supporting a broad freedom of assembly. There are basic differences between these positions as to what should be understood by the term 'mores' and the relationship between mores and rights.[15] The idea that 'by law, human will is capable of rationalising

---

12. Raymond Huard, 'Existe-t-il une "politique populaire"?', in Jean Nicolas (ed.), *Mouvements populaires et conscience sociale. XVIe–XIXe siècles*, Paris, CNRS, Université de Paris VII, Maloine, 1985, p. 58.
13. Yves Déloye, *Sociologie historique du politique*, Paris, La Découverte, 1997, pp. 103–104.
14. Rosanvallon, *Le sacre du citoyen*, p. 479.
15. Without going back to the general question of the relation between rights and mores — should rights adapt to mores or mores to rights? — see: Denis Alland, 'Les mœurs sont-elles solubles dans le droit?', *Droits*, 1994, vol. 19, pp. 3–9; Raymond Boudon, 'Penser la relation entre le droit et les mœurs', *L'avenir du droit. Mélanges en hommage à François Terré*, Paris, Dalloz, PUF, 1999, pp. 11–24; Danièle Lochak, 'Le droit à l'épreuve des bonnes mœurs. Puissance et impuissance de la norme juridique', in *Les bonnes mœurs*, Paris, PUF, 1994, pp. 15–53.

rights, and rights are able to transform mores',[16] is at the heart of the project to educate citizens through taking part in assemblies. The republican discourse is based on the conviction that the evolution of mores is inevitable not only through education, but also through the practice of freedom partly directed by the law. The People are undoubtedly immature, but will not remain so for long, provided they are well guided, learn good democratic habits and relinquish those acquired under an authoritarian regime.

'In the process of setting themselves up, and in order to last, republican institutions need republican mores',[17] wrote Jules Barni in 1872 in his *Manuel républicain*. The book was 'commissioned' by Gambetta in 1870 and is representative of the theoretical work of republicans at the end of the Empire and during the installation of the Republic.[18] 'There is no long-lasting republic worthy of the name without mores of freedom', Barni added later.[19] These republican habits in the shape of free mores are built up, Barni insists, through instruction: it is the 'duty [of any truly republican government] to establish and maintain a vast system of public instruction'. Yet this only produces results in the long-run, and when complemented by a moral education. Republican institutions contribute to this process because they 'contain their own moralising virtue'.[20] The political assembly has a central place among these institutions, alongside instruction, in the reform of public mores.

Believing in the progress of political habits

Under the Second Empire, those demanding true freedom of assembly based their arguments on the English case, where the People were not suspect in any way and where citizens could meet freely to discuss public issues. In response, the promoters of the draft law affirmed, in the Legislative Body or in the press, that the English model of assembly was not applicable to France due to the difference between political mores in the two countries. 'Is the character of the two Peoples not […] different?' asked Pinard on 18 March 1868.[21] The first distinctive element of British mores was a 'respect for the law that we do not have', stated the Minister of the Interior. In a series of letters on British and French political mores published

---

16. Jean Carbonnier, *Essais sur les lois*, Paris, Répertoire du notariat Defrénois, 1979, p. 213, and cited in Irène Théry, 'Le droit et les mœurs, un enjeu politique. La refonte du code civil et le paradoxe de la situation française', *L'Année sociologique*, 1993, vol. 43, p. 111.
17. Jules Barni, *Manuel républicain*, Paris, Germer-Baillière, 1872, p. 97.
18. Serge Audier, *Les théories de la république*, Paris, La Découverte, 2004, pp. 54–55; Mirelle Gueissaz, 'Jules Barni (1818–1878) ou l'entreprise démopédique d'un républicain moraliste et libre-penseur', in *Les bonnes mœurs*, Paris, PUF, 1994, p. 237.
19. Barni, *Manuel républicain*, p. 103.
20. Jules Barni, *Ce que doit être la République*, Publication de l'Union Républicaine de la Somme, no. 1, 1872, (3rd edn.), pp. 11, 19–20. The texts take up the developments reported in the *Manuel Républicain*.
21. *Le Moniteur Universel*, 19 March 1868, p. 414.

in September 1868 in *Le Constitutionnel* the imperialist writer Fernand Giraudeau stated that in England 'the law is sacred. There is no problem enforcing it, it works, so to speak, by itself'.[22] The assumption being that in France we find the precise opposite:

> Do we respect the law? Alas, *Monsieur*, in our country, the law is the thing that is least respected. It is enough to prohibit something for all Frenchmen to have an immediate and compelling urge to do it.[23]

Moreover, unlike the French, the English 'respect the police', affirms Pinard, and 'faced with a constable's white baton the docility of the crowd is proverbial', writes Giraudeau.[24] Another difference stressed is that the English have a practical sense in comparison to the French, who have developed a taste for theories and abstract issues. Above all it is moderation and preference for reform rather than revolution that distinguishes the British from the French. The British had 'the patience to wait [...] peacefully for reform', declared Pinard, and 'pursue their aims only through lawful and regular ways, [and] never snatches anything', affirmed Giraudeau.[25] In general, the French are portrayed as being inclined to passion. 'One knows [their] character is easily inflamed', declared Jean-Baptiste Josseau, a member of the commission which established the draft of the 1868 law.[26] It is a question of two national stereotypes whose traits had been magnified and whose differences took precedence over their similarities.[27]

This discourse ends with the insistence on the entrenched nature of these differences in mores. There is nothing contingent about it, peculiar to a period. The term 'mores', here, is similar to that of race. 'For 2,000 years, we have been inconstant, unsteady, and incapable of sustained effort. For 2,000 years we could not be corrected: so sturdy defects are [...] defects of race, organic defects, defects which are more or less incurable', wrote Giraudeau.[28] This type of rhetoric sometimes acknowledged that the troubled mores of the French were also a product of tradition and history. It is argued that these are simply too deep-rooted to be changed with the help of rights. It is the law that must adapt to mores, not in the sense that it should follow their development, but that it should take account

---

22. Fernand Giraudeau, 'Nos mœurs politiques. Lettre II. Les mœurs de l'Angleterre', *Le Constitutionnel*, 3 September 1868.
23. Giraudeau, 'Nos mœurs politiques. Lettre V. Les mœurs de la France', *Le Constitutionnel*, 9 September 1868.
24. Giraudeau, 'Nos mœurs politiques. Lettre II'.
25. Giraudeau, 'Nos mœurs politiques. Lettre II'.
26. *Le Moniteur Universel*, 17 March 1868, p. 399.
27. On the definition and use of national stereotypes, see: Sylvaine Marandon, 'Français et Juifs dans la conscience anglaise', in Jean Pirotte (ed.), *Stéréotypes nationaux et préjugés raciaux aux XIXe et XXe siècles. Sources et méthodes pour une approche historique*, Louvain-la-Neuve, Collège Erasme / Leuven, Nauwelaerts, 1982, p. 4.
28. Giraudeau, 'Nos mœurs politiques. Lettre V'.

of the passionate character of the French, and prevent these bad habits from being expressed and disturbing public order. This means that freedom of political assembly is not feasible. The French are not the English, and therefore cannot benefit from a similar freedom. 'We make laws for France', declared Peyrusse on 14 March 1868;[29] 'freedom is something relative measured against the conditions of each People's and has to adapt to mores of a country and the constraints of public order'.[30]

On the contrary, under the Empire, republicans' reference to French mores and to their comparison with those found elsewhere rests on a proclaimed optimism regarding their ability to adapt to a regimen of freedom, and particularly by the action of rights and thus the laws of the country. It is a different notion of mores. The latter are more of an acquired habit, and can be modified by apprenticeship in a new form of behaviour, rather than being consolidated features that one can only observe, boast of or deplore. On 1 December 1868 the influential editor of *Le Temps*, Edmond Scherer, denounced the theory aiming 'to show that the government under which France lives at present is the only one of which it is worthy or capable'. For Scherer, the distinction between mores and institutions is 'a logical abstraction', because the two are in fact linked. 'Will the introduction of universal suffrage not direct us towards changes [to political habits in France]?'[31] he asks by way of example.

It is significant that neither the debates in the Legislative Body nor the articles in the republican press on the rights and practice of assemblies claim that the behaviour of the Anglo-Saxons and the French are inherently different. The example of Britain is used to show that freedom of assembly and public order are reconcilable. Arguing against those who defend a system of order based on prevention, Scherer states: 'it is enough to look beyond our borders to find examples of total freedom, compatible with full security'.[32] *Le Temps* contains several accounts of open-air British meetings with tens of thousands present, all of which went off peacefully. The difference between the two countries is presented as a difference of institutions rather than popular temperament. Cucheval-Clarigny wrote in a liberal newspaper: 'Our political mores are not as bad as some would like us to believe', and 'with a part of mores, we must also take into account institutions'.[33] On the other side of the Channel or the Atlantic, things did not always go perfectly and assemblies could also develop trouble. When this is mentioned in France, it is to show that the liberal system elsewhere did not necessarily collapse for this reason, and that these problems did not have serious consequences either for order or for freedom. *Le Siècle* argues that the example of what happens where assemblies are free suggests that 'facts rather than words

---

29. *Le Moniteur Universel*, 15 March 1868, p. 388.
30. *Le Constitutionnel*, 6 September 1868.
31. *Le Temps*, 1 December 1868.
32. *Le Temps*, 30 March 1862.
33. *La Presse*, 10 December 1868.

show that freedom remains the best guarantee of order among all Peoples and all States'.[34] From this perspective, the comparison between French and Anglo-Saxon mores, to show the inability of the French to live under a regimen of freedom comparable to those found elsewhere, is simply inappropriate.

Comments in the liberal press on the first assemblies held under the 1868 legal provisions often suggest that the perfect compatibility between the nature of the French People and the exercise of freedom of assembly had been tested, and that the French would quickly behave as worthy citizens. According to *La Presse*:

> [With] the law on public assemblies enforced in Paris, immediately after its proclamation, a rather large number of assemblies, dealing with very different subjects, had already been held: none has caused the least disorder.[35]

Other newspapers, such as *Le Siècle*, repeatedly praise the exemplary behaviour of the participants: 'With its admirable instinct, the people of Paris understood the importance and the decisive nature of the test attempted at the moment. Perfect order, calm and restraint reigned everywhere', writes Louis Jourdan, a chief political editor.[36] And he adds: 'citizens feel that they regain possession of an inalienable right, and prove themselves worthy of freedom'. Anatole de la Forge, another editor of *Le Siècle*, writes that 'everything went off calmly with propriety and dignity' in public assemblies in Paris and that 'some learn to listen (a rare quality), while others try the apprenticeship of the word'.[37]

However the republican discourse on the need for the People to serve an apprenticeship of freedom developed rapidly, especially from autumn 1868 with the monopolisation of public assemblies by the extreme left.[38] It is not that the French, on account of their temperament, were unsuited for life under a regime of political freedom, but simply that they had not yet acquired the necessary maturity to prevent freedom from leading to disorder. This was because they had lived for so long under a regime prohibiting this apprenticeship. In January 1869, Édouard Laboulaye, a great admirer of the American Republic[39] and defender of a liberal Republic under the Empire, particularly in his many lectures, opened a meeting he was chairing with a speech on the exercise of freedom of assembly:

---

34. *Le Siècle*, 21 September 1868.
35. *La Presse*, 2 August 1868.
36. *Le Siècle*, 28 July 1868.
37. *Le Siècle*, 3 August 1868.
38. On this evolution, see: Robert D. Wolfe, *The Origins of the Paris Commune. The Popular Organizations of 1868–1871*, PhD dissertation, Cambridge MA, Harvard University, 1966, pp. 41–49, and Dalotel, Faure and Freiermuth, *Aux origines de la Commune*, pp. 34–35.
39. Édouard René Lefèbvre de Laboulaye inspired the idea to offer the United States a statue representing freedom, the so-called 'La Liberté éclairant le monde'.

A recent law has restored the right of assembly. It is said that the first exercise of this new freedom has been accompanied by ferment and confusion. I would hardly be surprised were it true. A People to whom freedom is rendered is like a sick man long confined when exposed to fresh air. The first day, it goes to his head.[40]

The mores did not seem as flawless as the first meetings had led to be expected, because the French had developed bad habits in seeing their options of political expression compressed by the Empire. Suddenly, the People were unsettled by freedom and did not know immediately how to behave. Mores are nothing other than habits. According to *Le Siècle* on 10 September 1868:

> The years that have elapsed [...] were unable to train us in this necessary practice [of freedom], and the generation which grew up in the midst of this long silence needs [...] to be familiarised with public life with its rights and obligations.

This insistence on the immaturity of the public does not only focus on disorders in meetings. It also allows republicans to react to the progressive socialist monopoly of public reunions, to explain the echo of revolutionary theories. These 'unfortunate exaggerations', wrote Rousselle and Limousin in their *Manuel des réunions*, occur because: 'we have lost the habit of free discussion and common action'. Under a regimen of freedom, 'our civic education would have been realised', and 'the surest and most judicious conquests are those won slowly and with wisdom'.[41] In early 1869 it was often repeated that there was no need for alarm, because the recurring practice of assemblies would allow the People to learn the mores of freedom. In the words of Charles Delescluze:

> That restraint was lacking, that discipline has not been faultless, that inexperience or introversion of the largest number made speaking the privilege of a few, all this may be true. Yet we know that the best things have difficult beginnings, that everything requires an apprenticeship.[42]

As soon as the lungs are accustomed to fresh air, 'breathing will become calmer and more regular'.[43] The first effects of this apprenticeship would soon be apparent. From this perspective the institutions could thus exert a binding force. It was no longer a question of simple prohibition in order to prevent, in the name of safeguarding public order, in a country whose mores were not adapted to a free political life. Instead, it meant regulating popular participation in public life in order to encourage the development of civil mores.

---

40. *Le Journal des Débats*, 14 January 1869.
41. André Rousselle and Charles Limousin, *Manuel des réunions publiques non politiques, publiques électorales, électorales privées*, Paris, A. Le Chevalier, 1869, p. 10.
42. *Le Réveil*, 23 January 1869.
43. *Le Siècle*, 22 February 1869.

This discourse was maintained and became better defined at the start of the Third Republic. In the debate on the adoption of the 1881 law we can detect two positions in the republican camp, around a cleavage discussed previously. In the first, the supporters of absolute freedom rejected any reference to a difference between the mores of the French and those of the English or Americans, as a way to justify regulating participation in assemblies. 'We are not looking for imaginary differences to excuse us for not having known how to be free. Human nature is the same everywhere', declared Louis Blanc on 26 January 1880.[44] They also denied that the law had the legitimate authority to train good citizens that the Republic would govern: what they wanted was absolute freedom, after which the mores would follow automatically. 'Children learn to walk by walking, and People learn to be free by practicing freedom', said Blanc two days earlier.[45] Note the parallel, not necessarily intentional, between People and children.

Meanwhile, the law's promoters stressed the unrefined nature of French mores and the fact that the Republic would be weakened if the law did not take this into account. Naquet, in particular defended this idea. On 24 January 1880, he affirmed that 'as a result of the special state of mores, of minds, [...] we cannot be obliged to simply do away with all the laws that govern and regulate freedom of assembly'.[46] But in this case mores are more or less synonymous with habits. It is a question of something contingent, that the Republic can shape. The idea of an apprenticeship in freedom by practising freedom persisted, as did the fear that apprenticeship was at risk and that institutions would be weakened by complete freedom. Once the law had been adopted this idea remained central in the republican camp. It was then a matter of taking up a position against the opponents of the Republic, who affirmed that the progress of mores by the practice of freedom was a republican illusion. Several articles appeared in the royalist press after 1881, insisting on the intolerance and violence of the electoral assemblies in September. Under the pseudonym Jean de Nivelle the journalist Charles Canivet exclaimed: 'Well then, what nice electoral mores!', and mocking those who announced a rapid evolution of mores alongside freedom of assembly:

'Keep calm', say the optimists, 'this will sort itself out. We are only beginning to exercise freedom, it is quite normal that there be some excesses. In a few years time this won't occur, and everything will run smoothly'.[47]

Indeed the republican press continued to demonstrate confidence. On 19 August 1881, following the assembly in rue Saint-Blaise where Gambetta was offended by the racket of the public, Auguste Vacquerie condemned the event in *Le Rappel*, especially for the 'joy' it would give the Republic's enemies:

---

44. *Journal Officiel*, 27 January 1880, p. 870.
45. *Journal Officiel*, 25 January 1880, p. 758.
46. *Journal Officiel*, 25 January 1880, p. 754.
47. *Le Soleil*, 5 September 1881.

Leave it to them, they have so little. They will soon realise that Tuesday's incident has little to do with freedom of assembly, and that it is instead, the product of the long period during which freedom of assembly did not exist.

And the journalist expressed faith in the progress of mores:

The right of assembly is still a novelty; it starts, but lacks experience. It will not delay in getting adjusted, in getting hold of itself, in winning respect for itself. The first time we try to swim, we become agitated, we beat our hands and feet, we splash our neighbours, we injure them if they come near. Some days later, we know how to swim, our movements are regular and our agitation ceases.

Reacting to the same assembly, an editorial affirmed that: 'it is not in a few weeks, or even some years, that a People can develop a new temperament; education in freedom is very slow'.[48] Concerns and complaints about the state of political mores were sometimes heard in the republican press; but in the 1880s the great majority continued to affirm that the apprenticeship would be made, perhaps taking a little more time than first envisaged.

The necessary reform of 'mores of authority'

'We are not afraid [...] to say that it is above all the mores of the authority that must adapt to freedom', wrote the journalist Léon Plée in an article entitled 'The Mores of Freedom'.[49] Under the Empire, the republicans had not been content to express their trust in the evolution of mores through the practice of assemblies. The apprenticeship of mores worthy of a free country would require that the police and government authorities themselves have the same experience in advance. If the authorities persist in treating the People as it is treated under a despotic government, assemblies will continue to be characterised by disorder and physical and verbal violence. It was not enough to adopt a law establishing a slightly more liberal regime for freedom of assembly. Authority had to abandon the mores of the authoritarian Empire. Only on this condition would the People acquire the necessary maturity. Here too, the idea is not that the authorities or the police are necessarily, or by nature, authoritarian, but rather that they had acquired bad habits since 1852, that they used in response to government instructions, which did not promote progress.

The first criticism concerned the role of the police officer in public assemblies. Dalotel, Faure and Freiermuth noted: '[His] presence [...] and then [that] of stenographers in the assembly rooms is the occasion for meetings to define themselves in relation to power'. They specify that 'after a certain period of neutrality a verbal confrontation begins which suddenly will be transformed in

---

48. *Journal des Débats*, 19 August 1881.
49. *Le Siècle*, 8 February 1869.

1869–1870 by the physical intervention of the forces of law and order'.[50] The republican press gives a rather unflattering image of this figure of authority, presented as incompetent, not particularly intelligent and unfamiliar with the law. This was especially the case when a police officer dissolved electoral assemblies because the orator strayed from his official subject even though any question could be addressed in such assemblies. Some failed, they say, to understand that there was nothing subversive in the words of a speaker which could have led to a warning or put an end to an assembly. The remarks of journalists were, of course, ironic because speakers intentionally kept up their anti-government allusions in public assemblies supposed to be non-political. In May 1869, after a warning, an electoral assembly at which Jules Ferry took part was disbanded. The event sparked this remark: 'This is freedom of discussion in our electoral assemblies. It depends on the caprice of a young man wrapped up in a scarf, who may have digested his dinner badly, and who has at his discretion a meeting of 2,000 voters'. The author requests that government: 'At least send to our meetings intelligent commissioners. We are sure they exist'.[51]

From this perspective, it is the police who are the main cause of disorder, primarily due to their mere provocative presence. Speakers do indeed try to demonstrate their ability to defy their authority, and the public is amused by the ridicule. Gustave de Molinari greets the progress of participants' behaviour in public assemblies, but remarks that the presence of the police and the 'duels between the commissioner and the *bureau*' put a break to it.[52] The idea is that commissioners merely excite speakers and public alike. In the words of Anatole de la Forge, 'the sight of their uniforms is like a red rag to a bull'.[53] Far from intimidating participants, the presence of the police pushed them to be more daring: revolutionary ideas, taken as signs of immaturity by republicans, would develop as a reaction to the provocation constituted by the police presence.

The liberal press insisted that assemblies became stormy basically after repeated advertisements and the increase in dissolutions as of 1869. Without this they would have remained calm. Unwarranted dissolutions sparked off participant protest and could degenerate into clashes with the police. This occurred during a public assembly in Belleville on 10 October 1869, described in the aforementioned *Observations sur la pratique de la loi du 6 juin 1868*, as 'one of the most important of the period of public assemblies'. While the commissioner requested the disbanding of the meeting following the speaker's remarks, 'the *bureau*, supported by the assembly, protests [...], and refuses to disperse'. This refusal led to police entering the room and clashing with participants.[54] Charles Du Bouzet, editorial secretary of *Le Temps* criticised the version of events

---

50. Dalotel, Faure and Freiermuth, *Aux origines de la Commune*, p. 128.
51. *Le Temps*, 9 May 1869.
52. *Le Journal des Débats*, 22 September 1869.
53. *Le Siècle*, 4 February 1869.
54. APP/Ba/1520.

conveyed by the conservative press that laid great responsibility for the outbreak of violence on participants in the assembly.[55] According to the liberal press, if there was disorder, it was due to the intervention of the authorities; without them, participants would discipline themselves and eliminate violence from meetings. Following the Belleville incidents, which motivated government to announce its decision to resort to Article 13 of the 1868 law, allowing 'the police prefect in Paris, the prefects in the *départements* to adjourn any assembly likely to disturb order or to endanger public safety', the journalist Ulysse Ladet deplored the return to authoritarian practices:

> Instead of leaving the field free for these popular meetings, getting rid of the irritating presence of the police commissioner, and in this way compelling meetings to discipline and control themselves, it […] suits [government], following an incident which would have ended peacefully like many others without the sudden intervention of the armed forces, to reinstate the former regime of silence. The latter has been, in fact, so successful, and it is indeed the good way […] to accustom the masses to the discussion of their interests and to the practice of freedom.[56]

Police intervention is particularly denounced when it gives rise to physical clashes with participants. The liberal press notes the difference between the administrative and policing tradition in France with countries where freedom is respected. Elsewhere, rather than intervening by force to stop or prevent an assembly which is not a risk to public order, but is believed to be illegal, the illegal act is registered and justice is left to do its job in applying the appropriate penalty. The criticism returns in a series of articles by Cucheval-Clarigny in the liberal newspaper *La Presse* in September 1868 during the Nîmes trial. The latter is motivated against organisers of an electoral assembly held in the five days before the election, not declared by the organisers because of its allegedly private character, which was contested by the administration. After participants refused to obey the police summons to disband, the room was cleared by force. Beyond their limited understanding of what constituted a private meeting, the author criticised the administration and the police for not having acted as 'everywhere else but in France'.[57] That is, by recording the infringement and 'leaving the task of asking citizens who have broken the law to account for themselves to justice'. In 'free countries', one has 'trust in the law', whereas in 'despotic countries', one 'resorts to force', echoed *La Presse* the following day. If there is a difference between British and French mores, it lies in the administration 'still imbued with despotic traditions of the *Ancien Régime*', 'immobile in the midst of universal progress, [and without] the mores of freedom'[58].

---

55. *Le Temps*, 13 October 1869.
56. *Le Temps*, 14 October 1869.
57. *La Presse*, 2 September 1868.
58. *La Presse*, 3 September 1868.

A more serious accusation is that the police and government made no attempt to restore calm in assemblies, or even that the disorder actually benefited government. In the first months of this experience of freedom, the government did nothing to eradicate the disorder, and would even encourage and provoke it. This was taken as the proof that the French, in contrast to their British neighbours, could not assemble freely without being a serious threat to public peace. Their unruly assemblies with their violent arguments attacking the foundations of society may have encouraged anxious voters to take refuge in Empire candidates, rather than voting for those advocating an extension of freedoms. In this way the police are blamed for not having stepped in to assure that freedom of assembly was not endangered by those deliberately seeking to disturb it. The police are basically concerned with supervising opinions and do not intervene except to prevent the success of anti-Empire speeches. For freedom of assembly to adapt in France the police must focus their action on those who cause the disorder in assemblies. Louis Jourdan writes that the police in France have 'a political character', making it different from the British police which 'deals exclusively with ensuring public safety and guaranteeing citizens the exercise of their rights'.[59] The *bureaux* of assemblies could not count on it to eject the very few disturbers from the room where the majority of participants wished to assemble peacefully. If the police do not intervene to prevent disturbances it may mean that government has a vested interest in assemblies going wrong. Are disturbers acting on behalf of government? Are people paid to deliver the most violent speeches? The republican press tends in this direction: 'The exaggerations, the extravagances of which one complains, are they not provoked by those to whom they are most directly useful, and who, objecting to the right of assembly, have an interest in making it seem impracticable?', asks Louis Jourdan.[60]

The fact that the government allows the law to be broken without reacting for a period of several months is also highly criticised. This is not a display of its liberalism, because its 'clemency' is followed by a period of severity. Starting in early 1869 there is an increase in the number of dissolutions, trials of organisers and speakers in assemblies, and bans on assemblies with an 'anti-assembly offensive' launched before the elections of May–June 1869.[61] For some months before this repression, assemblies had been allowed to operate on a *laissez-faire* basis. 'I reproach government', writes Pressensé in a critical pamphlet, already mentioned, 'for having tolerated the open violation of the law for over six months'. Pressensé argues that it let speakers 'become accustomed to political and religious digressions', a way for the government to make 'a stock […] of red rags'.[62] The fact that violent speeches are made and that assemblies sometimes end

---

59. *Le Siècle*, 10 September 1868.
60. *Le Siècle*, 22 February 1869.
61. Dalotel, Faure and Freiermuth, *Aux origines de la Commune*, pp. 35–36.
62. Edmond De Pressensé, *Les réunions publiques à Paris et les élections prochaines*, Paris, Librairie Meyrueis et Librairie Le Chevalier, 1869, pp. 17–19.

in chaos is encouraged by government as a way to arouse fear. This is reinforced by the accounts of assemblies spread by the government press, or by August Vitu's inaccurate pamphlet, *Les réunions publiques à Paris*, which claims that 'every evening the most extravagant and criminal talk, a mixture of stupidity and perversity in equal doses, is reeled off to an immense public [...]'.[63]

Government therefore let orators speak freely, only to condemn them some months later. The theme of the 'mousetrap' was developed in 1869 by the extreme left and the moderate republicans. It appears in several issues of *La Lanterne*, the radical opposition newspaper founded by Henri Rochefort, who 'used [his] spirit of derision to make a systematic critique of the government'.[64] On 13 March 1869 we read that:

> The proclamation of this famous right of assembly was nothing more than a mousetrap set by [the police prefect] M. Piétri, to lay his hands on men who, knowing how to speak in public, could in moments of ferment transport the People to dangerous displays [of feeling]. The Empire is the police.

Faure and Fontaine de Rambouillet also talk of a 'mousetrap' and a 'raid' when referring to the condemned speakers. For the authors 'it seemed that one gathered [the speakers] in order to count them better and, on the eve of elections, to alarm the mass of voters by violent speech so that they throw them in pro-government votes'.[65] The apprenticeship of freedom of assembly by the People was thus described as having been checked by the undeveloped mores of authority. The latter continued to be traits of a regime with no trust in freedom. Republicans believed in the reform of undeveloped popular mores through the practice of assemblies. For this to succeed, the People had to be trusted and the mores of authority had to be changed. The People also required models of conduct.

Replacing rules by models

The rejection of assemblies in the form of club meetings, which republicans had long criticised, was encoded in the law of 1881. For most of the opportunist republicans, these go against the deliberative ideal of open meetings and present the risk of becoming intermediary bodies intervening between citizens and government. Paradoxically, this refusal to reopen political clubs weakens the mission to regulate the formation of popular civic behaviour through participation in assemblies. In fact, in contrast with assemblies held in the last three decades of the nineteenth century, those organised by clubs could be regulated by rules imposing specific attitudes that must be adopted by participants, some codes

---

63. Auguste Vitu, *Les réunions électorales à Paris. Mai 1869*, Paris, Editions Dentu, 1869, p. 8.
64. Christophe Charle, *Le siècle de la presse (1830–1939)*, Paris, Seuil, 2004, p. 114.
65. Faure and Fontaine de Rambouillet, *Le peuple et la place publique*, p. 172.

of behaviour which had to be accepted.⁶⁶ We are taken back to the question of the formation of mores by participation in assemblies at the outset of the Third Republic, due to the cleavage between radical republicans defending freedom of association with freedom of assembly, and the law's promoters, in particular the opportunist government, wanting the right of assembly to be regulated and insisting that the clubs remain banned. Under the Empire, as under the early Republic, the great majority of republicans did not explore the idea that meetings organised by clubs could have demopedic advantages that simple assemblies regulated by the few rules imposed by law did not have. In the years 1880–1890 above all, faced with continuing disorder in assemblies, it was repeatedly stressed that the opportunist republicans in power should have listened to the radical deputies and left assemblies to organise as clubs.

Criticism returns regularly in the radical newspaper *La Justice*. Edouard Durranc, admirer of Clemenceau, wrote:

> One of the most certain symptoms of the evil from which democracy has suffered for some years, is the difficulty it has in trying to develop mores of freedom. [...] If the first experiences were rather disappointing, this was to some extent the fault of men; it is even more the fault of the law that banned clubs, that is, serious assemblies. [...] We must ask ourselves if the law which is supposed to have granted the right of assembly, did actually grant it. I say that it only did so very imperfectly. This law gives me the right to gather, at all events, in a closed and covered place, as many people as the room can contain, and nothing more. This is not a popular meeting; this is a crowd, with all the violence that a handful of disturbers can cause. We see that this alleged right of assembly gives above all the right to prevent all assemblies. When one discussed this law in 1881 [...] the Chamber had only one aim: banning clubs.⁶⁷

This virtue of clubs in the formation of mores of freedom went unrecognised by non-radical republicans. A debate started between *La Justice* and the moderate republican newspaper *Le Temps*. Several articles in *La Justice* denounce the fact that the moderate republican press seems to have been gradually admitting that the adoption of good political mores was bankrupt, and refused to see that the problem was primarily caused by the 1881 law, which was their own work, the work of the moderates in the Chamber. The journalists of *Le Temps* could not accept the idea that the way to resolve the increasingly frequent incidents in assemblies was the club, which 'would be [according to *La Justice*] an organised assembly, disciplined, master of itself'.⁶⁸ *Le Temps* recalls the reasons which led the legislator

---

66. For Jacobin clubs of Provence under the Revolution, see: Paula Cossart, 'S'assembler en Provence sous la Révolution. Légitimité des réunions des sociétés populaires comme mode de participation collective du peuple au débat public (1791–1794)', *Annales Historiques de la Révolution Française*, 2003, vol. 331, pp. 57, 77.
67. *La Justice*, 13 September 1889.
68. *Le Temps*, 6 August 1893.

to reject it in 1881: it was a question of dealing with freedom of assembly and not freedom of association, and 'clubs had a bad reputation'. On 6 December 1886, an article on this issue, also in reply to *La Justice*, stated:

> You can think what you want about clubs. If we understand by this associations that meet periodically and peacefully, we have nothing against them; but what seems to us to go beyond the limits of the illusion allowed in politics, is the idea that clubs may resolve everything [...].

Each time the conclusion was that the radicals were not in a position to talk about good mores when they had contributed, with their indulgence towards the agitators, the 'revolutionaries', to citizens' bad practices. Without resorting to assemblies such as those organised by the clubs whose participants were subject to regulation likely to help model their conduct, what is needed to allow the rapid development of good mores is the organisation of assemblies that could be taken as models.

The republican position at the end of the Empire, faced with the progressive monopolisation of assemblies by socialists and communists, is a warning which continues into the first years of the Republic: do not abandon the privilege of assemblies to them. 'Everyone must use the right of assembly recognised by law. This is the true way to suppress deviations'.[69] Calm assemblies held by moderate republicans had to show that meetings can and must be meetings worthy of citizens. Accounts of assemblies in the liberal press demonstrated the virtues of example in the apprenticeship of good mores: 'Giving a good example, this is [...] the best guarantee of, and perhaps the best propaganda for, republican feeling', affirmed Jules Barni.[70] Some meetings are seen as being able to put an end to the risk of a bad use of the right of assembly. An Orleanist newspaper reports that this idea is not confined to the republican opposition, even when assemblies are held by republicans:

> M. Jules Simon must speak [...] in an assembly presided over by M. Saint-Marc Girardin. [...] M. Jules Simon has chosen the subject of *Duty*. This title alone reveals the speaker's intention of contesting with brilliance socialist doctrines preached for some months by all the clubs in the capital. [...] The nature of the assembly where M. Jules Simon must speak is such as to restore the free exercise of the right of assembly harmless, because the aim is to set a prompt remedy for evil, and to correct the effect of foolishness uttered elsewhere by simpletons and the ignorant, by a sensible, moral, generous, and truly eloquent education.[71]

After having affirmed that 'with the exaggerations of language that have emerged here and there, and severe measures taken by the authorities to disband

---

69. *La Presse*, 3 February 1869.
70. Barni, *Ce que doit être la République*, p. 21.
71. *Le Journal de Paris*, 14 February 1869.

some clubs, one would think that the popular forums would not be long in disappearing',[72] Henri Vigne noted with satisfaction that the 'excesses of the first assemblies gave way to lectures by the most elevated spirits of our time', and spoke of 'an emulation which will bear fruit'. He gives the example of an assembly 'where M. Eugène Pelletan dealt with one of the most pleasant subjects, the question of women, before an attentive and concentrated audience'. The public in the room, depicted in an engraving alongside the article shows the distance between such assemblies and those usually attended by citizens (see Figure 4.1).

The assemblies cited in the republican press as models of order and good behaviour, are paradoxically often lectures where only one or two people speak and where entry is not always free. Even if these characteristics reduce the size of the public,[73] they are still presented as able to help impress good habits on the masses. Thus, when trying to find the concrete means to generate political mores for the People, the republican ideal of the assembly as a meeting which is open to all and is contradictory and deliberative, moves into the background. In this way, the latter can remain the ideal model of assembly in a democratic regime, whilst accepting at the same time that it is also by organising other types of assemblies that we can contribute to the formation of patterns of behaviour expected of participants effectively. For example, the journalist Eugène Yung gives a very favourable account of an assembly organised in the Valentino meeting room to listen to a lecture by Jules Favre.[74] According to Yung, several conditions helped guarantee calm among participants. First, the assembly took place on a Sunday afternoon, which meant 'a peaceful public, because it took place in the daytime with a lively and well disposed audience, because it is a Sunday'. Then there was the chance to 'pay something at the door as a good deed': the public 'enters, conscious of carrying out a good action, and you then have the most excellent audience a speaker can dream of'. In the words of the meeting's chairman, Laboulaye: 'there is no room for discussion'; it is thus far from the deliberative model whose importance has already been stressed. For Yung, one must nevertheless 'make the public understand the benefit that assemblies [of this type] render to the cause of freedom'.

In the same article it is argued that it was above all Jules Favre's speech which got the better of potential interrupters, of the 'small, tight and unfriendly battalion', whose 'haranguers monopolise evening public assemblies'... 'Like all others they applauded the illustrious orator'. The liberal press echoes the idea that if orators speak correctly to the assembled people, then the latter will behave well, even when what is said is hard to accept. Obviously things do not go as smoothly when republicans take the risk of speaking in public assemblies organised by socialists and communists. Nevertheless speakers must provide the example by avoiding

---

72. *L'Illustration*, 13 March 1869.
73. Iouda Tchernoff, *Le Parti républicain au coup d'État et sous le Second Empire*, Paris, A. Pedone, 1906, p. 327.
74. *Journal des Débats*, January 1869.

162 | From Deliberation to Demonstration

Figure 4.1: 'Paris. A public assembly in the Theatre of the Prince Imperial. According to a sketch by M. Pignard', L'Illustration, 13 March 1869

demagogy and telling the truth with dignity and respect for their audience. 'It is remarkable that the Parisian public never gets angry with the frankness of language, when this language, albeit severe, remains courteous', wrote Anatole de la Forge,[75] about a speech made by Jules Simon in a public assembly. The public of assemblies is induced to behave in a turbulent, noisy and violent way partly because of speakers who, for the sake of easy success, excite the crowds with their declamations. It is thus hoped that with the repetition of exemplary assemblies — as a consequence of the attitude of speakers, chairman, *bureau* or public — the behaviour of participants will eventually comply with the expected civic wisdom.

The role of emotion

During a speech, the orator tends to create a listening relation through which he tries to reinforce sympathies and antipathies. He can do this better if he behaves with enthusiasm and becomes the symbolic bearer of shared passions. A particular communication is established here between the orator and his public, a circle of interactions in which the public is invited to share the

---

75. *Le Siècle*, 2 March 1869.

feelings expressed, to find in the speaker's tone, in the nuances of his feelings, the legitimised image of his own feelings.

Pierre Ansart points out in this description that emotions play a key role in what takes place in political meetings. He specifies that it is not a question of assemblies where the speaker is supposed to convince his public, but where the public is in general already convinced. At the end of the Second Empire and in the early years of the Republic, those who propose the assembly as an ideal form of popular participation promoting public opinion and putting aside direct action, are a long way from finding such an 'exemplary place of transmission of political affects' in assemblies.[76]

The debate that one wants to see taking place in assemblies relies instead on an exchange of arguments that do not appeal to emotions. It is a question of convincing or being convinced by the use of reason and not manipulating or being manipulated by an interplay of emotions. The eloquence practiced in assemblies must thus correspond to a 'mastered exercise of reason'.[77] Generally speaking, one of the elements of the apprenticeship in civic wisdom called for by republicans to stabilise representative government, is the ability to master one's uncontrolled emotions, often referred to as 'passions' and which impede the use of reason. Yves Déloye, bringing together the expectations found in the manuals of moral and civic instruction of the Third Republic and the treatises on civility studied by Norbert Elias, shows that 'the individual-citizen to whom manuals are addressed […] joins the courtier in his need for self-control and to manage his feelings'. Thus, the '"good citizen" […] knows how to govern his passions and master his emotions'.[78] In the republican press the accounts of assemblies rarely valued displays of emotion. Instead they boast of the 'calm', 'moderation', 'peaceful' character of participants in assemblies — terms which cropped up regularly. At the same time they criticised the 'amateurs of emotion'[79] seen in other assemblies, generally those of revolutionary parties, where 'all is fever, passion, ardour'.[80] Not only were revolutionary assemblies no longer the norm, but they were deemed unlikely to persist with the practice of freedom which brought a decline of the passions.

Déloye stresses the insistence found in Gambetta's speeches on the control that a citizen must exercise over his emotions. Meetings in which Gambetta takes part are not 'held only for people to attend, but also and especially to take part in regulating their emotions, in obliging them to express themselves in a way that

---

76. Pierre Ansart, *La gestion des passions politiques*, Lausanne, L'Âge d'Homme, 1983, p. 23.
77. Nicolas Roussellier, 'La diffusion de l'éloquence en France sous la IIIe République', in Fabrice D'Almeida (ed.), *L'éloquence politique en France et en Italie de 1870 à nos jours*, Rome, École française de Rome, 2001, p. 45.
78. Yves Déloye, *École et citoyenneté. L'individualisme républicain de Jules Ferry à Vichy*, Paris, Presses de la FNSP, 1994, p. 26.
79. *La Presse*, 13 November 1868.
80. *La Presse*, 11 February 1869.

reinforces the republican imperative of the mastery of the self and its passions'.[81] The discourse of the speaker thus contains a genuine 'lesson aimed at tracing the legitimate ways to appraise merit in a republican society', made of a distrust *vis-à-vis* all 'movements of collective crowd enthusiasm' for the benefit of a 'more moderate register of public recognition of his action'.[82] This 'grammar of respect' rests on the assumption that one must show democratic restraint in regulating one's feelings. This need for citizens to master their emotions is particularly anticipated in the 'assemblies of free men, that is, men who know how to control their feelings', as specified by Gambetta in a speech in 1872.[83] Here the speaker appears to rally to the republican standard of controlling emotions, particularly in assemblies, as a required condition of citizens' behaviour.

I chose to study Gambettist assemblies in order to further analyse the role of emotion in political meetings.[84] They are indeed an exemplary illustration of the difficulties encountered by republicans in the attempt to reconcile the important place of emotion in some assemblies organised by their leaders and the discourse on the necessary mastery of this emotion when citizens meet to debate public issues. Olivier Ihl has retraced the way in which this tension is managed in celebrations organised in the 1880s: 'Deployment of gaiety, the first republican celebrations [...] paradoxically prompted an apprenticeship of self-mastery'.[85] Nicolas Mariot also studied the way in which 'republicans justify [...] and explain [the] "rejoicing" of crowds', in presidential tours; analysing the tours of Sadi Carnot between 1884 and 1894, he stressed that 'all along the route, [the President] repeated that acclamations must not be addressed to himself, but to the Republic, or to the philosophical abstractions that support it'.[86] From Gambetta's first assemblies until his death in 1882, the question of the role of emotion in politics comes up repeatedly in commentaries on the charismatic leader's use of eloquence. Here I focus on the comments that instigate this practice, on the perception of the use of emotion by a republican leader, without trying to know whether or not it was truly felt.

---

81. Yves Déloye, 'Le charisme contrôlé. Entre grandeur et raison. La posture publique de Léon Gambetta', *Communications*, 2000, vol. 69, p. 164.
82. Déloye, 'Le charisme contrôlé', pp. 160–161.
83. Cited in Déloye, 'Le charisme contrôlé', pp. 160–161.
84. Paula Cossart, 'L'émotion: un dommage pour l'idée républicaine. Autour de l'éloquence de Léon Gambetta', *Romantisme*, 2003, vol. 119, pp. 47–60.
85. Olivier Ihl, *La fête républicaine*, Paris, Gallimard, 1996, p. 123.
86. Nicolas Mariot, '"Propagande par la vue". Souveraineté régalienne et gestion du nombre dans les voyages en province de Carnot (1888–1894)', *Genèses*, 1995, vol. 20, pp. 31, 39.

Making a People of Citizens | 165

The omnipresence of emotion in Gambettist assemblies

In the stormy assembly of 16 August 1881 in rue Saint-Blaise, Gambetta was forced to step down due to the noise from the public, but not without first having struck the table with his cane and calling the interrupters 'drunken slaves', and 'loudmouths'.[87] The next day *La Justice* stated that 'an event of undeniable importance took place yesterday in Belleville'.[88] The assembly had a strong and immediate impact in the press and was recalled long after Gambetta's death.[89] He had never before been defeated in an encounter with the public. His eloquence was constantly portrayed as compelling and described by supporters and critics alike as an intensely used gift. Gambetta's eloquence rested on the transmission of emotions between orator and public, and empowered his words. In rue Saint-Blaise there was still emotion, on the platform and in the room, but it lacked the communicative passion that had made previous assemblies such a success. On the contrary, emotion was used as a weapon by a part of the audience.

The press gives two opposing interpretations of this assembly. For Gambetta's critics, its failure is an emblem of political death. Gambetta had a single ability: an enchanter's eloquence which relied on the manipulation of the audience's emotions. The assembly of 16 August was the sign that it no longer worked, and that Gambetta no longer knew how to move the People. The fact that this occurred in an assembly is presented as just deserts for a man who had built his success on being acclaimed in meetings by an audience excited by words. On 17 August 1881 the royalist newspaper *Le Clairon* wrote:

> It is good, it is right, to use a little slightly modified proverb taken rather roughly from the Scriptures that he, who strikes by the word, perishes by the word, and that the king of invective collapses in the midst of universal slanging match.

For pro-Gambetta republicans, however, this assembly means neither declining popularity nor flagging eloquence. A small group of well-organised obstructionists, intransigents or Bonapartists, had simply prevented Gambetta from speaking, claims a Gambettist newspaper,[90] and 'they had instructions to brawl', denounces an other.[91] Without this, Gambetta's eloquence would have been effective, everyone would have been moved and everyone would have applauded.

---

87. Gérard Bourdin, 'Preface', *Les grands orateurs républicains. Gambetta*, Monaco, Hemera, 1949–1950, pp. 198–200.
88. *La Justice*, 17 August 1881.
89. At the inauguration of a monument to Gambetta in place du Carrousel in Paris, on 13 July 1888, Eugène Spuller spoke of the 'cruel wound' that Belleville had inflicted on its friend. See: Émile Labarthe, *Gambetta et ses amis*, Paris, Éditions des Presses Modernes, 1938, p. 251.
90. *La Petite République Française*, 20 August 1881.
91. *Le Voltaire*, 18 August 1881.

In their narratives, Gambetta's biographers present his successive speeches as key milestones.[92] The speeches are so important because Gambetta is presented as a man of exceptional eloquence, with an unwavering ability to arouse strong emotions. What then is the source of the impact of Gambetta's speeches, in particular those held during assemblies, where emotion is more intense and where his eloquence acts most strongly? Gambetta's reputation as a popular orator first appears in the testimony of those who had an image of him but without ever having heard one of his speeches. Many, evoking his memory after his death, recall that they had admired his speeches as young men. On 31 March 1912, at a commemorative ceremony in Jardies, where Gambetta lived and died,[93] Raymond Poincaré, then President of the Council stated: 'We, adolescents saw Gambetta as the embodiment of the Republic and repeated the most fiery passages of his speeches from Amiens, Abbeville, Château-d'Eau'. As Gambetta recalls, it was with a speech that he 'burst onto the world stage', in 1868, with a plea — an indictment against the Empire — for the republican Delescluze prosecuted for having organised a subscription to erect a monument 'to the memory of Alphonse Baudin, representative of the people, who died on the barricades of faubourg Saint-Antoine on 3 December 1851'.[94] Gambetta recalls the image of a man who preferred direct contact with people in assemblies to self expression through writing.

Speeches made in Gambetta's memory stress his reputation as a compelling orator. On 2 April 1938 at Cahors, Albert Sarraut, then senator and Minister of State, recalls what was so 'magnetic' in Gambetta's eloquence.[95] In a speech at the Sorbonne on 6 April 1938, Jean Zay, born after Gambetta's death, and the Minister of National Education and Arts of the *Front populaire,* recalls, the 'irresistible force' of his words.[96] There is a real 'magic' — a term often used in his biographies[97] — in Gambetta's words to which everyone is forced to yield, even when they are *a priori* opposed to the ideas articulated. At the end of October 1876, at a meeting in the Graffard hall, Boulevard de Ménilmontant, the pro-Gambetta press recalls what was 'one of his most splendid oratorical triumphs'.[98] The speaker was even applauded 'by those who had come to express their anger'; 'they acclaimed the

---

92. See two more recent biographies: Pierre Barral, *Léon Gambetta. Tribun et stratège de la République (1838–1882)*, Paris, Privat, 2008; and Jean-Marie Mayeur, *Léon Gambetta. La Patrie et la République*, Paris, Fayard, 2008.
93. Mayeur, *Léon Gambetta. La Patrie et la République*, pp. 290–291.
94. Daniel Halévy and Émile Pillias (eds), *Lettres de Gambetta, 1868–1882*, Paris, Grasset, 1938.
95. Labarthe, *Gambetta et ses amis*, p. 367. He did not speak from direct experience, being only ten years old when Gambetta died.
96. Labarthe, *Gambetta et ses amis*, p. 359.
97. See, for example, Pierre Chanlaine, *Gambetta, père de la République*, Paris, Tallandier, 1932, pp. 127, 133.
98. *Le Siècle*, 29 October 1876.

man they had promised to disgrace and scoff at!'[99] The testimony of Clovis Hugues, a deputy on the extreme left and not particularly in favour of Gambetta illustrates the impossibility of withstanding the speaker (even though this testimony does concern an address to the National Assembly):

> When Gambetta mounted the platform, I hid myself in the corridors; I did not want to hear him, he knocked me down so much, he upset me; he would be able to make me vote against my convictions; yet one day I remained at my desk, [and] decided to face the monster. That day, he was more striking than ever. His head afire, threatening gestures, thundering voice, finally unleashed like a hurricane, he gave the impression of a force of nature. The entire Chamber [...] applauded. Me, I clenched my two hands to my desk in order not to do [the same] as everyone else. — Why don't you clap, Clovis, my neighbour asked. — Ha! I replied, can't you see that I am weeping![100]

Given the impossibility of withstanding Gambettas' speeches, the only way opponents can avert the influence over an audience is to prevent him from speaking. Police reports describe the efforts made to obstruct the speeches by 'uproar', or 'a never-ending series of questions', and this, they say explicitly, 'to prevent Gambetta embarking on developments that would ensure his success',[101] and 'to forbid him all force of popular eloquence'.[102] Any assembly where Gambetta is present seems to exert miraculous effects due to the orator's perceived eloquence. The authors of police reports constantly recall the 'deep sensation',[103] the 'huge result',[104] of those assemblies. One unique assembly is depicted as enhancing the popularity of the speaker to its pinnacle, bringing '[his] influence and glory [...] to a climax'.[105]

The effectiveness of Gambetta's eloquence is linked to the fact that it is imbued with passion. Opponents and supporters alike recognise its warmth, vigour, and often spirited character which an 1876 pamphlet describes as '[smelling] explosive powder while others smell oil'.[106] Some physical characteristics of the orator, which are presented as partly determining his manner of speaking, would help explain the passionate nature of the tone. The voice is marked by emotion: 'a deep voice, vibrant, moving',[107] and 'a tremendously resounding voice which

---

99. *XIXe siècle*, 30 October 1876.
100. Comments reported in: Paul Brulat, *Histoire populaire de Léon Gambetta*, Paris, P. Paclot, 1909.
101. APP/Ba/919/1876: Rapport, police municipale, Paris, 14 octobre 1876.
102. APP/Ba/919/1876: Rapport, police municipale, Paris, 29 juillet 1876.
103. APP/Ba/918/1875: Rapport 'Chaisson', Paris, 27 avril 1875.
104. APP/Ba/918/1875: Rapport, Paris, 28 avril 1875.
105. APP/Ba/918/1875: Rapport, Paris, 5 avril 1875.
106. APP/Ba/919/1876: *Les portraits de Kel-Kun*, 1876: 'II. M. Gambetta, député'. E. A. Texier, editor-in-chief of *L'illustration* and chronicler on *Le Siècle*, signed his work with the pen name Kel-Kun.
107. APP/Ba/917: Camille Pelletan, 1877 (press cutting, without title or newspaper name).

made the walls shake and that one could hear roaring at a distance',[108] writes Camille Pelletan — who had distanced himself from Gambetta to become one of the leaders of the radicals, moving away from the opportunists, while Gambetta went on to become one of their leaders. Gambetta's strong, powerful voice is also described as 'warm'[109] and 'melodic'.[110] Some feel that the man's physique also reinforces the passionate expression, and Émile Labarthe recalls the benefits of a 'robust physique' and a 'leonine head'.[111] In much the same way, Pelletan writes:

> The heavy body, stocky and powerful, drawn in broad strokes, briefly, the black beard, short and rude, prominent eyes, the resonant mouth, an imperious frown in his eyebrows. One would say that nature deliberately shaped him on a massive and striking model, to be seen on the grand political theatre, as these tragic masques of Antiquity, calculated to bring to the benches of the hemicycle, both the expression and the accent of passions.[112]

Those who want to belittle Gambetta's success with crowds insist on the idea that he is the embodiment of passion. Gambetta has 'the gift of exciting the crowd, because he is the personification of the populace', reports an important catholic anti-republican publication.[113] His gestures also show too much passion, and it is often remarked that he comes from the South of France, described as 'the land of gestures *par excellence*' by 'one of the classical essayists at the end of the nineteenth century: a political writer with a scientific medical training casting a clinical eye over the political society of his time', Charles Hacks.[114]

One indication that this eloquence is closely linked with emotion is that it cannot be aroused without it; it needs a passionate environment, irrespective of whether this is favourable or not, in order to function. Gambetta is not as good an orator in salons or lectures as when in contact with the people in huge assemblies. In a radical newspaper, d'Alton-Shée, former radical candidate in Paris,[115] mentions a speech made by Gambetta whilst touring.[116] Shée assures that Gambetta knew that 'his voice, stifled in this narrow theatre of Versailles, free under the sky, in contact with the inspired crowd, recovers all its breadth and all its power'. It seems that Gambetta is indeed aware of this need to be face to face with a crowd. In a letter

---

108. Cited in Pierre Antonmattei, *Léon Gambetta. Héraut de la République*, Paris, Michalon, 1999, p. 403.
109. Jacques Chastenet, *Gambetta*, Paris, Fayard, 1968, p. 252.
110. Gabriel Hanotaux, 2 April 1938, speech in Nice. Cited in Labarthe, *Gambetta et ses amis*, p. 397.
111. Gabriel Hanotaux, 2 April 1938, speech in Nice, p. 44.
112. APP/Ba/917: Camille Pelletan, 1877.
113. *La Défense sociale et religieuse*, 11 October 1877.
114. Yves Déloye, 'Le geste parlementaire. Charles Hacks ou la sémiologie du geste politique au XIXe siècle', *Politix*, 1992, vol. 20, pp. 129–130.
115. Pierre Albert, *Histoire de la presse politique nationale au début de la Troisième République (1871–1879)*, vol. 2, Lille, ANRT, 1980, p. 1,549.
116. *Le Peuple souverain*, 4 October 1872.

of 26 October 1876 to his lifetime companion Léonie Léon, about an assembly in Belleville, Gambetta writes: 'I cast my eyes on the sketch that I have traced in front of you of this painful harangue. I feel in a state of sullen embarrassment [...]; it seems that I am unable to produce far from the heat of the audience'.[117] An 1876 police report on the electoral clash with Naquet in Marseilles, recounts a contradictory assembly at which the two men took part. The author of the report suggests that Gambetta's oratorical genius, nonexistent at the beginning, was not roused until faced with a strong reaction from his opponent: 'To develop all his talent, he needs protest, harassment, and even insults'. At the end of the assembly, the acclaim and applause were not for Naquet.[118]

The emotion at the heart of Gambetta's eloquence permeates the assemblies as the meeting unfolds and in the reactions that his words provoke. The assemblies are perceived by observers, journalists, police and politicians alike as a form of combat. The metaphor of battle is often used and assemblies at which Gambetta takes part are frequently described as 'oratorical conflicts'.[119] In some of these meetings the speaker is faced with opponents, but these episodes seem to matter less than the ardour of Gambetta's face-to-face contact with the crowd. The victory is sometimes easy, such as in an assembly in Belleville in 1876 that provoked a comment likening the speaker with another well-known warrior: 'Monsieur Gambetta came, spoke, won'.[120] Longer combats are described more frequently, where the speaker is:

> First calm, becoming animated by degrees as the conflict gets angry, until finally, the battle definitively engaged, he throws himself into the fray with all his oratorical passion, tossing his head above the raised crowd.[121]

This to and fro between speaker and crowd was depicted as an exchange of strong emotions. According to the report in a pro-Gambetta newspaper, there was '[something that] moved within' the farmers attending a banquet at La Ferté-sous-Jouarre in 1872, listening to him for the first time.[122] The emotion caused by the speeches is described as general and intense. A benevolent commentator writing in a radical journal relates the effect of a speech at a banquet in Lyon: 'The waves of this burning eloquence penetrated all hearts, each was moved, even tears came to the eyes'.[123] Gambetta knows how to create emotions using eloquence and is won over in return by the sentiment emanating from the crowd. A police report, relating the content of an article in *The Times*, states that: 'His Southern nature' could

---

117. Halévy and Pillias (eds), *Lettres de Gambetta*.
118. APP/Ba/919/1876: Rapport '6', Paris, 27 février 1876.
119. See, for example: Georges Clemenceau, 26 avril 1909, in Labarthe, *Gambetta et ses amis*, p. 264.
120. *Le XIXe siècle*, 30 October 1876.
121. APP/Ba/917: Camille Pelletan, 1877.
122. *Le Rappel*, 16 July 1872.
123. *Le Petit Lyonnais*, 1 March 1876.

'inflame on contact with a sympathetic audience'.[124] A centre-right newspaper reported a speech he gave in Cherbourg thus:

> It seems that he allows himself to be won over at the end by this contagion of feelings and the need to pour out his soul has been stronger than the desire — sincere, we wish to believe — not to overshadow the official representative of the Republic.[125]

The idea often crops up that when faced with collective emotion, Gambetta 'surrenders himself' to his public, 'abandons himself' to emotion, and 'gives himself' completely, expressions used by all types of observers. This transmission of emotions between speaker and participants is recalled by Clemenceau in 1909 when paying homage to Gambetta:

> Oration is like a living, changing creature that spreads from soul to soul animated by some mysterious emotional communication. Emotion produces emotion: this is an undeniable fact. 'Cry if you want to make me cry' [...]. Thus, Gambetta gave himself in order to receive, that is, so that the audience gave itself in turn.[126]

Emotions in the service of republican ideas?

In the 1870s the place of emotion in Gambettist assemblies is much debated by pro-Gambetta republicans; particularly in response to opponents of the Republic, monarchists, catholics and Bonapartists, who argue that the omnipresence of emotion in assemblies rules out the idea of Gambetta as a potential statesman. This is due to the perceived exploitation of popular sentiment through emotional exaggeration. Faced with these criticisms, republicans (the republican radicals are more silent on this issue) built a line of argument which allows space for emotions in assemblies. Far from being uncontrolled, a 'good' emotion can be found in both the orator and his public, an emotion inspired and directed by loyalty to the values and institutions of the Republic.

Gambetta is accused of being guilty of excessive emotion in his assemblies. His 'clumsiness' and 'violence' are typical of a man without self-control, and his eloquence is portrayed as weighty: opponents interpret what supporters call 'power' and 'force' as 'heaviness' and 'vulgarity'.[127] These attacks are often based on the idea that Gambetta's 'vulgar' manners reflect his humble origins. Heaviness is also deemed to be a consequence of the fact that some speeches are given after a banquet. The emphasis is on the association between the heaviness of the meal and Gambetta's words. According to Paul Granier de Cassagnac, a newspaper editor and heavy critic of the Repulican government, 'before a table covered with

---

124. *The Times*, 3 October 1872.
125. *Le Salut Public*, 22 August 1880.
126. Labarthe, *Gambetta et ses amis*, p. 280.
127. See, for example: 'M. Gambetta', *Le Gaulois*, 3 June 1872.

meat and wine', the speaker pronounced his 'fat, heavy phrases' in Angers in 1872.[128] The food and wine are always described as abundant, while republicans, by contrast, emphasise the lightness of the meal: 'It is pointless to say that the banquet, of a more than spartan sobriety, had a secondary role in the assembly'.[129] Food and alcohol would go to participants' and speakers' heads, and be responsible for their continual lack of restraint in the pursuit of sensory pleasure. If Gambetta's discourse is easily overrun by emotion, it is ironically suggested that this is because it takes place after drinking. *La République Française* is mocked for its account of a discourse in Lille on 15 August 1877, that Gambetta 'was very moved': 'For anyone who knows the habits of Monsieur Gambetta, this emotion, which occurs after a banquet [...] is easily explained. Loyalty compels us to recognise that, this time, it was not obliged to carry off the speaker.'[130]

The description of Gambetta as lacking self control, and thus unable to govern, does not stop at mere ridicule. He is accused of being a fanatic unable to control his violence. The day after an assembly, journalists of the catholic, legitimist and Bonapartist press, all rush to reveal every time that he had lacked restraint. The 'furious attacks [...] on clericalism' are deplored;[131] the 'oratorical violence', is condemned.[132] His inability to curb his passion is said to deprive him of the ability to govern the country. Alexandre Dumas *fils* writes that 'he shows none of the signs by which we recognise a leader: he is striking as one we recognise as an eternal rebel, and thus eternally defeated'.[133] Gambetta, it seems, could never be a responsible statesman.

The critics say that handling the emotions of a crowd involves risk. Gambetta inflames the masses by launching passionate declamations. He is described as someone who pushes the crowd to violence, and then abandons it to its madness, thus he is finally equally responsible for it. To support this theory, his political opponents refer to the Paris Commune. The Bonapartist newspaper *Le Combat* writes:

> At the start of the socialist and communist movement that brought this terrible civil war, [...] Gambetta took refuge in Saint Sebastian, in Spain. From his refuge, he waited impassively through the bloody days that dishonoured the country, and whose heroes were the same men who he had bribed and poisoned with his venomous talk and his 'smuggler's eloquence' in clubs and public assemblies.[134]

---

128. *Le Pays*, 13 April 1872.
129. *Le Peuple Souverain*, 16 July 1872. On the 'morality of the republican *agapes*' and their importance in 1872, see: Olivier Ihl, 'De bouche à oreille. Sur les pratiques de commensalité dans la tradition républicaine du cérémonial de table', *Revue française de science politique*, 1998, vol. 48, (3–4), p. 405.
130. *Le Pays*, 18 August 1877.
131. *La Défense sociale et religieuse*, 1 October 1877.
132. *Le Français*, 17 October 1872.
133. *Le Gaulois*, 12 October 1877.
134. *Le Combat*, 21 July 1877.

Throughout his career, Gambetta is accused of 'making promises to the masses' in his speeches 'to satisfy their hates and lusts' as reported in a conservative newspaper,[135] of '[stirring up] the populace', and of 'speaking [...] a language like a red rag to a bull'.[136]

The critique of the pre-eminence of passion in assemblies is also linked to the fact that it was present throughout France. Thus the speaker is accused of seeking a popular plebiscite. It is argued that the objective is not to convince, but to be acclaimed. Gambetta's letters show that the animated welcome of the masses, especially during assemblies held during tours of French cities, 'is pleasant to him'.[137] But the press which attacks Gambetta alleges that this is his sole aim. A Bonapartist newspaper stresses that before speaking in an assembly, the orator would 'carefully prepare his audience, as a theatre director on an opening night'.[138] Critics affirm that Gambetta prefers private assemblies, at which only supporters are allowed to participate. It is also suggested that the cities visited are chosen so as to ensure enthusiastic crowds. On a visit to Chambéry the press claim: 'We know a number of *départements* where the "great citizen" carefully avoided appearing — and where he would have got more pitchforks than bouquets'.[139] It is even alleged that Gambetta paid the public for applause and acclaim. The same newspaper reports that in an assembly in Saint-Étienne not only had 'the audience been carefully selected', so that 'no discordant cry [would mingle with] the concert of adulation prepared to caress the ears of the great man', but that 'brawlers' had also been paid 'to acclaim Gambetta'[140]. The latter tries to appear popular by the display of the crowd's passionate reception, be it sincere or not. The speaker is often described as behaving like a demagogue, open to almost every compromise: 'It is true that M. Gambetta is not in the least embarrassed to adjust his current opinion to the opinion of that of his audience'.[141] This is a picture of a manipulator. It is no longer a question of the ardent speaker losing self-control. In order to reach power through a popular plebiscite, Gambetta would work to be acclaimed by all. Examining Gambetta's tours of the provinces, Nicolas Mariot writes: 'We can easily imagine how a provincial tour in full daylight, openly resembling a traditional "royal journey", could risk heavy criticism'.[142] The comparison of the way the discourse of the speaker raises applause and praise in assemblies with the way that kings and emperors are acclaimed is an idea mentioned frequently by the press, and is even made by republicans at times. Gambetta is accused of

---

135. *Le Soir*, 30 September 1872.
136. *La Défense sociale et religieuse*, 11 October 1877.
137. Odile Sassi, *Léon Gambetta. Destin et mémoire. 1838–1938*, PhD dissertation, Paris IV, 1999, p. 53.
138. *L'Ordre*, 30 October 1876.
139. *Le Pays*, 25 September 1872.
140. *Le Pays*, 22 September 1872.
141. *Le Constitutionnel*, 27 September 1872.
142. Nicolas Mariot, *Conquérir unanimement les cœurs. Usages politiques et scientifiques des rites. Le cas du voyage présidentiel en province, 1888–1998*, PhD dissertation, Paris, EHESS, 1999, p. 404.

making plebiscitary use of the right of assembly, and is described as a 'Ceasar of the Republic' by a legitimist newspaper in Lyon.[143]

Faced with these attacks, how do republicans commenting on Gambetta's assemblies manage to legitimate the displays of often exaggerated emotion? Yves Déloye shows that Gambetta's speeches call on citizens to control their emotions.[144] In this apparent paradox is the orator an agitator playing with people's emotions, or their educator teaching them to master themselves in order to become citizens? Déloye is interested in Gambetta's speeches, impassioned political pleas and printed texts, without directly taking into account the very unfolding of assemblies, and the way in which these speeches are delivered. This may help explain the gap between the omnipresence of live emotion observed in Gambettist assemblies and the concern for restraint. However there is also a justification used by pro-Gambetta republicans, and by the speaker, in resolving this apparent paradox between a clear role of emotion in assemblies and the desire that men's loyalty to republican ideas be based on reason.

Emotion plays a distinctive role in Gambetta's eloquence in assemblies, but does it contradict the notion of assemblies as places where men learn why they should adopt republican ideas, with the help not only of the orator's knowledge, but also through personal reflection? The answer is based on an argument, still used after Gambetta's death, intended to show that the speaker's use of eloquence imbued with strong emotions does not corrupt civic reason. There may be a link, evident in the specific case of the Gambettist word, between emotion and reason, which do not always conflict. Many stress that the characteristic emotion of Gambetta's speeches is possible, and even laudable, because it comes from his strong belief in this body of arguments and concrete ideas which constitute the Republic. Very occasionally the republican press runs an article denying the role of emotion, claiming that Gambetta's 'words […] are marked by reason and not political passion'.[145] Yet this is more an attempt to reconcile emotion and reason, the first is found within the second, and flows from it. This is 'the sincere and profound conviction' that 'inspires' Gambetta's 'grand and beautiful language', with its 'waves of burning eloquence'.[146] The speaker sincerely believes and is inflamed by true arguments. The logical consequence is that, far from being overcome by emotions, Gambetta is actually in control of himself. 'He remains profoundly master of his spirited eloquence; he can launch it into a gallop, knowing that he can stop point blank, or suddenly turn back; it is a sort of impetuous tactic, a brutal calculation, measured and reflected ardour' wrote Pelletan.[147] Indeed, the republican justification for the passionate eloquence of the speaker relies largely on this notion of 'measured and reflected ardour'.

---

143. *La Décentralisation*, 7 August 1881.
144. Déloye, 'Le charisme contrôlé', pp. 157–172.
145. *La Liberté*, 28 April 1872.
146. *Le Petit Lyonnais*, 1 March 1876.
147. APP/Ba/917: Camille Pelletan, 1877.

The speaker's emotion is also legitimated because it is placed at the service of republican ideas. It helps citizens to understand them and reinforces them. Gambetta, says Pelletan, has the 'gift of giving expression to pure ideas, a movement, an impetus, a driving force that gradually wins the crowd'.[148] Eloquence is 'in the service of reason, justice and truth', and for this reason, 'will always find the way to [our] hearts'.[149] 'Language of an honest man inflamed by a passion for justice and truth', the speaker's eloquence is reinforced by the fact that the hearts and minds of the meetings' participants are directly linked. Gambetta's success is that he knows how to mix 'logical arguments specific to the demonstration' with the 'stirring tones needed to persuade'.[150] Claude Nicolet has shown that not only Gambetta, but also Ferry and Clemenceau use rhetorical practices 'to prove something, to say something in order to convince and not to defeat', and adds that 'emotion — even lyricism, in the case of Gambetta — only comes after rational conviction'.[151]

We can still ask whether this discourse compromises the claim that in a republican assembly a skilled and convincing orator does not impose ideas on the audience, but enlightens them to discuss, think for themselves, and be helped in this by a man qualified to contribute to their instruction. Those who continually stress that Gambetta did not impose any ideas by resorting to impassioned eloquence reply in the negative: the platform reveals what listeners already know and believe, but in a confused way, and one which Gambetta helps to clarify. The discourse of the speaker in assemblies constitutes a form of maieutics favoured by the use of emotion. 'He had the gift [...] of translating into strong images, bright formulas, confused feelings dispersed in the depths of the soul, deliver the minds and reveal to them the latent truths within themselves', wrote Labarthe after his death.[152] Gambetta uses emotion not to impose ideas, but to help draw out what is already in the mind of the public. The reflective character of support is not to the detriment of participants in assemblies. Pro-Gambetta republicans thus justify what may at first seem to be a contradiction between two elements: the recurring call, by Gambetta and many pedagogues of the Republic, to an audience to master its emotions, and the fact that a speaker's eloquence seems to give a prominent place to strong emotions.

Yet the speaker's emotion is not the only issue at stake. Yves Déloye reminds us that the emotion seen in the audience of assemblies also poses the problem of '*democratic restraint*, the only thing compatible with informed reason'.[153] Displays of lively popular enthusiasm, particularly during Gambetta's tours of

---

148. APP/Ba/917: Camille Pelletan, 1877.

149. *Le XIXe siècle*, 30 October 1876.

150. Bourdin, 'Preface', *Les grands orateurs républicains*, p. 1.

151. Claude Nicolet, *L'idée républicaine en France. Essai d'histoire critique*, Paris, Gallimard, 1982, pp. 258–259.

152. Labarthe, *Gambetta et ses amis*, p. 41.

153. Déloye, 'Le charisme contrôlé', p. 163. The italics are Déloye's.

France, are not welcomed by some republicans. A police report from October 1878 states that 'generally we are strongly critical, especially in the republican world, of the ovations received by Monsieur Gambetta, [...] we ask with concern what plans lie behind the tours that some compare with those of Prince Napoleon in 1852'.[154] The denunciation of the Gambettist trend of 'Ceasarism', recurrent among the Republic's enemies, is not limited to their remarks. Gambetta's supporters argue that crowd applause should not be taken as a sign of unbounded enthusiasm, but as a way for participants to indicate that they understood the issues being discussed. This effort to reintroduce the legitimating action of reason in the Gambettist practice of assemblies is difficult to sustain in the face of such intense applause and acclaim.

To justify displays of public emotion, Gambetta and his republican supporters interpret it as being directed not to the speaker, but to the Republic. In his speeches, Gambetta might ask the audience quite simply to restrain its applause, declaring that their exaggeration is unworthy of true citizens. When describing his assemblies the republican press frequently emphasises these calls to moderate their enthusiasm. Nicolas Mariot notes that if the applause and acclamations continue, the speaker hastens 'to reject the shouts chanting his name in order to have them addressed to the institutions which he promotes'.[155] This is a transfer of feeling from himself to the republican ideas that he develops and which transcend men. Referring to the same way of justifying displays of public emotion, Gambetta takes up the accusation of being a 'travelling salesman', on account of so many trips.[156] In a discourse at Le Havre on 18 April 1872, he declared:

> There are also people, I say men of spirit, my faith! Who believed they would show their mettle by calling me a *travelling salesman*! [...]. If they thought that they injured anything in my vanity or my self-esteem, in repeating this joke, they were cruelly... I would say grossly, mistaken! I do not blush; I am indeed a traveller and a salesman of democracy. This is my job, the People entrusted it to me.[157]

The effusion of public sentiment is not directed at Gambetta *qua* individual, who is effectively only a travelling salesman selling republican ideas and is not in search of a popular plebiscite. Republicans supporting the speaker, beginning with Gambetta, make the traces of public emotion acceptable. This emotion, they argue, is in fact not directed at the speaker, but at the Republic.

---

154. APP/Ba/922/1878: Rapport '32', Paris, 11 octobre 1878 (written between two assemblies, in Romans and Grenoble).
155. Nicolas Mariot, *Conquérir unanimement les cœurs*, p. 402. See also: John Patrick Tuer Bury, *Gambetta and the Making of the Third Republic*, London, Longman, 1973, p. 111.
156. See for example: 'Encore lui', *Paris Journal* (23 April 1872, n.s.). This newspaper defends the idea that 'health can only come from a union of all conservatives among which, [...] the journal included bonapartists'. Pierre Albert, *Histoire de la presse politique nationale au début de la Troisième République (1871–1879)*, vol. 2, Lille, ANRT, 1980, p. 861.
157. Account of the speech given in *Le Figaro*, 22 April 1872.

In the republican discourse, the emotion that marks Gambetta's assemblies is presented as being in the service of the republican idea broadcasted, explained and preached in speeches throughout France. Gambetta's defenders regard and remember him as a 'great lay preacher',[158] marked by 'his need for apostolacy',[159] with a determination to 'lead [the masses] to the faith, to the republican mystique',[160] and to 'catechise citizens'[161] with 'his civic apostolacy'.[162] Gambetta does not pretend to be God, as claimed by those criticising the rise in the number of assemblies leading to excessive enthusiasm; he is more of an apostle, the 'apostle of the Republic'.[163] When Gambetta uses passionate eloquence in an assembly, it is not to reap the emotion of participants for personal gain, but to direct it towards the republican ideal which he knows how to render understood and cherished. As for those taking part in assemblies, they would attend out of a feeling of duty: that of learning together. At the banquet of la Ferté-sous-Jouarre: '[the peasant] comes [...] as if performing a duty, just as people in the cities or countryside, seek the light, the truth, each time that it comes within their reach'.[164] In the early years of the Republic and when opposing barriers to freedom of assembly under the Empire, republicans see assemblies as a tool to train people to become wise citizens, citizens able to assemble without excessive passion or violence.

---

158. Joseph Reinach, *La vie politique de Léon Gambetta*, Paris, Alcan, 1918, p. 32.
159. Jacques Chastenet, *Gambetta*, Paris, Fayard, 1968, p. 201.
160. Pierre Chanlaine, *Gambetta, père de la République*, Paris, Tallandier, 1932, p. 127.
161. Henri Thurat, *Gambetta. Sa vie, son œuvre*, Paris, Bibliothèque des Communes, 1883, p. 296.
162. Eugène Spuller, speech of 13 July 1888. Labarthe, *Gambetta et ses amis*, p. 251.
163. APP/Ba/922/octobre–décembre 1878: *M. Gambetta. Notes biographiques*, Paris, Mme Veuve Roger Editeur, 1878.
164. *Le Rappel*, 16 July 1872.

Chapter Five

Resistance to the Civilisation of Political Mores

On 4 September 1893 *Le Temps* published a front-page article entitled 'Electoral Mores'. In this article the intention was no longer to boast about their inevitable progress or to seek evidence of their existence. On the contrary, it gave a concerned account of their incontestable 'decline'. In Paris electoral mores had become, principally, 'savage mores'. The author of the article declared that they 'have already killed freedom of assembly that we worked so hard to attain and which is no longer of any use', and fears the threat they pose to government. The republican ideal of popular participation in political life through deliberation in assemblies had not been realised in practice. From the late 1880s it appeared that 'the meeting is [not] this place of civic education that republicans could once boast'.[1]

Resistance to the mission to civilise mores is not only a question of behaviour in assemblies. More generally speaking, it has been emphasised that if 'the Republic is first and foremost characterised by the promotion of new political mores', these are 'continually faced by displays of disbelief, or worse, by transgressive practices'.[2] Taking the vote as a tool of republican acculturation, Yves Déloye and Olivier Ihl observe that 'there is great reluctance to adopt the qualities of the citizen's role'. Indeed, 'in the very room where the vote takes place, deviations from the rules to neutralise violence are rare'; yet disturbances become more intense when we move away from this sphere. Déloye and Ihl refer above all to disorder on the streets during electoral periods, interpreting this as a 'display of a rebellious citizenship, a citizenship opposed to peaceful voting', and a 'noisier citizenship [which] emerges [...] outside the circle of euphemised forms of political activity or in any case on its margins'.[3] But republicans see the assembly as an integral part of these 'euphemised forms of political activity'. In the same way as with the case of the sphere of voting, it is affirmed that there must be an apprenticeship in codes of conduct which transform individuals into 'good' citizens. Thus resistance to the mission of civilisation of mores appears also within the use made of legitimate forms of participation; forms of participation that

---

1. Michel Offerlé, 'La mobilisation électorale en milieu urbain. L'exemple de la France à la fin du XIXe siècle', 2e Congrès national de l'Association Française de Science Politique, Grenoble, 1984 (no page numbers).

2. Jacques Chevallier, 'Bonnes mœurs et morale républicaine. Présentation', in *Les bonnes moeurs*, Paris, PUF, 1994, pp. 186–187.

3. Yves Déloye and Olivier Ihl, 'La civilité électorale: vote et forclusion de la violence en France', *Cultures & Conflits*, 1993, vols. 9–10, pp. 86–93.

republican legislation had once encouraged to provide support for government. At the turn of the century, there was a veritable 'misappropriation', a 'deviant appropriation' of this form of participation.[4] Behaviour in meetings, the use made of freedom of assembly, moves it away from the ideal that had seemed attainable in the early years of the Republic and for whose signs one was still on the look out.

This development of what are seen as 'bad mores' endangering the Republic occurs alongside a move to deviate guilt and responsibility from the People itself. It was vital for the republicans in government to affirm that it was not citizens in general who rebelled against the apprenticeship in civic mores — then one would get closer to the reasoning of government supporters under the Empire. It was instead stated that some specific groups had invented bad forms of conduct which were then taken up by the masses as harmful habits. The Boulangists, anarchists, nationalists and particularly the anti-Dreyfusards, and to a lesser extent the socialists, are all branded as responsible for a situation where it had become difficult to meet together to discuss (in the 1880s opportunist republicans also pointed the finger at the radical republicans). These groups are dealt with together in a speech which distinguishes them from those who 'still believe in the use of debate and reason'.[5] Despite their differences, they are lumped together and accused of refusing pacification. 'Quite often, in democratic regimes radicalisation is taken as a threat from *outside*, [...] often associated with the intrusion of groups with extremist ideological convictions and repertoires of action'.[6] Republicans believe that these are the groups that create detrimental habits in the practice of freedom of assembly. These habits then expand to the point that we can speak of mores, and these mores may prevent men from profiting from potential virtues of assemblies.

> Many works have been able to show how citizens, as new voters, were able collectively and individually, to use republican freedoms in an ambivalent way, while hearing the *basso continuo* of the threat of the *Grand Soir*, [and] how they have invested these new repositories of 'citizenship' [...] in diverting them from their limited dimensions, enlarging them, giving them unexpected or unusual significance. In co-producing them.[7]

As for assemblies, we can see this co-production in some uses of freedom defined by the 1881 law, diverting it from the protected role of peaceful debate to the point where moderates begin to fear contradictory assemblies, and largely to give up the organisation of public meetings. The mores that republicans describe

---

4. To use Alain Garrigou's expressions on the vote in *Histoire sociale du suffrage universel en France. 1848–2000*, Paris, Seuil, 2002 (edited and revised by Garrigou), p. 242.
5. *Le Temps*, 5 August 1893.
6. Annie Collovald and Brigitte Gaïti, 'Introduction', in Collovald and Gaïti (eds), *La démocratie aux extrêmes. Sur la radicalisation politique*, Paris, La Dispute, 2006, pp. 12–13.
7. Michel Offerlé, 'Périmètres du politique et coproduction de la radicalité à la fin du XIXe siècle', in Annie Collovald and Brigitte Gaïti (eds), *La démocratie aux extrêmes*, pp. 266–267.

as bad when commenting on this use leave a lasting mark on the form taken by assemblies. It made them a collective mode of action, a means of protest, or a declaration of strength of opinion much more than a place of debate. Part of this behaviour gradually became typical of all assemblies, so that their stigmatisation became progressively less intense than in the last two decades of the century, when they still came into direct conflict with the fledgling venture to civilise democratic mores.

The author of the article in *Le Temps* cited at the beginning of this chapter, when he examines the origins of what he sees as a decline in mores, goes back to the Boulangist movement. Whilst it was not ultimately successful, it still left a profound mark on the political behaviour of the French by effect of imitation. But what do these incriminated practices consist of?

> We have learnt then how to recruit *the soldiers of uproar and systematic violence*, how one can set up a so-called public assembly, what tactics it takes to drown out a candidate's voice or prepare him, on the contrary, ovation, in a word the art of intimidating honest people, regimenting men of action and *dazzling universal suffrage*.[8]

There are then two 'deviances' in relation to the republican mission of civilisation of mores by taking part in assemblies, which become clear starting in the mid-1880s and particularly in the 1890s. On the one hand, there are the practices by the 'soldiers of uproar and systematic violence', who resort to noise or violence in order to suppress discussion and to prevent the expression of divergent opinions. On the other hand, the use of what can be described as assemblies-cum-demonstrations; that is, the organisation and participation in meetings in order to assert the force of a preconceived opinion by means of the gathering, to 'dazzle universal suffrage', as the journalist put it.

Organised intolerance

The scenes of disorder in assemblies, the noise and the violence, do not date to the end of the 1880s. Throughout his description of assemblies during the closing years of the Empire, the author of the lengthy police report in 1875 on 'the results of the application of the 1868 law' attests — albeit in a biased manner — that it did not promote freedom.[9] It insists that the speakers most welcomed by the public are those using the most violent language. Ignace Horn, an economist and moderate republican journalist, 'was very successful' as a speaker until 'more violent speakers arrived [...] and his popularity fell as fast as it had risen' (June 1868). Those taking part in assemblies are portrayed as intolerant, not allowing everyone to speak. 'Freedom of discussion was impossible; the interruptions followed one another', writes the author for the month of October 1868. Generally, he speaks

---

8. The italics are the author's emphasis.
9. APP/Ba/1520.

of 'interruptions' or 'insults' made by participants. Assemblies are often 'stormy' or 'turbulent' — the two most frequently used expressions in the report. Even physical violence is not ruled out. We are reminded of assemblies that 'almost generated into brawls several times' in January 1869 and of violent 'fights' in the wake of a disbanded assembly in October 1869. Disorder is present in assemblies from the relative liberalisation of imperial legislation onwards.

What changed at the end of the 1880s, and particularly in the 1890s, was primarily the republican discourse. It could no longer attribute responsibility for this kind of behaviour to previous badly drafted legislation or governmental mores. Neither could it claim that it was only a question of time, and that mores of freedom need months or years to acclimatise. Bad mores were no longer perceived as the continuation of habits inherited from despotic regimes. They were rather considered as a new element that emerged under the Republic, through the detrimental action of groups whose practices progressively contaminated the masses. However, we should point out that the progressive decline of optimism for education in civic mores through the assembly has its own rationale. If disorder and oral and physical violence are already typical of assemblies at the end of the Empire, we can see, especially in the 1890s, a systematic use and stepping-up of disturbances. These are no longer the sole outcome of placing individuals with different opinions in the same room. Instead they seem to be the product of deliberate attempts to prevent the adversary from speaking. Furthermore, violence became more intense, in the words spoken and in the fights then typical of assemblies.

The systematic use of obstruction

From the mid-1880s onwards many meetings were disturbed by noisy groups trying to block out the voices of speakers. These obstructive practices became increasingly common and disturbed public assemblies a great deal in the 1890s. Organising an assembly in this period — especially if public, but also when it is private, because private assemblies can also be disrupted — meant having to reckon with attempts to sabotage by 'interrupters' or 'obstructionists' as they are called in police and press reports. The fact that the terms had become part of the vocabulary of observers of assemblies to describe those preventing orators from speaking is proof that the phenomena had become an everyday matter. Some groups seem to be more responsible than others for these widely spread obstructionist practices. A number of moderate republican commentators emphasise that one reaps what one sows, and that bad mores spread first to the masses, but then rebounded back to those who introduced them. For example, when Naquet deplored being a victim of obstructionism during an electoral campaign in Le Vaucluse on 25 August 1895, *Le Temps* recalled that he had taken part in Boulangist propaganda some years earlier; and 'nothing', said the author, 'contributed to [...] the spread [of these deplorable mores] as much as Boulangism'.[10] In much the same way, Jean Jaurès complained that 'his voice was drowned out in public assemblies and that obstruction and

---

10. *Le Temps*, 25 August 1895.

uproar were organised against him'. *Le Temps* replied that 'responsibility for the introduction of these brutal processes in public assemblies' could also be traced to 'socialist revolutionaries'.[11] In the 1890s obstruction reaches such a point that, at a time without microphones and loudspeakers, it seems that no-one could be confident not to be interrupted and prevented from giving a speech due to noise.

Emerging out of the clamour of earlier assemblies, we find a new element of obstruction in the shape of premeditation. When *Le Temps* deplored the spread of bad mores, it referred to 'the *premeditated* organisation of uproar and disorder'.[12] Planned and prepared beforehand, the noise was the work of an organisation. At the end of the 1880s, the commotion in assemblies was no longer just a spontaneous reaction of discontent by a few individuals faced with an opinion differing from their own and against which they demonstrated their disagreement. These forms of protest could have been considered as legitimate forms of expression. For example, on 11 May 1880, during debates in the Chamber, Théophile Marcou, a defender of absolute freedom of assembly and protesting against the idea that the police could dissolve an assembly on the grounds of turmoil, argued that this was sometimes welcome:

> In all popular assemblies there are ardent men who, sometimes, utter highly unsuitable words, and these words provoke protest; discussions, noise, turmoil. [...] It can get to the point, — and we have sometimes seen it here, — that the turmoil created in an assembly has a justifiable cause.[13]

Obstruction differs from this benevolent description because it is premeditated turmoil, decided before the assembly, and not a reaction to words uttered during its course. It is impossible in this case to find reassurance in debate. In his speech, Marcou adds, with the optimism typical of statements of the era, that turmoil will inevitably give way to calm due to 'good public sense, [and] the general reason that controls all assemblies'. By contrast, at the turn of the century, we recognise that disturbers do not attend in order to debate. They have made a prior decision to prevent a particular speech from being delivered through excessive noise, or even to prevent the assembly from being held. Police and press accounts stress that some attend assemblies 'with the recognised intention of disturbing them'.[14]

For a long time militant anarchists were considered the main obstructionists, described as the 'killjoy of meetings' in *Le Matin*.[15] Indeed, many police reports on private assemblies of some of their propagandist groups reveal that since the mid-1880s a strategy of obstruction is prepared prior to the assemblies they intend to attend. In November 1884 an informer wrote that, in an assembly held the day

---

11. *Le Temps*, 11 May 1897.
12. *Le Temps*, 25 August 1894.
13. *Journal Officiel*, 12 May 1880, p. 5,123.
14. AD BDR/1M/866/Réunions publiques, associations, 1893: Note au commissaire central, 10 août 1893.
15. *Le Matin*, 31 July 1887.

before by an anarchist group from the 15th *arrondissement*, 'Druelle [...] added that at the first assembly organised by the Guesdistes it was necessary to bring all *en masse*, to try to disrupt their session'.[16] In the 1880s, however, Eugène Sabin-Druelle is denounced as an *agent provocateur* and police spy. The affair was never cleared up, but 'what is certain is that in 1884, reports signed by Sabin reach the police prefecture'.[17] A police surveillance dossier of a meeting organised by the Boulangists some years later in August 1891 at the Cirque d'hiver, contains several reports which testify to the meticulous preparation made by anarchists planning to disrupt the rally. Several meetings were held beforehand to ensure a good number of well-positioned obstructionists, and so that the uproar could be unleashed by all of them simultaneously.[18]

A police report of 16 September 1889 stated that 'the Boulangists of the 10th *arrondissement* intend to go this [same evening] in large numbers to [an] assembly [...] to create a racket and impose their own agenda'.[19] In the late 1880s the Boulangists turned overwhelmingly to obstructionism, and were accused by the moderate republicans of having contributed to the spread of this practice among the masses. Here too, obstruction appears to have been well-organised. The Boulangists even resort to recruiting people specifically to create a racket at assemblies in order to drown out the voices of their opponents. Jean-Yves Mollier comments on the habit of hiring pedlars in the Boulangist cause:

> In deciding to recruit men who are not asked to be convinced by ideas that they will be induced to defend, to remunerate them for their work, to support the candidatures of the movement but also to try to prevent opponents from expressing themselves, we seriously risked altering the democratic life established with difficulty less than two decades ago.[20]

In 1888, the anti-Boulangist republican deputy Maxime Lecomte denounced the electoral mores introduced by Boulanger and his supporters in the North, a region where he was deputy and later senator: '[the Boulangists] have killed freedom of assembly in the North'.

> In the North, people have a calm temperament; they respect public speech, love liberty, and also tolerate contradiction. The farm-labourer and the worker express this in their frank and clear language: *let people talk*. The Boulangists have changed all that.

---

16. APP/Ba/1522/Meeting du 23 novembre 1884 salle Lévis: Rapport, 22 novembre 1884.
17. *Dictionnaire biographique du mouvement ouvrier français. 3. 1871–1914*, CD Rom.
18. APP/Ba/1531/Meeting Franco-Russe, 17 août 1891.
19. APP/Ba/1462/1889. Élections diverses. Réunions, 1ᵉʳ arr.: Rapport de l'officier de paix, préfecture de Police, police municipale, 2e brigade de recherches, cabinet, 1ᵉʳ *bureau*.
20. Jean-Yves Mollier, *Le camelot et la rue. Politique et démocratie au tournant des XIXᵉ et XXᵉ siècles*, Paris, Fayard, 2004, p. 126.

Lecomte recounts how obstruction is organised for public electoral assemblies, attesting to the necessary preparatory work:

> The Boulangist newspaper sellers [...], arrived early, spread out into the bars, warming-up the zeal of those they met, delivered small suitable lectures, in a style which was both emblematic and familiar, hired some recruits and, at the appointed hour, moved to take up strategic points in the room and to arrange their stooges. The interruptions [...] and the songs in response to agreed signs. [...] We find and recognise these hired interrupters in all important assemblies.[21]

In 1895 the political writer and moderate republican Henry Leyret opened a bistrot near Belleville in the anarchist milieu in order to 'carry out a study of the working-class milieu, [chosing] to go "among them"'.[22] In a chapter from his book *En plein faubourg* dedicated to public assemblies, Leyret notes that 'the platform of harangues wavers, compromised by Boulangism, which had perfected, and this is the most lasting memory of its passage, the art of organising pandemonium in public assemblies'. If the 'platform of harangues wavers', it is because it has been 'undermined by the "comrades", who taught people to respond to loud words with blows'.[23] If we are to believe Bruce Fulton, government too did not hesitate to incite the police do the same and to prevent Boulangists from speaking during the 1889 electoral campaign.[24] However I found no documentary traces of such governmental practices.

Ten years later, during the Dreyfus affair, obstruction had become an integral part of people's political habits. It was once again the object of an organisation prior to the sessions of assemblies. Several reports of surveillance of the *Ligue des Patriotes* testify to this: 'Between 1897 and 1900 the *Ligue* stood in the forefront of anti-Dreyfusard and nationalistic forces crowding the meeting halls and streets of Paris'.[25] On 1 May 1899 a police observer wrote:

> This evening before the meeting in the Mille Colonnes hall, activists from the *Ligue des Patriotes*, the *Jeunesse antisémite* and the *Parti républicain socialiste français*, will go in groups in the cafés of rue de la Gaité near the

---

21. Maxime Lecomte, *Le boulangisme dans le Nord. Histoire de l'élection du 15 avril*, Paris, À la librairie illustrée, 1888, pp. 140–141, cited in Jean-Charles Chapuzet, *Le général Boulanger et le boulangisme. Des passions politiques à l'oubli (1886–2005)*, PhD dissertation, IEP Paris, 2005, pp. 120–121.

22. Caroline Granier, *'Nous sommes des briseurs de formules'. Les écrivains anarchistes en France à la fin du XIXe siècle*, PhD dissertation, Paris VIII, 2003, http://raforum.apinc.org/article.php3?id_article=2470

23. Henri Leyret, *En plein faubourg (mœurs ouvrières)*, Paris, G. Charpentier et E. Fasquelle, 1895, pp. 217–218.

24. Bruce Fulton, 'The Boulanger Affair Revisited. The Preservation of the Third Republic', *French Historical Studies*, 1991, vol. 17, (2), p. 319.

25. Peter M. Rutkoff, 'The *Ligue des Patriotes*. The Nature of the Radical Right and the Dreyfus Affair', *French Historical Studies*, 1974, vol. 8, (4), p. 586.

hall. As soon as the assembly begins, they will enter and, as soon as Jaurès speaks, they will try, by interrupting, to provoke fights in order to prevent the speaker from continuing with his speech.[26]

This means that obstruction is not an individual action. According to the *Journal des Débats* of 26 January 1889, Boulangists 'plan to […] interrupt Jacquist speakers' in electoral assemblies in Paris 'in groups'.[27] A police report stated that it was 'a group of *sans-patrie*' who disturbed the progress of a contradictory electoral assembly in Marseilles on 1 May 1898.[28] The practice of group obstruction collides directly with the ideal of citizens' participation in public life through assemblies. Republicans praising its merits consider participants as having come to debate public issues after abstracting themselves from all links outside the framework of the assembly. On the contrary, obstructionists attend assemblies in group, inspired by a common idea which has been agreed beforehand, and which they have no intention of changing, or of trying to convince others of the value through debate. These groups go from around ten to several hundred individuals, depending on the size of the assembly to be disturbed. It is no longer a question of isolated individuals uniting in the course of the assembly to make noise and to challenge the speaker. When the assembly opens, if obstructionists sometimes disperse in the room, they generally stay grouped together. The *Journal des Débats* reported that the obstructionists 'massed in a corner of the room', making it easier for them to coordinate actions and physically defend themselves.[29]

Police and press observers describe noise in a rather general way. They refer to 'noise',[30] 'turmoil',[31] 'uproar',[32] or 'row'[33] drowning out the voice of a speaker. This intense noise is produced by organised shouting, and is identical in many assemblies. Frequently, the reports and articles do not specify the exact nature

---

26. AN/F7/12451/Ligue des patriotes. Rapports, 1899: Rapport d'un correspondant, 1er mai 1899. The *Parti républicain socialiste français*, whose influence was declining, represents the patriotic and anti-semitic extreme left. The *Jeunesse antisémite* is a league that first appeared in 1893. See: Bertrand Joly, 'The Jeunesse Antisémite et Nationaliste, 1894–1904', in Robert Tombs (ed.), *Nationhood and Nationalism in France. From Boulangism to the Great War. 1889–1918*, London, Routledge, 2001, pp. 147–158.

27. *Journal des Débats*, 26 January 1889.

28. AD BDR/1M/870/Réunions publiques, 1898–1899: Rapport du commissaire de police du 6e arr. au commissaire central, 1er mai 1898.

29. *Journal des Débats*, 20 January 1889.

30. APP/Ba/1462/1889. Élections diverses. Réunions, 1er arr.: Rapport, préfecture de Police, police municipale, 1re brigade de recherches, cabinet, 1er *bureau*, 20 septembre 1889 (réunion électorale, préau des écoles, impasse des Provençaux).

31. APP/Ba/614/Élections de 1885. Réunions du 8 janvier au 31 août 1885: Rapport, préfecture de Police, police municipale, 1re brigade de recherches, cabinet, 1er *bureau*, 20 juin 1885 (réunion bonapartiste, salle Favié).

32. 'Les réunions électorales', *Journal des Débats*, 21 January 1889.

33. APP/Ba/62/Comités bonapartistes, 1874–1886: Rapport, 11 juillet 1885, n.s. (réunion salle Wagram).

of the shouting, only mentioning the 'vociferation'[34] of obstructionists and their 'booing'.[35] 'Loud whistling' coming from the obstructionists was reported at an electoral assembly in Marseilles in 1893.[36] A police observer at an electoral assembly in La Ciotat writes that 'cries, whistling and songs are heard and for a while this prevented the speaker from making himself heard'.[37] Songs sung in chorus are another form of vocal obstruction. This was developed by the Boulangists who stifled the voice of their opponents with songs praising the merits of General Boulanger and criticising or mocking their opportunist adversaries. On 21 January 1889 the *Journal des Débats* reported an electoral assembly organised in Neuilly where the committee supported Jacques: 'Hardly had [the] former mayor of Neuilly, tried to form the *bureau*, [...] than the revisionists burst into popular refrains'. Consequently, 'discussion could not take place', and in the end 'the supporters of M. Jacques left the room'. But this example was also followed by the republicans, who had their own songs against the General or who intoned *La Marseillaise* to interrupt Boulangist speakers. In the same way, at the end of the 1890s, the anarchists sang *La Carmagnole* when they wanted to drown out a speaker's voice in Marseilles.[38]

The primary aim of this noise was to prevent a speaker from being heard by the audience, and if the obstruction was really effective, to persuade him to leave the platform. Silencing the adversary had also become a way to demonstrate his unpopularity or the incompetence of his supporters. In public electoral assemblies the demonstration is sometimes weakened by the vote on candidates, generally made at the end of the meeting, which may show that a candidate prevented from talking still had the majority of votes. On 24 January 1889 the *Journal des Débats* stated that:

> The candidature of M. Jacques is acclaimed each day in most public electoral assemblies. The scene is always the same: supporters of General Boulanger or citizen Boulé interrupt speakers, filibuster, and, when the time to vote comes, it turns out that they were only a small minority in the room.[39]

This remark is characteristic of those who condemn the development of obstructive practices. Obstructionists often attained their primary aim, to prevent one or other speaker from speaking, but were only a minority and their success merely revealed their intolerance and their violence. One should not deduce the popularity of a group from its success in obstructing others.

---

34. 'Les réunions électorales', *Journal des Débats*, 20 January 1889.
35. 'Mœurs électorales', *Le Temps*, 25 August 1895.
36. AD BDR/1M/866/Réunions publiques, associations, 1893: Note au commissaire central, 10 août 1893.
37. AD BDR/1M/865/Réunions et associations, 1885: Rapport du commissaire de police au préfet, La Ciotat, 24 septembre 1885.
38. See, for example: AD BDR/1M/870/Réunions publiques, 1898–1899: Rapport du commissaire de police du 6e arr. au commissaire central, 1er mai 1898.
39. *Journal des Débats*, 24 January 1889.

In the case of anarchists, obstruction often goes further: it can prevent an assembly from being held, and sometimes even take it over afterwards. Obstructionists then often use physical force to convince speakers and members of the *bureau* to leave the platform. At the end of the century, anti-semitic and nationalist assemblies were the favourite target of this form of obstruction. In Marseilles, in February 1898 a private meeting of the *Ligue antisémitique* with 250 people was overrun by around fifty anarchists. After having attempted in vain to gain entry with fake letters of invitation, they entered by another entrance in the *brasserie* where the assembly was being held: it was subsequently interrupted.[40]

The government is sometimes accused of provoking this obstruction by paying people to make a noise so that potentially harmful meetings end in disorder. The police then intervene to put an end to the outbursts that often accompany verbal obstruction, and are thus seen to be restoring public order. Nationalist and anti-semitic assemblies where anarchists came to obstruct are often followed by accusations of so-called government manœuvres, either by their organisers or by a sympathetic press. They claim that the anarchists are only police spies paid to shout. Obstruction would not necessarily be the expression of a political disagreement but rather a desperate attempt by government to deflect attention from its own overwhelming crises. On 7 January 1893, *La Libre Parole,* a 'newspaper [animated by] its anti-semitic campaigns, its reports on financial scandals and its continual attacks on government and parliamentarians', describes a nationalist assembly in Tivoli Wauxhall hall as follows: 'At 10.15, the police spies massed, and all shouting, "Long live anarchy!", mounted the platform'.[41] This was the pretext for the police to intervene: 'Uniformed agents burst into the room uttering cries like wild beasts'. The journalist denounces what he refers to as a 'police ambush', to which the opportunist government had resorted in order to 'save the corrupt politicians and thieves of Panama'. However if we are to believe police informers, the obstructionists in this assembly are actually anarchists.[42]

When it is a question of obstruction of electoral assemblies organised by republicans, the republican press insists on the contempt for universal suffrage revealed by these practices. They are opposed to the need of electors to have a clearer picture before the vote through discussions held in assemblies. On 23 January 1889 *La Justice* reported that at the time of the election campaign in la Seine:

> The Boulangists, always friends of the *lumières*, have found a new trick to enlighten the electoral body on the merits of their candidate. When they cannot

---

40. AD BDR/1M/869/Réunions publiques, 1898 janvier–avril: Rapport du commissaire central au préfet des Bouches-du-Rhône, 2 février 1898.
41. Claude Bellanger, Jacques Godechot, Pierre Guiral and Fernand Terrou (eds), *Histoire générale de la presse française*, Paris, PUF, 1972, vol. 3, pp. 343–344.
42. APP/Ba/1531/Meeting de la salle Tivoli Wauxhall hall, 7 janvier 1893: Rapports 'Barbier' et 'Jules', 7 janvier 1893.

drown out the voice of their contradictor with their row, they force the public to retreat by cutting the gas pipes and plunging the room into darkness.[43]

The process of obstruction is described as a display of intolerance and denounced as the sign of a dangerous lack of reason. 'You must not be mistaken here: being incapable of reason, means admitting to being incapable of living in freedom. It is not reasonable to replace a speech with noise', according to *Le Temps*; 'You stifle my voice with your howling. What does that prove? That you are right and that I am wrong? No, only that you have stronger lungs than mine'.[44] Responding to a speech with uproar, instead of arguing, is considered as much more serious when the obstruction disturbs electoral assemblies which are vital for informing voters. These new mores that suffocate discussion by an organised racket are 'real violence done to universal suffrage'.[45]

Besides the condemnation of obstructionism, protection is organised against it. Public assemblies held by moderate republicans became scarcer. When in December 1886, the *Alliance républicaine* tried to hold a public meeting, it was disturbed by anarchists. A month later, a private assembly was organised and we read in *Le Temps* on 18 January 1887: 'speakers could speak with ease in a room of friends and develop questions that could not be dealt with in the previous meeting'.[46] The development of obstructive practices compelled occasionally moderate republicans to take refuge in private assemblies, sometimes very large, but not opened to the public. 'First in Paris and then in cities with large working-class populations, the public assembly becomes the privileged, if not unique, means of expression for [...] socialists, radicals, nationalists or Boulangists', notes Michel Offerlé.[47] One can also respond to noise with noise, obstructing in order to counter the obstruction. But when the way to combat the noise of one's opponents is to take refuge in a private assembly or to resort to making noise oneself, we are a long way from the ideal of a citizens' gathering where the adversary's ideas are defeated by the formulation of arguments based on reason.

The failure to pacify political mores

Alain Garrigou stresses that the '[electoral] campaigns [under the Third Republic] often take place in a tense atmosphere, marked by fights and the use of weapons'. He also suggests that violence did not disappear at the turn of the century, but that it was distinct from 'the old community violence', insofar as it '[opposes] more frequently the groups of activists mobilised by the election'. Without breaking completely with 'ordinary' violence, its characteristic is to '[continue] on a new

---

43. *La Justice*, 23 January 1889.
44. *Le Temps*, 11 May 1897.
45. *Le Temps*, 25 August 1893.
46. *Le Temps*, 18 January 1887.
47. Offerlé, 'La mobilisation électorale en milieu urbain'.

more specifically political basis'.[48] We can observe the presence of this politicised violence in assemblies, electoral or otherwise. The desire to pacify political mores by creating a place where conflicts are resolved through deliberation is faced with intensified resistance in gatherings at the end of the century. My research for this period is largely based on assemblies in two large cities, Paris and Marseilles, and so I cannot report on possible differences in assemblies taking place in small towns or the countryside. Still, a real difference is suggested by a few contemporary observers. In an article in *Le Matin* entitled 'The Law and Mores', Jules Simon mentions electoral campaigns taking place in villages, and remarks how quiet the meetings are, and how one can still find 'the mores of the golden age'.[49] He claims that there is a striking contrast with the 'new mores' that have ruined assemblies in Paris and large cities in general. This study focuses on these new violent mores that typify assemblies in large cities, rather than on the possible survival of calmer democratic assemblies somewhere else. Olivier Fillieule considers that there is political violence — in the case of street demonstrations — when:

> The assembly of persons for political ends [...] has the effect of causing bodily wounds and/or material damage in the public or private domain and tends to modify the situation of protagonists in a situation where blows are exchanged.[50]

Here I adopt this definition by outcome, and distinguish physical violence — that is, actions during or at the end of assemblies whose effect is 'bodily wounds' or 'material damage' — from oral violence, or calls to commit such actions.[51]

At the end of the century oral anarchist violence had become very important from this perspective insofar as it raised anxious questions about the possible links between incitement to violence in speeches in assemblies and the occurrence of actual physical violence. Anarchists, however, were not the only ones to call for violent action in assemblies — without wanting to move the two phenomena closer together, there is the question of nationalist assemblies and their instigation to anti-semitic violence. In anti-Dreyfusard assemblies in 1898, police informers talk of 'appalling violence' in speeches which 'could, without exaggeration, be considered as incitement to civil and religious war'.[52]

---

48. Garrigou, *Histoire sociale du suffrage universel en France*, pp. 122, 126–127.
49. *Le Matin*, 25 September 1889.
50. Olivier Fillieule, *Stratégies de la rue. Les manifestations en France*, Paris, Presses de Sciences Po, 1997, p. 98. See also: Olivier Fillieule, 'L'émergence de la violence dans la manifestation de rue. Éléments pour une analyse étiologique', *Cultures & Conflits*, 1993, vols. 9–10, pp. 267–291.
51. The definition excludes insult, although its use was developing at that time. Mollier talks of the Dreyfus affair as 'the climax of manipulation of insult in politics under the Third Republic'. See: Jean-Yves Mollier, 'Quand les camelots se politisent et manient l'insulte...', in Thomas Bouchet, Matthew Leggett, Jean Vigreux and Geneviève Verdo (eds), *L'insulte (en) politique. Europe et Amérique latine du XIXᵉ siècle à nos jours*, Dijon, Éditions Universitaires de Dijon, 2005, pp. 58–61.
52. Pierre Birnbaum, *Le moment antisémite. Un tour de France en 1898*, Paris, Fayard, 1998, p. 47.

Caroline Granier asks what 'making propaganda' meant for anarchists at the end of the nineteenth century, and reminds us that for them 'it is first a question of men who must be changed, trained, educated'. She wrote that they 'try to make individuals (convinced, not believers, according to Jean Grave's distinction), handling people with logic and reason and not by feelings'.[53] Alexander Varias also stresses that the anarchists close to the thought of Jean Grave defended the idea that 'knowledge and reason were instrumental in the process of change'.[54] This is a current of anarchism influential in the 1880s and which had some repercussions on the form taken by assemblies. In effect, since 'anarchism [is not] a dogma', since 'it is not so much a question of creating followers as of informing, so that individuals can choose in all freedom, build up an opinion', assemblies must logically leave room for discussion. Thus, they are often contradictory: 'It means reflecting together and not just uttering good words'.[55] On this point, if their aims differ, the conception that anarchists have of assembly is compatible with the republican ideal. A key difference, however, is the fact that for anarchists discussion must be fully free, and without an organising authority. They often reject the selection of a *bureau* imposed by law: there are many examples of assemblies without a *bureau* where speakers insisted that the rejection of authority should be absolute.[56] The organisers of these assemblies are then sometimes fined for violation of the 1881 law.[57] When a *bureau* is set up, it is often artificial in nature. A report on an 1893 assembly in Marseilles states:

> One of the conveners [...] opens the session more or less in these terms: 'In order to confirm to a certain law of 1881, I invite three persons of my general staff to take their places in the *bureau* and when we have these three puppets in place we can start our assembly'. Three anarchists who were only waiting for this invitation, climbed onto the rostrum to take place.[58]

Anarchist assemblies enter into open conflict with the republican enterprise of pacification of mores through participation in assemblies above all when the

---

53. Caroline Granier, '*Nous sommes des briseurs de formules*'. *Les écrivains anarchistes en France à la fin du XIXᵉ siècle*, PhD dissertation, Paris VIII, 2003, http://raforum.apinc.org/article.php3?id_article=2470. In particular, Jean Grave developed this theory in *La société mourante et l'anarchie*, Paris, Tresse et Stock, 1893.
54. Alexander Varias, *Paris and the Anarchists. Aesthetes and Subversives at the Fin-de-Siècle*, Basingstoke, Macmillan, 1997, p. 88.
55. Granier, '*Nous sommes des briseurs de formules*'.
56. See, for example: APP/Ba/1502/Propagande anarchiste par la parole: Rapport du contrôleur général, 19 février 1882, 'réunion anarchiste'; Rapport, Paris, 24 janvier 1883, réunion organisée par les groupes anarchistes, salle Rivoli.
57. See, for example: AD BDR/1M/866/Réunions publiques, associations, 1893: Rapport du sous-préfet d'Aix au préfet des Bouches-du-Rhône, 13 février 1893; AN/F7/12504/Agitation anarchiste. Tournées de conférences. 1882–1898: Rapport du commissaire de police du 6e arr., Bordeaux, 10 mai 1897.
58. AD BDR/1M/866/Réunions publiques, associations. 1893: Rapport du commissaire de police au commissaire central, 15e arr., 5 août 1893 (réunion café de la concorde, 255 bd. national).

speeches made are a direct call to commit acts of violence and, when these acts occur, they glorify this violence. In the early 1890s 'oral violence frames [...] the anarchist gesture' in assemblies.[59] The 1876 International Anarchist Congress in Bern launched the slogan of propaganda through facts, implemented from 1877 onwards in Italy, and reaffirmed by the London Anarchist Congress in July 1881. It was no longer a matter of simply educating the masses through spoken or written propaganda. The virtues of this are not denied; but it was not sufficient. Anarchists are encouraged to resort to 'action [that] engenders and spreads ideas'.[60] The French libertarian movement adopted choices made by the London Congress in formulating a model of anarchist action based largely on violence. The actual transition from words to actions proved rare in the 1880s, and it was not until 1892–1894 that we see the development of what Jean Maitron describes as a 'real terrorist epidemic'.[61]

Although propaganda through facts was not put to practice until the early 1890s, a direct incitement to violent action had already developed in the speeches of assemblies in the 1880s. In 1883 a police informer for an assembly organised by 'the anarchist initiative of Paris', stated that:

> A [...] working-class citizen, or rather a comrade, [...] replies [...] that in the coming revolution workers must use all the means that modern science puts at their disposal, such as petrol and dynamite.[62]

Reactions in the republican press to these calls to violence are rare. On 26 February 1886, an article in *Le Temps* on lectures by Louise Michel and Pyotr Kropotkin considered it deplorable that the social philosophy expounded in their assemblies was accompanied by 'a perpetual call to revolt and violence'. For the author of the article, 'it is regrettable [...] that under cover of freedom of assembly or freedom of the press, acts similar to a provocation to civil war are committed with impunity'.[63] The term 'with impunity' is excessive: we have seen that the Press Law of 29 July 1881 had already stipulated that speakers in public assemblies could be arrested for 'instigating crimes and offences'.[64] This is sometimes put into practice. In November 1887, for example, the Assizes Court of Aisne fined three anarchists and sentenced one to a year's imprisonment and the others to three months, for incitement to murder and pillage during two public assemblies. Devertus, editor of *Le Cri du Peuple*, and the most severely condemned, 'invited his audience to eliminate exploiters, to pickpocket their neighbours, to cut off protruding heads,

---

59. Pierre Éric Martin, *Le mouvement anarchiste français et la violence politique. 1892–1894*, Master of Advanced Studies dissertation, IEP Paris, 2002, p. 109.
60. Granier, '*Nous sommes des briseurs de formules*'.
61. Jean Maitron, *Le mouvement anarchiste en France*, Paris, Maspero, 1975, vol. 1, p. 212.
62. APP/Ba/1502/Propagande anarchiste par la parole: Rapport '34', 29 juillet 1883.
63. *Le Temps*, 26 February 1886.
64. Franck Laidié, 'L'insulte en politique saisie par le droit', in Thomas Bouchet, Matthew Leggett, Jean Vigreux and Geneviève Verdo (eds), *L'insulte (en) politique*, pp. 259–268.

to fire on officers in the case of war'.[65] In the 1880s, nevertheless, the republican press and police observers tend to minimise the importance of speeches calling for violence, as seen in the recurrent comments insisting that there was little echo of violent speeches in public assemblies. For example, an 1885 report states that: 'The discourse was not of great interest and was delivered to a rather scant public, yawning with boredom; the anarchists themselves left to chat with their comrades who had been arrested the week before and then released'.[66] The predominant conviction was that men could 'say what they liked', because the wild ideas expressed would disappear in the face of the public's common sense.

Things changed in the early 1890s, primarily due to a wave of anarchist attacks in France. Some incidents had 'long focussed attention of contemporaries, militants and historians of anarchism, due to their spectacular nature, and the well-publicised trials that followed'.[67] They focus on a small number of figures: Ravachol, who, among other things, in 1892, set off a bomb at the home of solicitor general Bulot who had condemned comrades who took part in the tumultuous parade in Clichy on 1 May 1891; Jules Léauthier, who in 1894, assassinated a restaurant client wearing a military decoration (who turned out to be a Serbian minister); Auguste Vaillant, who set off a bomb in the Chamber on 9 December 1893; Émile Henry, who threw a bomb into a café near Saint-Lazare station on 12 February 1894 and when arrested, claimed to be responsible for the 8 November 1892 attack on the 'des Bons-Enfants' police station; or Sante Caserio, who assassinated President Sadi Carnot on 24 June 1894. But the anarchist violence in this period was not limited to these spectacular events.[68] The early 1890s were marked by the perpetration of many other less well-known dynamite attacks, and by an intense 'use of arson as a means of revolutionary struggle'. Pierre Éric Martin refers to this as 'inter-individual violence', that is, aggression against persons believed to embody the social order that anarchists oppose, together with a great deal of 'material violence' (attempts to derail trains, damaging gas pipes, throwing stones at prisons, and so forth).[69]

In parallel, there is an increase of oral violence in speeches during assemblies. 'If anarchist violence is primarily physical violence, it is still linked to oral and written forms that precede (incitation and excitation), and succeed it (apologies)'; 'propaganda in words is [...] systematically conceived as the counterpart of propaganda in fact'.[70] We also see the emergence of the new idea that the impact of

---

65. Taken from the article 'Trois anarchistes en cour d'assises', *Le Temps*, 26 novembre 1887.
66. APP/Ba/1502/Propagande anarchiste par la parole: Rapport, 24 décembre 1885, n.s. (regarding a public contradictory assembly held the day before by anarchist groups in the Graffard meeting room).
67. Martin, *Le mouvement anarchiste français*, p. 51.
68. See, in particular: Jean Maitron, *Le mouvement anarchiste en France*, Paris, Maspero, 1975, vol. 1, pp. 206–250.
69. Martin, *Le mouvement anarchiste français*, pp. 83–98.
70. Martin, *Le mouvement anarchiste français*, pp. 82, 109.

this propaganda must be taken seriously given the potential link between words and actions. The assemblies of 1892 are marked by the explicit incitement of anarchist speakers to act violently. In a speech delivered on 28 May 1892 in the salle du Commerce in Paris, Jean Pausader, known as Jacques Prolo, declared: 'Anarchists have all it takes to succeed: they hold the most terrible weapon, a weapon that I do not need to name, here it is!' The police report stated that he: 'pulled a stick of dynamite out of his waistcoat pocket', which caused a 'general enthusiasm'.[71] This valorisation of propaganda through facts is decided in assemblies preparatory to public meetings. On 18 August 1892, a surveillance report pointed out that:

> The group of anarchist propaganda has taken the initiative of holding several meetings in support of the revolutionary movement. These meetings, according to the agenda distributed last Saturday, will be very violent and will only preach heroic deeds of individual action.[72]

Speakers glorified attacks committed by anarchists who are then held up as a model. In particular there is the figure of Ravachol. In the report of 8 May 1892 on an assembly of the same propagandist group, it is recorded that Renard announced that he 'intended to organise a forthcoming meeting to inform people about the incentive which Ravachol had acted on in his propaganda by facts', and that 'Bruneau, in turn, also said that 'a meeting was going to be organised soon to glorify the conduct of Ravachol and Pini'.[73] In his study of speeches made by two militant anarchists in the assemblies of 1892 and 1893, Pierre Eric Martin found 'the same systematic discourse and apologetics exclusively centred on violence and the exaltation of acts of violence'.[74]

The violence of speeches held in assemblies during the years when anarchist attacks increased was no longer considered with serenity by the republican power which was one of the targets. On this point Richard David Sonn likens the anarchist movement to other 'extremist groups' of the time, such as the Boulangists or nationalists on the grounds that 'they are opposed, and opposed violently, to the particular form of State took in the Third Republic'.[75] For François Beaudenon, 'nothing, in republican ideology and accomplishments, found favour in the eyes of the anarchists'.[76] He nevertheless stresses that there were

---

71. APP/Ba/1531/Meeting organisé par les anarchistes à la salle du commerce, 28 mai 1892: Rapport, préfecture de Police, cabinet, 1er *bureau*, 29 mai 1892.
72. APP/Ba/1502/Propagande anarchiste par la parole: Rapport, 18 août 1892, 'Correspondance anarchiste'.
73. APP/Ba/1502/Propagande anarchiste par la parole: Rapport, Paris, 8 mai 1892 (réunion, 104 rue Oberkampf, salle des grandes caves). Vittorio Pini was condemned in 1892 to five years' imprisonment and Ravachol was executed in 1892.
74. Martin, *Le mouvement anarchiste français*, p. 115.
75. Richard David Sonn, *Anarchism and Cultural Politics in Fin de Siècle France*, Lincoln, University of Nebraska Press, 1989, p. 34.
76. François Beaudenon, *Entre ordre et liberté. Le combat républicain contre l'anarchisme. 1880–1900*, MAS, IEP Grenoble, 1997, pp. 60, 62.

'complex, and quite ambiguous, bonds' between the anarchist movement and the Republic. 'If anarchism presents itself as a doctrine which breaks resolutely with the republican political tradition, the outcome of 1789 or 1793, this separation will never be either definitive or total', writes Gaetano Manfredonia.[77] Alexander Varias also stresses that in spite of their criticism 'anarchists still viewed the Third Republic as a progressive force when compared to the autocracy of the Second Empire and the narrow elitism of the July Monarchy', and that 'some anarchists came to its defence when it was attacked by reactionaries'.[78] In any case, when the government starts to consider that there is a link between words publicly calling for violence and concrete actions of violence, the republican axiom 'do not let anything be done, but let everything be said'— recalled as the 'M. Grévy's watchword' in *La Petite Gazette* on February 1886 — is no longer convincing.[79] In 1893 and 1894 three repressive laws were adopted. The attack on Vaillant was followed by the vote of the 'law amending Articles 24, pars. 1, 25 and 49 of the law of 29 July 1881 on the press' of 12 December 1893, and of the 'law on criminal associations' of 18 December 1893. After Carnot's assassination, the 'law to repress anarchist intrigues' of 28 July 1894 was passed. The legislation in question is described by their opponents as '*lois scélérates*', i.e. 'iniquitous laws', 'special laws' which were 'excessive and uncivilised',[80] unworthy of a free country. The reaction of the public powers to the attacks changed the regime of freedom of expression in assemblies. It meant that the notion that anything could be said in a political meeting without endangering public order, and that the latter even had an interest in assuring a full freedom in the matter, was progressively ditched. In the early 1890s, the words pronounced in assemblies were no longer perceived as appropriate 'safety valves against explosions',[81] but on the contrary, as triggering violence. Certainly, the 1881 Press Law had already set limits to what could be said in assemblies, but the 1893–1894 legislation went much further. Without going into detail, it introduced heavier penalties and a new procedure, but also a new crime. The 1881 law only aimed the direct provocation of facts described as crimes, but the law of 12 December 1893 also punished speakers engaged in eulogising such facts with up to five years' imprisonment, which was perceived as an indirect provocation.

Legal experts defending this new legislation insisted that '[the law] strikes [...] *acts* and not *opinions*'. These are the words, for example, of René Garraud, lawyer in the court of appeal and professor of law at the University of Lyon. In 1895 he went on to argue for a 'struggle against criminality by moral and religious

---

77. Gaetano Manfredonia, *Études sur le mouvement anarchiste en France (1848–1914)*, PhD dissertation, IEP Paris, 1990, vol. 3, p. 197.
78. Varias, *Paris and the Anarchists*, pp. 82–83.
79. *La Petite Gazette*, 12 February 1886.
80. Francis De Pressensé, un juriste, and Émile Pouget, *Les Lois Scélérates de 1893–1894*, Paris, Éditions de la *Revue blanche*, 1899, p. 9.
81. *Le Rappel*, 20 May 1869.

education, medical hygiene, just as much as by repression in the strict sense of the word',[82] and wrote:

> One can be anarchist, profess anarchist opinions, make them circulate, even publicly, by word of mouth and in the press, without falling foul of the law: there is no such thing as an *anarchist crime*. But what one cannot do is to *prepare an attack*, by inciting directly or indirectly to commit it, or approving those who have committed it.[83]

Guillaume Loubat, public prosecutor in Saint-Étienne, begins his study of the laws against anarchists by referring to the 'many attacks that have occurred in succession for some years'.[84] In the first place these attacks justified the new legislation. Oral violence was presented as encouraging physical violence, and as a result speakers in assemblies were no longer protected from repression, especially since these laws were applied quite strictly.[85]

The 'iniquitous laws' did not enjoy unanimous support during the debates preceding their adoption. Dominique Cochart highlights the divergences which emerged among republicans. In particular, Maurice Lasserre, president of the commission of enquiry on the draft law and its *rapporteur*, considered that the exceptional situation justified limiting freedom in the name of public order, whereas Henri Brisson rejected the plan, calling on the government to continue to trust in public opinion. The ideas of the latter remain close to those dominant in the Chamber during the debates which led to the 1881 law.[86] Nevertheless, these divergences did not prevent the laws from being voted on rapidly. Their adoption revealed a resolve to exclude violent action as a possible expression of legitimate protest. This was not a break with the republican ideal dominant until the 1880s, but it did mark the end of an era in which republicans were convinced that reason would necessarily prevail in open debate, and that there was thus no need for alarm about violent words uttered in assemblies. It is a '[reactivation of] a notion such as the crime of opinion', contrasting with the liberal tradition.[87] Jean-Pierre Machelon talks of a 'break with the philosophy of the 1881 law', that is, here with the Press Law but which also concerns verbal crimes made in assemblies.[88] In the early

---

82. J. Richardot, 'Garraud (Jean-René)', in Michel Prevost, Jean-Charles Roman d'Amat and Henri Tribout de Morembert (eds), *Dictionnaire de biographie française*, vol. 15, Paris, Letouzey & Ané, p. 554.
83. René Garraud, *L'anarchie et la répression*, Paris, L. Larose, 1895, p. 25.
84. Guillaume Loubat, *Code de la législation contre les anarchistes*, Paris, Chevalier-Marescq, 1895, p. 7.
85. Martin, *Le mouvement anarchiste français et la violence politique*, p. 124. See also: De Pressensé, un juriste, and Pouget, *Les Lois scélérates*, pp. 31–53.
86. Dominique Cochart, 'Eléments de réflexion sur les rapports entre ordre moral et républicanisme, in *Les bonnes mœurs*, Paris, PUF, 1994, pp. 245–249.
87. Beaudenon, *Entre ordre et liberté*, pp. 30, 34.
88. Jean-Pierre Machelon, *La République contre les libertés? Les restrictions aux libertés publiques de 1879 à 1914*, Paris, FNSP, 1976, p. 430.

1890s, oral propaganda was considered dangerous because it could bring with it violent action, even if speeches did not call for it directly.

What are the effects of these laws on the speeches made in assemblies? In 1895, Guillaume Loubat was delighted to note the 'considerable results' produced by the law of 12 December 1893: 'It curbs [...] the fiery sermons that the doctors of anarchy disseminated in their lectures.' He adds 'From this day, these prudent apostles were afraid', and 'speakers kept silent, knowing that at the first outburst they would be arrested'.[89] Direct incitement to commit violent actions and the glorification of these acts disappear from the accounts of public anarchist assemblies that I have consulted. The prefect of Bouches-du-Rhône claims to observe the change as of 31 December 1893, in a report to the Minister of the Interior on the anarchist organisation in Marseilles. After having listed the places and main speakers of anarchist assemblies, he writes:

> The propaganda begun in 1891 by Sébastien Faure has returned. For the last eight days, this particularly dangerous anarchist has re-established himself in Marseilles. His lectures have resumed with much success. Nevertheless, if his ideas remain the same, the form is singularly changed. This is one of the fortunate effects of the recently adopted laws.[90]

Some years later, in 1896, the threat seemed so well assimilated that a commissair could write in his report on an assembly in Marseilles that 'a man called Gros talked for around ten minutes, succinctly expounding the theory of anarchy, obviously refraining from violent language and incitement to revolt by explosive means'.[91] Speakers can, however, show their audience that they do not extol propaganda just because of the law. In a public assembly in Arles in 1898, Henri Dhorr states in his speech:

> I do not call for revolution, but I say that at present a revolutionary push seems near; it seems to be imminent; a storm is brewing. An iniquitous law lies in wait for us, but I shall say nothing that would make me fall into the nets of this robber's law.[92]

It is also likely that verbal violence had a strong hold in private assemblies, despite the fear of police spies. Here, there would be an undesired effect of laws against anarchist propaganda. In a report to the Minister of the Interior in December 1893, the prefect of Gironde noted that 'until then, anarchist assemblies had for the most part been public and contradictory', before going on to state that

---

89. Loubat, *Code de la législation contre les anarchistes*, pp. 7–8.
90. AN/F7/12504: Agitation anarchiste. Tournées de conferences, 1882–1898: Rapport du préfet des Bouches-du-Rhône au Ministre de l'Intérieur, direction de la sûreté générale, 31 décembre 1893.
91. AD BDR/1M/867/Partis et mouvements politiques. Réunions publiques, 1896: Rapport du commissaire de police au commissaire central, 26 avril 1896.
92. AD BDR/1M/869/Réunions publiques, janvier-avril 1898: Rapport du commissaire central au sous-préfet, Arles, 26–27 février 1898.

'since the new measures taken by the government and chambers, it was decided [by the anarchists] that these assemblies would henceforth be secret and with only a few people attending'.[93]

This verbal violence was accompanied by an escalation of physical violence in gatherings. In the 1890s in particular, brawls, which already occurred in earlier political assemblies, assumed a different form. We witness the appearance of more intense, frequent and organised violence. The fact that this is decided in advance and consequently intentional, stands out particularly in reports on private anarchist assemblies preparing public meetings. A report on an assembly of a group of Marseillais anarchists in 1893 states: 'one activist said it was useful to arm oneself with a bat before going to assemblies given by the different factions quarrelling over the spoils of power'.[94] Preparation is also made in the nationalist camp. The report on an assembly of the *Ligue des Patriotes* in 1898 asserts:

> Déroulède has [...] given instructions to place the police at the entrance and in the meeting room. These instructions, to be kept in all assemblies given by the League, mean letting in the Dreyfusards who will turn up to disturb assemblies, to surround them and to 'give them what they deserve'.[95]

The development of prepared violence, and the reactions it causes, is similar to what can be observed for the practice of obstruction; and the same groups are often implicated in fights.

In the 1880s, the most frequent fights in assemblies were between anarchist and socialist militants, and between militants of different schools of socialism. The stormy assembly held in the Palais de la Bourse on 20 September 1885, convened by the *Parti ouvrier révolutionnaire* of Jean Allemane (then a 'possibiliste'), was mentioned in Chapter One. When it came to setting up the *bureau*, a fight broke out between blanquists and anarchists. A great deal of ink flowed after this assembly as a result of revolver shots being fired causing injuries.[96] Fights of this sort are frequent in socialist assemblies. Setting up the *bureau* is always the first occasion for altercations between socialist groups working to impose their own representatives. But this type of incident 'disappeared [quite rapidly] for assemblies organised by the socialists'. Indeed, 'the electoral map of Paris is fixed, the boundaries between the groups are recognised or at least tolerated,

---

93. AN/F7/12504/Agitation anarchiste. Tournées de conferences, 1882–1898: Rapport du préfet de Gironde au Ministre de l'Intérieur, direction de la sûreté générale, Bordeaux, 17 décembre 1893.

94. AD BDR/1M/866/Réunions publiques, associations, 1893: Rapport du commissaire de police au commissaire central, 9 août 1893, réunion anarchiste au bar Isnard, place Saint-Michel.

95. AN/F7/12451/Ligue des Patriotes, septembre–décembre 1898: Rapport, préfecture de Police, Paris, 6 décembre 1898, réunion privée gymnase Pascaud.

96. See the police reports and press clippings in: APP/Ba/617/Réunion électorale tenue au Palais de la Bourse le 20 septembre 1885 par le comité électoral ouvrier des 1er et 2e arr. Fédération des travailleurs socialistes de France, Parti ouvrier: possibilistes.

militants have acquired the *savoir faire* needed to keep command of the *bureau*'.[97] When these fights are condemned by republicans in government, particularly in the press, they refer them especially at the fringes of politics. Physical violence had always been a question of 'revolutionaries' — the various socialist factions are confused with the anarchists under the same label — unable to debate seriously and always coming to blows. 'Revolutionaries still fought among themselves', reports *Le Temps* in 1885 about an assembly in Belleville.[98] In December 1884 the *Journal des Débats* reported on an assembly in Paris where 'revolutionary socialists and anarchists insulted each other, blows were exchanged, and benches were thrown over each other's heads'.[99] Putting an end to discussion by physical violence in these assemblies is highlighted, with the underlying idea that socialists thus betray their inability to express a serious political claim.

In 1889 Jules Simon deplores the fact that in 'Paris and large cities, people discuss with blows, imitating the cries of animals, breaking tables, throwing chairs', and that 'when an electoral assembly is announced, the police prepare cells in the prison of the *Conciergerie*, and the public assistance prepares beds in hospitals'. For him, 'it is M. Boulanger who inaugurated or developed these new mores'.[100] Many regret that, instead of the desired pacification, assemblies testified to a degradation of popular political mores. These mores had become more violent, and it would be the Boulangist movement that marked the real turning point. The habit of resorting to violence spread with the General. Assemblies held for the legislative election of la Seine in January 1889 were effectively marked by frequent episodes of violence, with only a few meetings left undisturbed. The newspapers which support neither Boulanger, nor Jacques — the latter being the candidate supported by the government — give the impression that fights are a general phenomenon. In January the catholic newspaper *La Croix* reported frequent accounts describing a daily scrum. For example on the 17 of the month: 'Each evening Jacobins and Boulangists hold small assemblies and nearly all end in punch-ups or blows with sticks'. 'There were brawls in five or six other meetings, this is the outcome of yesterday evening's assemblies', summed up a journalist on 20–21 January.[101] The pro-Jacques press affirms that the most serious violence is caused by the General's supporters. 'Boulangist attack in a public assembly', runs the title of *Le Matin* on 22 January on a contradictory public assembly in a school hall where an attempt was made to wound Emmanuel Arène, republican deputy, when he responded to a Boulangist speaker. The account given in the article is quite eloquent:

---

97. Michel Offerlé, *Les socialistes et Paris, 1881–1900, des communards aux conseillers municipaux*, PhD dissertation, Paris I, 1979, pp. 446–447.
98. *Le Temps*, 23 September 1885.
99. *Journal des Débats*, 4 December 1884.
100. *Le Matin*, 25 September 1889.
101. *La Croix*, 17, 20, 21 January 1889.

M. Arène was speaking when a very serious incident occurred. A Boulangist, who had repeatedly interrupted M. Arène, perched himself on one of the windows of the schoolroom, but from the outside, with the help of a ladder, and threw a solid object with the form of a large paving stone onto the platform in the direction of the Corsican deputy, which hit the nape of the neck of a voter seated in front of M. Arène. The wounded elector gave a cry and his wound gushed blood over the *bureau* and over the neighbours of this unfortunate man. Indescribable chaos ensued. The electors, indignant about this cowardly attack, immediately began to search for this miserable wretch.[102]

The use of violence to put an end to oral contradiction, the description of the wounded man as 'a voter', the insistence on the brutality of the action, and the fact that it triggered the indignation of 'electors', all relegated the Boulangists to the side of barbarity, far from electoral civility. If they '[make every effort] to disturb assemblies and to provoke murderous scrums', it is due to their 'supreme desire to put an end to civil discussion', states *La Justice* regarding the same meeting.[103] The explanation given for this attitude is that the Boulangists fear contradiction and want to prevent all discussion by transforming assemblies into battlefields.

The agitation caused by nationalists at the end of the century constitutes a new and major form of resistance in the enterprise of the pacification of mores through participation in assemblies. The 'patriotic' assemblies organised particularly around the Dreyfus affair are marked by significant acts of violence. These first occur during assemblies. In an assembly organised on 17 January 1898 by nationalists and anti-Semites in Paris, 'a general scrum ensued: blows with sticks and fists were exchanged, they fought with flags, there are many wounded and smashed skulls', according to Pierre Birnbaum.[104] Violence in assemblies continued the following year. In an assembly organised in Marseilles by the *Ligue des Patriotes* on 5 February 1899, a police report mentions several revolver shots.[105] During a nationalist assembly in Paris on 28 December 1899, a brawl started, in the words of a police informer, between 'republicans' and 'socialists' against 'nationalists and patriots': 'We could hear the noise of windows and mirrors, shouts, cursing, and blows in the midst of the dark. […] The damage must be immense and with a great many wounded'.[106]

What is even more serious is the violence at the end of anti-Dreyfusard assemblies, particularly in January and February 1898, and sometimes in the form

---

102. *Le Matin*, 22 January 1889.

103. *La Justice*, 24 January 1898.

104. Pierre Birnbaum, *Le moment antisémite. Un tour de France en 1898*, Paris, Fayard, 1998, p. 20.

105. AN/F7/12466/Affaire Dreyfus. Réunions, Bouches-du-Rhône: Rapport du commissariat spécial au Ministre de l'Intérieur, 1ᵉʳ février 1899.

106. AN/F7/12458: Surveillance des nationalistes dans le département de la Seine, juin–décembre 1899: Rapport, 29 décembre 1899, n.s.

of anti-Semitic riots.[107] Although this violence does not only occur when leaving assemblies, the latter were an important opportunity to trigger it. In Paris, leaving a hall where obstructionists had been shouting hate-filled slogans for hours on end, rather than dispersing, groups got together to go to the Jewish quarter despite an impressive police presence. For example, following an assembly on 17 January 1898 shops in rue des Rosiers became the target of attacks.[108] Violence also flared up after an assembly between militants of the organising group — either for or against Dreyfus — and their opponents waiting for them outside.[109] These encounters seem inevitable when two opposing groups hold assemblies on the same day. On 5 December 1898, a private assembly of the *Ligue des Patriotes* with 500 people was held at the Pascaud gymnasium, while at the same time a contradictory public assembly organised by Sébastien Faure was being held at the meeting room of the Pré aux Clercs, with 1,500 people. According to a police observer, in the nationalist assembly, 'the audience set off in small groups towards the salle du Pré aux Clercs'. In the pro-Dreyfus assembly, it was announced that 'Déroulède's gang [was] in the street waiting for the assembly to end'. Sébastien Faure then declared: 'we must [...] hunt down these fanatics'. The session was suspended.

> At the exit, the organisers of the assembly found themselves in the presence of a group of patriots, led by Déroulède [...]. Companion Lucas, on arriving in the street, fired two revolver shots in the direction of the patriots, who were driven back by the police to allow the anarchists to leave and thus avoid a collision.[110]

It is these violent clashes that gave rise to internal security patrols organised in 1898 and 1899 by pro-Dreyfus assemblies. In May 1899 the author of a report on an assembly for the release of Lieutenant-Colonel Picquart indicates that the assembly was calm as a consequence of 'the large number of people engaged for the occasion by the friends of Dreyfus'.[111] But their organisation was far less accomplished than in nationalist assemblies; on 23 January 1898 *Le Temps* reported an anti-Semitic assembly with:

---

107. Stephen Wilson, 'The Antisemitic Riots of 1898 in France', *The Historical Journal*, 1973, vol.16, (4), pp. 789–806; Zeev Sternhell, *La droite révolutionnaire. 1885–1914. Les origines françaises du fascisme*, Paris, Gallimard, 1997, pp. 297–318.
108. Birnbaum, *Le moment antisémite*, pp. 22–23.
109. Vincent Robert, *Les chemins de la manifestation. 1848–1914*, Lyon, Presses Universitaires de Lyon, 1996, pp. 337–340.
110. AN/F7/12451/Ligue des Patriotes. Rapports, septembre–décembre 1898: Rapport du préfet de police, cabinet du préfet, 6 décembre 1898.
111. AN/F7/12466/Affaire Dreyfus. Divers, révision: Rapport, Paris, 11 mai 1899.

A row of security guards wearing tricolour armbands who stood along the stairs that led to the room on the first floor. In the meeting room itself around fifty butchers from la Villette and members of anti-Semitic groups supervised the public.[112]

These were mostly agents from the *Ligue des Patriotes* who guaranteed order in these nationalistic assemblies and escorted 'patriot' speakers in the early twentieth century.[113] In the words of a 1902 report, they were those 'who take on the role of the police'.[114] The police intervene mainly to prevent street violence.[115] To this we can add measures to 'disarm' combatants. In 1899, *Le Temps* reported that following scenes of violence in a nationalist assembly, 'M. Lépine, the police prefect, gave very strict instructions to prevent anyone from henceforth carrying a cane or stick from entering public assemblies'.[116] With massive police mobilisation or a particularly strong dispersion of groups, the press supporting the assembly organisers resorted to denouncing what was considered to be an attempt by government to divert people from its own weaknesses by provoking riots. As with acoustic obstruction, the government and police are accused of paying spies to stir up fights.

From the end of the 1880s, the civilising mission of the People's political mores by participation in assemblies had not produced the anticipated results. There was no diffusion of attitudes of tolerance, calm and control of passions. The militants of some groups prevented deliberation by obstructing speeches that they rejected and resorting to violence. However, it is precisely these groups which then make the most frequent use of freedom of assembly. Commentators on animated assemblies, particularly in the republican press, stress that the mores had even evolved, but in the opposite direction. The virtuous citizen that republicans, until the first years after the law of 1881, hoped would assemble and multiply, seemed to desert assemblies so that 'peaceful citizens […] have gradually forgotten the way [to public assemblies]'.[117] 'All citizens of reflective humour, irrespective of their opinion, are careful not to take part [in assemblies]', affirmed *Le Temps*.[118] The place of these peaceful citizens had been taken by individuals unable to accept contradiction, and who tried to silence their adversaries by noise or by force. We are faced with the recognition of the failure to implement pacific discussion in assemblies.

---

112. Éric Fournier, *La Cité du sang. Les bouchers de La Villette contre Dreyfus*, Paris, Libertalia, 2008, p. 148.

113. See, for example, AN/F7/12451/Ligue des Patriotes, 1889–1907: Rapport d'un correspondant au sujet de la LDP, Paris, 22 juin 1901.

114. AN/F7/12451/Ligue des Patriotes, 1889–1907: Rapport d'un correspondant au sujet de la LDP, Paris, 22 février 1902.

115. See, in particular: Jean-Marc Berlière, 'Du maintien de l'ordre républicain au maintien républicain de l'ordre? Réflexions sur la violence', *Genèses*, 1993, vol. 12, pp. 6–29.

116. *Le Temps*, 24 décembre 1899.

117. Roger Arnette, *La liberté de réunion en France. Son histoire et sa législation*, Paris, Arthur Rousseau, 1894, p. 237.

118. *Le Temps*, 31 March 1896.

The impact of unanimous gatherings: the return of crowds

The end of the century is also marked by the progressive recognition of the inevitable division of opinion in parties not coming to consensus on a notion of the public good. What we see is the disappearance of the ideal of a People able to assemble around a politics based on reason, an 'erosion of the original monism', even within the republican camp: 'We begin [...] to consider structural divergences even within the republican world, as legitimate'.[119] A new conception of public opinion replaces that prevailing hitherto, that is, an opinion where division is admitted or at least recognised. This is the expression of a particular use of freedom established by the 1881 law. Political rallies are developed which bring together only people sharing an opinion formed prior to the assembly. The objective is thus not to convince participants by debate and exchange of arguments, but by gathering convinced individuals around the same idea in order to demonstrate its force. The journalist from *Le Temps*, who on 4 September 1893 imputed the spread of practices of intolerance in assemblies to Boulangism, denouncing the 'soldiers of uproar and systematic violence', also criticised the fact that some political groups organised assemblies to give the impression that the party was powerful and to 'dazzle universal suffrage'.[120] At the end of the nineteenth century it becomes increasingly clear that to convince citizens of the accuracy of their views by use of assemblies, many political groups no longer concentrate on mobilising arguments and confronting them with potential formulated criticism. Instead it became a question of impressing public opinion by demonstrating that many people already shared the same ideas.

From contradictory assemblies to meetings-cum-demonstrations

Olivier Fillieule points out that 'nowadays [...] common sense as much as learned speeches frequently use the word "*manifestation*"[121] for street parades, to the exclusion of many other forms of action'. He broadens the definition. By '*manifestation*' Fillieule means 'all activity of a temporary nature by people in an open public or private place and which contains the expression of political opinions directly or indirectly'. It thus applies to more activities than just street parades and processions, but it still excludes 'political assemblies and meetings held in a room or in a closed space'.[122] The definitions of the word '*manifestation*'

---

119. Pierre Rosanvallon, *Le peuple introuvable. Histoire de la représentation démocratique en France*, Paris, Gallimard, 1998, pp. 233, 235; see also: Raymond Huard, 'Aboutissements préparés et cristallisations imprévues. La formation des partis', in Pierre Birnbaum (ed.), *La France de l'affaire Dreyfus*, Paris, Gallimard, 1994, p. 93.
120. *Le Temps*, 4 September 1893.
121. As we are analysing the etymological evolution of the term in dictionaries, and to avoid confusion, we have chosen to keep the word 'manifestation' in French, instead of using its English translation (demonstration) until later in the chapter.
122. Olivier Fillieule, *Stratégies de la rue. Les manifestations en France*, Paris, Presses de Sciences Po, 1997, pp. 41–44.

given by dictionaries from the second half of the twentieth century imply this exclusion. The 1963 *Grand Larousse Encyclopédique* gives a definition which begins as follows: 'An action to make something manifest; the result of this action: a manifestation of an opinion, a feeling. [...] Collective and public demonstration in favour of an opinion; a public expression of a claim'. So far, the definition does not necessarily exclude political assemblies defined as organised, static and away from the public highway, which gather together participants and where one or more speakers deliver speeches. But the definition continues by indicating that:

> A '*manifestation*' is a momentary gathering of people, organised, in a given place, on the public street, disordered and static, with a protesting or symbolic character and most frequently accompanied by shouts, chants, and the bearing of symbols [and specifying that] when it moves a '*manifestation*' becomes a procession.[123]

Henceforth, a '*manifestation*' is defined as the expression of opinion on the public street, and not in a meeting room.

At the end of the nineteenth or in the early twentieth century, several dictionary definitions of the word give it a broader meaning, and do not rule out considering private or public assemblies taking place outside the public street as '*manifestations*'.[124] In 1863, the 'Littré' defines '*manifestation*' as a 'popular movement, gathering to manifest some political intention'.[125] In 1870 Maurice La Châtre's *Nouveau dictionnaire universel* begins with the following definition: 'Action by which one publicly expresses one's thought, one's opinion'. Yet he was among those who earlier gave the most importance to the idea that '*manifestations*' mainly take place on the street.

> If [...] they are the effect of discontent, '*manifestations*' result in considerable gatherings stationed on the streets of big cities and public places, in assemblies of bands of citizens, roaming the city, calling others to arms, erecting barricades and preparing to resist an oppressive power.[126]

This aspect of the definition may be inspired by the author's commitment to anti-Empire forces; 'La Châtre defines himself as anti-royalist and republican, and does not hesitate to reveal his communist convictions'.[127] In Larousse's *Grand dictionnaire universel du XIXe siècle* where the word '*manifestation*' appears in

---

123. *Grand Larousse Encyclopédique*, vol. 7, Paris, Librairie Larousse, 1963.

124. On the disappearance of the religious meaning of the word in these definitions, see: Fillieule, *Stratégies de la rue*, pp. 40–41.

125. Émile Littré, *Dictionnaire de la langue française*, Paris, Hachette, 1863–1869, cited in Vincent Robert, *Les chemins de la manifestation. 1848–1914*, Lyon, Presses Universitaires de Lyon, 1996, p. 9.

126. Maurice La Châtre, *Nouveau dictionnaire universel*, Paris, Docks de la Librairie, 1870, p. 592.

127. A.-M. Hetzel, 'Maurice La Châtre (1814–1900)', *Musée virtuel des dictionnaires*, (accessed 6 June 2006) http://www.u-cergy.fr/dictionnaires/auteurs/la_chatre.html

1873, we find the idea of a public event, but not that of a demonstration on the street. It is defined as a 'production outside, [an] act by which something becomes visible, tangible, apparent', and as a 'collective public demonstration, a public expression of an opinion, of a desire'.[128] In much the same way, in the 1878 edition of the *Dictionnaire de l'Académie française*, '*manifestation*' is defined as an 'action by which one manifests something', the verb '*manifester*' returning to the fact of 'making it known, uncovered, brought to light'. We read there that the word 'refers to [...] gatherings or movements whose aim is to manifest the feelings of a party'.[129] There is no direct reference to action on the street. The second volume of the *Dictionnaire général de la langue française du commencement du XVIIe siècle à nos jours*, published in 1900 by Hatzfeld and Darmester, defines '*manifestation*' as 'an action to make manifest, to make perceptible, tangible' and as a 'popular demonstration'.[130] These broad definitions of '*manifestation*' echo the use of the word at the time. When used for a demonstrative event taking place on the public street, police and press observers often take care to point this out: 'The exploiters of confusion will profit from recent events in Tonkin to try [...] to organise disorder through *street demonstrations*', states an article in the republican newspaper *National* on 1 April 1885.[131] The same applies to militants. Rather than lectures, '*the demonstration in the street* is better', claims a militant anarchist in an assembly of his propaganda group in 1892.[132] The term '*manifestation*' — that I now translate using its English equivalent 'demonstration' — was then currently used for assemblies in a room, when these were non-contradictory assemblies to demonstrate the strength of the organising group.

When the Republic was set up, these assemblies-cum-demonstrations were not very widespread and caused little apprehension among their reporters. They were principally organised by groups supposed to have little popular weight, and trying hard to hide this fact. From the end of the 1870s, the legitimists organised assemblies to reflect the strength of the royalist camp, and which their promoters and pro-legitimist journalists describe as demonstrations. On 21 January 1879 at an assembly in Paris, the catholic newspaper *La Défense* discusses a 'demonstration' of the royalist party through which 'it affirms itself in Paris'.[133] The assembly, which was private, was only attended by Parisian royalists and 'their political friends in the *départements*', but the author insists that the public was nevertheless massive:

---

128. Pierre Larousse, *Grand dictionnaire universel du XIXe siècle*, Paris, Administration du grand dictionnaire universel, 1875, pp. 1,078–1,079.
129. *Dictionnaire de l'Académie française*, Paris, F. Didot, 1878, 7th edn., pp. 163–164.
130. Adolphe Hatzfeld and Arsène Darmesteter (with A. Thomas), *Dictionnaire général de la langue française du commencement du XVIIe siècle à nos jours*, vol. 2, Paris, Ch. Delagrave, 1900, p. 1,462.
131. APP/Ba/1528/Dossier: Meeting dit des 'Affamés', le 1er avril 1885, place de l'Opéra: 'Les excitateurs', *Le National*, 2 avril 1885.
132. APP/Ba/1502/Propagande anarchiste par la parole: Rapport 'Barbier', 9 septembre 1892.
133. *La Défense*, 21 January 1879.

'2,000 men squashed into a space made to hold 1,200 spectators at most'. The assembly of so many people in a single room is used to affirm the party's vigour and presented as such by the press. On 26 July 1881, at an assembly in Lyon in the form of a banquet preceded by a lecture, a journalist on the centre-right and pro-legitimist newspaper, *Le Salut public*, spoke of a 'double and important legitimist demonstration'. It was held to draw attention to the weight of the party advocating a return of the monarchy. 'We must show that we exist', said a legitimist to a police inspector in 1881.[134]

These assemblies are also characterised in police reports with the word 'demonstration', without indicating whether their authors hold it from their promoters themselves. In an 1885 report a commissioner in Tarascon, announcing a royalist banquet, points out that it 'will have, it appears, the character of a veritable demonstration'.[135] A decade earlier, a police informer indicated that to 'focus attention on their party', legitimists 'intend to hold a demonstration on the 15th of this month on the feast of St. Henri'. It was a mass to which the press '[will enlist] supporters of this cause to […] take part in large numbers'.[136] These meetings are expected to assemble as many people as possible. They are not organised to convince those taking part, but to deliver proof of the strength of the party: the legitimist press takes care to echo this. Police observers often emphasise the failure of this sort of enterprise, and in the words of an 1879 report, 'the *vendéenne* demonstration which took place yesterday in Challans was noisy and crowded, but was not really very politically important'.[137] Generally the authors of reports do not express concern about the effects of such assemblies.

Opponents of legitimists thus used the term 'demonstration' in a derisory sense to describe them. On 20 November 1879, the intransigent republican newspaper *Le Mot d'Ordre*, reported a banquet and before the assembly took place, published the following letter:

> The legitimist demonstration is getting prepared, without the city of Challans, whose population is republican, being the least bit disturbed. We know what to expect from demonstrators. M. Baudry d'Asson […], M. de la Maronnière, M. de la Rochefoucauld, and other advocates of divine right, will bring all who value them from far and wide, put them in a large room to make speeches to them and make them vote by acclamation a petition, drafted beforehand […]. They will be pleased to call it a demonstration of 'the royalist *Vendée*'.

The simple fact that some hundreds or thousands of supporters gathered together does not signify that people are obliged to believe in the popularity of

---

134. APP/Ba/403/Menées légitimistes, 1881: Copie du rapport de l'officier de paix, 12 juillet 1881.

135. AD BDR/1M/865/Partis et mouvements politiques. Réunion et associations, 1885: Rapport du commissaire spécial au préfet, Tarascon, 18 août 1885.

136. APP/Ba/401/Affaires concernant les menées légitimistes: Rapport, 15 juillet 1876.

137. APP/Ba/402/Affaires concernant les menées légitimistes, 1879: Rapport, préfecture de Police, police municipale, 1re brigade de recherches, 20 novembre 1879.

their ideas and to be concerned about this type of gathering; particularly because the position of republicans in government was still to 'let speak', as folly would disappear on its own when it came to light.

> Neither the crisis of Boulangism, nor the Dreyfus affair itself, [...] made current events [the problem of assemblies]. [...] Despite the high number of assemblies held, despite the hatching of associations, circles, leagues, parties, authorised or not, open or secret — and that hold assemblies — despite the political malaise, the silent and profound spasms that try to shake and overturn a controversial government, not yet firmly established, the question of assemblies is no longer current.

The legal theorist Menanteau thus affirmed the success, albeit temporary, of the liberal law of 1881, with the idea that during the 1880s and 1890s, what would constitute the major problem facing freedom of assembly — confusing it with association — did not have to be faced. Menanteau argued that the period of Boulangism or of the Dreyfus affair did not witness the emergence of 'the problem of assemblies', because he compared them to the situation at the time of writing in 1937. For Menanteau, it is the birth of parties that causes the confusion between association and assembly and makes the appearance of assemblies dangerous for public peace. From then on 'mass concentrations have taken an appearance and meaning different from those typical of assemblies', so that 'the aim pursued is not so much to debate opinions, but the very fact of concentration, the result of intimidation and political pressure': 'meetings [are no] more assemblies where we discuss, but unilateral exhibitions'.[138] It is surprising that Menanteau refused to see the early signs of this evolution at the end of the nineteenth century. The period of Boulangism and the Dreyfus affair are in effect marked by the increase of assemblies to demonstrate strength by the numbers attending and to impress the outside world rather than convince participants. One of the basic differences with the situation in the interwar period is that this use of freedom of assembly did not then lead to a critique of the 1881 law and to a restriction of freedom of assembly. On the contrary, this is expanded again in 1907. At the end of the century, the deviant forms — in the sense that they do not correspond to the republican ideal of a sphere of debate — taken by assemblies, are indeed interpreted by those who criticised them as the consequence of the spread of bad mores, rather than as a legislative weakness.

If the Boulangists faced their opponents in contradictory assemblies, they also developed assemblies to rally their own followers. That is particularly the case of banquets arranged around the General during his provincial travels, for example in Tours on 17 March 1889:

---

138. Maurice Menanteau, *Les nouveaux aspects de la liberté de réunion. Essai sur les caractères juridiques et politiques de la liberté de réunion en France*, Paris, Librairie technique et économique, 1937, pp. 23–34.

At four o'clock a great banquet began in the garage of a car manufacturer. Eighteen tables of sixty-eight places each were placed perpendicular to a table of honour, raised on a rostrum and 150 metres long. An orchestra played the *Pious-Pious d'Auvergne* and other refrains, taken up in chorus by the dinner guests, beating the rhythm with forks and knife handles. The General gave his speech with dessert.[139]

Large assemblies with hundreds of followers were held regularly in Paris. For example, in 1889 the Pascaud gymnasium hosted private assemblies for 400 Boulangists on 15 September, 800 on 19 September, 1,500 on 4 October, etc.[140] Referring to the street rallies of the General's supporters, Patrick H. Hutton remarks that 'for some contemporary observers, it was these large rallies rather than the electoral plebiscite which lent Boulangism its mystique and through which the Boulangist legend grew'. By mobilising people to come and constitute a mass in the assemblies, the Boulangist movement was helped by the *Ligue des Patriotes*, or former league members after the latter was dissolved. Its support was particularly active in Paris where the League 'constitutes a force-in-being to cheer at public rallies'.[141] In the same period, the republicans also increasingly organised private assemblies. The difference with Boulangist propaganda is that their aim seems, above all, to be to protect themselves against obstruction. I have found no evidence in the republican press of articles celebrating the gathering of a large number of like-minded people in a private assembly.

Things change at the end of the century with the split over the Dreyfus affair. The shows of force on one side met with counter-demonstrations on the other. On 26 September 1898 a journalist for the republican newspaper *Petit Bleu*, referred to 'the [excitement] in the parties' with concern:

> One day it's M. de Pressensé who officiates [...] in a room in the suburbs; another day, it's M. Sébastien Faure, and then, it's the turn of M. Paul Déroulède who parades his eloquence in avenue de la Grande Armée [...]. Each speaker confides his passions, his hatred, his enthusiasm, his anger and his rancour to an audience who marries them all the more gladly because it is made up of friends. These are monologues that, in the absence of practical utility, at least reveal a rather alarming state of mind.[142]

---

139. Adrien Dansette, *Le boulangisme*, Paris, Fayard, 1946, p. 264. On Boulanger's provincial tours and the comparison made with presidential tours, see Nicolas Mariot: *Conquérir unanimement les cœurs. Usages politiques et scientifiques des rites. Le cas du voyage présidentiel en province, 1888–1998*, PhD dissertation, EHESS, 1999, pp. 146–183; and Nicolas Mariot, '"Propagande par la vue". Souveraineté régalienne et gestion du nombre dans les voyages en province de Carnot (1888–1894)', *Genèses*, 1995, vol. 20, pp. 24–47.

140. APP/Ba/1462/1889. Élections diverses. Réunions: Rapport, préfecture de Police, 2ᵉ brigade de recherches, cabinet, 1ᵉʳ *bureau*, Paris, rapports, 15 et 19 septembre, 4 octobre.

141. Patrick H. Hutton, 'Popular Boulangism and the Advent of Mass Politics in France, 1886–1890', *Journal of Contemporary History*, 1976, vol. 11, (1), pp. 90–93.

142. *Le Petit Bleu*, 26 September 1898.

Resistance to the Civilisation of Political Mores | 207

Figure 5.1: 'The meeting of the Ligue des Patriotes', *L'Illustration*, 1 October 1898

The turmoil caused by the Dreyfus affair and beyond it nationalist agitation in the *Belle Époque*, undermines the notion of the assembly as a place of apprenticeship in debate. Large nationalist assemblies are organised, particularly by the *Ligue des Patriotes*. With regards to the one referred to in the *Petit Bleu* on 25 September 1898 at the Guyenet riding school, the day afterwards, 'all the newspapers reported it', states *L'Illustration* of 1 October, with a drawing depicting Paul Déroulède on the platform with Maurice Barrès by his side (Figure 5.1). On 26 September, the patriotic press systematically emphasised the massive character of this demonstration: 'Yesterday [...] the grand patriotic meeting took place, organised under the chairmanship of M. Paul Déroulède. It was a memorable demonstration where over 4,000 Frenchmen took part', states *Le Jour*; 'A patriotic demonstration', runs *Le Petit Caporal*, mentioning a 'grandiose assembly, where 6,000 citizens acclaimed the *Patrie*'; 'Impressive patriotic demonstration', observes *Le Gaulois*. Many other assemblies of this sort are organised, always followed by articles emphasising them in the nationalist press. The opposition press borrows the term 'demonstration' from the organisers of these assemblies, but only in ridicule. In *Le Siècle* of 26 September Lucien Victor-Meunier begins his account of the assembly with the affirmation that 'the "*grandiose demonstration*" that the opponents of the revision wanted to organise yesterday, failed miserably, it will be difficult to contest this, even for the most resolute of liars that the general staff keeps in its pay'. He concludes: 'In the midst of general indifference, in other words, public contempt, the "*grandiose demonstration*" by the anti-semitic

Boulange burnt out pitifully'. As for him, the number of people assembled was not really impressive and had been exaggerated by the nationalist press; moreover, the assembly lost its importance because it was private.

Yet at times the Dreyfusard assemblies also take the form of rallies to show the force of their camp. The republican newspaper *Le Courrier du Soir*, claims that it is the 'demonstrations for or against a retrial for Dreyfus', that '[worry] the government', and so much more so since they 'no longer take place in public or private assemblies, but on the street';[143] it is always the spill-over onto the street that causes the most concern. However the numerous police reports of assemblies for a retrial in 1894 testify a fear of indoor demonstrations in support of Dreyfus. The assemblies of the two camps increased and enlarged, reacting to one another, creating an agitation considered to be dangerous. A report announcing an assembly in Nantes in December 1898 claims that it is only 'to have a counterweight to anti-semitic and nationalist demonstrations announced' that 'socialist assemblies [have] been organised at the last minute'.[144] It was a question of not leaving the adversary alone to vaunt his importance. Relating the plan of Parisian socialists to hold 'a series of meetings [...] to free Picquart', in 1899 a police informer wrote: 'we hope to act on public opinion, and to force government's hand'.[145] We cannot completely rule out that the action on the opinion mentioned here refers to being convinced by the speech given; but it is also more likely to be a question of rallying people already active in Dreyfus' cause and to have an impact on public opinion by a show of numbers. After the first meeting of the series, the report writer worries about its consequences: 'In this sort of assembly heads get overheated and spirits get overexcited. This is certainly the clearest result of [the meeting held] the day before yesterday'.[146] The speakers at assemblies protesting against Dreyfus' sentence defended themselves against the accusation of trying to stir up public opinion. On the contrary, they claimed that their intention was to inform and educate participants, in contrast to patriotic speakers who simply tried to excite crowds. The police commissaire relating an 1899 assembly organised with the patronage of the *Ligue des droits de l'homme* in Orléans, wrote that '[Pressensé] has shown that he did not come to agitate, but to work for the public salvation, by making known how Dreyfus had been condemned by the greatest injustice'.[147] Moreover, in contrast to anti-Dreyfusard assemblies, pro-Dreyfus meetings were generally public and potentially contradictory.

---

143. *Le Courrier du Soir*, 5 October 1898.

144. AN/F7/12466/Affaire Dreyfus. Réunions, 1898–1899: Rapport de M. Brulat, commissaire spécial, police spéciale des chemins de fer et des ports, Nantes, 11 décembre 1898.

145. AN/F7/12466/Affaire Dreyfus. Réunions, 1898–1899: Rapport, Paris, 10 mai 1899.

146. AN/F7/12466/Affaire Dreyfus. Réunions, 1898–1899: Rapport sur le meeting de la rue Cadet, 12 mai 1899.

147. AN/F7/12466/Affaire Dreyfus. Réunions, 1898–1899: Rapport du commissaire de police au préfet, Orléans, 8 janvier 1899.

Assemblies that muster followers to one and the same cause were regularly described as 'demonstrations' in the last decade of the nineteenth century. This is also the period when the word 'meeting' began to supplant 'assembly' in the words of organisers published in the press or in police reports. The term 'meeting' was occasionally used before — and sometimes and sometimes adapted to the French language, as in the word 'métingue' — but it was increasingly used at the end of the century, when the assembly became a show of force. It is first recorded in the dictionaries of the nineteenth century, where the definitions given make it the equivalent of a public assembly. However the meeting is first presented as something essentially British. In the *Dictionnaire politique* of Eugène Duclerc and Laurent-Antoine Pagnerre, published in 1842 to divulge the republican ideology, meetings are seen as an English particularism that France could only envy.[148] The word then took on a more general sense and detached itself progressively from its origin. In the Hatzfeld and Darmester dictionary in 1900, 'meeting' is defined as 'a popular assembly organised to deliberate on a political issue', and its English etymology is just recalled.[149] In this way the word is gradually adopted as the equivalent of 'public assembly', separating it from its English origins, but the dictionary definitions keep the notion of assembling 'to deliberate'. However, actors in the period tend to make 'meeting' synonymous with large assemblies of people supporting the same cause. A 1898 report on the steps taken in Angers by a militant anarchist looking for a room for a protest meeting in favour of Dreyfus notes that 'he had to find spacious premises, because his intention was to let the assembly degenerate into a "colossal meeting" to use his words'.[150] In 1945, the legal expert Marcel Le Clère described this transition from assembly to meeting:

> The 'freemason's lodge' where the idea hung over, was substituted by the mass wherein lies the force, and the secret, and the personal vote retreats before the spectacular and collective sanctification of the elected. *The meeting has replaced the assembly.*[151]

Le Clère places the phenomena in the interwar period. We nevertheless observe a development of this type of assemblies, often described as demonstrations or meetings which rally followers of the same opinion, since the end of the nineteenth century.

---

148. Eugène Duclerc and Laurent-Antoine Pagnerre, *Dictionnaire politique, Encyclopédie du langage et de la science politique*, Paris, Pagnerre, 1842.

149. Hatzfeld and Darmesteter (with Antoine Thomas), *Dictionnaire général de la langue française*, p. 1,494.

150. AN/F7/12466/Affaire Dreyfus. Réunions, Belgique et France. Maine-et-Loire: Rapport du commissaire spécial, Angers, 29 décembre 1898.

151. Marcel Le Clère, *Les réunions, manifestations et attroupements en droit français et comparé*, Paris, Impr. Petites Affiches, 1945, p. 5.

Participants become crowds

These end-of-century assemblies-cum-demonstrations are marked by an image of participants as one vast and profoundly cohesive body. Here we are far from the original notion of assembly as a place to compare opinions. The accounts of nationalist assemblies in the pro-nationalist press often use the term 'crowd' without a negative connotation. An article in *Le Jour* in 1898 mentions that 'M. Paul Déroulède has translated the sentiments found in the crowd's enthusiasm into a magnificent language'.[152] In the same edition of the newspaper, another article discussed this assembly saying that 'the spectacle of this crowd of 4,000 Frenchmen was not without its own grandeur when M. Paul Déroulède, very eloquently pointed out who the traitors were, [and the crowd] clenched their fists, quaking with indignation'.[153] The unanimity that prevails in the crowd is always emphasised. It is 'the thoughts of all patriots', that are expressed by the speakers, to use terms from *La Libre Parole*.[154] This unanimity highlighted by journalists takes the form of a show of enthusiasm of all participants: 'The entire audience, without exception, proved, by their incessant applause, that they understood the importance of this wonderful assembly from the national perspective'.[155] The public of assemblies is described as acting as a sole man, without expressed differences.

This image of the public in assemblies makes us wonder how crowd phenomena were perceived at the time. In the introduction to this book I emphasised the fear of crowds when the institutions of the Third Republic were set up; the constraints imposed on forms of participation in political life that complement the vote in the shape of a concern to 'prevent the strength of the People from becoming the brutality of the crowd'.[156] Yet it is only at the turn of the century that the two most important works on the fear of the crowd in collective psychology were published. Gustave Le Bon's *Psychologie des foules* (1895),[157] and Gabriel Tarde's *L'opinion et la foule* (1901, collecting articles from 1893, 1898 and 1899).[158] After an attempt to master crowds through participation in assemblies amongst other things, comes a warning of their dangers. In revealing the dangers of crowds, Le Bon and Tarde refer more or less directly to the political assemblies of their time: 'far more than the prophets of the twentieth century, they are witnesses, limited, but significant, to what marked the three decades up to the Great War', write Yvon Thiec and Jean-René Treanton.[159] In the *Psychologie des foules*, Le Bon describes political

---

152. *Le Jour*, 26 September 1898.
153. *Le Jour*, 26 September 1898.
154. *La Libre Parole*, 17 November 1903.
155. *Le Jour*, 26 September 1898.
156. Pierre Rosanvallon, *Le sacre du citoyen. Histoire du suffrage universel en France*, Paris, Gallimard, 1992, p. 497.
157. Gustave Le Bon, *Psychologie des foules*, Paris, Alcan, 1895.
158. Gabriel Tarde, *L'opinion et la foule*, Paris, Alcan, 1901.
159. Yvon J. Thiec and Jean-René Treanton, 'La foule comme objet de "science"', *Revue française de sociologie*, 1983, vol. 24, (1), pp. 133–134.

electoral assemblies as places where the violent, intolerant and irrational character of the crowd emerges:

> As regards the influence that reasoning could exercise on the mind of voters, we need to have never read the account of an electoral assembly to not know the subject. Affirmations, invective, sometimes blows are exchanged, never reason. If there is a moment's silence, it is because one of those present with a difficult character announces that he is going to ask the candidate one of those awkward questions which always delights the audience. But the satisfaction of opponents did not last long, because the voice of the previous speaker is soon drowned out by the cries of their adversaries.[160]

To support this Le Bon reproduces extracts of press accounts — although without specifying which — on socialists and anarchist assemblies. The latter are not considered to be the only guilty party, and the observations are generalised as phenomena typical of crowds which can be found in all assemblies:

> Let us not imagine that this type of discussion is specific to a particular class of voters, and the result of their social status. In all anonymous assemblies, even one exclusively made up of men of letters; discussion easily takes the same forms. I have shown that men in a crowd tend towards intellectual equalisation, and every moment we find evidence of it.

After having painted this picture of electoral assemblies, the conclusion is as follows:

> In similar conditions we might ask how an elector can form an opinion? But asking a similar question would delude strangely on the degree of freedom which a collectivity can enjoy. The opinions of crowds are imposed, never reasoned.[161]

Some years later, the sociologist Gabriel Tarde, even without referring to assemblies directly, did refer to contemporary examples to support his ideas. He evokes 'contemporary French, Boulangist or anti-Semitic crowds',[162] and describes how the crowd 'rushes, adoring, to the feet of its human idols', giving *inter alia* the example of Boulanger. Tarde notes that the public of an assembly corresponds to what he means by the word 'crowd': 'We say: a theatre public, the public of a meeting; here, public means crowd'. He adds:

> There is no word, in Latin or in Greek, that corresponds to what we mean by 'public'. There are words to designate the People, the assembly of armed or unarmed citizens, the electoral body, all types of crowds.

---

160. Gustave Le Bon, *Psychologie des foules*, Paris, Alcan, 1895.
161. For this, and earlier citations see: Le Bon, *Psychologie des foules*, pp. 164–166.
162. Tarde, *L'opinion et la foule*.

It was above all the Dreyfus affair that inspired Tarde's theory of the transition from 'crowds' to 'publics'. He envisages the public as an 'evolved form of sociality and association based on a suggestion at a distance', and 'a purely spiritual collectivity [...] a scattering of physically separated individuals whose cohesion is purely cerebral'. In contrast to Le Bon, Tarde states that the modern era is one of publics formed by the press and conversation, and no longer one of crowds.

Commenting on Tarde's work, several authors see the Dreyfus affair as the epitome of the transition from 'crowd' to 'public'. Olivier Bosc focuses on the evolution which took place between the period of Boulangism, 'the theatre of great public demonstrations', and that of the Dreyfus affair:

> What was the role of crowds in the affair? Not much. The latent hostility of the crowd gathered in the courtyard of the military school to see captain Dreyfus stripped of his rank, the enthusiastic crowd who welcomed him when he left the court in Rennes, did not weigh heavy in the progress of the affair. It is well and truly the public, the opinion in its different expressions, that occupied the forefront of the scene and became the stake in the clash between Dreyfusards and anti-Dreyfusards.[163]

According to Dominique Reynié, the Dreyfus affair was indeed a 'quarrel of "publics"'.[164] The fact that political meetings are at the centre of this book and that Tarde himself refers to contemporary 'anti-Semitic crowds', commits me to moderate this cleavage between Boulangism and the Dreyfus affair, between an era of large rallies, and an era of indirect influence, mostly through the press.

Le Bon's analyses are echoed in the political world where their success is explained as 'a sort of prop for democratic disillusion and a remedy for the fear of great numbers'.[165] The new science is presented as a way to make crowds governable. For moderate governments this is also a way to resolve:

> the persisting paradox between the celebration of universal suffrage and the savagery of the masses in exonerating citizens for their behaviour. The crowd, that is, a situation, was guilty. Its crimes, moreover, presupposed the presence of ringleaders.[166]

---

163. Olivier Bosc, *La foule criminelle. Positivisme, politique et criminologie en Italie et en France à la fin du XIXe siècle. Scipio Sighele (1868–1913) et l'école lombrosienne,* PhD dissertation, Paris IX, 2001, pp. 276–277.

164. Dominique Reynié, 'Théories du nombre', *Hermès,* 1988, 2, pp. 100–101.

165. Rosanvallon, *Le peuple introuvable,* pp. 10–11.

166. Garrigou, *Histoire sociale du suffrage universel en France,* p. 135.

Le Bon's reasoning is typical of the elitist conservative liberalism of his time.[167] His writings and more broadly the developments in crowd psychology certainly influence the way assemblies are perceived. This appears in the writings of legal experts on the right of assembly. Until the end of the nineteenth century, there was a certain trust in the ability of the 1881 law to regulate the participation of the masses in public life. At the turn of the century, even if we continue to think that republican framing of the right of assembly is effective, the dangers of the crowd are also pointed out. In 1911, Nucé de Lamothe affirmed that 'assemblies are likely to become dangerous'[168] with reference to Le Bon. His theses are perceived as giving scientific support to the idea that emotion tends to supplant reason among participants. In a crowd, 'isolated beings sense, if not a will distinct from their own, then at least a group strength which forms above them', wrote Menanteau in 1937.[169] This unified will tends to dominate individual strength and to push assembled individuals to direct action. Legal experts also rely heavily on Tarde's writings. In 1910 Fournier-Poncelet recalls that he: 'had established that, in a crowd, persons of weak or easily suggestionable character, could commit crimes under the influence of pervading excitement, alien to them in the isolated state'.[170] In the early twentieth century, these jurists agreed that an individual in a crowd taking part in an assembly is capable of acts that he would not commit on his own.

Among the causes of this phenomenon, they first consider the fact of mental contagion. 'In a crowd, all feeling, all action is contagious [...] to the point that it is very easy for the individual to sacrifice his personnel interest to the collective interest', noted Pierre Brisse in 1937.[171] Then there is the idea that the individual, when grouped with others in a crowd, loses awareness of his actions. In 1901 Girieud wrote: 'The individual in a crowd undergoes [...] a sort of lessening of his moral faculties comparable in some way to that produced by drunkenness'.[172] As a result, a man in a crowd is extremely suggestible. Legal experts emphasise the key role of leaders, able to guide a crowd where each man abdicates their own will. Finally, and most importantly, the individual behaves differently in a crowd because

---

167. Benoît Marpeau, *Gustave Le Bon. Parcours d'un intellectuel. 1841–1931*, Paris, Éditions CNRS, 2000; Marcia Christina Consolim, 'Gustave Le Bon e a reação conservadora às multidões', *Anais do XVII Encontro Regional de História. O lugar da História*, 2004, http://www.fflch.usp.br/dh/anpuhsp/downloads/CD%20XVII/ST%20II/Marcia%20Cristina%20Consolim.pdf (accessed 6 June 2006).

168. Henri Nucé de Lamothe, *La liberté de réunion en France. Réunions publiques proprement dites. Réunions publiques cultuelles. Réunions privées*, Toulouse, Impr. Sebille, 1911, p. 200.

169. Maurice Menanteau, *Les nouveaux aspects de la liberté de réunion. Essai sur les caractères juridiques et politiques de la liberté de réunion en France*, Paris, Librairie technique et économique, 1937, p. 17.

170. Jean Fournier-Poncelet, *La liberté de réunion au XXe siècle. Étude de droit public comparé*, Faculté de droit d'Aix, 1910, p. 31.

171. Pierre Brisse, *Les attroupements et l'ordre public*, Paris, Dommat-Montchrestien, 1937, pp. 32–33.

172. Joseph Girieud, *Du régime des attroupements. Etude historique et critique*, Aix, Université d'Aix-Marseille, Faculté de droit d'Aix, typographe et lithographe B. Niel, 1901, p. 16.

he feels invincibly strong. This allows him 'to give in to instincts that he would have checked, if alone'.[173] For legal experts, this feeling of strength arises because the individual in an anonymous crowd relinquishes individual responsibility. 'In an assembly, we only encounter the inorganic milieu of "the crowd", so well and to such an extent that we cannot hold this crowd collectively responsible', wrote Fournier-Poncelet.[174] As a consequence there is the question of possible control to avoid a spill-over into action. Since repression cannot be exercised on a crowd, we are left with prevention. This solution was rejected by the government in 1881. The spill-over of assemblies into direct action thus continued to be a threat.

---

173. Girieud, *Du régime des attroupements*, 1901, p. 32.
174. Fournier-Poncelet, *La liberté de réunion au XXe siècle*, p. 33.

Part III

When a Show of Force Threatens Freedom of Assembly

Chapter Six

The Political Rally as a Party Showcase

The postwar witnessed the birth of leagues, parties, excessively militarised organisms, and for some the assembly became 'an exercise in mobilisation'. [...] To the thought succeeded the mass, to the oratorical demonstration the spectator counting.

This is what the legal expert Marcel Le Clère wrote in 1945.[1] From the end of the nineteenth century freedom of assembly had been used to demonstrate the strength of the organising group. But this evolution in the use of the right of assembly became increasingly established in the interwar period.[2] In 'the age of democratic control characterised by the role of parties [...] and by the discipline of engagement [...], rallies progressively replaced contradictory assemblies'.[3] Taking the assemblies of the two main parties on the left, the SFIO (*Section Française de l'Internationale Ouvrière*) and the PCF (*Parti Communiste Français*), we see that the rally becomes a vital means of propaganda.[4] In the interwar period the transformation of the assembly is affirmed as a way to demonstrate the force and cohesion of a party, contradiction and debate are unlikely to play any role here. The model of the rally was then characterised by what Philippe Burrin describes as '[the passage to] a politics which drifted into a liturgy and in which the masses, by their physical presence and their emotional participation, played a key role'.[5]

The SFIO and the PCF had rather different views on huge propaganda rallies. The PCF resorts to them wholeheartedly. The SFIO, on the other hand, often specialises in assemblies and makes the greatest use of them, but it primarily

---

1. Marcel Le Clère, *Les réunions, manifestations et attroupements en droit français et comparé*, Paris, Impr. Petites Affiches, 1945, p. 14.
2. Moving on from assemblies held at the turn of the century to those in the 1920s and 1930s, I omit the period of the First World War, where the right of assembly was subject to restrictions due to the state of siege: 'France [...] was to live under the regime of the law of 9 August 1849; more precisely, the military authority had the right "to ban [...] assemblies considered likely to excite or support disorder"', Michel Baffrey, *Le droit de réunion en Angleterre et en France*, Paris, Les Presses Modernes, 1937, p. 146.
3. Nicolas Roussellier, 'La diffusion de l'éloquence en France sous la IIIe République', in Fabrice D'Almeida (ed.), *L'éloquence politique en France et en Italie de 1870 à nos jours*, Rome, École française de Rome, 2001, p. 45.
4. The term 'meeting', much used in the 1920s and 1930s in French to denote large gatherings, is often replaced here by its closest equivalent in English, 'rally' (for large meetings).
5. Philippe Burrin, 'Poings levés et bras tendus. La contagion des symboles au temps du Front Populaire', *Vingtième siècle*, 1986, vol. 11, p. 18.

focuses on didactic assemblies for a rather limited public, sometimes within the party. Gilles Candar and Christophe Prochasson illustrate this for the period from the very beginning of the twentieth century until the end of the 1910s.[6] For the socialists: 'propaganda must educate and not be a question of psychological conditioning or even a simple recruitment technique'. In this way they distinguish between rallies and didactic assemblies; the latter being preferred for a long time: 'The socialists do not always penetrate as easily as one might think in a modern era where the masses start to take the stage'.[7] Yet if part of the SFIO is reluctant in the face of large rallies, in the interwar period we still witness an upgrading of socialist propaganda through the assembly which becomes 'less and less, an informative assembly where one goes to learn and debate' and 'ever more a display of party strength and the value of party ideas'.[8]

A question of numbers

In the interwar period the SFIO and the PCF defined a successful rally as a large meeting held in a crowded room. The number of spectators is a major criterion of success and figures largely in the accounts published by the partisan press.[9] Susan Herbst brings to light the development of a symbolic use of estimates of the size of rallies in the United States;[10] as in France, this is no longer a question of seeing it as a place to sound out opinion, as was the case in the nineteenth century. In *L'Humanité*, observers at communist rallies systematically stick to showing that they bring together a large number of people, an observation which also applies to a large proportion of the articles about socialist rallies in *Le Populaire*.[11] Commentators are obsessed with the number of spectators. There are stereotypes of partisan journalism in reporting rallies. To guarantee the presence of a large audience at a rally, its organisers must provide maximum advertising. Describing the transition of assemblies at the end of the nineteenth century when the public often reaches hundreds or thousands, to the rallies of the interwar period with tens of thousands, the legal expert Menanteau stresses that the birth of parties coincides exactly with 'the appearance of new tools of advertising, convocation and human concentration'.[12]

---

6. Gilles Candar and Christophe Prochasson, 'Le socialisme à la conquête des terroirs', *Le Mouvement Social*, 1992, vol. 160, pp. 49–50.
7. Candar and Prochasson, 'Le socialisme à la conquête des terroirs', pp. 49–50.
8. Gilles Candar, 'Propagande: à propos de Jean Longuet, Marcel Cachin, Lucien Roland et quelques autres...', *Cahier et revue de l'OURS*, 1993, vol. 211, p. 5.
9. The national partisan press focuses primarily on meetings held in Paris.
10. Susan Herbst, *Numbered Voices. How Opinion Polling Has Shaped American Politics*, Chicago, Chicago University Press, 1993, pp. 133–151.
11. My analysis here is based on articles taken from these two newspapers for 1938.
12. Maurice Menanteau, *Les nouveaux aspects de la liberté de réunion. Essai sur les caractères juridiques et politiques de la liberté de réunion en France*, Paris, Librairie technique et économique, 1937, p. 28.

The size of the public as criterion of success

When produced for the same rallies, police reports and articles in the partisan press fail to agree about figures on audience size.[13] On 8 May 1938, an SFIO rally was held at the Luna Park. A note sent to the police prefecture estimates that 'the festivity took place [...] with a public of 7,000–8,000 persons'.[14] The following day, *Le Populaire* ran the title: 'At the Luna Park for the *fête populaire* organised by the *Amicales socialistes*, 40,000 workers gave a warm welcome to socialist speakers'.[15] This is a well-known phenomena and the police are often criticised for their tendency to underestimate the scale of this type of event. On the other hand, it is also likely that journalists in the partisan press increase the real number of participants. The way that the numbers are cited in the newspapers is rather striking. Firstly, numeral figures are often used, and seem to draw more attention than numbers written in longhand. This is a characteristic of articles in *L'Humanité* which regularly announce rallies with tens of thousands of people. In *Le Populaire*, many articles emphasise the massive nature of the participation, but without evaluating it in numbers. The estimated figures or the remarks made about the size of the influx at a meeting can be highlighted by its inclusion in the title of the article or the first sentence. This is true for nearly all articles consulted in *L'Humanité* and some articles in *Le Populaire*. If there is no mention of the numbers present either in the title or in the first sentence, it is generally referred to several times throughout the rest of the article, particularly for communist rallies. The number itself can be repeated, particularly when the article starts on the front page and continues overleaf. On 23 January 1938, *L'Humanité* reported a meeting held at Courbevoie cited on the front page as 'an enthusiastic rally of 3,000 people', and on the second page where 'over 3,000 people filled the Aristide Briand meeting hall and occupied the surrounding area'.[16]

The emphasis on the multitude is completed by placing it in relation to the size of the room. A successful rally is where there is not enough space for all those wishing to take part. Wherever it takes place, it must be described as 'extra-full', 'full to busting', 'crowded' or 'packed', to use expressions from the press. Even if the room is large, it is still by definition too small, causing the public to overflow into the surrounding area. An account in *L'Humanité* on 20 March 1938 describes a rally at the Maison de la Mutualité:

---

13. About the 'work of constructing the importance and significance of numbers' in questions of collective action, see: Michel Offerlé, *Sociologie des groupes d'intérêt*, Paris, Montchrestien, 1994, pp. 110–118; and Donatella Della Porta and Mario Diani, *Social Movements. An Introduction*, Oxford, Blackwell, 2006, pp. 171–173.
14. APP/Ba/1956/SFIO, 1937–1938: Rapport, préfecture de Police, 8 mai 1938, 17h20.
15. *Le Populaire*, 9 May 1938.
16. *L'Humanité*, 23 January 1938.

> Well before the planned time, the surroundings [...] of place Maubert were criss-crossed with people walking around who then converged towards the lower part of rue Monge, towards *La Mutualité*. Without waiting, we go in. Already — it is not yet 14.30 and the rally does not begin until 15.00! — the stalls are full and there are only some free places in the galleries. Soon, all these few spaces will be taken, many activists remain standing, surrounding, both below and on the balconies, the first arrivals with an animated and dense barrier. The central row is finally filled up and in the corner, the table prepared for the press, also very full, is virtually the only island of resistance left to the pushing of impatient listeners to enter and became offended not to find room in the dense rally. Then there are many who stand for two hours in the corridors, keeping the doors open to listen to Thorez' speech.[17]

These constructions are found more occasionally in the socialist press while they are used in most of the articles in *L'Humanité*. This is the partisan journalistic task of making numbers count.

The audience also has to seem important in the smaller rallies. Two techniques are used by the press which are interlinked at times: regrouping several assemblies in a single article so that accumulation produces a mass effect that a sole relatively small rally cannot produce; or emphasising the tough constraints faced and stressing that this nevertheless does not stop a reasonable number of people from attending. Press reports must show that a lot of people attend, even when reporting smaller rallies. This sort of journalistic presentation works particularly well for propaganda tours: the audience of each rally adds up to a creditable score for the propagandist at the end of the series of assemblies. Articles of this type abound in the columns of *Le Populaire* under the heading 'Socialist Propaganda'. On 20 February 1938 the meetings held in la Manche by the permanent delegate of the SFIO for propaganda, Théo Bretin, are related as follows:

> Despite winter, despite the cold, his assemblies were followed and had many listeners. Naturally, in the middle of Chouans country [royalist territory], where for the clerics the key is abstention, and as for republicans, only the SFIO is organised, our friend's assemblies did not move the masses, but as a sign of things to come, not one took place without enthusiasm. They began at Carentan [...]. Then in Bréhal 200 listeners, a fervent and fraternal atmosphere; in Saint-James, where a section was set up, in Pontorson, in Saint-Hilaire-du-Harcouet 150 to 200 listeners; in Granville, a hundred listeners; in Bouillon, in Sartilly before around forty sympathisers, the first milestones; finally in Avranches, despite terrible weather, around fifty enthusiastic listeners.

---

17. *L'Humanité*, 20 March 1938.

Figure 6.1: L'Humanité, 9 April 1938 (left); Le Populaire, 27 November 1938 (right)

As Michel Offerlé notes for street demonstrations, the 'accommodation of estimates is also made by estimating the quality of this quantity'.[18] This evocation of the multitude is then coupled with an emphasis on the unanimous behaviour of the crowd. Thus 'making up numbers' is also 'giving body' — to use Emmanuel Fureix's expression about liberal funerals under the Restoration as a 'ritual of opposition'.[19] In the communist press and to a lesser extent in socialist newspapers, we often find terms describing the audience in the singular, such as: 'the hall', 'the assembly', 'the crowd' — the latter being used the most frequently. The character both gigantic and assimilative of it is stressed by the association of certain adjectives. *L'Humanité* speaks of crowds which are uncountable, ardent, immense, unanimous and compact, to cite terms used in many articles. If the public is immense, it must also be presented as united in its support for a speech: 'Popular Unanimous Will!' ran the title of *L'Humanité* on 16 January 1938. Two days later, at a rally at the Vélodrome d'Hiver, the public is described as acting 'as a sole man'. This public unity is also emphasised by photographs published alongside the articles. Of around fifty photographs illustrating accounts of rallies in 1938 in *Le Populaire* and fifty odd in *L'Humanité*, over half present the public as an indistinguishable crowd: the room is seen from above and at a distance (see Figure 6.1).

---

18. Offerlé, *Sociologie des groupes d'intérêt*, p. 117.
19. Emmanuel Fureix, 'Un rituel d'opposition sous la Restauration. Les funérailles libérales à Paris (1820–1830)', *Genèses*, 2002, vol. 46, pp. 78–79.

'Making noise' to 'bring in the crowds'

The account of an assembly of a communist committee preparing a rally to present a report on a mandate (*compte rendu de mandat*) states: 'We need to make noise before the report to bring in the crowds'.[20] To guarantee the success of a rally, particularly the presence of a large audience, organisers work hard to ensure good publicity. From the 1920s, both parties observed develop a mobilising expertise, and a body of mobilising mechanisms is used in the big cities in particular, such as posters, notes in the press, and distribution of leaflets. To attract participants to a series of rallies in August 1927, the *Bulletin d'information du Parti communiste* advises people to 'get to work on methods of agitation still little used', adding some original ways to announce them.

It was standard to make a call for rally participation via the press, the most mobilised newspapers being those linked to the party organiser. This method, generally coupled with postering, was considered an effective way to attract a large number of participants. A police report on three rallies organised by the PCF in 1926 specifies that these measures consist of 'daily appeals appearing in the Party organs and a poster [that] will be put up on the walls of Paris and its suburbs', after emphasising that 'the organisers have taken all measures necessary to assure the success of these assemblies'.[21] Announcing a rally in the press differs from using an 'advertisement' — to use a term employed by the administrative and police authorities in their surveillance reports. The partisan press may contain simple announcements informing the public that a meeting is to be held. In 1938, in *Le Populaire*, these are regrouped in the column 'Convocations', under the heading 'Festivities and Public Assemblies'. There are three or four indications about rallies (place, date, speaker, etc.). This type of announcement is also used in *L'Humanité*. On 11 January 1938, it published a list of 'large public meetings and account of mandate assemblies' to be held during the week. A series of rallies organised by the party leadership for a big national campaign is also regularly announced. Lists of this sort abound in *L'Humanité* in November 1938 for the rallies organised: 'against the Munich Diktat, against the Daladier decrees, [and] in defence of republican Spain'. The accumulation of these dozens of announcements of rallies tends to make participation in one of them a contribution to a broader protest movement. The objective is not only to inform the public about a meeting, but to stress its importance, thus promoting it as part of a nationwide campaign. For the larger rallies, often held in Paris, more developed propaganda is also published in the press.

In addition to a drive to mobilise participants already involved, posters are used as an announcement aimed at the larger public. In October 1927 a PCF memorandum states:

---

20. AN/F7/13103/Notes générales sur l'activité du PCF, Seine, 1925–1926: Rapport, 'comité du 38ème rayon', 1926.
21. AN/F7/13103/Rapport, 'Au sujet des trois meetings organisés par le comité d'action', 12 mai 1926.

It is not enough, to attract the usual public to the big meetings in our regions with a few posters. You have to paste up small propaganda posters, distribute leaflets in your factories, you must organise small workshops and local assemblies to prepare the success of the main meetings.[22]

Putting up posters is an important device for attracting a minimum number of people, but it is often only a first step and considered insufficient on its own. Taking a look at the work of small PCF cells nevertheless reveals a number of practical problems that even a simple collage of posters involves — the size of the area, the number of bill posters, problems of sabotage, the need for a minimum supply of material, etc. This explains why organisers of an assembly sometimes limit themselves in this respect. On 3 April 1926 the question of postering was discussed in the assembly of a PCF cell in the Paris area:

> Marcel, Pierre, Bertrand and Schreps have made a very good job postering and the cell thanks them. Yet the next must be more inclusive. [...] We need more bill posters. I have asked the [*Fédération Sportive du Travail*], and Maille [...] is ready to assist us. He has the material. From now on our team of bill posters must make [...] contact with him and some of his young boxers. Ideally, we should have a map of Conflans and divide the area by sector for installing and supervision. This is especially as we shall be much sabotaged for our next assembly. [...] The cell thanks comrade Muller of the *Jeunesses Communistes* for making a pot of glue which he offers our team of bill posters. [...] We beg comrade Schreps to press the business of the brushes so that our bill posters are all equipped.[23]

The extent of postering certainly depends on the size of the planned rally. The sources say little on this point, and those I found only deal with the PCF. The large rallies in Paris required several thousand posters: 5,000 posters were put up for the meeting at the Maison de la Mutualité on 31 July 1925.[24] The same applies for posters in a national campaign which groups several rallies together: '5,000 posters for convocations for rallies [are] put up throughout France' for the international week against the *Terreur blanche* of 1–7 December 1924.[25] As for the zone covered by postering, the organisers rarely stick to just the population of the city where an assembly will take place. A 1926 police report on three rallies organised by the PCF action committee states that walls in 'Paris and its suburbs' will be postered.[26] The *Bulletin d'information du Parti communiste* specifies that

---

22. AN/F7/13094/Circulaires PCF, 1926: Circulaire Région Est, octobre 1927, sur le 'mois syndical'.
23. AN/F7/13103/Notes générales sur l'activité du PCF. Seine, 1925–1926: Cellule 782, PV de la séance du 3 avril 1926.
24. AN/F7/13103/Circulaires PCF, 1925.
25. AN/F7/13092/Circulaires PCF, 1924: Circulaire du Secours Rouge International, novembre 1924.
26. AN/F7/13103/Notes générales sur l'activité du PCF. Seine, 1925–1926.

'the rally [...] must not only bring in workers from the city where it takes place, but must include the more remote villages or localities'.[27] It is difficult to know what precise locations are chosen for postering. Posters cannot be put up anywhere and a 1928 memorandum sent to secretaries of communist cells in the Lyon region stipulates that:

> A certain number of posters are put up on walls to broadcast this rally. [...] You must [...] instruct your comrades that they must stop sticking Party posters on top of those of the [commercial] agencies because all the Lyonnais agencies have warned us for the last time that if our comrades persist in sticking Party posters right in the middle of their notice boards, they will prosecute them in the courts.[28]

In 1924, in its 'instructions to federal secretaries for the campaign of the first anniversary of Lenin's death' the Agitprop section of the PCF specifies that 'given [the] importance [of posters supplied], they must be put up in the best places'.[29] But what are the best places? In 1927 the *Bulletin d'information du Parti communiste* provides a hint by saying that they must be put where they can be seen by as many people as possible: 'It is a question of [...] making [assemblies and demonstrations] as big as possible, and so to prepare them seriously. Posters should be put up near businesses in the most densely populated places'.[30] Posters must in any case be made to attract attention. A '*Schéma de causerie*' published in 1936 by *Les Cahiers du propagandiste* on the 'problem of socialist propaganda' insists that:

> Until recently, [publicity for public assemblies] was pitiful. Some sections have organised propaganda assemblies but with the maximum discretion. Invisible posters on walls, often handwritten and whose content is illegible.[31]

Postering is generally carried out for one to eight days before the date of the rally. Starting any earlier is unwise given the risk of sabotage by opponent activists. In 1935, Pierre Hanon, secretary of the Paris group of socialist students, relates the problems caused by the sabotage of their posters in an article in *La vie socialiste*: 'The morning of the meeting, we noticed that alas our wretched adversaries had systematically covered up posters that we had paid for with great trouble'. In 1926, in a communist rally in a Paris suburb, a speaker 'protested energetically against the sabotage of posters advertising the assembly, probably made by the "fascist

---

27. *Bulletin d'information du Parti communiste*, no. 8, 1926, p. 12.
28. AN/F7/13095/Circulaires PCF, 1928: Circulaire aux secrétaires de cellules, rayon de Lyon, 15 novembre 1928.
29. AN/F7/13092/Circulaires PCF, 1924.
30. *Bulletin d'information du Parti communiste*, no. 17, 1927.
31. 'Schéma de causerie', *Les Cahiers du propagandiste*, SFIO, 1936, vols. 20–21, pp.11–12, author unknown.

workers in the pay of capitalists"'.[32] This sort of damage is regularly noted by police observers. The report on a communist rally on 9 March 1926 at rue Danton in Paris, specifies that 'posters put up, especially in the 5th *arrondissement,* [have] for the most part, been ripped'.[33] Sabotage is a common practice, and means that posters cannot be put up too early. Jules Moch, socialist deputy and then Minister, wrote in his memoirs of having once taken the risk of announcing the venue of a rally with Léon Blum in Valence six weeks in advance, commenting: 'This is dangerous, because it leaves the time to prepare counter-demonstrations'.[34] Late postering also helps take the organisation of counter-demonstrations by surprise. I will return to this in Chapter 7.

Organisers also often plan a distribution of leaflets. The form of the distribution depends on the size of the rally, but the aim of having a large public is always evident. For a rather modest communist assembly estimated at around a hundred people, organised in Paris in 1934 in a café, leaflets were only distributed in the *arrondissement*.[35] In 1930, for a more important assembly — the police estimate was 400 people — leaflets were distributed in three *arrondissements*.[36] In the provinces, the distribution often extends to the entire city and even its periphery. For a meeting in Dunkirk in 1929, leaflets were distributed 'in Dunkirk and in the region'.[37] Naturally, the number of leaflets distributed also depends on the size of audience that the organisers want to attract. The SFIO printed 150,000[38] to announce a rally in the Vélodrome d'Hiver in December 1938, where the police expected 12,000–15,000 people[39] and where *Le Populaire* counted 40,000.[40] Specific locations are targeted for leafleting, and in the case of communist meetings, workers are one of the main targets. We are told that to inform the public of a meeting held in Nantes in 1929 'workshops and worksites in the city' were to be covered by the distribution of leaflets.[41] If leafleting is not limited to a distribution outside workshops, they stay in the privileged place. In the case of the SFIO, it aims at a larger public and runs a greater risk of missing its target. In 1938 a letter addressed to the police prefect by a person describing himself as 'an elderly Parisian of around eighty years of age, who as a private individual of no

---

32. AN/F7/13103/Notes générales sur l'activité du PCF. Seine, 1925–1926: Rapport, 4 octobre 1926, réunion au préau de l'école de la rue de Châtenay, Antony.
33. AN/F7/13103/Rapport, 8 mars 1926.
34. Jules Moch, *Une si longue vie*, Paris, R. Laffont, 1976, p. 60.
35. AN/F7/12963/Notes journalières de la préfecture de Police sur les réunions et manifestations, 1934: Rapport, 24 mars 1936.
36. AN/F7/13190/Affiches, tracts, papillons du PCF, 1927–1931: Rapport, 15 janvier 1930.
37. AN/F7/13190: Rapport, commissaire spécial, Dunkerque, 2 décembre 1929.
38. APP/Ba/1956/SFIO, 1937–1938: Rapport, 25 novembre 1938.
39. APP/Ba/1956/SFIO: Rapport, 1er décembre 1938.
40. *Le Populaire*, 3 December 1938.
41. AN/F7/13190/Affiches, tracts, papillons du PCF, 1927–1931: Rapport, commissaire central de police, Nantes, 7 novembre 1929.

importance, signed with nothing more than his initials', began: 'Here is a leaflet that my daughter received on returning home yesterday evening towards seven o'clock at Carrefour Buci from a brochure seller'. It was a leaflet announcing a socialist meeting. The letter ended by suggesting 'an immediate reply of preventive repressive action'.[42]

There are other, rarer, techniques for announcing rallies, such as driving a car or truck with loudspeakers in the environs of the place where it will be held. On 16 July 1938, the commissaire general of the commission of SFIO festivities wrote to the police prefect requesting authorisation to advertise a festivity organised by the federation of la Seine in Bry-sur-Marne in this way. This meant 'letting a car drive very rapidly through the main streets of the district of Nogent-sur-Marne. This car [...] will announce the programme of [the] festivity by loud-speaker'. The police chief of Nogent-sur-Marne gave the prefect his opinion on this authorisation, concluding that it should not be refused for three reasons: the car would drive 'very fast'; 'no stopping [...] will be tolerated on the public streets'; 'there have been precedents in the district'.[43] This way of announcing rallies was nevertheless rather infrequent, precisely because of the need for prior authorisation from the prefect. Sometimes placards are also placed on bikes, cars or trucks, a technique to which invites a PCF memorandum in 1926:

> In the days leading up to the demonstration or rally, we will organise teams of cyclists going round the surrounding villages or the industrial suburbs to announce rallies using placards [...]. We can also study the use of trucks decorated with placards inviting workers to take part in rallies.[44]

The use of this variety of ways to announce rallies testifies to the effort made by activists to assure that it will assemble a large public and the mastery of a *savoir-faire* for mobilising numbers.

Whatever the method of mobilisation used, the elements of a rally which are most clearly emphasised in order to attract a large audience are the names of the expected speakers. As far as posters go,[45] the party or group organiser is systematically mentioned, generally at the top of the poster, but in a relatively discrete way. Posters also print the place, date and hour of the rally. However this is not the most striking information. The objective of the meeting, if there is one, is also given and can take the form of a descriptive title such as: 'Foreign Policy and the Socialist Party', announcing a SFIO assembly on 15 December 1928 at Annecy. It can also take the form of a slogan: 'Fascism no! Communism yes!', proclaims the poster for a PCF assembly of 28 April 1934 in Modane. Explanations

---

42. APP/Ba/1956/SFIO, 1937–1938: Lettre du 26 avril 1938.
43. APP/Ba/1956/SFIO: Dossier sur l'autorisation d'annoncer une fête SFIO, juillet 1938
44. AN/F7/13093/Circulaires PCF: Circulaire no. 31, 6 août 1926.
45. This is based on a body of over fifty posters (20 for the SFIO, 23 for the PCF and 15 for the *Front populaire*), found in the very rich *fonds* in the Archives de Haute-Savoie: 1M/114–117/Affiches à caractère politique et général.

are frequently added in a less conspicuous typeface. When the meeting is part of a national campaign, posters often carry a relatively long explanatory text in small print. At the bottom of the poster we find the conditions of entry, as well as the public to which it is directed. We learn whether or not entry is free of charge, whether is it open to everyone or reserved for activists, and if women are welcome. These notes at the bottom of the poster are where we find any additional information to draw in a larger public: 'The hall is heated', announce the SFIO at the foot of a poster for an assembly of 11 November 1923 in Annecy. However, of all this information, the most important concerns the speakers. Their names are generally written in capital letters and bold print. In the 1938 *Almanach Populaire*, the socialist Théo Bretin, giving advice for a successful meeting, recalls that posters must 'make the name of the speaker clearly visible'. More specifically, 'he must look like a star; this will encourage the potential audience to come'.[46] Not all the names are emphasised in the same way: there are star speakers, or at least speakers that the organiser wants to present as such, and other speakers. When it is a question of mobilising for the largest rallies, the content of announcements in the press has strong similarities with that of posters. The element considered most likely to attract people is the presence of well-known speakers whose names are written so as to stand out from the rest of the advertisement. There is a hierarchy of speakers. The most famous are those written in larger print, sometimes with a portrait added, which the others do not have, or a portrait that is larger than the others, or placed differently, above or at the centre.[47] The same predominance of information about speakers can be found in leaflets. Their way of presenting various aspects of the rally, such as place, names of speakers, use of slogans and so forth, strongly resembles that of posters, except that the leaflet is more precise in the information given.[48]

If the presence of a famous speaker is highlighted, this is because it is indeed one of the main factors likely to attract a large number of people. To estimate the numbers likely to attend a meeting, police agents take into account the presence or absence of a well-known speaker first of all. A police report announcing a SFIO rally at the Vélodrome d'Hiver on 2 December 1938 states that 'due to the personality of the announced speakers, it seems likely that [the rally] will be a great success in terms of attendance'.[49] When an important speaker cancels his appointment, there is a significant difference between forecasts and estimations given after the rally. This is the case of a PCF rally at the Huygens gymnasium on 20 February 1926. Two days before the police had announced that 'given

---

46. Théo Bretin, 'La propagande', *Almanach Populaire*, 1938, p. 235.
47. *L'Humanité* and *Le Populaire* differ: in 1938, the PCF press used a great many photographs of speakers, whereas these are absent in the socialist press.
48. The text may be virtually identical in posters and leaflets announcing rallies. See, for instance: AN/F7/13190/Affiches, tracts, papillons du PCF, 1927–1931: Tract, affiche et rapport, Nantes, 7 novembre 1929.
49. APP/Ba/1956/SFIO, 1937–1938: Rapport, 1er décembre 1938.

the advertising which has recently appeared in *L'Humanité*, we should estimate that around 2,500–3,000 persons will respond to the organisers' call'.[50] The report submitted after the meeting mentions only 500 spectators, and specifies that 'caught in an electoral assembly', Marcel Cachin, who was announced as a speaker, had excused himself.[51] It is likely that people had been warned of his absence and that consequently a sizeable part of potential participants decided not to attend. For these people it seems that the main attraction at the rally was the presence of a key party figure.

Collecting signs of support

Observing meeting rooms in the interwar period I am struck by the passivity of the audience, or at least its absence of spontaneity. The public are largely spectators. Police reports reveal the lack of oral interventions and questions posed by participants. The latter, when they do not cause disorder or express violent reactions, are certainly not what primarily interests the police observer; but even in the most detailed reports, where the action seems to be related minute by minute, we find very little reaction from those in the room, contrary to what is seen in many assemblies at the end of the Second Empire or the beginning of the Third Republic. The questions are of course more numerous in small assemblies than in big rallies where the size of the hall and the acoustics make speaking difficult for an isolated participant — the use of voice amplification systems being limited to the speakers on the platform.

In the massive rallies typical of the period, the role of the public consists less in generating discourse than in showing its support for party speakers. In the socialist and communist press commentators insist not only on the massive character of participation in rallies, but also on the signs of approval from the assembled crowd, and its enthusiasm — a term which crops up frequently. Not only is the crowd innumerable, but it is also frequently described as 'passionate', 'ardent' and 'vibrant'. Party organisers try to present the image of a public united in the same emotion, using a range of mechanisms to stage key signs of support. The parties studied exert themselves until the participants are moved, or at least appear to be moved, and can be described as being moved. In his study of the funerals of presidents of the Republic, Pierre-Yves Baudot explains his decision to focus on the work of the organisers. Baudot stresses that the research is 'situated upstream of the production of emotions, on the creation of devices that allow organisers to collect them and, hence, give form to them', and states that 'genuinely felt emotions do not condition the organisers' perception of the effectiveness of their ceremony'.[52]

---

50. AN/F7/13103/Notes générales sur l'activité du PCF. Seine, 1925–1926: Annonce du 18 février 1926.
51. AN/F7/13103/Rapport, 21 février 1926.
52. Pierre-Yves Baudot, *Événement et institution. Les funérailles des présidents de la République en France (1877–1996)*, PhD dissertation, Paris I, 2005, p. 59.

Promoting communion in public enthusiasm

From police observations we can draw a repertoire of public expressions of support: starting with the applause generally made after a speech to indicate agreement with the ideas expressed, but also marking and stressing key points in the speech. The public also applauds speakers on their arrival or at end of a rally, particularly after a motion has been adopted. In meetings with a sufficiently small audience the proposal is often put to the vote by a show of hands. This is impossible in larger rallies; but the way motions are drafted still indicates that they would really express the voice of the entire public. In June 1933, a socialist rally in the festivity hall of Vienne ended with the adoption of the following motion:

> After having heard the admirable presentation by the speaker Léon Blum, the audience of around 1,800 people approves his statements: making a commitment to work with all the means in their possession for the success of the PS-SFIO.[53]

Rhythmic clapping is also used to pay homage to a speaker. A police report of 13 June 1928 on a SFIO rally in the Pyrénées Palace cinema in Paris, recounts that following a speech by Léon Blum: 'the entire room acclaims the speaker and Luquet [deputy, on the platform], pays him tribute and encourages the public to make a round of rhythmical applause in his honour'.[54]

Similarly, shouting is a show of support used to celebrate a particular speaker: 'Long live Blum!', cries the audience of the SFIO rally of 14 April 1935 in Asnières.[55] Another form of support is when the public repeats slogans aloud. They abound in communist rallies, and on 11 March 1936 in Saint-Ouen, cries of 'soviets everywhere!' and 'soviets, this is peace!' welcomed Maurice Thorez to the platform.[56] We find the same cries nine days later at a rally at the Maison de la Mutualité.[57] Then there is the dialogue that the public has with the speaker, when taking up his words. At a communist rally on 13 March 1936 in the festivity hall of Clichy, when a speaker mentioned 'sectarian politics championed by Doriot', the public responded by booing Doriot.[58] By intervening at the right time, the audience takes part in the success of the meeting.

---

53. AD Isère/55 M/4/Police générale. Réunions publiques et privées, conferences, 1925–1933: Rapport du commissaire spécial, Vienne, 14 juin 1933.
54. AN/F7/13080/Activité du Parti socialiste, Seine (1926, 1928–1932). Notes, rapports, extraits de presse: Rapport, 14 juin 1928.
55. AN/F7/13320/Réunions et manifestations diverses, 1934–1935: Rapport, 15 avril 1935, réunion au gymnase municipal d'Asnières.
56. AN/F7/12964/Notes journalières de la préfecture de Police sur les réunions et les manifestations, 1–15 mars 1936: Rapport, 12 mars 1936.
57. AN/F7/12965/Notes journalières de la préfecture de Police sur les réunions et les manifestations, 16–31 mars 1936: Rapport, 21 mars 1936.
58. AN/F7/12964/Notes journalières de la préfecture de Police sur les réunions et les manifestations, 1–15 mars 1936: Rapport, 14 mars 1936.

The same can be said for the practice of singing partisan songs. *L'Internationale* is sung frequently by the audience of communist rallies and is often used to open and close them, with the public leaving the room singing it. It is also used to greet a speaker and is generally sung when they arrive on the platform and then at the end of their speech. Finally, it can be sung in the middle of a rally, between two speeches, launched by a singer or a choir, with the hall taking up the refrain. At socialist and communist rallies the public sometimes sang *La Jeune Garde,* the anthem of the *jeunesse ouvrière de France*, written before the Tours Congress, or *The Red Flag*, which evokes the struggle of the Paris Commune. In the mid-1930s *La Marseillaise* made its first appearance at communist rallies. In his memoirs the communist deputy for la Seine, Georges Cogniot, recounts:

> I remember a rally in around mid-April [1936] at the school in rue de Boulets, with 2,500 people in the audience singing *L'Internationale* and *La Marseillaise* not only in the school hall [...], but also outside in the street, where a large part of the crowd had overflowed.[59]

Support is also shown through gestures. Whatever the party, there is a certain solemnity in the act of standing to welcome a speaker, to sing or to listen to a song. On 24 January 1926 at the Jean Jaurès gymnasium, a rally organised by the PCF opened with *L'Internationale*, performed by the *Harmonie ouvrière d'Ivry* 'to which the audience listens standing'.[60] Often the two practices are linked. At a communist rally of 14 October 1926 in the Artistic Palace in Saint-Maur, when Sadoul followed Duclos to the platform: 'the audience rose to its feet and sung *L'Internationale*'.[61] The increasing use of the action of standing at times accompanied by the gesture of a raised fist in the 1930s has been studied by Philippe Burrin and Éric Nadaud.[62] During a rally organised on 18 March 1936 by the SFIO at the Stella Palace in Paris, 'a record player plays *L'Internationale*, the audience listens standing, fists raised, and then takes up the refrain in chorus'.[63]

Applause, shouting, singing and gestures are all signs of party support that the press presents the day after when describing the crowd's enthusiasm. Whilst not suggesting that participants do not actually support ideas developed on the platform, we can nonetheless deviate from the purely expressive function of the sounds and gestures to detect in them an inherent element in the meeting, an

---

59. Georges Cogniot, *Parti pris*, vol. 1, Paris, Éditions sociales, 1976, p. 251.
60. AN/F7/13103/Notes générales sur l'activité du PCF. Seine, 1925–1926: Rapport, 25 janvier 1926.
61. AN/F7/13103/Rapport, 15 octobre 1926.
62. Philippe Burrin, 'Poings levés et bras tendus. La contagion des symboles au temps du Front Populaire', *Vingtième siècle*, 1986, vol. 11, pp. 5–20; Éric Nadaud, 'Le renouvellement des pratiques militantes à la SFIO au début du Front Populaire (1934–1936)', *Le Mouvement Social*, 1990, vol. 153, pp. 17–18.
63. AN/F7/12965/Notes journalières de la préfecture de Police sur les réunions et les manifestations, 16–31 mars 1936: Rapport, 19 mars 1936.

obligatory step. This is that rallies are also used 'to collect applause',[64] as a sign of party support. A show of public enthusiasm can thus be interpreted as an expected form of behaviour. The way rallies are narrated in the press — and, albeit to a lesser extent, in film propaganda or the memoirs of politicians, that is, the partisan presentations of rallies — reveals an emphasis on this vital aspect of their success. The public must show signs of support which are then regularly interpreted as belonging to the register of emotion.

The partisan press describes the public who come to hear party speakers from the perspective of passion. Meeting rooms would contain a vibrant assembly, an ardent crowd. This passion is described as directed towards certain speakers who are 'warmly' or 'passionately' applauded, who receive 'warm ovations' or 'frenetic applause'. Journalists affirm that some speakers touch 'the heart' of the audience with their words. On 9 May 1938 in Amiens, socialist speakers 'found the hearts and minds of assembled workers', states *Le Populaire* the following day.[65] In December 1938 *L'Humanité* announces that Duclos' presentation at the Maison de la Mutualité went 'right to the heart of the activists who filled the huge room to suffocating point'.[66] Generally, the press describes the 'feelings' of the crowd towards the speakers, and talks of 'ardent sympathy', 'deep affection', 'love' or even 'passion'. These feelings are described as addressed to a sacred person. The audience listens 'in a religious silence', when Léon Blum speaks at a rally in Lille on 13 November 1938, recounts *Le Populaire* the following day. Even the word 'worshipped' occurs several times in the press. The idea that the fervour of the crowd is such that it is difficult to describe is recurrent. On 21st November 1938 *Le Populaire* describes an 'indescribable enthusiasm'; on 9 October 1938, *L'Humanité* reveals an enthusiasm 'that words cannot translate'. The ways to express support in these partisan representations are rather distant from those on which the link between politicians and citizens should be based in the republican discourse at the end of the nineteenth century.

An article in *Le Populaire* on 3 December 1938 relates the arrival of speakers for a rally at the Vélodrome d'Hiver: 'It was a delirium. Blum arrived at the foot of the platform [...]. The crowd surrounded him, children bearing flowers, everyone trying to get near him'. The journalistic description of the public's movements towards the main speaker uses the image of people trying compulsively to get closer to him. This 'surge' takes place through the accentuation of the public's attention. A communist assembly was depicted in *L'Humanité* as 'seeming to hold its breath in order to follow Duclos' statement better'.[67] The press also insists on

---

64. An expression used by Jean Zay in a modest-sized rally organised by the *Parti radical* at *la Mutualité*. On the question of 'raking in the applause', he contrasted the aim of the rally in which he took part: 'comparing ideas'. AN/F7/12962/Notes journalières de la préfecture de Police sur les réunions et manifestations, 1930–1933: Rapport, 14 décembre 1933.
65. *Le Populaire*, 10 May 1938.
66. *L'Humanité*, 8 December 1938.
67. *L'Humanité*, 8 December 1938.

the actions interpreted as honouring the speaker, in particular the gifts offered to him, most often flowers. 'A magnificent red bouquet', relates *Le Populaire* on 3 December 1938, was offered to Léon Blum during an SFIO rally at the Vélodrome d'Hiver. The gifts offered often have a symbolic meaning: *L'Humanité* on 18 July 1938 relates that Marcel Cachin received a miner's lamp from miners of Aniche. Commentators emphasise that the gifts with which the delegations greet the speakers are a way to demonstrate their recognition and affection.

Beyond the actual spatial position of the speaker, who talks from a platform and is consequently above the public, the partisan press insists on his domination of the situation. The signs of support that come from the crowd are frequently depicted as 'ascending' or 'rising towards the speaker'. In parallel, the speaker is described as mastering the crowd, able to tame its displays of enthusiasm. A single gesture is enough for him to obtain the silence of those applauding. *L'Humanité* described Thorez' arrival at the microphone:

> When our director, [Marcel Cachin], said, in a profound silence: "*I now give the word to our secretary general, Maurice Thorez!*", the crowd [...] made a long ovation to our comrade and cried: "*Thorez to power! Open the borders!*" But, promptly, at a sign from Maurice, calm returned, and, in the midst of the general attention, our comrade began his report.[68]

Some speakers would try to control the feelings of the crowd in order to guide them through each stage of their speech. This is described in the same article (the reactions of the room are in italics):

> Eyes fixed on the speaker, everyone following his moves. Does he express his certainty of seeing the fascist offensive stopped in Aragon? *The cheers start.* Does he evoke Hitler's dream of encircling France, a threat on three frontiers at the same time? *Conscious of the danger, the mute listeners, have serious and tense faces.* If he denounces the godless phrases of *Mein Kampf* [...], *a shiver ran through the room, the condemnation and contempt for the author of these insanities are read in the expressions of all. And it is with anxiety that [the public] listens to Maurice Thorez* recalling the alarming list of retreats, concessions or betrayals that French diplomacy had operated or committed in the last three years.

In parallel the partisan press presents the people at the rally, speakers and public, as participants to a same communion. In 1938 *L'Humanité* recalls the: 'communion of the audience with the words of Maurice Thorez', or writes in a headline: 'When the Crowd and the Speaker Communicate' — about a meeting of the party general secretary.[69]

There is also a communion among those in the audience. For a rally to be successful in the eyes of commentators and organisers, it must depict a large and

---

68. *L'Humanité*, 20 March 1938.
69. *L'Humanité*, 5 February 1938 and 20 March 1938.

united audience. The communion on which journalists insist primarily takes the form of a shared emotion. The description of a meeting as a place of collective emotion is part of a stereotyped discourse in journalistic accounts of socialist and communist rallies. If the crowd acted as 'a sole man', it also had only 'one heart'.[70] When observers give their own impressions they mention emotion, precise moments during the rally, certain passages of speeches or certain songs, that are described as 'moving' and 'poignant'. But it is above all the emotion of the crowd that is affirmed: 'a deep emotion, that, visibly, each share in the assembled crowd';[71] a room '[raised] by emotion'.[72] Beyond sharing the same ideas, supporters' descriptions of public reactions thus give a central place to emotion. This 'entering into communion' on the part of the crowd is described as giving it strength beyond that of the simple aggregation of individuals. The word 'powerful' is one of the most frequently used to describe the different aspects of meetings, particularly in the huge rallies at the Vélodrome d'Hiver, or the Japy or Wagram halls, exactly those privileged by journalists in their accounts. The individual is described as transcending himself by participation in this public communion: 'each, on entering in this bath of virile and unanimous humanity felt stronger'.[73] The partisan press highlights the fact that in rallies something occurs that exceeds words.

The press description of this collective emotion should not make us lose sight of the fact that if police reports relate instances where participants applaud, shout, sing or stand, only those sources linked to the party organiser interpret these reactions by stressing the emotional approach as the veneration of speakers or the communion of participants. Moreover, even if I could find descriptions of emotional expression in non-partisan sources, I still cannot consider, starting from the description or observation of behaviour, that these are in fact support for the speaker taking the form of a shared sensation of participants. In other words, the observer cannot grasp what these individuals really think and feel. The problems posed by the 'sliding of the postulated behaviour of the believer which can be observed, to the existence of an individual belief expressed as a proposition on the world',[74] has been emphasised several times. According to Nicolas Mariot:

---

70. *Le Populaire*, 3 December 1938.
71. *L'Humanité*, 5 February 1938.
72. *Le Populaire*, 31 July 1938.
73. *Le Populaire*, 3 December 1938.
74. Nicolas Mariot, 'Morphologie des comportements et induction de croyances. Quelques remarques à propos de l'exemplaire circularité de la fonction intégratrice des rites', *Hypothèses 1997. Travaux de l'École doctorale d'histoire de l'Université Paris I-Panthéon Sorbonne*, 1998, p. 63.

When observing crowd behaviour from a distance, the imputation of intentions starting from behaviour seems illegitimate because the observer knows too little about the multiple social scenes facing him: his ignorance implies the generality of his conclusions.[75]

If participants in rallies during the interwar period probably agree with the ideas of the party organiser, we should nevertheless distrust the idea that they 'experience the same things together' and that it is 'from this community of feelings [that] the union of consciences emerges'.[76]

Techniques of staging: the theatralisation of rallies

To ensure that a rally is successful its organisers must attract the greatest number of participants possible. However since success rests not only on numbers but also on the expression of their support, the work of organisers also aims to control, orient and stimulate the enthusiasm of participants. This is the theatralisation of rallies.[77] We can distinguish several components such as the techniques intended to artificially generate a semblance of support, the introduction of increasingly relevant elements of the festivity and spectacle, the use of decorations and the symbolic marking of the space where the meeting is held, and the ways of staging speaker-stars. The organisers sometimes try to provoke public reactions directly. For example, activists are positioned around the room to lead the singing in the refrains of songs sung at the platform. During an internal assembly in 1926, a PCF cell noted for its festive assemblies that:

> It is necessary that, in certain cases planned and defined in common, the refrains of songs whose verses will be sung by comrades and artists [who are] good singers, be taken up in chorus; a well-disciplined group must thus be set up to meet this need.

The minutes of the assembly specify that 'it is not necessary to be a very good singer, this comes with practice. The aim is to get spectators to participate in our fervour'.[78] At times the positive reactions of the room are also inflamed in a 'dialogue' with speakers. For example, for a speech made by Léon Blum at the Vélodrome d'Hiver on 2 December 1938 during a SFIO rally, where a part is reported by a police observer:

---

75. Nicolas Mariot, 'Les formes élémentaires de l'effervescence collective, ou l'état d'esprit prêté aux foules', *Revue française de science politique*, 2001, vol. 51, (5) p. 728.
76. Nicolas Mariot, 'Le frisson fait-il la manifestation?', *Pouvoirs*, 2006, vol. 116, pp. 87–99.
77. Danielle Tartakowsky refers to the parallel movement of 'politicisation of theatre' and the 'theatralisation of politics' particularly in the 1930s. See: Noëlle Gérome and Danielle Tartakowsky, *La fête de l'Humanité. Culture communiste, culture populaire*, Paris, Messidor, Éditions sociales, 1988, p. 46. See also Paula Cossart, 'La communion militante. Les meetings de gauche pendant les années 1930', *Sociétés et Représentations*, 2001, vol. 12, pp. 131–140.
78. AN/F7/13103/Notes générales sur l'activité du PCF. Seine, 1925–1926: Procès-verbal de la session, 3 avril 1926.

The speaker then asks his listeners: — Are you better than two years ago? — NO — Did you feel at that time the weight of threats as those of today? — NO — Have we not done everything to unite the petit bourgeoisie, the middle classes, the agricultural labour, the workers? — The public replies YES (cries of 'Blum to power').[79]

Mobilisation is not just a job of encouraging participation understood as 'being present'; it continues during the rally in the form of actions by the participants, understood as a display of dedication. Both are directed towards press commentators, who then describe a full and enthusiastic room. However, the acceptance of techniques destined to stimulate what can only be described as an appearance of support is not obvious for a part of the political class which still considers the assembly as a place of discussion and a means of education. A part of the SFIO resisted the renewal of activist practices in the mid-1930s seeing in it a questioning of the *guesdiste* primacy of education. 'Socialism [...] must not just brush [us] on passing, leaving some phrases in memoirs. It must penetrate our entire being', wrote Georges Dumoulin in 1935 in *Le Populaire*.[80] If this resistance aims at the modernisation of propaganda techniques, it is accompanied by a distrust of the possible superficiality of reactions in the room. In an article of 1936 on 'the problem of socialist propaganda', René Cabannes notes that in the case of public assemblies one should 'distrust easy success, oft-repeated applause [which] are not always an obvious sign of understanding'.[81]

The increasing use made of a spectacle to accompany speeches can be linked to the transformation of assemblies into places to demonstrate party unity and to the will of stimulating displays of enthusiasm among participants. In the interwar period police observers of communist and socialist meetings are regularly informed of the presence of an artistic performance, a play or a film screening. Political parties certainly did not wait for this period to discover the role of festivities and spectacles in meetings. Thus, from the years 1900–1910:

> In spite of their intent to make propaganda a serious affair on principle where the appeal to reason steers away the ease of entertainment, a number of [socialist] demonstrations had a recreational or festive form.[82]

Nevertheless the interwar period remains characterised by an increased borrowing from the world of entertainment by organisers of political rallies. In his *Carnets*, in 1936, Lucien Roland complains that: 'the comedy, the theatre,

---

79. APP/Ba/1956/SFIO, 1937–1938: Notes rédigées au cours du meeting, 2 décembre 1938.
80. Cited in Éric Nadaud, 'Le renouvellement des pratiques militantes à la SFIO au début du Front Populaire (1934–1936)', *Le Mouvement Social*, 1990, vol. 153, (9–34), p. 26.
81. Renée Cabannes, 'Le problème de la propagande socialiste', *Les Cahiers du Propagandiste*, 1936, vols. 20–21, p. 11.
82. Candar and Prochasson, 'Le socialisme à la conquête des terroirs', pp. 33–63, 53–54.

are increasingly invading politics'.[83] The festivity is above all presented in rallies which commemorate an event or which are held in honour of political figures. It helps to give rallies 'a grandiose character', to use the expression of a report on the preparation, by the *Fédération socialiste de la Seine*, to commemorate Jaurès' death in 1926.[84] This use spread to other types of rallies. In January 1927, the central committee of the *Association Républicaine des Anciens Combattants* (ARAC) informs the section secretaries of an 'excellent method to introduce in this campaign in meetings, assemblies and lectures', referring to 'the distractions in the form of festivities, political concerts'.[85] In 1929, the *Matériaux pour la conférence d'entente*, published by the PCF Agitprop, points out that:

> Even in the various workshop assemblies, assemblies of sympathisers or trade unionists, in all lectures and youth assemblies, we need to introduce a recreational part in the programme. The use of theatre, living pictures [*tableaux vivants*], and revolutionary films must become widespread. Meetings-cum-festivities were thus organised for various campaigns such as the Liebknecht-Luxembourg-Lenin week.[86]

The PCF is not alone in recommending the use of festive elements to animate rallies. In 1938 in an article in *L'Almanach Populaire* on socialist propaganda where advice for the success of a public assembly is given, Théo Bretin points out that 'a lecture can be enlivened with songs, pieces of music, films, etc'.[87]

The PCF frequently resorts to theatre. A play is often part of a broader artistic programme, which complements speeches with theatre, song, dance and music. In this case the part dedicated to speeches is regularly placed between two more artistic components. A PCF rally at the Royal Cinéma in Bobigny on 24 February 1926 alternated a concert, then three speeches followed by a one-act social play.[88] When there are both songs and theatre, the meeting generally opens with the part dedicated to songs, followed by the speeches, and ends with the theatrical presentation. Sometimes the artistic part consists of a single play and the speech is often given during the interlude. During the communist rally of 25 August 1926 at the municipal theatre of Saint-Denis in commemoration of Jaurès' death, the four-act drama by Henri Pons, *Fraternité*, was staged, and the speeches took place between the second and third acts.[89] Theatre companies linked to the party

---

83. Cited in Gilles Candar, 'Propagande: à propos de Jean Longuet, Marcel Cachin, Lucien Roland et quelques autres...', *Cahier et revue de l'OURS*, 1993, vol. 211, p. 5.
84. AN/F7/13080/Activité du Parti socialiste. Seine (1926, 1928–1932). Rapport, 23 juin 1926.
85. AN/F7/13094/Circulaires PCF: Circulaire aux secrétaires de section du Comité central de l'ARAC, 18 janvier 1927.
86. AN/F7/13095/Circulaires PCF, 1928: *Matériaux pour la conférence d'entente* (Entente des Jeunesses communistes), section d'Agitprop, 9 et 16 juin 1929.
87. Théo Bretin, 'La propagande', *Almanach Populaire*, 1938, p. 236.
88. AN/F7/13103/Notes générales sur l'activité du PCF, Seine, 1925–1926: Rapport, 25 février 1926.
89. AN/F7/13103/Rapport, 26 août 1926.

are generally called on,[90] such as 'Octobre', 'Théâtre ouvrier', 'Le Nid Rouge', etc. However there are also performances by professional artists from Parisian theatres. At the communist rally on 30 January 1926 at the Maison des Syndicats, in rue de la Grange aux Belles, a comedy, *Depuis six mois*, was presented by Max Maurey, director of the Théâtre des Variétés, and performed by Jeanne Arnoux from the Sarah Bernardt theatre and Léon Bénédict from the Athénée.[91] This difference between two types of actors often matches the distinction between plays with a political character and those without. On 24 February 1926, during a rally in Bobigny, the play *L'Idée*, presented a strike and the treachery of a worker towards 'his brothers in poverty'.[92] The performance of this type of play — by far the most frequent — was clearly encouraged. In *Le Bulletin d'information du Parti communiste* of January 1927, a memorandum of Agitprop on the third anniversary of Lenin's death notes that it would be 'possible and useful' to 'present plays such as *Le Monstre* or *La Commune* by Vaillant-Couturier', deputy and chief-editor of *L'Humanité*, but also a playwright and poet.[93] Plays have a double use: as propaganda, they assume the role of a speech whilst presenting ideas in a way which is appealing; they can also lose their political character and basically become entertainment. The political nature of the rally is then provided by one or more speeches.

In the 1920s police reports generally mention plays performed, whereas in the mid-1930s we see the appearance and development of films. The use of the theatre faces the competition of cinema. The SFIO and the PCF call for it to be included in rallies,[94] and the progress of screenings seems to have as a corollary a reduction in the use of theatre. Generally speaking, there are two types of films, documentary and fiction. Documentaries of the funerals of famous people such as Lenin at PCF meetings,[95] or Jaurès at SFIO meetings are screened.[96] Others highlight the work

---

90. See the developments on 'the Agitprop' in: Jacqueline de Jomaron, *Le Théâtre En France*, Paris, A. Colin, 1992, vol. 2. On militant theatre in France in this period, see also: Danielle Tartakowsky and Alain Corbin, 'Théâtre et politique', *Revue française d'histoire des idées politiques*, 1998, vol. 8, pp. 227–400; Pascal Ory, *La belle illusion. Culture et politique sous le signe du Front Populaire. 1935–1938*, Paris, Plon, 1994, pp. 337–416.
91. AN/F7/13103/Notes générales sur l'activité du PCF. Seine, 1925–1926: Rapport, 31 janvier 1926.
92. AN/F7/13103/Rapport, 25 février 1926.
93. Arlette Schweitz, *Les parlementaires sous la Troisième République. II. Dictionnaire biographique*, Paris, Publications de la Sorbonne, 2001, pp. 201–203.
94. See, for example: J. P. Granvallet, 'La propagande cinématographique', *L'Almanach populaire*, 1939, p. 197.
95. APP/Ba/1939/Réunions ou soirées artistiques organisées par le PCF (1924–1928): Rapport, 11 novembre 1927, meeting salle du cinéma Lutétia; Rapport, 15 mars 1928, meeting salle du cinéma des Roses, L'Hay-les-Roses.
96. AN/F7/13084/Activité du parti socialiste, classement départemental (1926–1932). Rhône: Rapport, 2 août 1931, meeting SFIO (pour commémorer la mort de Jaurès), salle de la mairie du 3e arr., Lyon.

of the party in the municipalities for both the PCF[97] and the SFIO.[98] Fiction films naturally have themes linked with the ideology of the party organiser. The SFIO tends to screen pacifist films. For example, *Héros à vendre*, and a documentary, *Trafiquants de la mort*, always scheduled together, were shown several times in 1938.[99] Their projection was announced in *Le Populaire* on 9 January 1938, which presented them as 'two anti-war films'. The first was introduced as a Warner Brothers film, 'with the great star Richard Bartholomess' (Richard Barthelmess).[100] This American film was released in 1933 and deals with the after-effects of the war, but above all with the social consequences of the American Depression.[101] *Trafiquants de la mort* was presented in *Le Populaire* as a 'great documentary against arms dealers presented on the screen by a short speech by Roosevelt and another by Paul Faure'. The speeches made during rallies where these films are shown deal with the questions of war and peace. On 4 March 1936, at a communist meeting at the cinema Stephenson in Paris, after a private screening of *Le Miracle de St Georgeon* — a soviet film banned by the film censor in the French Minister of the Interior — the party candidate, Blache, gave a speech on the relations between the PCF and the Church.[102] The two parts of the assembly, film and speech(es), are linked by a common theme. Theatre and cinema may indeed distract or induce a rather facile enthusiasm; but they also publicise party ideas.

Partisan songs or airs are often performed. *L'Internationale* is frequently played by an orchestra or sung by professional singers. In SFIO meetings we find the Italian socialist song *Bandiera Rossa*, revolutionary songs such as *Ça ira* or *La Carmagnole*, songs of the Commune, or popular Spanish songs. In communist rallies the communard song *Le Drapeau Rouge*, *La Varsovienne*, a Polish song of the end of the nineteenth century which became popular in Russia in 1905 and 1917, or *The Red Army Song*. These are often sung or played by singers or orchestras linked to the party, such as the *harmonies*, musical groups in several communist and socialist municipalities, for example in Clichy for the PCF,[103] or Pantin for the SFIO.[104] The PCF's *Chorale de la Région Parisienne* was heard at a

---

97. AN/F7/13320/Réunions et manifestations diverses, 1934–1935: Rapport, 3 mars 1935, meeting PCF salle du cinéma Fantasio, Levallois-Perret (documentaire sur la municipalité de Bezons); Rapport, 11 avril 1935, meeting PCF cinéma Ivry-Palace, Ivry (documentaire sur la municipalité d'Ivry).

98. APP/Ba/1956/SFIO, 1937–1938: Rapport, 27 avril 1938, meeting au Succès Cinéma, Pré-Saint-Gervais (documentaire sur 'les réalisations socialistes à Boulogne-Billancourt').

99. APP/Ba/1956/SFIO, Rapport, 10 January 1938, meeting salle Pleyel; Rapport, 25 février 1938, meeting salle du cinéma Jojot, Noisy-le-Sec; Rapport, 27 février 1938, meeting au Ciné Pathé, Boulogne.

100. *Le Populaire*, 9 January 1938.

101. Jean Tulard, *Guide des films*, vol. 1, Paris, R. Laffont, 1990, p. 1,015.

102. AN/F7/12964/Notes journalières de la préfecture de Police sur les réunions et les manifestations, 1–15 March 1936: Rapport, 5 mars 1936.

103. AN/F7/13103/Notes générales sur l'activité du PCF. Seine, 1925–1926: Rapport, 14 février 1926.

104. AN/F7/13080/Activité du parti socialiste. Seine (1926, 1928–1932). Notes, rapports, extraits de presse: Rapport, 25 mars 1928, meeting SFIO salle des conférences, Pantin.

communist meeting on 14 October 1926.[105] *L'Harmonie socialiste de la Seine* took part in an SFIO rally on 28 July 1838, in the Wagram meeting hall.[106] The 'collectif Mai 36', 'popular movement of art and culture',[107] also frequently took part. The singing and the plays did not always have a political connotation. For example, when theatre, musical, cabaret or music-hall stars perform in their repertoire — sometimes freely, as was the case at a SFIO rally on 10 November 1938 at the Moulin de la Galette, where 'the artists who have so kindly given [...] their help' are duly thanked.[108] Police observers note that these songs, plays, and operettas were 'not of a political nature',[109] although pure entertainment was often mixed with more political chants and performances.

The theatralisation of meetings is also seen in the increasing use of decorations and in the symbolic marking out of the meeting room. In a letter addressed in response to a communist deputy requesting to use the hall of a boy's school in Vanves on Saturday 15 October 1938, to hold an account of mandate assembly, the prefect of la Seine reminded him 'that he must not [...] put up any decoration or symbol' in the school building.[110] Schools had to remain neutral places, and it was exceptional to find ornamentation, as was the case in a communist meeting of February 1937 in the hall of a girl's school in the 19th *arrondissement*:

> At the bottom of the school hall there is a huge red flag with the national colours at the upper left corner and communist symbols at the centre. Below are photos of Karl Marx, Lenin, Stalin, Duclos, Thorez and Cachin all lined up. Around the room are hung banners with the following inscriptions: 'All by the *Front populaire* — All for the *Front populaire*', 'For a free, strong and happy France, vote communist', 'For a clean municipal council, vote communist'.[111]

If schools are subject to restrictions, the other places where political rallies are held are characterised by an increasing use of decorations. The organisers see to it that the decor in the place where a rally is held help make it an occasion to stage a show of unity and jubilation. This effort is directed at those who write or read the press accounts, but certainly also towards participants themselves. Nicolas Mariot

---

105. AN/F7/13103/Notes générales sur l'activité du PCF. Seine, 1925–1926: Rapport, 15 octobre 1926, meeting à 'La Bellevilloise', rue Boyer.
106. APP/Ba/1956/SFIO, 1937–1938: Rapport, 29 juillet 1938.
107. Ory, *La belle illusion*, pp. 115–116.
108. See, for example, APP/Ba/1956/SFIO, 1937–1938: Rapport, 11 novembre 1938.
109. AN/F7/12966/Notes journalières de la préfecture de Police sur les réunions and manifestations, 8–19 février 1937 et 26–29 juin 1938: Rapport, 21 juillet 1937, meeting SFIO salle des fêtes, Vincennes; AN/F7/13080/Activité du parti socialiste. Seine (1926, 1928–1932). Notes, rapports, extraits de presse: Rapport, 25 mars 1928, meeting salle des conférences, Pantin.
110. ADP/Perotin/10441/57/1/33/Cabinet du préfet. Mise à disposition des locaux scolaires pour les comptes rendus de mandat des députés, 1938–1939: Lettre du préfet de la Seine au député M. Piguinier, 7 octobre 1938.
111. AN/F7/12966/Notes journalières de la préfecture de Police sur les réunions et les manifestations, 8–19 février 1937 et 26–29 juin 1938: Rapport 26 février 1937.

has studied the role of transformations in the sensory environment of individuals who participate in a ceremony, the way in which the decorations particularly allow to 'create the exceptional by dazzling the senses' and 'to bring the observer along the delicate paths of public support for the official subject of the event, slipping imperceptibly from the brightness of decor to the emotion of hearts'.[112]

Banners were regularly used with partisan slogans, as in a communist rally held in the mid-1920s in the Jean Jaurès meeting hall in Paris, where two banners overhung the stage where the speakers sat: 'Workers of the World, Unite' and 'Workers, Emancipate Yourselves'.[113] Banners can also be placed vertically on each side of the platform. At a rally to commemorate the tenth anniversary of the Russian Revolution the platform was framed by two banners: '1917' and '1927'.[114] They helped to highlight the importance of the platform as a place. Flags are another key element of decor which often enframes the platform. At an SFIO rally in 1937 in the 13th *arrondissement*, 'large red flags are placed on each side [of the platform]', whereas 'on the left […] hangs the flag of the 13th section', which organised the meeting.[115] Draperies are also used, particularly for covering the platform. In 1937, during a socialist rally at the Jean Jaurès gymnasium, the platform was 'hung with red'.[116] They can also take in the rest of the room: the police observer of a SFIO banquet in 1929 described 'the vast Jean Jaurès riding school arena, all hung with red drapery'.[117] Decorative pannels are also made, generally hung behind the platform.[118]

Starting in 1935–1936, we witness an evolution in decorations and in the use of symbolism. The descriptions of communist rallies in police reports reveal that the colour red starts to be accompanied with the national colours (blue, white, red). At the meeting of 10 February 1937, in Saint-Denis, 'flags in the national colours [are] framed by red flags'.[119] The descriptions of this union of the national colours and red abound in the press. On 7 December 1938 at the Maison de la Mutualité

---

112. Nicolas Mariot, *Conquérir unanimement les cœurs. Usages politiques et scientifiques des rites: le cas du voyage présidentiel en province, 1888–1998*, PhD dissertation, Paris, EHESS, 1999, p. 558; see also Mariot, '"Nos fleurs et nos cœurs". La visite présidentielle comme évènement institué', *Terrain*, 2002, vol. 38, pp. 79–96.

113. Roger-Violet/Politique française 1919–1939 EV PCF Défilés-Manifestations-Meetings/RV-474052: Picture, Meeting PCF salle Jean Jaurès, 1926–1927.

114. Roger-Violet/Politique française 1919–1939/RV-23378: Picture, 10e anniversaire de la révolution russe à Paris, 1927.

115. AN/F7/12966/Notes journalières de la préfecture de Police sur les réunions et les manifestations, 8–19 février 1937 et 26–29 juin 1938: Rapport, 18 février 1937, meeting SFIO, 8 rue Fagon.

116. AN/F7/12966/Rapport, 13 février 1937.

117. AN/F7/13080/Activité du parti socialiste. Seine (1926, 1928–1932). Notes, rapports, extraits de presse: Rapport, 1er juillet 1929.

118. Magnum/CAR37028 W00X4/X01 C Europe/France: Picture, Meeting de soutien aux républicains espagnols.

119. AN/F7/12966/Notes journalières de la préfecture de Police sur les réunions et les manifestations, 8–19 février 1937 et 26–29 juin 1938: Rapport, 11 février 1937, meeting PCF, 73 rue de la république, Saint-Denis.

there is 'an immense scarlet canopy hang[ing] in the vault which joins the back of the scene, also draped red with tricolour stripes'.[120] Miguel Rodriguez notes with reference to the May days: 'In 1936 there is a turning point when these signs, marks of opposition, [the red flag, wearing a dog rose, or singing *L'Internationale*], start to be accompanied by emblems representing the nation', and recalls 'the strategy of reconquest of national symbols that the party had begun the year before'.[121] The decorations of socialist rallies remain largely red, with flags, hangings and banners. The description of the Vélodrome d'Hiver during a rally in *Le Populaire* of 2 December 1938 is typical of the way in which ornamentation of halls is highlighted and interpreted in journalistic accounts:

> The decor itself [...] accentuated this character of popular revolt. Nothing but red, falling in elegant folds from the platform, surmounted by the three arrows, the party emblem. And, in the smoky atmosphere, snatched from the darkness capped by the beams of the spotlights, a series of immense red banners carrying the same emblem swayed slowly down the entire length of the nave.[122]

Other colours can be associated with this dominant red. For example, on 22 July 1938 at a socialist rally organised to protest against the attack on republican Spain, a police report states that 'the bandstand is decked out in Spanish colours'.[123] Communist meetings also frequently mix the Spanish colours with red and the national tricolour. At a rally organised in the Vélodrome d'Hiver to 'demand the opening of the frontier and free trade with republican Spain', the platform is described as 'soberly draped in red', and 'surmounted by a large canopy made up of the national French colours and the flag of Republican Spain, intertwined'.[124] The evolution in the decor of socialist rallies can be seen in its emblems more than anything else, with an increasing use of the three arrows.

> Originating in Germany, the 'three arrows' appeared for the first time in 1932 [...]. But it was really in 1934 that they imposed themselves after the arrival of Sergei Chakhotin, their probable creator, in France. [...] First used by the *Jeunesses [socialistes]*, they unfolded and are taken up by the entire party. [...] A veritable weapon against fascist propaganda, they become the rallying emblem of the *Front populaire*.[125]

---

120. *L'Humanité*, 8 December 1938.
121. Miguel Rodriguez, 'Le premier mai 1936 entre deux tours et deux époques', *Vingtième Siècle*, 1990, vol. 27, p. 58.
122. *Le Populaire*, 2 December 1938.
123. APP/Ba/1956/SFIO, 1937–1938: Rapport, 23 juillet 1938.
124. *L'Humanité*, 8 April 1938.
125. Fabrice D'Almeida, 'La SFIO, la propagande, les affiches (1945–1969)', *Cahiers et Revue de l'OURS*, 1993, vol. 211, p. 24.

The police descriptions of the decoration of meeting rooms confirm that the three arrows begin to appear in the mid-1930s. As of 1936–1937 they are seen in almost all rallies: on 20 February 1937, 'a crown with three arrows' hung above the platform;[126] on 2 December 1938, 'the Vélodrome d'Hiver was decorated with red banners with three arrows. The platform is decorated with a large red drapery with three arrows in the centre'.[127] These became routine elements of the apparatus of socialist rallies, in the same way as the hammer and sickle at communist rallies. The three arrows are also highlighted in the partisan press — in the articles and photographs printed alongside them.

Slogans also became an integral part of the 'decoration' in meeting rooms with inscriptions on flags, banners or placards. Police accounts mention these, but journalists go further, highlighting them as a summing-up of the ideas shared by participants. There are two types of slogans: general party slogans which are also used on other occasions; and slogans emphasising the purpose of a rally or series of meetings, and whose intention is more the defence of a particular cause. Slogans, such as 'Workers of the World, Unite', probably play on what has already been heard in the past, and are supposed to function as reminders, as echoes raised among participants. Other slogans may have a more external objective in their expression of protest, to explain why so many people are assembled under these banners: 'With the PC against the extension of military service, the two years and the war', declared a poster in 1935 in a meeting against the two-year law.[128]

On 26 April 1938, at Moulin de la Galette a police observer notes that 'a huge portrait of Jaurès' decorated the room of a SFIO meeting.[129] Portraits of leaders in the rooms honour the person represented or give importance to the politicians on the platform by their identification with prestigious ancestors or more important leaders. To allow this association, the portraits of people that one wants to link with the speaker are placed directly behind him, so that a glance includes both. The party presentations of assemblies again support this association by putting meetings not only into words in the press, but also into images in photographs or films. This worked well in the meeting recreated in Jean Renoir's 1936 film *La vie est à nous* — the penultimate sequence is a fictional meeting but the speakers are the real PCF leaders and the public are actors among other protagonists seen in earlier scenes.[130] Speakers on the platform stand before the portraits of Marx,

---

126. AN/F7/12966/Notes journalières de la préfecture de Police sur les réunions et les manifestations, 8–19 février 1937, 26–29 juin 1938: Rapport, 21 février 1937.

127. APP/Ba/1956/SFIO, 1937–1938: Rapport, 3 décembre 1938.

128. AN/F7/13320/Réunions et manifestations diverses, 1934–1935: Rapport, 15 avril 1935, meeting stade Lénine, Ivry. In April 1923, eighteen months' military service was adopted. In 1928 this was reduced to one year. In March 1935, the law extended it again to two years exceptionally, until 1939.

129. APP/Ba/1956/SFIO, 1937–1938: Rapport, 27 avril 1938.

130. Vidéothèque de Paris (Forum des Images), *La Vie est à nous* (producer, Jean Renoir; scriptwriter, J. Renoir, J.-P. Le Chanois, P. Vaillant-Couturier, A. Zwoboda; production, PCF, 1936). 'This film was produced by the French Communist Party for screening at rallies before the elections

Engels, Lenin, Stalin. The most striking sequence is Cachin's speech, placed in front of a portrait of Marx, with Lenin to the left, and Stalin to the right, and filmed in a circular movement that allows the appearance of the three men successively. The portraits may also pay homage to a party member. On 4 February 1938 at a communist meeting in the festivity hall of Boulogne-Billancourt, at the bottom of the scene, behind the rostrum was a portrait of Alfred Costes, secretary of the Paris metalworkers union; 'loved by the workers of the city of which he is [...] the representative in Parliament', whose 50th anniversary was celebrated later in the evening.[131] Costes was one of the speakers at the meeting.

Decoration is often concentrated around the platform, marking it off from the rest of the room. At electoral rallies in Brazil in 1988 and 1990, Moacir Palmeira and Beatriz Heredia observe:

> The platform — on high — sets a clear boundary between the spaces taken by the different participants in the event. [...] It marks the separation between a closed space (above) and an open space (below). Specific decor, bright lighting and disposal of microphones draw attention to those who must be seen.[132]

In socialist and communist rallies of the interwar period, the boundary between the platform and the rest of the room is marked particularly by the wealth of decoration that adorns the former, whilst the second is more austere. As highlighted in the partisan press, the platform sometimes stands out from the rest of the room on account of its colour: 'The platform, [...] forms a pocket of red against the sombre background of the room' writes a journalist describing the Vélodrome d'Hiver before the start of a communist rally.[133]

Yet staging political rallies goes further than this symbolic marking out of space; there is also a range of devices to theatricalise speakers, and more specifically the speaker-stars of the meeting. A rally is not only the place where ideas are defended, it is also where the leaders that incarnate them are celebrated. On this point there is a clear change in relation to rallies of the end of the nineteenth century where the acclamations directed towards a political personage were generally rejected, or had at the very least, to be justified. In the 1930s above all, the arrival and departure of the key speakers at a rally are carefully orchestrated. In the case of big rallies reported in the party press, speakers arrive from the front of the stage, not from the back. Sometimes their entry is postponed in relation to the arrival of the other people on the platform. At a communist rally at the Maison de la Mutualité on 18 January 1938, in the midst of the first speech 'Maurice Thorez took his seat in the *bureau*'. The next day *L'Humanité* insisted that he was 'greeted by a veritable ovation, a powerful *L'Internationale* and cries of "Thorez to power!" repeated a

---

that marked the advent of the *Front populaire*', http://www.forumdesimages.net/cgibin/rdoc/find?CritA=LIME (accessed 6 June 2006).

131. *L'Humanité*, 5 February 1938.
132. Moacir Palmeira and Beatriz Herédia, 'Le temps de la politique', *Études rurales*, 1993, vols. 131–132, p. 76.
133. *L'Humanité*, 17 January 1938.

hundred times over',[134] and it was only after this had calmed down that the first speaker was able to end his speech. The entry of these speakers is a key moment of the staging of the meeting, often made in the midst of applause from the room and to the sound of a partisan air. Similarly, the departure of a speaker before the end of the event is another opportunity for applause and anthem. However, if this deferred entry and anticipated departure are partially the result of a desire to stage specific moments of the rally, they are also sometimes explained by the fact that orators often give speeches at several different rallies in the same evening. The order of speakers is not neutral either: key orators generally address the public after several speeches, and often at the end of the meeting. It is good practice to make the public wait for the star speaker so that the acclamations for their arrival become more intense. Were this not the case the audience might not wait for the speakers that arrived later and the meeting room might be left empty.

The staging of these speakers also means shouting, singing and gestures that envelop their arrival on the platform and punctuate their speech. The big names stand out due to the ovations they receive from the moment they stand up to when they take the microphone. This welcome, although we cannot say that it does not testify at all to a real enthusiasm on the part of participants, does however reveal a degree of staging. According to the author of the police report on the rally organised by the *Fédération socialiste de la Seine* on 12 February 1937 at the Jean Jaurès gymnasium, each important speaker was greeted with a different song, leaving little room for spontaneity. Henri Salengro, later deputy of le Nord, is welcomed onto the platform to the sound of *L'Internationale*, 'sung by the audience accompanied by the Harmonie de la Fédération'. Then Blancho, deputy for the Loire-Inférieure and Under-Secretary of State for the *Front populaire,* is greeted by the *Jeune Garde*, whereas Paulin, deputy for Puy-de-Dôme and vice-president of the Chamber, arrives on the platform to the notes of the *Red Flag*.[135]

In the interwar period political rallies are a means of collective action used to demonstrate force and party unity, to persuade participants and to put pressure on public opinion. The success of a rally also relies on what takes place there, the way it takes place, and how this is then presented in texts and images. The demonstration has a double public: the immediate public of those present in the room, and the indirect public, which can be reached through the accounts of the demonstration once this has taken place, particularly in the press. This tableau of the partisan use of freedom of assembly in the 1920s and 1930s shows the extent to which the big cities and their conglomerations — particularly Paris and its suburbs — have shifted away from the notion of assemblies as a sphere where arguments are exchanged.

---

134. *L'Humanité*, 19 January 1938.

135. AN/F7/12966/Notes journalières de la préfecture de Police sur les réunions et les manifestations, 8–19 février 1937, 26–29 juin 1938: Rapport, 13 février 1937.

Chapter Seven

The Political Assembly in Danger

In an article on socialist propaganda Gilles Candar asserts that the political assembly underwent a period of 'crisis' in the interwar period.[1] This may come as a surprise after the portrait I have painted of the impressive gatherings of the 1920s and 1930s. But what Candar means by 'crisis' is that the 'assembly [had become] a question of relations of physical force' where the 'beautiful tumult' of prewar assemblies gave way to clashes, at times very violent, between parties. For Candar, this does not necessarily toll the bell for the 'impending end' of the assembly. Rather 'crisis' means that this form of participation was undergoing a period of transition, and during this period we witness a stepping-up of violence. We are also justified in speaking of a crisis of the political assembly in the interwar period in the sense of a relative decline; that is, as an indirect consequence of its transformation into a means to exert pressure and to demonstrate the strength and cohesion of parties.

The meeting has weak links with the outside world. While as a place of debate it does not suffer so much from this isolation, the situation is different when it becomes an element in the repertoire of collective action. If the aim of a gathering is not to compare ideas, but is instead to promote the visibility of its massive and united character, why not show its force more directly on the street? It is not so much a question of abandoning meetings for the benefit of processions, which are not often tolerated, as of a hybridisation of the two forms of grouping, in particular with the 'routinisation' of marches on the public highway of participants going to or leaving meetings. It is, above all, a use of street demonstrations as a way to counter a rally organised by an opponent party. Its indirect consequence is that freedom of assembly was seriously undermined in the 1930s. In the words of Claude-Albert Colliard in 1950, 'freedom of assembly underwent a very serious crisis after 1935'.[2] Colliard was referring to the legal and regulatory attacks which have impacted on it since this date, and to the routinisation of an administrative policy no longer respecting the provisions of the 1881 law. The crisis of freedom of assembly arose from the generalised use of the rally as a way to demonstrate party strength.

---

1. Gilles Candar, 'Propagande: à propos de Jean Longuet, Marcel Cachin, Lucien Roland et quelques autres...', *Cahier et revue de l'OURS*, 1993, vol. 211, p. 5.
2. Claude-Albert Colliard, *Précis de droit public. Les libertés publiques*, Paris, Dalloz, 1950, p. 371.

Demonstrating in a meeting room or on the street?

Assemblies in a room, or more generally in a place away from the public street, were protected under the 1881 law. From a legal perspective the attitude of the public authorities to street demonstrations falls into two distinct periods: before and after 1935. In 1938 Renaud Berthon describes the pre-1935 regimen as follows:

> It was not a crime to organise a procession or a demonstration without consulting the authorities. [...] Nevertheless, if the authorities were aware of a planned demonstration, they could ban it [...]. Once banned, the procession or demonstration would then be considered an illegal mob and thus could be disbanded with the use of force.[3]

On 23 October 1935 a decree amended the situation by subjecting demonstrations to the regimen of prior declaration — a minimum of three days before three organisers were to declare their names and addresses, and the day, time and route of the demonstration — and in this way giving authorities the right to ban any demonstration likely to disturb public order. Before and after 1935, the street was still a potential locus of expression for political opinions, contrary to the project of circumscription of public space planned under the early Republic. It is thus a question of a fluctuating tolerance depending on the period.[4]

Competition and confusion in the repertoire of collective action

In 1924, Camille Chautemps, the radical-socialist Minister of the Interior, sent a memorandum to prefects drawing their attention to 'the methodical organisation by communist and revolutionary groups of rallies held on the public thoroughfare outside workshops and factories, generally at a time when workers leave [the premises]', and reminding them:

> The legislation which recognises the right to free assembly for all citizens and provides for the largest application of this freedom of assembly, does not, however, allow to do it in public places or streets which must be reserved for traffic. Article 6 of the law of 30 June 1881 stipulates that 'meetings cannot be held on the public highway'. This is a basic rule for maintaining order and general calm.[5]

---

3. Renaud Berthon, *Le régime des cortèges et des manifestations en France*, Paris, Sirey, 1938, p. 88.
4. Danielle Tartakowsky, *Les manifestations de rue en France. 1918–1968*, Paris, Publications de la Sorbonne, 1997, pp. 23–442.
5. AD Haute-Savoie/4M/117/Mesures prises lors de réunions, meetings et manifestations publiques: Circulaire du Ministre de l'Intérieur aux Préfets, 25 septembre 1924.

In 1937 the legal expert Michel Baffrey welcomed this memorandum, declaring that it was 'in complete agreement with the spirit of the legislator'.[6] In the interwar period, this legal measure was sometimes applied in such a way that the ban also applied to meetings planned in places considered not sufficiently set apart from the public street. In 1936, the mayor of Fontenay-sous-Bois, who only had two meeting rooms, planned to authorise meetings in a covered market in his municipality for an electoral campaign. However the prefect refused authorisation on the grounds that 'the market, even if covered, is not completely closed, but simply surrounded by railings', and that 'in these conditions, any public assembly organised there would end up with the audience partly on the public highway'. He deduced that 'this practice would be likely to cause inconvenience for the maintenance of law and order on the street'.[7] Despite this possible restrictive interpretation in the application of the law, meetings are sometimes held in parks or public squares, that is to say, places which are neither covered nor strictly closed, but distinct from the street.[8] Indeed, we have seen that by stipulating only that 'assemblies cannot be held on the public thoroughfare', the 1881 law discards the imperial requirement that assemblies be held in 'closed and covered' locations. Nevertheless, the definition of what constitutes the public thoroughfare is subject to different interpretations. Does it only mean the street or also public squares? What about open spaces such as parks and gardens? The organisers of meetings tried to profit from this imprecision by adopting the narrowest notion possible, whereas they were sometimes faced with broader definitions. In July 1935 in Isère, a communist meeting was organised in the hall above the city's covered market by Alessandri, the 'great PC figure in Bourgoin'.[9] When leaving the room towards midnight, Alessandri and 300 participants marched through the market singing *L'Internationale*. They were stopped by a police captain who asserted that it was forbidden to sing on the public thoroughfare. The author of the report notes that Alessandri '[tried] to quibble and to play with words saying that the market was not a "public thoroughfare"'. Yet the 'captain's determination' and an 'attempt by the police to encircle [...] them' got the better of Alessandri's legal arguments and the rally was broken up.[10] Generally speaking, whatever the possible interpretations of the law, a meeting does not spread out into the public highway directly, unlike a demonstration.

---

6. Michel Baffrey, *Le droit de réunion en Angleterre et en France*, Paris, Les Presses Modernes, 1937, pp. 148–149.

7. ADP/Perotin/10441/64/2/75/Concession de locaux municipaux et scolaires dans les communes du département: Lettre du préfet de police au préfet de la Seine, 29 janvier 1936.

8. For example, in July 1938 the SFIO organised a meeting in place Trousseau in Paris. APP/Ba/1956/SFIO, 1937–1938: Rapport, 23 juillet 1938.

9. AD Isère/77M/2/Dossier sur la réunion communiste à Bourgoin, 7 juillet 1935: Lettre du sous-préfet de La-Tour-du-Pin au préfet de l'Isère (n.d., fin juin 1935).

10. AD Isère/77M/2/Dossier sur la réunion communiste à Bourgoin, 7 juillet 1935: Lettre du sous-préfet de La-Tour-du-Pin au préfet de l'Isère, 7 juillet 1935.

One way to reduce the isolated nature of rallies is to enlarge their acoustic space by using loudspeakers which relay speeches outside the closed space of the assembly. An article describes how those unable to enter the hall of a meeting at the Maison du Peuple in Angoulême, stood 'in front of one of the many loudspeakers so as not to miss anything in the speeches that were to be made'.[11] At an assembly in May 1935 in Saint-Denis, the PCF 'proposed [...] installing loudspeakers outside the room so that those who could not find a place inside could still listen to the speeches'.[12] However this type of practice was rare and only feasible when the organising party had the support of the municipality. Furthermore, I found no such examples in Paris. Thus, the boundary between the public thoroughfare and the rally is often too rigid for the latter to be a direct show of force. On the other hand, organisers have indirect ways of making it a demonstration. They can use the partisan press, in particular to publish a decision, or an agenda, adopted during a rally. This is very important for the PCF. In 1924 a memorandum accompanied by a resolution model specifies that the latter 'must be proposed in all factories assemblies and other meetings', then 'once voted, it should be communicated to *L'Humanité*'.[13] The resolutions adopted in several meetings are sometimes assembled to give the impression of a vast movement of revendication. On 18 January 1938 the front page of *L'Humanité* announced: 'from all over France, comes an avalanche of resolutions to express the passionate will of the masses'.[14]

The wish to use of modes of participation with a demonstrative dimension *vis-à-vis* the outside world — that we find mainly at the extremes of the political spectrum[15] — was still difficult to achieve in meetings which, in their immediate material sense, generally remained limited to a fixed space isolated from the public thoroughfare and that could only become a show of force *a posteriori* and on paper. In the case of the PCF, directives to federations and committees reveal a clear hierarchy of modes of collective action to which the party can resort. By the mid-1920s there was a certain determination to supplement meetings by street demonstrations. A 1924 memorandum calls on the federations to 'organise by [their] own means, in all the centres, public meetings, where possible, supported by demonstrations'.[16] In February 1926, an edition of the *Bulletin d'information du Parti communiste* dedicated to the campaign for amnesty stated that 'the regions

---

11. *La vie socialiste*, 2 September 1933.
12. AN/F7/13320/Réunions et manifestations diverses, 1934–1935: Rapport, 4 mai 1935.
13. AN/F7/13092/Circulaires PCF. 1924: Circulaire no. 46, *bureau* politique et *bureau* d'organisation, 11 septembre 1924. The term 'factory meeting' refers to assemblies of activists in the same unit of industrial production.
14. *L'Humanité*, 18 January 1938.
15. In the interwar period, it was very strong not only for the PCF but also for groups on the extreme right. On this question, see the accounts of PSF rallies in: Michel Winock, 'Retour sur le fascisme français. La Rocque et les Croix-de-Feu', *Vingtième Siècle*, 2006, vol. 90, pp. 3–27.
16. AN/F7/13092/Circulaires PCF, 1924: Circulaire no. 46, *bureau* politique et *bureau* d'organisation, 11 septembre 1924.

must organise public assemblies and street demonstrations'. The year before, the central section of Agitprop explained that 'a meeting is not the conclusion of [their] organised unrest, but serves to develop it'; 'every time this is possible we must organise a public demonstration'.[17] The memoranda speak of transforming meetings into street demonstrations. In July 1924, the memorandum to the federal committees on the 'international week against the imperialist war and the social betrayal' stated:

> Over 150 meetings will take place. In a good number of cities there will be large audiences. We must profit, wherever possible, to transform our meetings into street events. Processions will be organised with men, women and children. We will bring placards with our slogans.[18]

It was in the late 1920s that a greater value was explicitly attributed to demonstrations as opposed to indoor meetings. In March 1929, in the *Bulletin d'information du Parti communiste*, the central section of Agitprop gave directives for the campaign for the tenth anniversary of the International. It states that 'the organisation of meetings and workers' assemblies does not exclude the use of the highest forms of struggle during our campaign'[19]: it is a matter of street protest, and of creating a hierarchy between the two forms of action.

The year before, the Communist International made the conquest of the streets a 'strategic priority'.[20] In a first phase during the early 1920s street demonstrations were often only a supplement of meetings, and the stimulus came above all from the audience. According to Danielle Tartakowsky, although the demonstration becomes a privileged instrument of communist expression in 1923 and 1924 — a practice breaking with that of the socialists[21] — it generally remains a simple supplement to the meeting. From the end of 1931:

> The Communist Party and satellite organisations [...] agitate in the Paris Region less frequently than in the past, no longer choosing the street and preferring private or secluded spaces, but always in the open air, [...] to preserve the character of 'demonstration' [which is] increasingly difficult to keep in a closed room.[22]

However with the years 1934–1936 and the *Front populaire* the street demonstration acquires a central position: '[It] became a major expression of the culture of the *Front populaire* in gestation'.[23] The fact that a march on the public highway makes it easier to rally more people than an assembly in a room also

---

17. 'L'utilisation du meeting', *Bulletin d'information du Parti communiste*, no. 1, 25 juin 1925.
18. AN/F7/13092/Circulaires PCF, 1924: Circulaire no. 41 aux comités fédéraux, 15 juillet 1924.
19. AN/F7/13095/Circulaires PCF, 1929.
20. Tartakowsky, *Les manifestations de rue en France*, p. 193.
21. Tartakowsky, *Les manifestations de rue en France*, p. 115.
22. Tartakowsky, *Les manifestations de rue en France*, pp. 239–240.
23. Tartakowsky, *Les manifestations de rue en France*, p. 389.

explains why it was preferred. After having pointed out the 'importance of mass demonstrations as a vital part of the Popular Front experience', Julian Jackson stressed that even large meeting rooms were often too small to accommodate the crowds that came, causing the organisers of rallies to turn to sports arenas, such as the Vélodrome d'Hiver or the Buffalo stadium. Jackson later wrote that 'for the biggest Popular Front demonstrations stadia were too small'. As a result, 'it was in the street that the Popular Front showed its full strength'.[24]

Replacing the meeting within the repertoire of collective action does not only lead us to ask why a party decides to organise an assembly rather than another type of action, and emphasise that there is a hierarchy of collective forms of political expression. Indeed, the choice is not simply between different modes of action with clearly defined forms. The interwar period is marked by an increasing overlap between the two means of action, and by a blur of boundaries between meeting and street demonstration. The sections of a party sometimes give participants a *rendez-vous* to go to a meeting in a group. On 30 July 1922 the various sections of the PCF in Paris and its suburbs that organised a meeting at the Butte du Chapeau-Rouge in Pré-Saint-Gervais published calls in *L'Humanité* for participants to arrive in groups: 'Everyone on the station platform at 13h30. To go to Pré-Saint-Gervais', instructs the section of Bois-Colombes; 'Everybody to the meeting of the Pré-Saint-Gervais. *Rendez-vous* 14h30 at the town hall square', announced the Drancy section. The route taken by participants then has the appearance of a procession on the public highway, particularly if people are carrying flags. The intention of highlighting these marches is not to pretend that before the 1920s people always went to meetings separately, but to stress the routinisation of the practice, which is a sign of a growing desire to make meetings more visible.

The addition of a street march to a meeting is not so easily feasible everywhere. We see the emergence of local traditions in some regions where there is a greater lenience on the part of administrative and police authorities. Although it appears to be relatively rare in Paris, it seems to be normal to go to a meeting in procession in the surroundings of Lyon, for example. At a communist assembly at Oullins in 1921, the prefect of the Rhône assured the Minister of the Interior that he had 'advised the organisers that [he would not tolerate] any disorder on the street' and had 'taken the measures necessary to repress, if need be, any attempts of this sort'.[25] Despite this the public decided to go to the meeting in procession.[26] This practice is repeated in the region during this period, and not only for communist assemblies. It has also been the case for assemblies organised to commemorate

---

24. Julian Jackson, *The Popular Front in France Defending Democracy, 1924–1938*, Cambridge, Cambridge University Press, 1988, pp. 307–308.
25. AD Rhône/4M/268/Réunions électorales, 1913–1926: Rapport du préfet au Ministre de l'Intérieur, 28 juillet 1921.
26. AD Rhône/4M/268/Réunions électorales, 1913–1926: Rapport du commissaire spécial à la préfecture, 28 juillet 1921; Rapport du commissaire de police d'Oullins à la préfecture, 31 juillet 1921.

the death of Jaurès. On 30 July 1922, participants to the socialist meeting at the Fantasio theatre in Villeurbanne went in a procession 'at its head was the brass band of the 6th *arrondissement*, with its tricolour flag, followed by the red flags of the Party'.[27] On 3 August 1924, the participants at a rally organised by the PCF, SFIO and ARAC in the festivity hall of Villefranche formed a procession 'in which there were three red flags with trade union slogans'; the sub-prefect who edited the report did not appear to be unduly surprised by this display.[28] One sign of the routinisation in the region of these marches on their way to a rally is that in their reports police observers were now careful to mention, if such is the case, that 'no demonstration is planned'.[29] Yet this flexibility of administrative and police authorities diminished in the 1930s, mainly due to growing political agitation, the result of the conflicts between the left and the extreme right. Above all, the police feared what might happen in the wake of rallies, when spirits were heated. The report of the security services of the police prefecture of the aforementioned meeting on 30 July 1922 at Pré-Saint-Gervais indicates:

> The incidents, if they occur, will take place when the meeting ends and when the demonstrators set off towards the metro stations in the vicinity. It is still possible that, according to precedents, groups form around the Butte du Chapeau Rouge and that they go towards the town hall of Pré-Saint-Gervais and then towards one of the gates of Paris, banners at their head, with the intention of continuing the demonstration in the capital.[30]

In the Paris area this type of procession appears to be more frequent than those that form when going to a rally. Here too, the practice already existed at the end of the nineteenth century, but it became particularly recurrent in the interwar period. In *L'Illustration* of 4 February 1933, a photograph represented 'policemen on foot and horseback disbanding taxpayers at the end of their rally' (Figure 7.1).[31] In January an assembly was organised at the Magic City hall in response to a call from the national federation of taxpayers: 'A limited delegation had been authorised to go to the Chamber or the Élysée, but the police vigorously prevented the bulk of "the troops" from following', comments the author of the article. We can see in the photograph that participants are carrying placards for the parade. In fact, processions do not generally form spontaneously at the end of a rally, which is what seems to be feared in the extract of the report on the rally of 30 July 1922 at Pré-Saint-Gervais. The police are generally warned beforehand. At a communist meeting in 1926, originally planned for the town hall square in Ivry,

---

27. AD Rhône/4M/268/Réunions électorales, 1913–1926: Rapport, 1er août 1922.
28. AD Rhône/4M/268/Réunions électorales, 1913–1926: Rapport, 5 août 1924.
29. AD Rhône/4M/268/Réunions électorales, 1913–1926: Rapport, 31 juillet 1825, meeting du PCF et de l'union des syndicats, salle Oger, Lyon.
30. APP/Ba/1644/Meetings communistes place de la Réunion et au Pré-Saint-Gervais: Rapport, 28 juillet 1922, préfecture de Police, service des Renseignements Généraux.
31. *L'Illustration*, 4 February 1933.

252 | From Deliberation to Demonstration

Figure 7.1: 'The guard on foot and on horseback dispersing taxpayers at the end of their meeting', L'Illustration, 4 February 1933

but then held in a closed room due to bad weather, a communication was drafted three days before, specifying that 'on leaving the meeting, the audience will form a procession [...] and march'.³²

Counter-demonstrations

The routinisation of direct combat between opposing party activists by countering political rallies with street demonstrations, allows distinction between acts of violence in and around assemblies during the interwar period from those typical of assemblies at the end of the nineteenth century. When a group announces a rally its opponents sometimes organise a street demonstration at the same time in a nearby location. These reciprocal shows of force, a sort of 'arm wrestling', which end up in the street, are less likely to occur when the confrontation of political opponents takes place within the assembly itself. However, obstruction and violence are still typical of meeting rooms in the interwar period. A police report describes the public of an electoral assembly organised by the *Parti radical* in October 1922 in a school hall in rue d'Alésia with 1,200 people where communists were in 'the great

---

32. AN/F7/13103/Notes générales sur l'activité du PCF. Seine, 1925–1926: Rapport, 18 octobre 1926.

majority', the assembly was efficiently disturbed by their noise.³³ An obstruction is a success when party activists who lead it are sufficiently numerous in relation to those supporting the organising party. However it is useless in a rally gathering tens of thousands of people where the loud-speaker system would automatically drown out the noise of obstructionists. To ensure that its activists turned out in force at the meetings of its adversaries, the PCF — champion of obstruction in the interwar period, particularly of socialist assemblies³⁴ — often called on them to attend *en masse*. A police report of December 1930 states that 'the 10th section of the PC invited its followers to make a big turnout [for the SFIO rally on 11 December] "to impose there a communist contradiction"'.³⁵ Obstruction often results from unfruitful attempts to make communist speakers be heard — as well as those of the organising party. It frequently begins with the refusal of the party organiser to cede his rights on the meeting and can thus be triggered by the rejection of a request to put this to the vote of the *bureau*. At a socialist meeting at the Casino of Ivry in January 1932: 'where the communists, who were as numerous in the room as the socialists, demanded that the *bureau* be put to the vote', they are faced with the fact that the chairman had already 'been chosen by the local socialist section', a declaration which triggered 'a racket and shouting from the communists'.³⁶ Refusing to cede their rights on the meeting, chairmen also frequently decline to change the agenda. A report on a socialist meeting organised in 1931 in Nanterre, relates that when Georges Barthélémy, then general councillor of la Seine and socialist mayor of the neighbouring municipality of Puteaux, delivered an account of his mandate:

> Some [communists] demand the speaker to deal with the question of unemployment. M. Barthélémy pointed out therefore that the assembly had been organised by the Socialist Party, and it was not the job of the communists to alter the agenda. 'Those who are not content, he exclaims, can go and get some fresh air outside' [...]. He wanted to restart his speech later, but could not make himself heard.³⁷

How did the organising party react in the face of the obstruction led against it? In the frequent cases of SFIO rallies disturbed by the communists in the 1920s, there is stress put on the fact that the latter try specially to prevent socialists from holding public assemblies. On 13 November 1926, an article in *Le Progrès* on a rally in Lyon was described as 'exasperated' by communist obstruction. Paul Faure, gave up any attempt to develop his line of thought, and exclaimed:

---

33. AN/F7/12951/Notes 'Jean', 1918–1922: Rapport, 22 octobre 1922.
34. On the disturbance of socialist assemblies by communists in the 1920s and early 1930s in the Paris suburbs, see Aude Chamouard, *Le parti socialiste SFIO en campagne électorale: L'exemple de la banlieue rouge pendant l'entre-deux-guerres*, Master of Advanced Studies (MAS), Paris, IEP, 2004, pp. 111–115.
35. AN/F7/13080/Activité du parti socialiste. Seine (1926, 1928–1932). Notes, rapports, extraits de presse: Rapport, 12 décembre 1930, réunion SFIO salle du cinéma Palace.
36. AN/F7/13080/Rapport, 14 janvier 1932.
37. AN/F7/13080/Rapport, 23 novembre 1931.

Today we see in this very room where, you the disturbers, you want to stifle the voice of whoever does not think exactly according to your orders. Ah well! I declare flatly, you are not revolutionaries, you are the worst agents of reaction![38]

The criticism is also publicised by the diffusion of a protest resolution voted during the disturbed assemblies. In the case of the Lyon rally, the journalist affirms that socialist speakers managed to put to the vote and adopt the following motion: 'The 4,000 citizens gathered at the Alcazar in response to the call of the *Fédération socialiste du Rhône*, protest against systematic obstruction by a handful of disturbers.' The publication of press accounts of rallies, such as that in *Le Progrès*, was another way to complain about obstruction publicly. Sometimes posters were put up to this end. This was the case after the SFIO assembly of 12 June 1926, where Léon Blum came to give an account of his term in office, and was faced with communist obstruction. A police report recounts that 'in protest against these facts, the executive commission of the group of Charonne of the 20th section of the socialist party put up on the walls of the 20th *arrondissement*' 200 copies of a poster. The latter denounced 'communo-fascist methods' and recalled the risk of having to hold meetings behind closed doors:

> If [...] such events are repeated, we will be forced, to our great regret, to organise assemblies by special convocation [...] where the brigades of the party of demagogy will be mercilessly hunted down.[39]

As at the end of the nineteenth century vocal obstruction is sometimes accompanied by physical violence. The memoirs of those who took part in socialist rallies are full of descriptions of fights that they had with communists. Marcel Déat, who was then still an SFIO deputy, speaks of an 'epic battle', a 'savage fray' regarding a rally in 1929 at the Japy meeting hall.[40] The memoirs of Charles Pivert — a militant trade unionist and socialist, 'often Blum's bodyguard and part of all the internal security patrols of large demonstrations'[41] — abound with descriptions of this kind, leading their author to write: 'I cannot count the clashes with the communists'.[42] This type of conflict between two rival groups during a meeting is not necessarily very intense. Police reports often speak of 'fights' and 'rushes', without the officer supervising the assembly seeming to attach much gravity to the fact. The use of violence may also directly seek to prevent opponents' speeches by attacking a given speaker whilst on the platform.

---

38. AN/F7/13084/Activité du parti socialiste (1926–1932). Rhône: Article joint au rapport de police. *Le Progrès*, 13 novembre 1926.
39. AN/F7/13080/Activité du parti socialiste. Seine (1926, 1928–1932). Notes, rapports, extraits de presse: Série de rapports concernant la réunion, 12 juin 1926.
40. Marcel Déat, *Mémoires politiques*, Paris, Denoël, 1989, p. 220.
41. *Dictionnaire biographique du mouvement ouvrier français, 4, 1914–1940*, CD-Rom, Éditions de l'Atelier.
42. Charles Pivert, *Le parti socialiste et ses hommes. Souvenirs d'un militant*, Paris, France-éditions, 1950, pp. 43–44.

Albeit much rarer than the previous form, this is nevertheless lively conflict in the historical background of the 1930s, marked by the cleavage between extreme right groups and leftist parties. There are several cases of aggression or threats of aggression by extreme right groups at communist rallies where Jacques Sadoul is billed as a speaker. A police report warning of a rally on 9 March 1926 specifies that: 'due to the presence of Jacques Sadoul at this assembly, the organisers fear an interference from the *Camelots du Roi*',[43] an organisation close to *L'Action française* which took part in the disturbances of 6 February 1934 and which was dissolved along with the other leagues on the extreme right in January 1936. On 9 March, the *Camelots du Roi* managed to get into the room and to overrun the platform.[44] The announcement in *L'Humanité* of the assembly of 17 March, where Sadoul was still to speak, consequently does not specify the name of the speaker.[45] During a communist assembly of June 1926 in Paris aimed at 'group members of various revolutionary organisations from the Latin quarter, to consider a means of defence against fascism', it is significantly declared: 'Later [...] we will organise an assembly [...], where Sadoul will speak. Our combat groups will thus need to be well organised'.[46]

Internal security patrols were set up by the parties to avoid fights in public and to 'guarantee the protection of speakers'.[47] Activists are thus responsible for ejecting disturbers from the room. On 26 November 1930, during an SFIO assembly 'around twenty [communists], who were near the exit, were thrown out by the activists responsible for ensuring the peace of the assembly'.[48] Expulsion can thus prevent obstruction preemptively. In the early 1930s, the socialist federations set up internal security patrols to protect rallies against communist aggression, using the logic of self-defence which led to the creation of the TPPS (*Toujours Prêts Pour Servir*) of the *Fédération de la Seine* in summer 1934. These are the 'veritable shock troops of Parisian socialism', and their aims exceed the simple pacification of assemblies.[49] For its part, very early on the PCF had organised its own internal security patrols whose members recognised one another in rallies by wearing berets and carrying walking sticks. The film shot by the Albert Kahn film troupe of the rally organised on 7 August 1927 in Pré-Saint-Gervais in favour of Sacco and Vanzetti, shows them stopping the crowd from mounting the hillock

---

43. AN/F7/13103/Notes générales sur l'activité du PCF, Seine, 1925–1926: Note d'annonce, 8 mars 1926.
44. AN/F7/13103/Rapport, 13 mars 1926, réunion des groupes du service d'ordre du PCF, 120 rue de Lafayette.
45. AN/F7/13103/Rapport, 17 mars 1926.
46. AN/F7/13103/Rapport, 17 juin 1926, réunion PCF, rue Gracieuse.
47. AN/F7/13103/Note d'annonce de la réunion PCF du 9 mars 1926, salle des sociétés savantes.
48. AN/F7/13080/Activité du parti socialiste. Seine (1926, 1928–1932). Notes, rapports, extraits de presse: Rapport, 27 November 1930.
49. Éric Nadaud, 'Le renouvellement des pratiques militantes à la SFIO au début du Front Populaire (1934–1936)', *Le Mouvement Social*, 1990, vol. 153, pp. 22–23.

where the platform stood.[50] The question of the limit to pose to the militarisation of these groups is debated among both socialists and communists. A strong opposition of the secretariat of the SFIO on this terrain of self-defence manifests itself, as has been shown by Éric Nadaud in particular.[51] Albeit to a lesser extent than in the SFIO, there is a certain reticence in the PCF regarding an over-strong militarisation of groups responsible for guaranteeing order in rallies. The question of 'the presentation of groups in blue jackets' during an ARAC rally in May at the Huygens gymnasium was debated at an assembly of PCF surveillance groups in the Paris area in 1926. A member in the audience opened the discussion by criticising 'this totally military obligation'. A second member proposed just 'wearing a beret and walking stick as well as a distinctive badge'. A third confirmed that the 'colour of the jacket was a bad choice'.[52] The extreme right organised impressive internal security services. *L'Illustration* of 21 July 1934 (see Figure 7.2) published two pictures: one representing members of the *Camelots du Roi*: 'determined-looking, wearing berets, [who] guarantee order' in an assembly of *L'Action française*; and in the other, an assembly of the *Ligue republicaine nationale* in the Wagram room, where the stage is protected by a group of *Jeunesses patriotes* with 'a martial bearing' as is described in the accompanying paper.

In the interwar period meetings are still characterised by the sort of obstruction and violence that had been typical of assemblies at the end of the nineteenth century. This makes it difficult to identify in these events an expression of a 'brutalisation of political life' as the outcome of the 'importation of aggressive behaviour in the political field in the wake of the First World War'.[53] Moreover, it is not so much the progress of rallies which causes disorder, at times even serious disorder. On the contrary, the fact that they often take the form of massive gatherings and are equipped with loudspeakers, causing obstruction and generally any form of disturbance by opponent activists, is much more difficult than in the past and at times impossible, within the meeting room. What is new is the practice of responding to a planned rally by one party with the organisation of a rally or demonstration by another opponent party at the same time and in the same locality.

---

50. Espace Albert Kahn: *Paris vu par les opérateurs d'Albert Kahn. 1913–1928*, 1982: Manifestation en faveur de Sacco et Vanzetti, 7 août 1927.
51. Nadaud, 'Le renouvellement des pratiques militantes à la SFIO', pp. 26–30.
52. AN/F7/13103/Notes générales sur l'activité du PCF, Seine, 1925–1926: Procès-verbal de réunion, 5 juin 1926.
53. It is for instance the interpretation proposed by Aude Chamouard with reference to the work of George L. Mosse. See: Chamouard, *Le parti socialiste en campagne électorale*, p. 130; George L. Mosse, *Fallen Soldiers: Reshaping the Memory of the World Wars*, New York, Oxford University Press, 1990.

The Political Assembly in Danger | 257

Figure 7.2: Camelots du Roi guaranteeing order in an assembly of the Action française (top); Jeunesses Patriotes protecting the platform during an assembly of the Ligue républicaine nationale (bottom). L'Illustration, 21 July 1934

In 1937, the legal expert Menanteau writes:

> Assemblies being no longer places of discussion, but unilateral exhibitions, led to violent responses and we rapidly got to the point where all assemblies, even the most peaceful, have indirectly become a threat for public order due to the hostile demonstrations they attract. Examples are hundreds. [...] Simple private assemblies, or even [...] a simple spectacle, can cost lives, and have incalculable consequences.[54]

First of all, there are a great many rallies and counter-rallies that set extreme right groups against PCF activists. An urgent appeal for mobilisation generally precedes the counter-rallies. In Levallois on 11 June 1926, a propaganda assembly was organised by the *Faisceau* — France's first openly fascist league, set up in 1925 as a synthesis of nationalism and socialism, but which broke up three years later. Communist activists in the area decided to hold an assembly at the same time and in the same municipality. They put up posters which declare:

> Stand up, workers of Levallois! We will not let fascists enter our revolutionary city without responding tit for tat. Come to the rally on Friday 11 June at 20h30 in the *maison commune*, 28 rue Cavé. Agenda: the fight against fascism!

L'Humanité of 11 June published the following short paragraph: "'No, you are not communist" say the fascist posters. The workers will reply at the public assembly, 28 rue Cavé [...].' The agenda of counter-rally is generally centred on the need to fight their opponents. In this case problems occured when leaving rallies. The police report announcing a communist assembly on 20 October 1926 in a school hall at Levallois-Perret specifies that: 'at the same time, in the Levasseur room [...] at Levallois-Perret, *L'Action Française* is organising an assembly' and: 'it is said that there will be incidents on the way out and that an "event" has been set up by *L'Action Française*'.[55]

Yet the most serious clashes were cases where a demonstration on the public highway was organised to protest against a rally. The practice first developed in the 1920s. I have mentioned the memorandum that the Minister of the Interior, Chautemps, sent to prefects on 25 September 1924, calling for a ban on assemblies on the public highway. Two other memoranda on assemblies followed. The second, of 7 November, deals partly with the troubles occurring within meeting rooms. The Minister asked that freedom of assembly be protected by '[putting] an end to the scheming'. He recalled 'the recent incidents in many cities where agitators have systematically disturbed public assemblies and have thus seriously attacked a citizen's basic right'. In particular he requested prefects to 'facilitate

---

54. Maurice Menanteau, *Les nouveaux aspects de la liberté de réunion. Essai sur les caractères juridiques et politiques de la liberté de réunion en France*, Paris, Librairie technique et économique, 1937, p. 34.
55. AN/F7/13103/Notes générales sur l'activité du PCF, Seine, 1925–1926: Rapport, 19 octobre 1926.

the accomplishment of their mission to the *bureaux* which [...] are responsible for maintaining order in assemblies'. He also points to what takes place around the assembly in stressing the need to 'take, together with Messrs mayors, any provisions likely to prevent tumultuous incidents on the public thoroughfare on entering and when leaving these assemblies'. The third memorandum on 13 February 1925 was to put an end to clashes between participants in rallies and counter-demonstrations. Stressing that the '[tumultuous] incidents [on the public thoroughfare] are particularly dangerous when there are groupings announcing their intention to organise demonstrations against the authors or audience of some assemblies', the Minister invites the prefects to 'distance [...] the demonstrators of opposing parties and prevent all contact between them'. For this, he calls on the organisers of both assemblies and counter-demonstrations. The first must organise the departure of the audience 'in small groups which will be directed to routes indicated beforehand and who must disperse immediately' as a precaution. The second must choose a route far away from the location of the assembly for their procession, and must also have an internal security patrol 'to assure respect of the plan stipulated in agreement with public authority'. Finally, there is an appeal for the mobilisation of a sufficiently large police force, responsible if need be, for setting up 'roadblocks' to avoid a 'collision' between opposing groups.[56] These memoranda are often praised by legal experts for having protected freedom of assembly against the threat of counter-demonstrations. In 1950 Claude-Albert Colliard wrote that they 'limited themselves to defend freedom of assembly by advising, in the case of counter-demonstration, setting up police roadblocks to protect the assembly and to channel processions and demonstrations towards other remote places'; adding that 'for a decade, these three liberal memoranda were enough to guarantee the maintenance of order, without endangering freedom of assembly'.[57]

The clash between rallies and counter-demonstrations is most clearly seen in the tragic events that took place at Clichy on 16 March 1937, often regarded as the cause of the *Front populaire*'s fall from power.[58] That evening, in response to a call by the socialist mayor of Clichy, Charles Auffray, the communist general councillor, Naile, and the communist deputy, Honel, a leftist counter-demonstration was organised to protest against a PSF (*Parti social français*) assembly of the Colonel La Rocque. The *Front populaire* government, often accused by the conservative press of bullying the opposition — I will come back to the practice which gave rise to these critiques later on — refused to ban the assembly preventively. However

---

56. Memoranda reproduced in: Baffrey, *Le droit de réunion en Angleterre et en France*, pp. 149–152.
57. Colliard, *Précis de droit public*, p. 369.
58. Irwin M. Wall, 'French Socialism and the Popular Front', *Journal of Contemporary History*, 1970, vol. 5, (3), p. 15; André Chérasse, *La Hurle. La nuit sanglante de Clichy, 16 et 17 mars 1937*, Paris, Pygmalion, 1983, p. 1; Dominique Borne and Henri Dubief, *La Crise des années 30. 1929–1938*, Paris, Seuil, 1989, p. 183; Frédéric Monier, *Le Front Populaire*, Paris, La Découverte, 2002, p. 62.

violent clashes took place between the demonstrators and the police block. The police fired on the crowd. The toll was heavy with six deaths and 200–300 wounded. There is a stark cleavage between the interpretations of what took place and the responsibilities of each in the leftist press — here *L'Humanité* and *Le Populaire* — and in the rightist, conservative and extreme right press — here *Le Temps*, *Le Figaro*, *L'Illustration* for the conservatives and *L'Action française*, for the extreme right. Differences certainly exist among the newspapers of the latter group, even if as Fabrice d'Almeida points out 'the moderate ideology was broadly fed by the ghost of the anti-communist, nationalist and xenophobe extreme right', and it is precisely here that: 'political moderation flirts [...] with extremism'.[59]

The right-wing press stressed that the PSF assembly, was not a strictly political assembly, but much more a simple cinema screening. Although organised by the PSF, it nevertheless would have had no strictly political aim, particularly because no speeches were planned. *Le Figaro* on 17 March referred to a 'merely recreational meeting'. The following day it said:

> The assembly at cinema 'Olympia' was not of a political nature. It was a question of screening a film to the benefit of charity works of the *Parti social français*, no speech was to be given. Neither Colonel La Rocque nor party leaders would take part. Women and children were welcome. No assembly has ever been less 'provocative'.[60]

On 27 March *L'Illustration* spoke of 'a private assembly of a non-political nature', and of 'a recreational spectacle'. *Le Temps* on 18 March stressed that it was a question of a simple and un-threatening 'private assembly': 'The PSF had organised [...] a purely recreational film viewing [...]. No speakers were planned'. Naturally enough there is a similar statement in *L'Action française* on 17 March: the assembly 'should only be recreational', it was a question of a 'film screening'. This position is in line with Colonel La Rocque's declaration to the press, who refers to 'the strictly artistic and family nature of the assembly', as recalls *Le Temps* on 21 March. By contrast, the communist and socialist press report it rather differently. The headline in *L'Humanité* on 17 March was that 'La Rocque had organised a rally' at Clichy, that we were dealing with 'a provocation by the *Croix-de-Feu*'. The provocation was all the more evident given that the assembly had not been organised in a symbolically neutral location, but 'in the proletarian centre of Clichy', as stressed Vaillant-Couturier on 24 March. We find the same accusation of provocation in *Le Populaire* on 17 March directed at 'an assembly organised by the *Parti social français* in a working-class area with the help of outside shock troops'. The newspaper challenged the right's assertion that there would be no speeches and that no party leader would attend. The same edition of

---

59. Fabrice D'Almeida, 'Terreurs de la France modérée. Les affiches du Centre de propagande des républicains nationaux dans l'entre-deux-guerres', *Sociétés et Représentations*, 2001, vol. 12, pp. 253–267.

60. *Le Figaro*, 17 and 18 March 1937.

17 March adds that 'according to public rumours, La Rocque was supposed to be there in person.' The leftist press went on to stress that this assembly was part of a series of non-propagandist rallies — indeed, how could they hope to convince the worker population of Clichy of their arguments? — they are instead 'exercises in mobilising shock troops to the locality', as one reads in *Le Populaire* on 21 March. Furthermore, adds the same article '[the] day of the Clichy assembly, five other PSF assemblies took place in the region of Paris, of which two [...] were destined to support, if need be, the "demonstration" at cinema Olympia'. When a debate was opened on the matter in the Chamber on 23 March, this was precisely what Léon Blum suggested in a speech reproduced in *Le Populaire* the following day. He admits that 'on its own, the assembly was nothing'.[61] However, he then went on to explain that it had been understood as part of the plan of mobilisation exercises through assemblies launched by the leagues, adding that 'the emotion [was] all the more easier to explain when the place chosen was a city where the body of the population is hostile, and as a consequence the assembly could not be justified on propagandist grounds'.

There are also diverging explanations for the way in which the rally and counter-demonstration had slipped towards violence. For the conservative and extreme right press, the communist crowds are responsible. *Le Figaro* talks of 'communist bands', of 'communist demonstrators with their hateful shouting that filled the place and the nearby streets, throwing projectiles', and of 'literally unleashed screaming masses'.[62] *L'Illustration* reports 'the fury of demonstrators';[63] *Le Temps*, 'howling fury', 'madmen'.[64] These then were the demonstrators, the crowd excited by the communist leaders who had fired the first shots. The police had only responded in self-defence, claims *Le Temps*, and did 'its duty' in protecting the departure of members of the PSF from the room.[65] Things are even more clear-cut in the pages of *L'Action française*, where the victims turn out to be the forces of law and order: '[With] the agents of law and order [...] barring the way, [the people of Jouhaux, Vaillant-Couturier and Marceau Pivert] massacred them'.[66] The 'five Clichy martyrs', as *L'Humanité* called them (six deaths in all), and 200 wounded, are nevertheless workers who took part in the counter-demonstration. It is thus not surprising that the communist press begins by attacking the police which must '[purge] their ranks as soon as possible'. Responsibility for the drama should not be sought in the 'peaceful' counter-demonstration, but among the police who fired on the demonstrators, and among the fascists who not only provoked the worker population of Clichy by meeting there, but who also fired the first shots.

---

61. *Le Populaire*, 24 March 1937.
62. *Le Figaro*, 17 March 1937.
63. *L'Illustration*, 27 March 1937.
64. *Le Temps*, 18 March 1937.
65. *Le Figaro*, 20 and 18 March 1937.
66. *L'Action française*, 17 March 1937.

For historian Irwin M. Wall, 'the charges of fascist instigation of the Clichy riots, repeated *ad nauseam* in the left-wing press, were not unreasonable'.[67] *L'Humanité* reports: 'The witnesses establish fascist and police responsibilities very clearly'.[68] In *Le Populaire*, the accusations against the police are less harsh than those against the PSF. The importance of the opened legal enquiry is stressed in order to understand what happened: 'What sad fatality caused the eruption of such a severe collision between the police forces of the *Front populaire* government and worker elements of the same *Front populaire*?', asks the Deputy Secretary General of the SFIO, Jean-Baptiste Severac on 18 March. Other articles in *Le Populaire*, for example on 20 March, evoke 'failures in police command', rather than a malicious intent of police force against workers. It is suggested that the first shots were probably fired by PSF activists in order to provoke a riot. Léon Blum notes in his already mentioned speech that even if the call for a counter-demonstration by the socialist mayor of Clichy amounted to 'an error', that evening 'everything occurred as if "someone" wanted a bloody outcome'.

The interest of the extreme right would have been to undermine the credibility of a government unable to guarantee law and order. The columns of *L'Action française* repeat that the lesson to be learnt from the drama is that 'one must not play with the masses', in the words of Léon Daudet on 18 March, and that 'when we wet the appetite of the masses in movement, [...] we do not really know how things will end'. This opinion is expressed with a violence marked by the newspaper's anti-Semitism. Blum's experience 'slides in the blood of the unfortunate that it has itself excited'; 'Whatever he does, this Jew, who brought us to the brink of the civil war, can only generate what he himself represents, that is, disorder', reports *L'Action française*.[69] For the left the consequence is not the weakening of government. On the contrary, the communist attacks stop rapidly in the press to emphasise the union of the *Front populaire*: 'The *Front populaire* came out stronger from its new trial', affirms Vaillant-Couturier in *L'Humanité*.[70] The lesson to be drawn from the drama is not the failure of government, which subsequently won a vote of confidence from the Chamber, but the need to ban the activity of fascist leagues, of which the PSF was nothing but a reincarnation. Léon Blum suggests this in his speech to the Chamber. The accusation is rejected by the conservatives and extreme right, who affirm that the PSF has the characteristics of a genuine party. *Le Temps* describes a 'party in no way different from other legally constituted political parties'.[71] The PSF parliamentary group responded by submitting a draft law '[introducing] new or heavier penalties against anyone who directly or indirectly provokes a rally or takes part in a demonstration against a

---

67. Wall, 'French Socialism and the Popular Front', p. 15.
68. *L'Humanité*, 18 March 1937.
69. *L'Action française*, 17 March 1937.
70. *L'Humanité*, 24 March 1937.
71. *Le Temps*, 18 March 1937.

legitimate or regularly authorised assembly', as announced *Le Figaro*.[72] Indeed, the drama of Clichy revives the debate on the attacks on freedom of assembly under the *Front populaire*. In particular, it raises the question of counter-demonstrations as a way to exert pressure on government and administration. Undeniably, the preventive bans of assemblies had been multiplied during the interwar period in the name of maintaining public order; that is, when a party announced the organisation of a counter-demonstration.

Preventive banning: the Republic against freedom?

The 1881 law, amended in 1901 and 1907, makes political assemblies free by denying government or administration the right to ban them preventively. For fifty years, the assertion contained in Article 1 of the law — 'public assemblies are free' — corresponded to the reality of right of assembly. In the 1930s this was no longer the case when repeated attacks on freedom of assembly were mainly justified by the threat of fascist mobilisation. The renewed interest of legal experts in the right of assembly in the 1930s is a symptom of this. They denounced the new constraints on freedom of assembly and stressed their illegality. In 1937 Baffrey claimed: 'Proclaiming that freedom no longer exists is banal. [...] Freedom of assembly seems the most moribund of all freedoms'.[73] The same year Menanteau declared that 'legal experts no longer dare write the word freedom with the sense we still gave it at the beginning of the century, as something absolute, proud, reassuring'.[74]

In the writings of legal experts this reprobation is more or less explicitly bound to a rejection of the time of 'the masses'. This is particularly true for Joseph Barthélémy, who wrote most on the question and whose theories were referred to by every legal commentary of the period that I have consulted. The denunciation of the crisis of freedom of assembly largely took the form of an aversion *vis-à-vis* the *Front populaire* government, accused of being mainly responsible. This is expressed in strictly legal writings, particularly in Barthélémy's *Précis de droit public* of 1937,[75] but also in the many articles that he published in *Le Temps*. Attacks on freedom of assembly are not the only object of criticism: 'In his tribune of *Le Temps*, Barthélémy denounced the economic and social reforms, which increased sharply in 1936, one by one and without any subtlety.'[76] Retracing the route of this defender of liberal democracy who gradually moved towards reactionary politics,[77] Frédéric Saulnier insists on his radical rejection of the *Front populaire* and an 'aversion to massification' that brought 'him, the liberal, [to take]

---

72. *Le Figaro*, 20 March 1937.
73. Baffrey, *Le droit de réunion en Angleterre et en France*, p. 178.
74. Menanteau, *Les nouveaux aspects de la liberté de réunion*, p. 257.
75. Barthélémy, *Précis de droit public*, Paris, Dalloz, 1937.
76. Gilles Martinez, 'Joseph Barthélémy et la crise de la démocratie libérale', *Vingtième Siècle*, 1998, vol. 59, p. 35.
77. Joseph Barthélémy was minister of Justice in the Vichy government between 1941 and 1943.

a reactionary drift during this period'.[78] This indictment of the *Front populaire* government, seen as the symbol of the entry of politics in the era of the masses, is not unique. Many other legal experts affirm that if freedom had been in a state of crisis since the 1930s, it was 'during the years 1936–1937 that it succumbed'.[79] Their observations are not purely of a legal nature, it is also a question of a strongly conservative discourse against the *Front populaire* government. Unfortunately, there is too little biographical information available on these legal experts to allow me to put in perspective their evolution and these attitudes regarding freedom of assembly — by '[determining] what the relations are between the legal field and the political field, the social recruitment of the professions concerned and their doctrinal attitudes'.[80]

Jurisprudence and regulations against the liberalism of republican legislation

In his *Précis de droit public* Barthélémy emphasises that the 'movement of authoritarian reaction' in the 1930s in matters of 'group freedom' arose from the fact that assemblies had become a way to 'make an impression on Parliament, government and the bourgeois classes by mass demonstrations', and that consequently what we see is the opposition of 'the masses *vs.* the masses'.[81] The idea is largely shared by those writing on the right of assembly at the time. In particular, they denounced the new confusion produced by mass demonstrations; that is, confusion between assembly and association due to the birth of parties and their role as powerful organisers of huge rallies; and confusion between public and private assemblies — assemblies gathering together party members can be defended as private, even when there are thousands of supporters. Indeed, in the interwar period, the zone of transition between assemblies which are strictly private and rallies open to the crowd is rather blurred. This is the case for assemblies where the membership card of the organising party is requested on entry to what may be huge assemblies which do not differ at all in their aspect from the so-called public assemblies with only mere sympathisers. Menanteau notes that 'a huge open-air communist party or PSF assembly at the Parc des Princes for example, would be very difficult to consider as private, even if one is required to present a document'. Moreover, 'the scale of the party and the assembly are beyond all practical control'.[82] This confusion made the 1881 law

---

78. Fédéric Saulnier, *Joseph Barthélémy. 1874–1945. La crise du constitutionnalisme libéral sous la IIIe République*, Paris, LGDJ, 2004, pp. 475, 473–478.
79. Baffrey, *Le droit de réunion en Angleterre et en France*, pp. 178–179.
80. Christophe Charle, 'Pour une histoire sociale des professions juridiques à l'époque contemporaine. Note pour une recherche', *Actes de la Recherche en Sciences Sociales*, 1989, vol. 76, (76–77), pp. 117–118.
81. Barthélémy, *Précis de droit public*, p. 115.
82. Menanteau, *Les nouveaux aspects de la liberté de réunion*, p. 6.

inappropriate for the new forms taken by assemblies which had become a show of force. A criticism sometimes levelled against idealist legislators of the late nineteenth and early twentieth century is that they were unable to take into account the prospect that assemblies might not be places limited to discussion eternally. 'Hadn't [this liberal government] shown itself to be utopian and unviable?', asked Menanteau in 1937, suggesting that a regime of absolute freedom, based solely on weak repressive measures, necessarily makes governors unable to maintain public order and pushes them towards arbitrary decisions suppressing freedom for lack of regulatory capacity.[83] Faced with the disturbances caused by these assemblies which the law was no longer able to control, governments issue a series of rulings, decrees and memoranda putting an end to the absolute character of freedom.

On 24 February 1930, the mayor of Nevers issued a by-law, which in the name of safeguarding public order, banned a public literary conference planned by René Benjamin in the city. Benjamin, who had 'never concealed his monarchist sympathies and his lack of admiration for secular education',[84] choosing Nevers, provoked the protest of the local section of the national union of schoolteachers, declaring that it would oppose this public assembly with all the means available, particularly by a counter-demonstration. To remedy this ban, the lecture was transformed into a private assembly by the city's cultural union. In response, the mayor issued a new ruling to ban it, again in the name of preserving public order, for which he was responsible according to law of 5 April 1884 on municipalities. The problem is that even if the law effectively makes the mayor responsible for avoiding potential disorder caused by an assembly, it does not give him the preventive powers to carry this out.[85] These decisions to ban the assembly were brought before the Conseil d'État by René Benjamin and the president of the cultural union of Nevers. The Conseil had to judge on the nature of preventive powers of a mayor against an assembly. The government commissioner accepted the petition and the Conseil d'État subsequently annulled the two by-laws in its judgement of 19 May 1933.

The famous 'Benjamin judgement' was taken as a sign of the judge's liberalism when faced with an arbitrary use of administrative power. Even if the intervention came late, wrote several legal experts, it nevertheless confirms recognition of the idea that 'whoever wants to speak is within his right [to do so]', to use Barthélemy's expression.[86] The jurisprudence of the Conseil d'État was 'the safeguard [...] of freedom of assembly against the arbitrary use of power by the police authorities'.[87] The interpretation seems to have prevailed to the present in the Conseil d'État, which commented on the judgement as follows:

---

83. Menanteau, *Les nouveaux aspects de la liberté de réunion*, p. 160.
84. Marcel Le Clère, *Les réunions, manifestations et attroupements en droit français et comparé*, Paris, Impr. Petites Affiches, 1945, p. 28.
85. Léon Morgand, *La Loi municipale, commentaire de la loi du 5 avril 1884 sur l'organisation et les attributions des conseils municipaux*, Paris, Berger-Levrault, 1884–1885, pp. 36–39, 49–50.
86. Barthélemy, *Précis de droit public*, p. 129.
87. Menanteau, *Les nouveaux aspects de la liberté de réunion*, p. 198.

In the *Benjamin* judgement, the Conseil d'État put all its weight behind freedom of assembly [...] in exercising rigorous control of infringements which can be legally brought against it using police measures, particularly to maintain public order. As indicated by the government commissioner, following an often used formula: 'freedom is the rule, restriction of the police is the exception'. [...] With the legal precedent produced by the *Benjamin* judgement, the Conseil d'État affirmed its role as guardian of public and individual freedoms in the face of possible attacks caused by the exercise of the police's administrative powers.[88]

The prevailing interpretation is that the Conseil d'État thus recalled that administrators cannot suppress a freedom recognised and organised by law. This judgement is nevertheless the first breach of the inviolability of freedom of assembly. In considering, according to the text of the judgement, that 'from the inquiry it appears that the likelihood of disorder invoked by the mayor of Nevers did not present a degree of seriousness such that he was unable to, without banning the lecture, maintain order in issuing police measures that he had a duty to take', the judge implied that the mayor could have legitimately banned the lecture had the risk of disorder been more serious. If the risk of disorder likely to be provoked by holding an assembly is considered sufficiently severe, the assembly can be banned beforehand by a simple administrative ruling. In the 1930s, noting however that the Conseil d'État had '[acknowledged to the police] the formal right to intervene to limit and, if necessary, to suppress the best defined freedoms',[89] most legal experts did not seem to fear that a municipal rule can go against the law.[90] It was only in the postwar period that the violation of the law was clearly disapproved. In 1950, Claude-Albert Colliard wrote that the Benjamin judgement 'introduced an important exception to the principle of freedom of assembly' and that 'despite the success of the applicant, in this case the principle posed by the judgement is not a liberal principle', since it 'gives the administration the power to suppress a freedom recognised and regulated by law'. The main problem is that 'it is not simply the current disorder that allows [...] the ban; it is also the likelihood, the threat of disorder'.[91]

The consequence emanating from the *considérants* of the Benjamin judgement was not immediately evident. In the following years the Conseil d'État repeatedly renewed the same type of reasoning, thus revealing a conception of freedom of assembly quite remote from that of the legislators at the outset of the Third

---

88. *Analyse des grands arrêts du Conseil d'État et du Tribunal des conflits*, http://www.conseil-etat.fr/ce/jurisp/index_ju_la21.shtml (acessed 6 June 2006).

89. Marcel-Louis Degrenne, *Les réunions et les pouvoirs de police*, Caen, Caron & Cie, 1938, p. 150.

90. Achille Mestre, who annotated the Benjamin judgement in the *Recueil Sirey* in 1934, immediately denounced this possibility. He wrote that 'while sanctioning the violation of a freedom, the Benjamin judgement can be added to the file on the crisis of liberalism'. Cited in Claude-Albert Colliard, *Précis de droit public. Les libertés publiques*, Paris, Dalloz, 1950, p. 369.

91. Colliard, *Précis de droit public*, pp. 368–369.

Republic. This is the case of another famous judgement: the Bucard judgement on 23 December 1936. At the end of 1935 the *Parti franciste* planned a series of assemblies in the *département* of Bas-Rhin. The prefect banned them all by rulings, irrespective of their character. Marcel Bucard, leader of this fascist party, challenged these rulings for their excessive force and submitted them to the Conseil d'État.[92] The '*considérants*' to the final judgement stated that:

> Considering that the principle of freedom of assembly was unable to foil the need to preserve law and order with which it should be reconciled; that it falls to the competent authorities to take measures to control safety and public peace and even, if safeguarding public order so demands, to ban assemblies [...].

Through this preamble (*considérant*), it is recognised that the prefect legitimately banned all types of meetings, withdrawing their former inviolability, even thus for private assemblies. In February 1936 the prefect of the *Nord* department banned a banquet, justifying his decision on the grounds that the organisers were members of dissolved leagues and that this meant a risk of disturbing the peace. The organisers appealed to the Conseil d'État whose judgement annulled the decision. The grounds for the Bijadoux judgement on 5 February 1937 were that the prefect did not demonstrate that he lacked the necessary means to maintain law and order without banning the assembly. Here too, it acknowledges 'the possibility of a ban based on the tendentious notion of "state of necessity"'.[93] With this series of judgements, the Conseil d'État thus asserts the principle that freedom of assembly is the rule, which should not be undermined by prohibiting a meeting, if order can be guaranteed by other means: then the ban must be the exception. Yet in so doing, it implicitly acknowledges that assemblies can be banned beforehand when the risk of disorder is deemed sufficiently serious. Thus the liberalism of the legislation of the late nineteenth and early twentieth centuries was no longer respected.

However it is above all the interpretation of the decree of 23 October 1935 in the Paganon Memorandum of 27 October that extends the powers of administrators and reduces freedom of assembly. Without returning to the nature of this decree, we should recall that it subjected 'all processions, marches, people gatherings and, in general, all demonstrations on the public street' to prior declaration. It only mentions assemblies in order to recall the ban on holding them on the public thoroughfare. In the guise of applying this decree, aimed exclusively at street rallies, the memorandum to prefects from the Minister of the Interior, Joseph Paganon, banishes the notion of freedom of assembly. By a slip, it passes from the word 'demonstration' (*manifestation*) to the word 'assembly' (*réunion*) to describe groupings to which the ban should be applicable. At the time legal experts were less divided on this blow to the legal regimen governing assemblies than to those emanating indirectly from the judgements of the Conseil d'État; this is not

---

92. See, in particular: Baffrey, *Le droit de réunion en Angleterre et en France*, pp. 179–180.
93. Le Clère, *Les réunions, manifestations et attroupements en droit français et comparé*, p. 30.

unrelated to the fact that bans based on this memorandum would basically take place under the government of the *Front populaire*, criticised by a large part of them. In 1937 Barthélémy stresses that:

> Administrative instructions, particularly those issued by M. Paganon, Minister of the Interior, on the subject of the application of the decrees, immediately went much further than the decrees themselves.[94]

In the previous year, he had denounced an 'erosion of freedom' in *Le Temps*:

> This decree, on the wishes of the Minister of the Interior, took advantage of a legal loophole. The prefects were invited to prevent all assemblies, even in closed and covered places, that could have external repercussions. There is no assembly without arrivals, even scattered, and above all without leaving as a crowd. Freedom of assembly is dead.[95]

In 1937 Menanteau also pointed the finger against the erroneous substitution of the term demonstration (*manifestation*) with that of assembly (*réunion*) in the memorandum to prefects and included it in a series of memoranda that 'exaggerate [...] the preventive powers of the administration'.[96] In 1938, Degrenne noted that 'in a very curious way' the statutory law of 1935 has been 'interpreted' by a ministerial memorandum.[97] Later, in 1950, Colliard wrote more firmly that the Paganon Memorandum: 'denotes the anti-liberalism of the central administration and its ministers', and that 'since [it] [...] the arbitrary use of administrative power has been the rule'.[98] It is largely on the basis of the memorandum's content that the administration began to increase the number of bans on assemblies that, even if not spilling out onto the street, were deemed likely to cause trouble, particularly due to the opposition that they might provoke.

An arbitrary power justified by the threat of fascist mobilisation

The arbitrary use of administrative power regarding right of assembly did not date to the legal precedents and ministerial memoranda of the 1930s. A mayor could already hamper the organisation of an assembly by refusing to grant a place to hold it. In 1925, the PCF asks the municipal council of Asnières for authorisation to use the municipal gymnasium to hold a protest rally against the war in Morocco. The mayor, Leclere, refused the authorisation on the grounds of the 'biased nature of the assembly'. Profiting from the absence of Leclere, the committee went on to make a new request, this time to the deputy mayor, Audouy, presenting the planned assembly no longer as strictly political, but as 'a protest assembly against

---

94. Barthélémy, *Précis de droit public*, p. 129.
95. *Le Temps*, 17 November 1936.
96. Menanteau, *Les nouveaux aspects de la liberté de réunion*, pp. 215, 217.
97. Degrenne, *Les réunions et les pouvoirs de police*, p. 222.
98. Colliard, *Précis de droit public*, pp. 368–369.

the recent price increases [of the Paris public transport]'. The authorisation was granted and, once obtained, the communists announced in their posters that the rally would be against the war in Morocco.[99] The practice of refusing to grant a place to hold an assembly already existed before, but increased in the 1930s. It is subsequently frequently the case that a mayor refuses to grant use of a meeting room on the grounds of the unrest that this would cause and the fact that a rally would aggravate the situation or more simply because he was an opponent to the party organising the rally. In 1936, the prefect of la Seine asked the mayor of Bois-Colombes to book the municipal theatre for an SFIO rally where the of Minister of Sports and Leisure, Léo Lagrange, would participate. The mayor initially refused on the pretext of only conceding rooms during electoral periods.[100] Yet in the last instance he consented, but in his letter gave a different reason to justify his previous refusal:

> Out of respect for the Minister and yourselves, I consent to grant the hall. I must however accompany my acceptance with the following explanations: during the electoral campaign and in the months before it the municipality of Bois-Colombes showed the greatest liberality in making this room available for political parties [...]. Nevertheless, the municipality [...] noted the dangerous tension for public order which reigns in people's spirits and which may increase rather than diminish. [...] The increase of political assemblies cannot [...] but set the French against each other and harm public order. We have acted in a spirit of appeasement; I am consequently surprised by the intervention of higher authorities in a contrary sense.[101]

The same argument is used to legitimate the refusal to grant access to schoolyards in the centre of Vanves to the communist deputy Piginnier for an assembly to report on his mandate in 1938.[102] The mayor explained in a letter to the prefect of la Seine:

> At a time when the government of the Republic requires all French to adjust to painful discipline and to accept sacrifices to restore order in the country's affairs, so seriously compromised since communist interference manifests itself with impunity, it seems to me inadmissible that a municipal magistrate, mindful of his duties and responsibilities, becomes the accomplice of the

---

99. ADP/Perotin/10441/64/2/73/Opposition politique dans les communes: Lettre du préfet de la Seine au Ministre de l'Intérieur, 5 octobre 1925.

100. ADP/Perotin/10441/64/2/77/Concession de locaux municipaux et scolaires dans les communes du département: Lettre de Charles Bernard, secrétaire de Bois-Colombes de la SFIO, au préfet, 2 juillet 1936.

101. ADP/Perotin/10441/64/2/77/Lettre du maire de Bois-Colombes au préfet de la Seine, 4 juillet 1936.

102. ADP/Perotin/10441/57/1/33/Mise à disposition des locaux scolaires pour les comptes rendus de mandat des députés: Lettre du préfet de la Seine à M. Piginnier, 3 décembre 1938.

Communist Party allowing it in whatever form to publicly sabotage the work of recovery undertaken by government.[103]

Thus the arbitrary use of administrative powers already emerges in the question of using municipal rooms and the reasons given for refusal. For motives of political opinions, what is granted to some is refused to others. This type of practice worsened in the 1930s. Yet it was not exclusively attributable to the government of the *Front populaire*.

However freedom of assembly also suffered from an increase in the use of preventive bans by the administration, starting in the mid-1930s. In 1937 the legal expert Baffrey announced the demise of freedom of assembly established by legislators in 1881: 'The texts that guarantee it remain, but they are treated with such contempt, that we can suppose that they are conserved as vestiges of a past, now destroyed!'[104] In the wake of the Paganon memorandum, that is, basically under the *Front populaire*, many rallies were banned. These bans were declared either by the government, or the mayor or prefect of wherever the assembly was to take place.[105] The press regularly reports the prohibitions of one assembly or another — directed mainly against the extreme right. These are routinised to the point that they are often simply notified; whatever the political colour of the newspaper, if the bans sometimes spark criticism, they are frequently purely informative. On 19 March 1937 *Le Populaire* declares: 'Ban on a Doriotist assembly in Marseilles. Marseilles, 18 March. Doriot, and Sabiani, had announced a big assembly in Marseilles on Sunday. This assembly is banned'.[106] In periods when bans were particularly numerous, conservative or extreme right newspapers, such as *L'Action française*, *Le Figaro* or *Le Temps* ran a column entitled 'Banned Assemblies'.

Some legal experts distinguish three stages in this wave of bans which occur in rapid succession in early 1936. In the first, bans are made on assemblies where members of dissolved leagues or associations are expected to participate. They sometimes affect banquets and this seems particularly to shock legal experts. 'In a period where the right of assembly did not exist, the government of Louis-Philippe hesitated a great deal before banning banquets', wrote Barthélémy.[107] In a second stage, there are the bans on assemblies organised by groups deemed to be a threat for public order. Menanteau specifies that these are 'groups whose claims tended to impose direct action operations'.[108] This is the case of assemblies organised

---

103. ADP/Perotin/10441/57/1/33/Mise à disposition des locaux scolaires pour les comptes rendus de mandat des députés: Lettre du maire de Vanves au préfet de la Seine, 23 novembre 1938.
104. Baffrey, *Le droit de réunion en Angleterre et en France*, p. 178.
105. As the obligation of prior declaration had been suppressed in 1907, the authorities were now warned by the meetings announcement to the participants or by police informers.
106. *Le Populaire*, 19 March 1937.
107. Barthélémy, *Précis de droit public*, p. 130.
108. Menanteau, *Les nouveaux aspects de la liberté de réunion*, p. 218.

by the agrarian party then under the empire of Dorgères,[109] or of the *Ligue des contribuables*, a conservative movement against increased taxation, which became more radical with the crisis.[110] Finally, we come to the third, and most important, stage of assemblies' prohibitions: those due to a counter-demonstration announced by an opposing party. It develops under the *Front populaire*; bans which until then had been relatively limited, increased.

Opponents frequently announce a counter-demonstration, not so much to protest against the rally as to exert pressure in the form of blackmail to force the administrative authorities to declare a ban on the proposed assembly. In the words of Menanteau:

> When an assembly is announced, the opposing parties alert their members, launch a provocative campaign in the press, put up posters, distribute leaflets, and decry the impudence of those wanting to enjoy their rights.

He added that:

> After the excitement, when one expects that the seeds of hatred will produce the fruits of violence, an appointed group requests the police authority a ban in order to maintain the necessary public order.[111]

The mobilisation campaign led the authorities to believe that violence, as the outcome of a confrontation between two parties in the same place, might be particularly critical. Thus the administrative authorities increasingly preferred to ban an assembly rather than to block a counter-demonstration effectively.

The prohibitions of assemblies were sufficiently numerous to be presented as a legitimate means for government to maintain order. In a speech to the Chamber when debates opened after the events of Clichy, Léon Blum affirmed: 'Police authority, whether it be that of the municipality, the prefecture, or government, can be brought to ban assemblies organised by perfectly legal organisations, in the name of public order'.[112] As early as 1936, there was talk about the 'authorisation' of assemblies. In October 1936 a government communiqué attempted to explain why after having 'banned' a PSF assembly, it 'authorised' a communist assembly, and announced that the government was 'determined not to authorise demonstrations and rallies likely to provoke opposite actions and reactions and to further alarm the public spirit in Paris and the region of Paris'.[113] On 2 February 1937 *Le Temps* reports how the municipal council of Evreux deliberated on whether or not to 'authorise' a PSF assembly. On 19 March 1937 *Le Figaro* speaks of a

---

109. Édouard Lynch, 'Le Parti agraire et paysan français entre politique et manifestation', *Histoire et sociétés*, 2005, vol. 13, pp. 54–66.

110. Pierre Milza, 'L'ultra-droite des années 1930', in Michel Winock (ed.), *Histoire de l'extrême droite en France*, Paris, Seuil, 1994, p. 160.

111. Menanteau, *Les nouveaux aspects de la liberté de réunion*, p. 226.

112. Speech republished in *Le Populaire*, 25 March 1937.

113. 'Un communiqué de l'Intérieur', *L'Oeuvre*, 6 October 1936.

'government authorisation' to the benefit of an assembly. This return to the system of authorisation was particularly striking as the ban on all rallies was the rule, and only some had government approval to hold them. An extensive practice of preventive prohibitions amounted to the *de facto* administrative authorisation only for those assemblies which they favoured. In some periods we see a reinstatement of a system of prior authorisation. This was the case in October 1936 when the government decided to ban all assemblies of any party in the region of Paris. The PCF announced its plan to hold fifty-two assemblies in Alsace-Lorraine on 11 October. Finally, the government decided to 'authorise' only ten of the planned assemblies. This provoked a critical reaction from the three legal experts already considered here: 'The government has gone from the faculty to ban assemblies to the faculty to authorise them', wrote Barthélémy.[114] 'It seems to us', comments Menanteau, 'that we are returning from a rule of law to the previous rule of police and authorisation'.[115] And Baffrey is indignant about the fact that the government 'assumes not only the right to forbid, but the right to allow'.[116]

This practice of repeatedly banning assemblies was blamed for the fact that not all of the parties were treated with the same severity by the authorities. Menanteau criticised the fact that the 'susceptibilities of public order are capricious',[117] and that they depend on the party organising the assembly. Barthélémy went so far as to say that 'there are no assemblies except for friends of the majority'.[118] Indeed, during periods of high tension between communist and extreme right activists, the assemblies most frequently banned were those of La Rocque's PSF and Doriot's PPF (*Parti Populaire Français*). This was even though communist rallies as well as those of the extreme right could be considered a threat to public order, if a ruling is based on the potential disorder on the street after a call to counter-demonstrate by the opponent party. The day after the Clichy drama the government banned several rallies of the extreme right. Precisely because it had been accused of partiality in its bans, the government did not ban the PSF assembly in Clichy, despite the pressure to do so from the city's socialist and communist authorities. 'As a public safety measure the government banned three rallies of the so-called "national front" of fascist disturbers', approved *L'Humanité*.[119] However at the same time it authorised a communist rally at the Vélodrome d'Hiver.

---

114. Barthélémy, *Précis de droit public*, p. 131.
115. Menanteau, *Les nouveaux aspects de la liberté de réunion*, p. 221.
116. Baffrey, *Le droit de réunion en Angleterre et en France*, p. 187.
117. Menanteau, *Les nouveaux aspects de la liberté de réunion*, p. 220.
118. *Le Temps*, 22 September 1936.
119. *L'Humanité*, 10 October 1936.

A characteristic example of this 'double attitude of power in what concerns freedom of assembly'[120] — to use the terms of a journalist critique in *L'Illustration* — is found in the form of duels organised between the PCF and the PSF starting in October 1936: the threat of counter-demonstration was not as effective for all of the parties that used it. The PSF announced the organisation of an assembly in the Vélodrome d'Hiver on 2 October 1936. The SFIO and the PCF then launched an appeal for a counter-demonstration. On 2 October *L'Humanité* stated:

> Workers of the *Région Parisienne*: Colonel La Rocque and his *Croix-de-Feu*, camouflaged as the *Parti Social Français*, announce their intention of rallying in one of the most proletarian areas of our great Paris (in the Vélodrome d'Hiver). The times are too grave to tolerate such a provocation. Stand up everybody for a powerful counter-demonstration. [...] The *Comité Régional de Coordination* (Socialist Party, Communist Party).[121]

Consequently, a ruling to ban an assembly was made against the rally organised by La Rocque.[122] The PSF therefore resumed the process and announced a counter-demonstration on 4 October, the day when the PCF also planned to hold a rally, this time in the Parc des Princes. The PSF appeal took a form almost identical to the one of the leftist parties:

> Socialist and patriotic workers of the *Région Parisienne*: Cachin, Jacques Duclos and Maurice Thorez, fascists of Russian soviets, announce their intention of rallying in one of the most peaceful areas of our great Paris (in the Parc des Princes). The times are too grave to tolerate such a provocation. Stand up everybody for a powerful counter-demonstration. [...] The Executive Committee of the PSF.[123]

However, no ruling to ban the assembly was made, but a police presence of 20,000 men was mobilised in order to avoid clashes between participants in the assembly and counter-demonstrators.[124] Both the conservative press and the extreme right press denounced this protection of a communist assembly, when the PSF rally had been banned. 'The communists are assembled under the protection of 20,000 agents and anti-riot police', runs the title of *L'Action française* on 5 October. The idea that the police could be at the service of government and simultaneously protect leftist assemblies — rather than public order — was also implicit in the cover of *L'Illustration* on 10 October 1936, which shows that: 'in London, the police charge fascists and counter-demonstrators alike', while in Paris, only 'demonstrators of *Parti social français*' were charged by the police

---

120. *L'Illustration*, 10 October 1936.
121. *L'Humanité*, 2 October 1936.
122. 'Réunions interdites', *L'Action française*, 3 October 1936.
123. Reproduced in Menanteau, *Les nouveaux aspects de la liberté de réunion*, p. 227.
124. 'Un meeting communiste au Parc des Princes', *L'Oeuvre*, 4 October 1936.

(see Figure 7.3).¹²⁵ An article comparing the two situations describes how 'passers-by, "neutrals", watched curiously as, for the first time, police and troops were placed at the disposal of communist organisations'.

Yet this disparity of treatment did not mean that the *Front populaire* was, in the last instance, an authoritarian government and an enemy of public liberty. We need to focus on the context of the struggle against fascism during which these bans and authorisations occurred. The rise of the extreme right in France, and in Europe in general, brought within it enough to render alarming the vast nationalist mobilisations, and all the more so when the memory of the activity of the leagues was not far. The justification for banning assemblies made by Léon Blum's government and the press supporting its action tend in this direction. It was first claimed that extreme right rallies were not genuine political assemblies, but paramilitary exercises of mobilisation. This aspect is promoted by authors who today defend the PSF's affinity with fascism, in particular, Robert Soucy, who insists on the idea that La Rocque was accustomed to the fact that 'his shock troops obey him blindly'.¹²⁶ Michel Winock, who rejects the comparison of the PSF to a fascist movement, nevertheless recognises that there is 'nothing more disturbing [...], than these massive mobilisations at times fixed secretly [...] where activists arrive by car or motorbike, or these parades opposing supporters of the *Front populaire*'. However, according to Winock it is advisable to replace them in a strategy to 'provoke a show of strength', and to 'show its force', without seeking 'physical clashes'. This should be done in a way that does not allow us to deduce assimilation to 'paramilitary fascist forces'.¹²⁷ The left in power nevertheless insisted on this aspect of rallies organised by the extreme right in order to justify bans. The PSF assembly forbidden on 2 October 1936 'only constitutes an exercise of mobilisation in view of the civil war'.¹²⁸ Following this banned assembly, and the communist assembly authorised two days later, a government communiqué reported in *Le Populaire* on 6 October 'specifies the paramilitary character of the *Parti social – Croix-de-Feu*;¹²⁹ and denounces its methods of mobilisation that have nothing in common with the public action of a political party'.¹³⁰ The communiqué from the Minister of the Interior, Roger Salengro, brought together the modes of organisation for the planned PSF assembly and the counter-demonstration organised at the occasion of the communist rally in the Parc des Princes, and spoke of 'a rally by rapid and secret call-up, presupposing an organisation, a hierarchy, a militaresque discipline', a 'mobilisation of groups', and 'gathering around given

---

125. *L'Illustration*, 10 October 1936.
126. Robert J. Soucy, *Fascismes français? 1933–1939. Mouvements antidémocratiques*, Paris, Autrement, 2004, p. 165.
127. Michel Winock, 'Retour sur le fascisme français. La Rocque et les Croix-de-Feu', *Vingtième Siècle*, 2006, vol. 90, pp. 7–8.
128. *Le Populaire*, 5 October 1936.
129. This is a play on words associating the PSF with the Croix-de-Feux.
130. *Le Populaire*, 6 October 1936.

Figure 7.3: 'In Paris, around the Parc des Princes, where the communist meeting is being held, the police charged the counter-demonstrators of the Parti Social Français' (top). 'In London, the police charge fascists as well as counter-demonstrators'. L'Illustration, 10 October 1936

points'. Thus we cannot not make 'any analogy [...] with a public assembly organised publicly by a political party'.[131] We find the same idea in 1937 in the analyses of the events at Clichy. *Le Populaire* affirmed that PSF assemblies were not ordinary political assemblies but 'exercises of mobilisation',[132] characteristic of nothing other than a fascist league disguised as a party. The leftist press affirmed that the extreme right tried to provoke a civil war with these assemblies.

The legal denouncement of repeated attacks on freedom of assembly in the late 1930s is largely the result of the deep-rooted anti-communism of the legal experts referred to above. The example serving as a foil, used to show that where one would arrive by progressively suppressing public freedoms, is not a fascist country, but soviet Russia. The descriptions used to talk about communism reveal a violent rejection: 'What we must fear is that the lack of reaction in the public opinion will encourage government to increasingly stifle the right of assembly. Inevitably, this will lead to the regime of soviet Russia', wrote Baffrey. If we refer to Raphaël Alibert — a legal expert who later, as Minister of Justice, signed the first *Statuts des juifs* of 3 October 1940 — stressed that 'in Russia, the right of association and assembly are severely prohibited for the most tepid government's opponents, but the assemblies of sympathisers are favoured'.[133] After having denounced the fact that 'the right of assembly is practically suppressed', in *Le Temps*, Barthélémy talks of 'the monstrous soviet Babel'.[134]

The transformation of the uses of the assembly, primarily by making it an expression of the strength of the organising party, moves it further away from its original pacificatory ideal, still strong in the early years of the Third Republic. An assembly organised by a party now becomes a mere 'provocation'. This term crops up repeatedly in the press, both right-wing and left-wing. It was no longer a question of debate in assemblies, or even seeing it as a means of propaganda to convince participants. As a unilateral demonstration of a party strength and cohesion, the political rallies generate violent reactions by its opponents. The attacks on freedom of assembly are a major consequence of this.

---

131. 'Un communiqué de l'Intérieur', *L'Oeuvre*, 6 octobre 1936.
132. See, in particular: J.-M. Hermann, 'Pourquoi Clichy? Les provocations et les intentions des Croix de Feu', *Le Populaire*, 17 mars 1937.
133. Baffrey, *Le droit de réunion en Angleterre et en France*, pp. 195–196.
134. *Le Temps*, 22 September 1936.

Conclusion

The idea that politics could no longer be conducted without taking the masses into account stands out, while the French republicans who expressed themselves on the right of assembly shared the conviction that freedom of assembly, which allowed the formation of public opinion, was the corollary of democratic government. I have shown that this discourse can be heard not only when they contest the limits set by the Second Empire, but also when they developed the laws for the foundation of the Republic once in power. An essentially repressive regime was set up to regulate freedom of assembly: most preventive measures in force under the Empire were discarded. Nonetheless, it was not simply decided that citizens could assemble freely and without any limitations; a regulation of freedom remained, essentially justified by the fact that the rules led not so much to its limitation, but above all to its protection.

The same law that declared in 1881, in its first article, that 'Public meetings are free', also introduced a first restriction on freedom of assembly: the ban on assembling on the public highway. This was primarily a way to ensure that the assembly remained an instrument which avoided political participation through action, as the republican framing of freedom of assembly excludes the street from the places where the crowd can gather. At the beginning of the Third Republic the nature of speeches delivered in assemblies counted less than keeping participation in assemblies in the domain of discourse. Action was something to be avoided, above all violent action, and particularly on the street. Compared with the Empire the difference of the new conception of the boundary between assembly and the outside lay primarily in the fact that republicans considered the assembly as a place where virtually all opinions could be expressed. This was provided as the opinions expressed did not incite directly to violent action, and above all, remained within one and the same sphere. The main corollary is that disorder outside the assembly is considered less acceptable because citizens have already been granted a place where they can express their discontent. Throughout the period studied, assemblies have been marked by a series of heterogeneous issues. These constitute as differing definitions of politics in assembly, in its models and counter-models, but rallies are always understood in a spatial perspective. As in a Greek tragedy, it is a question of unity of place. The aim is to circumscribe assemblies in limited, controllable and controlled spaces in order to avoid open violence. As the counter-model is the street, we see that a basically urban model was considered.

The mission of the type of public opinion promoted by republican policy of regulation of mass participation was to be unified through reason. As a result of deliberation among citizens in assemblies, this opinion would be pacified in moving towards the common good. At the basis of this perspective there is a belief affirmed in reason, and the often expressed conviction that reason will always have the upper hand in a deliberation. We have seen that the value given to deliberation does not mean involving citizens directly in decision-making.

Moreover, it is possible to disqualify opinions deemed politically extreme in the name of a consensus on the declared notion of public good. Until the end of the nineteenth century republicans in power considered that it was only because it did not solely gather together those of the same opinion, *a fortiori* members of an association, that the assembly did not constitute a danger for representation. Otherwise, the division of the public according to group interests might prevent the realisation of the pacific outcome expected from citizens' deliberation. In rallying those united around the same cause, the assembly would also constitute a threat, that of competing with public powers.

The form taken by political meetings did not correspond perfectly to the ideal model of deliberation understood as the free and reasoned discussion of the assembled citizens, where each participant would employ arguments based on reason and listen carefully to those of his opponents. Nevertheless, it is still significant that the most legitimate and most widespread form of assembly at the beginning of the Third Republic was the contradictory assembly, where individuals with differing opinions confronted each other directly through discourse. In the last instance, to the concern of circumscribing gatherings, we must add another central concern: the selection of actors populating the space of political assemblies. This is a question of favouring the increase of the number of people who have initially opposing opinions, and to eliminate those united beforehand by common positions and interests. This is because any reabsorption of rival opinions must occur through discussion, and harmony and consensus must be the outcome of an interactionist confrontation, and these dynamics must contribute to a pacification of mores. The quasi-Darwinian process affecting opinions is placed under the patronage of reason, understood in a specific sense. The main vector of this conception of reason is a great principle, the principle of contradiction. At the same time, the political assembly must be a place where very particular goods are produced, namely consensual opinions.

What links the republic to assemblies in the republican discourse is largely the fact that assemblies were a way to enlighten citizens on the vote, when electors consult among themselves and interact with candidates. I have shown how the development of electoral assemblies from the end of the Second Empire can be linked with the emergence of a new political caste, where the electoral campaign is based on an organisation, that of committees, and putting forward opinion as a legitimatory principle. This is also because the assembly serves republican government as a way to anticipate the disturbances likely to arise in elections under universal suffrage. It is a way to test the opinion of the electorate in an era where there is still a fear of potential surprises produced by the polls. In other words, the will to make a factory for consensus is accompanied by another ambition. Political assemblies are in fact seen as laboratories, since they allow government and candidates to test arguments, to observe the reactions of electors, and to predict the electoral future. They also allow the electorate to examine candidates, to test their professions of faith and to support particular political choices. The empirical observations are thus conducted bilaterally. The experimental device developed is symmetrical insofar as actors present hold the role of both the observer and the observed.

Moreover, I have shown the importance of the republican *leitmotiv* according to which the authoritarian governments that the People had previously experienced prevented them from learning how to be free. If the People are not entirely composed of autonomous and rational individuals that the Republic can govern, this is because it lacks the necessary maturity, and not because it is by nature incapable of behaving reasonably. Civic wisdom is not something that takes root immediately. It will take time for the People's new political mores to become embedded. The administration and police must reform their own behaviour, and some assemblies should serve as a model. We have seen that this civic behaviour, to which apprenticeship assemblies are expected to contribute, is a question of mastering emotions and of reducing uncontrolled passions. Starting with the example of Gambettist assemblies, I have highlighted the difficulties met by republicans having to justify the clear role played by emotion in assemblies where some of their leaders took part, whilst simultaneously insisting on the rejection of passions and the control of emotions on the part of citizens. Thus, the republicans are particularly concerned with the question of the 'scenic' rules of political assemblies, once their means have been defined, particularly the place and the actors, and their objectives. It is in this sense that great emphasis is placed on the definition of interactionist norms. Reason is also invoked here, even if it takes on a new appearance: that of a bastion against the passionate dimension of behaviour, which is also that of a flamboyant pedagogism, since it is no less than to learn freedom by behaving reasonably in assemblies.

I have stressed the fact that from the 1890s onwards there are many who agree that the hope for participation by the People in the form of peaceful deliberation no longer seemed realistic. The problem lies in new mores which should, once established, lead to a deviated use of the freedom granted in 1881. Some intolerant or violent behaviour, which was condemned by the republican project of civilisation of political mores, far from disappearing or slackening has been amplified and its use has become systemic, thus limiting any real prospect of peaceful discussion. I have also shown that one can trace two connected forms of deviance in relation to the republican project of civilisation of political mores, which become clear as of the end of the 1880s and in the 1890s. First, the organised and systematic use of noise or violence designed in particular to prevent discussion and the expression of opposing opinions and then, resorting to what I have described as assemblies-cum-demonstrations. The latter consist of the organisation of, and participation in rallies whose primary purpose is to demonstrate the force and mass support behind a previously formed opinion. I have focussed on socialist and communist assemblies in the interwar period, and have highlighted how a number of them are organised as demonstrations of force, and described as such particularly in the partisan press. The force involved is shown by the number of people assembled and by the presence of signs of their consent and enthusiasm. This may or may not be sincere, but what seems to matter most is to make it patent and to demonstrate that the crowd is united in one and the same emotion. Commentators of assemblies will make it systematically stand out as a fundamental issue.

To conclude, I have shown that from the moment that it became a question of demonstrating the massive and unified character of partisan rallies, the assembly whose links with the outside are weak by comparison, competes with street demonstrations. In the last instance, the urban spill-over cannot be eliminated, and even has the indirect consequence of limiting freedom of assembly. Assemblies remain one of privileged theatres of political experience. As in a Greek tragedy, violence contained in the unity of place could not be re-absorbed. On the contrary, incited by some forms of street violence which in turn they helped to nurture, political assemblies did not prove equal to the initial ambitions of republicans since these gatherings had become shows of force. In so far as interactions could not be governed by the ideal rules originally intended to govern them, the use of these devices — spatial (unity of place), industrial (producing consensus), and experimental (laboratories) — was diverted. The dual conception of reason was substituted by a double deployment of force: that of numbers, and also the manifest and organised enthusiasm of those taking part in rallies. These two forces acted in concert to kindle a mimetic vocation in public opinion. Two parallel processes are at work here: a restricted development of forms of deliberation giving way to intimidatory games and propagandist actions; and the transformation of laboratories of democracy into showcases of political parties.

Bibliography

Ackerman, Bruce and Fishkin, James (2003) 'Deliberation Day', in J. Fishkin and P. Laslett (eds) *Debating Deliberative Democracy*, Oxford, Blackwell, pp. 5–30.
Adams, Brian (2004) 'Public Meetings and the Democratic Process', *Public Administration Review* 64(1): 43–54.
Agulhon, Maurice (1970) *La République au village. Les populations du Var de la Révolution à la IIe République*, Paris, Plon.
— (1977) *Le cercle dans la France bourgeoise, 1810–1848*, Paris, A. Colin.
— (1980) '1830 dans l'histoire du XIXe siècle', *Romantisme* 28–29: 15–27.
— (1988) 'Associations et histoire sociale', *Revue de l'économie sociale* 14: 35–44.
— 1992) *1848 ou l'apprentissage de la République. 1848–1852*, Paris, Seuil.
— (1998) '"La République au village". Quoi de neuf ', *Provence historique* 194: 423–433.
— (2000) 'Présentation', in *La politisation des campagnes au XIXe siècle. France, Italie, Espagne, Portugal*, Rome, École française de Rome, pp. 1–11.
Albert, Pierre (1980) *Histoire de la presse politique nationale au début de la Troisième République (1871–1879)*, Lille, ANRT.
Alfandari, Elie (2005) 'La liberté d'association', in R. Cabrillac, M.-A. Frison-Roche and T. Revet (eds) *Libertés et droits fondamentaux*, Paris, Dalloz, 2005, pp. 401–405.
Alland, Denis (1994) 'Les mœurs sont-elles solubles dans le droit?', *Droits* 19: 3–9.
Altschuler, Glenn. C. and Blumin, Stuart. M. (1997) 'Limits of Political Engagement in Antebellum America. A New Look at the Golden Age of Participatory Democracy', *The Journal of American History* 84: 855–885.
Amann, Peter H. (1960) 'Prelude to Insurrection. The Banquet of the People', *French Historical Studies* 1(4): 436–444.
— (1975) *Revolution and Mass Democracy. The Paris Club Movement in 1848*, Princeton NJ, Princeton University Press.
— (1975) 'The Paris Club Movement in 1848', in R. Price (ed.) *Revolution and Reaction. 1848 and the Second French Republic*, London, Croom Helm, pp. 116–131.
— (1976) 'Political Justice in the Second French Republic', *The Journal of Modern History* 48(4): 87–124.
Ameline, Henri (1868) 'Commentaire de la loi de 1868 sur les réunions politiques', *Revue pratique de droit français*, 344–407.
Aminzade, Ronald (1993) *Ballots and Baricades. Class Formation and Republican Politics in France, 1830–1871*, Princeton NJ, Princeton University Press.

Andrieu, Claire, Le Béguec, Gilles and Tartakowsky, Danielle (eds) (2001) *Associations et champ politique. La loi de 1901 à l'épreuve du siècle*, Paris, Publications de la Sorbonne.
Ansart, Pierre (1983) *La gestion des passions politiques*, Lausanne, L'Âge d'Homme.
Antonmattei, Pierre (1999) *Léon Gambetta. Héraut de la République*, Paris, Michalon.
Arnette, Roger (1894) *La liberté de réunion en France. Son histoire et sa législation*, Paris, Arthur Rousseau.
Audier, Serge (2004) *Les théories de la république*, Paris, La Découverte.
Bacot, Paul (1994) *Dictionnaire du vote. Elections et délibérations*, Lyon, Presses Universitaires de Lyon.
Badonnel, Eric (2004) '*Une politique expérimentale'. L'action politique et l'opinion publique chez Jules Ferry. Une approche locale de ses pratiques électorales*, MAS, ENS-EHESS.
Baffrey, Michel (1937) *Le droit de réunion en Angleterre et en France*, Paris, Les Presses Modernes.
Baker, Keith Michael (1990) *Inventing the French Revolution: Essays on French Political Culture in the Eighteenth Century*, Cambridge, Cambridge University Press.
Balme, Richard and Chabanet, Didier (2002) 'Introduction. Action collective et gouvernance de l'Union européenne', in R. Balme, D. Chabanet and V. Wright (eds) *L'action collective en Europe*, Paris, Presses de Sciences Po.
Barbet, Denis (1991) 'Retour sur la loi de 1884. La production des frontières du syndical et du politique', *Genèses* 3(3): 5–30.
Bardout, Jean-Claude (2000) *L'histoire étonnante de la loi 1901. Le droit d'association en France avant et après Waldeck-Rousseau*, Lyon, Juris-Service.
Barni, Jules (1872) *Manuel républicain*, Paris, Germer-Baillière.
— (1872) *Ce que doit être la République*, Publication de l'Union Républicaine de la Somme, no. 1, (3rd edn.).
Barral, Pierre (2008) *Léon Gambetta. Tribun et stratège de la République (1838–1882)*, Paris, Privat.
Barrows, Susanna (1981) *Distorting Mirrors: Visions of the Crowd in Late Nineteenth-century France*, New Haven CT, Yale University Press.
Barthélémy, Joseph (1937) *Précis de droit public*, Paris, Dalloz.
Barthélémy, Martine (2000) *Associations. Un nouvel âge de la participation?*, Paris, Presses de Sciences Po.
Baudot, Pierre-Yves (2005) *Événement et institution. Les funérailles des présidents de la République en France (1877–1996)*, PhD dissertation, Paris I.
Beaudenon, François (1997) *Entre ordre et liberté. Le combat républicain contre l'anarchisme. 1880–1900*, M.A., IEP Grenoble.
Bécarud, Jean (1973) 'Noblesse et représentation parlementaire. Les députés nobles de 1871 à 1958', *Revue française de science politique* 23(5): 972–993.

Becker, Howard S. (1963) *Outsiders. Studies in the Sociology of Deviance,* New York, The Free Press of Glencoe.
Bellanger, Claude, Godechot, Jacques, Guiral, Pierre and Terrou, Fernand (eds) (1972) *Histoire générale de la presse française,* vol. 3, Paris, PUF.
Bellis, Mary (n.d.) 'The History of Loudspeakers – Speakers', Online. Available http://inventors.about.com/library/inventors/blloudspeaker.htm (accessed 6 June 2006).
Benoist, Charles (1934) *Souvenirs, 1902–1933, vie parlementaire, vie publique,* vol. 3, Paris, Plon.
Benoît, Bruno (2002) 'Réflexion sur le phénomène associatif', *Cahier Millénaire3,* 1(26): 9–18.
Berlière, Jean-Marc (1993) 'Du maintien de l'ordre républicain au maintien républicain de l'ordre? Réflexions sur la violence', *Genèses* (12): 6–29.
— (1996) *Le monde des polices en France. $XIX^e–XX^e$ siècles,* Bruxelles, Complexe.
Berthon, Renaud (1938) *Le régime des cortèges et des manifestations en France,* Paris, Sirey.
Bessette, Joseph. M. (1997) *The Mild Voice of Reason. Deliberative Democracy and the American National Government,* Chicago, Chicago University Press.
Birnbaum, Pierre (1998) *Le moment antisémite. Un tour de France en 1898,* Paris, Fayard.
Blondiaux, Loïc (1998) *La fabrique de l'opinion. Une histoire sociale des sondages,* Paris, Seuil.
— (2001) 'La délibération, norme de l'action publique contemporaine?', *La Revue Projet,* CERAS 268, http://www.ceras-projet.com/index.php?id=1868, pp. 1–6.
— (2004) 'Prendre au sérieux l'idéal délibératif: un programme de recherche', *Swiss Political Science Review* 10(4): 158–169.
— (2004) 'Démocratie participative et démocratie délibérative. Une lecture critique', Université du Québec: Montreal. Online. Available http://www.chaire-mcd.ca/publications/conferences/Blondiaux-conf1-novembre-2004.pdf (accessed 6 June 2006).
— (2008) *Le nouvel esprit de la démocratie. Actualité de la démocratie participative,* Paris, Seuil, *République des idées.*
Blondiaux, Loïc and Sintomer, Yves (2002) 'L'impératif délibératif', *Politix* 57: 17–35.
Bohman, James (1996) *Public Deliberation. Pluralism, Complexity, and Democracy,* Cambridge (MA), MIT Press.
— (1998) 'The Coming of Age of Deliberative Democracy', *The Journal of Political Philosophy* 6(4): 400–425.
Borne, Dominique and Dubief, Henri (1989) *La Crise des années 30. 1929–1938,* Paris, Seuil.
Bosc, Olivier (2001) *La foule criminelle. Positivisme, politique et criminologie en Italie et en France à la fin du XIXe siècle. Scipio Sighele (1868–1913) et l'école lombrosienne,* PhD dissertation, Paris IX.

Bouchet, Thomas (2004) 'Les sociétés secrètes pendant la monarchie censitaire', in Jean-Jacques Becker and Gilles Candar (eds) *Histoire des gauches en France*, vol. 1, Paris, La Découverte, pp. 161–168.

Boudon, Raymond (1999) 'Penser la relation entre le droit et les mœurs', *L'avenir du droit. Mélanges en hommage à François Terré*, Paris, Dalloz, PUF, pp. 11–24.

Bourguet, Marie-Noëlle (1989) *Déchiffrer la France: la statistique départementale à l'époque contemporaine*, Paris, Edition des Archives contemporaines.

Bourdin, Georges (1949–1950) 'Préface et commentaires', *Les grands orateurs républicains. Gambetta*, Monaco, Hemera.

Boutier, Jean and Boutry, Philippe (eds) (1992) *Les sociétés politiques. Atlas de la Révolution française*, vol. 6, Paris, EHESS.

Boutry, Philippe (1990) 'Des sociétés populaires de l'an II au parti républicain. Réflexions sur l'évolution des formes d'association politique dans la France du premier XIXe siècle', *Storiografia Francese ed Italiana a confronto sul fenomeno associativo durante XVIII e XIX secolo*, Turin, Fondazione Luigi Einaudi, pp. 107–135.

Bouvard, Louis (1869) *Les réunions électorales à Besançon et à Pontarlier et les candidats à la députation par un électeur de la 1ère circonscription du Doubs*, Besançon, Imprimerie J. Roblot.

Brisse, Pierre (1937) *Les attroupements et l'ordre public*, Paris, Dommat-Montchrestien.

Bruant, Aristide (1889–1895) *Dans la Rue. Chansons et monologues*, Paris, A. Bruant.

Brulat, Paul (1909) *Histoire populaire de Léon Gambetta*, Paris, P. Paclot.

Bunzl, Martin (2004) 'Counterfactual History. A User's Guide', *American Historical Review* 109(3): 845–858.

Burdeau, Georges (1972) *Les libertés publiques*, Paris, LGDJ.

Burrin, Philippe (1986) 'Poings levés et bras tendus. La contagion des symboles au temps du Front Populaire', *Vingtième siècle* 11: 5–20.

Bury, John. P. T. (1973) *Gambetta and the Making of the Third Republic*, London, Longman.

Candar, Gilles (1993) 'Propagande: à propos de Jean Longuet, Marcel Cachin, Lucien Roland et quelques autres...', *Cahier et revue de l'OURS* 211: 3–5.

Candar, Gilles and Prochasson, Christophe (1992) 'Le socialisme à la conquête des terroirs', *Le Mouvement Social* 160: 33–63.

Carbonnier, Jean (1979) *Essais sur les lois*, Paris, Répertoire du notariat Defrénois.

Caron, Jean-Claude (1980) 'La société des Amis du Peuple', *Romantisme* 28–29: 169–180.

— (2004) 'Les clubs de 1848', in Jean-Jacques Becker and Gilles Candar (eds) *Histoire des gauches en France. vol. 1, L'héritage du XIXe siècle*, Paris, La Découverte, pp. 182–188.

Caubet, Jean-Marie-Lazare (1893) *Souvenirs (1860–1869)*, Paris, Léopold Cerf.

Chamouard, Aude (2004) *Le parti socialiste SFIO en campagne électorale. L'exemple de la banlieue rouge pendant l'entre-deux-guerres*, M.A., IEP.

Champagne, Patrick (1990) *Faire l'opinion. Le nouveau jeu politique*, Paris, Éditions de Minuit.
Chanlaine, Pierre (1932) *Gambetta, père de la République*, Paris, Tallandier.
Chapuzet, Jean-Charles (2005) *Le général Boulanger et le boulangisme. Des passions politiques à l'oubli (1886–2005)*, PhD dissertation, IEP Paris.
Charle, Christophe (1987) *Les élites de la République. 1881–1900*, Paris, Fayard.
— (1989) 'Pour une histoire sociale des professions juridiques à l'époque contemporaine. Note pour une recherche', *Actes de la Recherche en Sciences Sociales* 76(76–77): 117–119.
— (2003) 'Les parlementaires. Avant-garde ou arrière-garde d'une société en mouvement?', in J.-M. Mayeur, J.-P. Chaline and A. Corbin (eds) *Les parlementaires de la Troisième République*, Paris, Publications de la Sorbonne, pp. 45–63.
— (2004) *Le siècle de la presse (1830–1939)*, Paris, Seuil.
Chartier, Roger (1990) *Les origines culturelles de la Révolution française*, Paris, Seuil.
— (1990) 'Opinion publique et propagande en France', in *L'image de la Révolution française. Communications présentées lors du Congrès mondial pour le bicentenaire de la Révolution, Sorbonne, Paris, 6–12 juillet 1989*, Paris, Pergamon, pp. 2,345–2,356.
— (1998) *Au bord de la falaise. L'histoire entre certitudes et incertitudes*, Paris, Albin Michel.
Chastenet, Jacques (1968) *Gambetta*, Paris, Fayard.
Checkoway, Barry (1981) 'The Politics of Public Hearings', *Journal of Applied Behavioral Science* 17(4): 566–582.
Chérasse, André (1983) *La Hurle. La nuit sanglante de Clichy, 16 et 17 mars 1937*, Paris, Pygmalion.
Chevallier, Jacques (1994) 'Bonnes mœurs et morale républicaine. Présentation', in *Les bonnes mœurs*, Paris, PUF, pp. 185–190.
Clunet, Edouard (1909) *Les associations au point de vue historique et juridique*, vol. 1, Paris, Marchal et Billard.
Cochart, Dominique (1994) 'Éléments de réflexion sur les rapports entre ordre moral et républicanisme', in *Les bonnes mœurs*, Paris, PUF, pp. 245–249.
Cochin, Augustin (1921) *Les sociétés de pensée et la démocratie moderne. Études d'histoire revolutionnaire*, Paris, Plon.
Cogniot, Georges (1976) *Parti pris*, vol. 1, Paris, Éditions sociales.
Cohen, Joshua and Sabel, Charles (1997) 'Directly-Deliberative Polyarchy', *European Law Journal* 3(4): 313–342.
Colliard, Claude-Albert (1950) *Précis de droit public. Les libertés publiques*, Paris, Dalloz.
Collovald, Annie and Gaïti, Brigitte (2006) 'Introduction', in A. Collovald and B. Gaïti (eds) *La démocratie aux extrêmes. Sur la radicalisation politique*, Paris, La Dispute, pp. 11–17.
Consolim, Márcia Christina (2004) 'Gustave Le Bon e a reação conservadora às multidões', *Anais do XVII Encontro Regional de História. O lugar da História*, Universidade Estadual de Campinas. Available http://www.

fflch.usp.br/dh/anpuhsp/downloads/CD%20XVII/ST%20II/Marcia%20 Cristina%20Consolim.pdf (accessed 6 June 2006).

Constant, Charles (1881) *Code des réunions publiques, des réunions électorales et des réunions privées. Commentaire pratique de la loi du 30 juin 1881 à l'usage des préfets, sous-préfets, maires, juges de paix, ainsi que des organisateurs de réunions publiques ou privées*, Paris, A. Durand and Pedone-Lauriel.

Corbin, Alain (1992) 'Préface', in Édouard Lynch, *Entre la commune et la nation. Identité communautaire et pratique politique en vallée de Campan (Hautes-Pyrénées) au XIXe siècle*, Toulouse II, Archives des Hautes-Pyrénées.

— (2002) *Le monde retrouvé de Louis-François Pinagot: sur les traces d'un inconnu, 1798–1876*, Paris, Flammarion.

Cossart, Paula (2001) 'La communion militante. Les meetings de gauche pendant les années 1930', *Sociétés et Représentations* 12: 131–140.

— (2002) 'Se réunir', in V. Duclert and C. Prochasson (eds) *Dictionnaire critique de la République*, Paris, Flammarion, pp. 1,113–1,119.

— (2003) 'S'assembler en Provence sous la Révolution. Légitimité des réunions des sociétés populaires comme mode de participation collective du peuple au débat public (1791–1794)', *Annales historiques de la Révolution française* 331(1): 57–77.

— (2003) 'L'émotion: un dommage pour l'idée républicaine. Autour de l'éloquence de Léon Gambetta', *Romantisme* 119: 47–60.

— (2010) 'Lecture critique: Historiciser les expériences délibératives. L'éducation civique par la discussion aux Etats-Unis (années 1820 – années 1830)', *Revue française de science politique* 60(1): 136–141.

— (2012) 'À quoi servent les meetings dans une campagne électorale?', *Mediapart*.

— (2012) '2012, la guerre des meetings de plein air', *Atlantico*.

Cossart, Paula, Talpin, Julien and Keith, William (2012) 'Comparer les pratiques délibératives à travers les époques: une aberration historique?', *Participations* 2(3): 5–47.

Couprie, Claude (1905) *L'association déclarée d'après la loi de 1901*, Paris, Impr. de H. Jouve.

Courtine, Jean-Jacques (1990) 'Les glissements du spectacle politique', *Esprit* 9: 152–164.

Cowans, Jon (2001) *To Speak for the People. Public Opinion and the Problem of Legitimacy in the French Revolution*, New York/London, Routledge.

Cumenge, Germain (1881) *Dissertation sur le droit de réunion lue à la séance solennelle de rentrée des avocats stagiaires le 5 décembre 1880*, Toulouse, Douladoure-Privat.

D'Almeida, Fabrice (1993) 'La SFIO, la propagande, les affiches (1945–1969)', *Cahiers et Revue de l'OURS* 211: 21–24.

— (2001) 'Terreurs de la France modérée. Les affiches du Centre de propagande des républicains nationaux dans l'entre-deux-guerres', *Sociétés et Représentations* 12: 253–267.

Dalotel, Alain, Faure, Alain and Freiermuth, Jean-Claude (1980) *Aux origines de la Commune. Le mouvement des réunions publiques à Paris. 1868–1870*, Paris, F. Maspero.
Dalton, Russell J. [1996] (2002) *Citizen Politics. Public Opinion and Political Parties in Advanced Industrial Democracies*, New York, Chatham House Publishers, Seven Bridges Press.
Dansette, Adrien (1946) *Le boulangisme*, Paris, Fayard.
D'Arcy, François and Saez, Guy (1985) 'De la représentation', in F. D'Arcy (ed.) *La représentation*, Paris, Economica, pp. 7–31.
Dayan, Daniel (1992) 'Les mystères de la réception', *Le Débat* 71: 146–162.
Déat, Marcel (1989) *Mémoires politiques*, Paris, Denoël.
De Certeau, Michel (1990) *L'invention du quotidien. 1. Arts de faire*, Paris, Gallimard.
De Falloux, Alfred (1888) *Mémoires d'un royaliste*, Paris, Perrin & Cie.
Degrenne, Marcel-Louis (1938) *Les réunions et les pouvoirs de police*, Caen, Caron & Cie.
De Jomaron, Jacqueline (1992) *Le théâtre en France*, vol. 2, Paris, A. Colin.
Delattre, Eugène (1863) *Devoirs du suffrage universel*, Paris, Pagnerre.
Della Porta, Donatella and Diani, Mario [1999] (2006) *Social Movements. An Introduction*, Oxford, Blackwell.
Déloye, Yves (1992) 'Le geste parlementaire. Charles Hacks ou la sémiologie du geste politique au XIXe siècle', *Politix* 20: 129–134.
— (1994) *École et citoyenneté. L'individualisme républicain de Jules Ferry à Vichy. Controverses*, Paris, Presses de la FNSP.
— (1997) *Sociologie historique du politique*, Paris, La Découverte.
— (1997) 'Idée républicaine et citoyenneté. L'expérience française (1870–1945)', in J.-M. Lecomte and J.-P. Sylvestre (eds) *Culture républicaine, citoyenneté et lien social*, Dijon, CRDP de Bourgogne, pp. 67–83.
— (1998) 'L'apprentissage de la citoyenneté', *Cahiers français* 285: 76–82.
— (2000) 'Le charisme contrôlé. Entre grandeur et raison. La posture publique de Léon Gambetta', *Communications* 69: 157–172.
— (2002) 'Des incidents électoraux. Éléments pour une autre histoire du suffrage électoral', in M. Bernard, P. Bourdin and J.-C. Caron (eds) *L'incident électoral de la Révolution française à la Ve République*, Clermont-Ferrand, Presses Universitaires Blaise Pascal, pp. 19–43.
Déloye, Yves and Ihl, Olivier (1993) 'La civilité électorale: vote et forclusion de la violence en France', *Cultures & Conflits* 9–10: 75–96.
— (2000) 'Deux figures singulières de l'universel: la République et le sacré', in Sadoun (ed.) *La démocratie en France*, vol. 1, Paris, Gallimard, pp. 138–246.
De Molinari, Gustave (1871) *Les clubs rouges pendant le siège de Paris*, Paris, Garnier Frères.
— (1872) *Le mouvement socialiste et les réunions publiques avant la révolution du 4 septembre 1870*, Paris, Garnier Frères.
De Pressensé, Edmond (1869) *Les réunions publiques à Paris et les élections prochaines*, Paris, Librairie Meyrueis et Librairie Le Chevalier.

De Pressensé, Francis (un juriste) and Pouget, Émile (1899) *Les Lois scélérates de 1893–1894*, Paris, Éditions de la *Revue blanche*.
Deschanel, Émile (1870) *Les conférences à Paris et en Province*, Paris, Librairie Pagnerre.
Dictionnaire de l'Académie française (1878) 7th edn, Paris, F. Didot.
Dictionnaire biographique du mouvement ouvrier français, Le Maitron 2, 1864–1871, CD Rom, Éditions de l'Atelier.
Dictionnaire biographique du mouvement ouvrier français, Le Maitron 3, 1871–1914, CD Rom, Éditions de l'Atelier.
Dictionnaire biographique du mouvement ouvrier français, Le Maitron 4, 1914–1940, CD Rom, Éditions de l'Atelier.
Doggan, Mattéi (1967) 'Les filières de la carrière politique en France', *Revue française de sociologie* 8(4): 468–492.
Dompnier, Nathalie (1992) *La clef des urnes. La construction socio-historique de la déviance électorale en France depuis 1848*, PhD dissertation, IEP Grenoble, Université Grenoble II.
Dubois, George (1869) *Commentaire théorique et pratique de la loi du 6 juin 1868 sur les réunions publiques*, Paris, Imprimerie et Librairie Générale de Jurisprudence.
Duclerc, Eugène and Pagnerre Laurent-Antoine, *Dictionnaire politique, Encyclopédie du langage et de la science politique*, Paris, Pagnerre, 1842.
Dynneson, Thomas L. (2001) *Civism. Cultivating Citizenship in European History*, New York, Peter Lang.
Elias, Norbert (1969) *The Civilizing Process*, vol. I. *The History of Manners*, Oxford, Blackwell.
— (1976) *La Dynamique de l'Occident*, Paris, Calmann-Lévy.
Estèbe, Jean (1982) *Les ministres de la République. 1871–1914*, Paris, FNSP.
Fabreguettes, Polydore (1884) *Traité des infractions de la parole, de l'écriture et de la presse*, Paris, A. Chevalier-Marescq.
Faget de Casteljau, A. de (1905) *Histoire du droit d'association de 1789 à 1901*, Paris, A. Rousseau.
Faure, Émile and Fontaine de Rambouillet, Anatole (1869) *Le peuple et la place publique. Historique du droit de réunion*, Paris, Décembre-Alonnier.
Feyel, Gilles (1999) *La presse en France des origines à 1944. Histoire politique et matérielle*, Paris, Ellipses.
Fillieule, Olivier (1993) 'L'émergence de la violence dans la manifestation de rue. Éléments pour une analyse étiologique', *Cultures & Conflits* 9–10: 267–291.
— (1997) *Stratégies de la rue. Les manifestations en France*, Paris, Presses de Sciences Po.
Fishkin, James (1991) *Democracy and Deliberation. New Directions for Democratic Reform*, New Haven CT, Yale University Press.
— (1997) *The Voice of the People. Public Opinion and Democracy*, New Haven CT, Yale University Press.
Ford, Caroline C. (1993) *Creating the Nation in Provincial France. Religion and Political Identity in Brittany*, Princeton NJ, Princeton University Press.

Forstenzer, Thomas R. (1981) *French Provincial Police and the Fall of the Second Republic. Social Fear and Counterrevolution*, Princeton NJ, Princeton University Press.
Fournier, Éric (2008) *La Cité du sang. Les bouchers de La Villette contre Dreyfus*, Paris, Libertalia.
Fournier-Poncelet, Jean (1910) *La liberté de réunion au XXᵉ siècle. Étude de droit public comparé*, Université d'Aix-Marseille, Typographie et lithographie Barlatier.
Franceschini, E. (1993) 'Combes (Jean-Louis)', in Jean-Charles Roman D'Amat (ed.) *Dictionnaire de biographie française*, Paris, Letouzey & Ané, vol. 9, pp. 367–368.
Fretel, Julien (2004) 'Le parti comme fabrique de notables. Réflexions sur les pratiques notabiliaires des élus de l'UDF', *Politix* 17(65): 45–72.
Fretel, Julien and Lefebvre, Rémi (2004) 'Retour sur un lieu commun historiographique. La faiblesse des partis politiques en France', *Journées AFSP Science politique/Histoire*, http://www.afsp.msh-paris.fr/activite/ diversafsp/ collhistscpo04/hist04fretel.pdf.
Fulton, Bruce (1991) 'The Boulanger Affair Revisited. The Preservation of the Third Republic', *French Historical Studies* 17(2): 310–329.
Fureix, Emmanuel (2002) 'Un rituel d'opposition sous la Restauration. Les funérailles libérales à Paris (1820–1830)', *Genèses* 46: 77–100.
— (2004) 'Banquets et enterrements', in J.-J. Becker and G. Candar (eds) *Histoire des gauches en France*, vol. 1, Paris, La Découverte, pp. 197–209.
Furet, François and Ozouf, Mona (eds) (1988) *Dictionnaire critique de la Révolution Française*, Paris, Flammarion.
Gainot, Bernard (2001) *1799, Un nouveau jacobinisme? La démocratie représentative, une alternative à Brumaire*, Paris, CTHS.
Garraud, René (1895) *L'anarchie et la répression*, Paris, L. Larose.
Garrigou, Alain (1992) *Le vote et la vertu. Comment les Français sont devenus électeurs*, Paris, Presses de la FNSP.
— (2002) *Histoire sociale du suffrage universel en France. 1848–2000*, Paris, Seuil.
Gauchet, Marcel and Raynaud, Philippe (1995) 'La République enlisée', *Le Banquet* 6: 174–188.
Gaxie, Daniel and Lehingue, Patrick (1984) *Enjeux municipaux. La constitution des enjeux politiques dans une élection municipale*, Paris, PUF CURAPP.
Gérome, Noëlle and Tartakowsky, Danielle (1988) *La fête de l'Humanité. Culture communiste, culture populaire*, Paris, Messidor, Éditions Sociales.
Gervais, Louis (1913) *Du droit de réunion en France et en Angleterre*, Université de Montpellier, Impr. De Firmin et Montane.
Girieud, Joseph (1901) *Du régime des attroupements. Etude historique et critique*, Université d'Aix, Typographe et lithographe B. Niel.
Goujon, Pierre (1993) *Le vigneron citoyen. Mâconnais et Chalonnais, 1848–1914*, Paris, CTHS.

Gould, Roger V. (1995) *Insurgent Identities. Class, Community, and Protest in Paris from 1848 to the Commune*, Chicago, University of Chicago Press.
Granier, Caroline (2003) '*Nous sommes des briseurs de formules*'. *Les écrivains anarchistes en France à la fin du XIXe siècle*, PhD dissertation, Paris VIII, http://raforum.apinc.org/article.php3?id_article=2470.
Grave, Jean (1893) *La société mourante et l'anarchie*, Paris, Tresse et Stock.
Gueissaz, Mireille (1994) 'Jules Barni (1818–1878) ou l'entreprise démopédique d'un républicain moraliste et libre-penseur', in *Les bonnes mœurs*, Paris, PUF, pp. 215–244.
Guillemin, Alain (1982) 'Aristocrates, propriétaires et diplômés. La lutte pour le pouvoir local dans le département de la Manche 1830–1875', *Actes de la Recherche en Sciences Sociales* 42: 33–60.
Guionnet, Christine (1997) *L'apprentissage de la politique moderne. Les élections municipales sous la Monarchie de Juillet*, Paris, L'Harmattan.
Gunn, John A. W. (1989) 'Public Opinion', in T. Ball, J. Farr and R. L. Hanson (eds) *Political Innovation and Conceptual Change*, Cambridge, Cambridge University Press, pp. 247–265.
Gutmann, Amy and Thompson, Dennis F. (2004) *Why Deliberative Democracy?*, Princeton NJ, Princeton University Press.
Habermas, Jürgen [1962] (1989) *The Structural Transformation of the Public Sphere: An Inquiry into a Category of Bourgeois Society*, Cambridge, Polity.
— [1992] (1998) *Between Facts and Norms. Contributions to a Discourse Theory of Law and Democracy*, Cambridge MA, MIT Press.
Haine, W. Scott (1996) *The World of the Paris Café. Sociability among the French Working Class, 1789–1914*, Baltimore, Johns Hopkins University Press.
Halévy, Daniel (1930) *La fin des notables*, vol. 1, Paris, Grasset.
Halévy, Daniel and Pillias, Émile (1938) *Lettres de Gambetta, 1868–1882*, Paris, Grasset.
Halpérin, Jean-Louis (ed.) (1996) *Avocats et notaires en Europe. Les professions judiciaires et juridiques dans l'histoire contemporaine*, Paris, LGDJ.
Haroche, Claudine (1993) 'Retenue dans les mœurs et maîtrise de la violence politique', *Cultures & Conflits* 9–10: 45–59.
Harvey, David W. (2003) *Paris, Capital of Modernity*, New York, Routledge.
Hatzfeld, Adolphe and Darmesteter, Arsène (with A. Thomas) (1900) *Dictionnaire général de la langue française du commencement du XVIIe siècle à nos jours*, vol. 2, Paris, Ch. Delagrave.
Hauriou, Maurice (1893) *Précis de droit administratif contenant le droit public et le droit administratif*, Paris, L. Larose et Forcel.
Hazareesingh, Sudhir (2001) *Intellectual Founders of the Republic. Five Studies in Nineteenth Century French Political Thought*, Oxford, Oxford University Press.
Hayat, Samuel (2006) 'La République, la rue et l'urne', *Pouvoirs* 116: 31–44.
Herbst, Susan (1993) *Numbered Voices. How Opinion Polling Has Shaped American Politics*, Chicago, Chicago University Press.

— (1995) 'On the Disappearance of Groups: 19th and Early 20th Century Conceptions of Public Opinion', in T. L. Glasser and C. T. Salmon (eds) *Public Opinion and the Communication of Consent*, New York, The Guiford Press, pp. 89–104.
— (1995) 'Election Polling in Historical Perspective', in P. J. Lavrakas, P. V. Miller and M. W. Traugott (eds) *Presidential Polls and the News Media*, Boulder, Westview, pp. 23–33.
Hetzel, Anne-Marie. (n.d.) 'Maurice La Châtre (1814–1900)', *Musée virtuel des dictionnaires*, http://www.u-cergy.fr/dictionnaires/auteurs/la_chatre.html (accessed 6 June 2006).
Heurtin, Jean-Philippe (1999) *L'espace public parlementaire. Essai sur les raisons du législateur*, Paris, PUF.
Heymann-Doat, Arlette and Calves, Gwénaële (2005) *Libertés publiques et droits de l'homme*, Paris, LGDJ.
Huard, Raymond (1982) *Le mouvement républicain en Bas-Languedoc, 1848–1881*, Presses de la FNSP, Paris.
— (1985) 'Existe-t-il une "politique populaire"?', in J. Nicolas (ed.) *Mouvements populaires et conscience sociale. XVIe–XIXe siècles*, Paris, CNRS, Université de Paris VII, Maloine, pp. 57–68.
— (1991) *Le suffrage universel en France (1848–1946)*, Paris, Aubier.
— (1994) 'Aboutissements préparés et cristallisations imprévues. La formation des partis', in P. Birnbaum (ed.) *La France de l'affaire Dreyfus*, Paris, Gallimard, pp. 87–119.
— (1996) *La naissance du parti politique en France*, Paris, Presses de la FNSP.
— (2000) 'Political Association in Nineteenth Century France. Legislation and Practice', in N. Bermeo and P. Nord (eds) *Civil Society Before Democracy. Lessons from Nineteenth-Century Europe*, Lanham, Rowman & Littlefield, pp. 135–153.
Hutton, Patrick H. (1976) 'Popular Boulangism and the Advent of Mass Politics in France, 1886–1890', *Journal of Contemporary History* 11(1): 85–106.
Ihl, Olivier (1996) *La fête républicaine*, Paris, Gallimard.
— (1998) 'De bouche à oreille. Sur les pratiques de commensalité dans la tradition républicaine du cérémonial de table', *Revue française de science politique* 48(3–4): 387–408.
— [1996] (2000) *Le vote*, Paris, Montchrestien.
Imbert, Jean (1984) 'Passé, présent et avenir du doctorat de droit en France', *Annales d'histoire des facultés de droit* 1: 11–34.
Ion, Jacques (1997) *La fin des militants?*, Paris, Éditions de l'Atelier.
Jackson, Julian (1988) *The Popular Front in France Defending Democracy. 1924–1938*, Cambridge/New York, Cambridge University Press.
Jardin, André and Tudesq, André-Jean (1973) *La France des notables. 1. L'évolution générale. 1815–1848*, Paris, Seuil.
Jensen, Richard (1969) 'Armies, Admen and Crusaders. Types of Presidential Election Campaigns', *The History Teacher* 2(2): 33–50.

Joana, Jean (1999) *Pratiques politiques des députés français au XIXe siècle. Du dilettante au spécialiste*, Paris, L'Harmattan.
Johnson, Martin Philip (1996) *The Paradise of Association. Political Culture and Popular Organizations in the Paris Commune of 1871*, Ann Arbor, University of Michigan Press.
Joly, Bertrand (2001) 'The Jeunesse Antisémite et Nationaliste, 1894–1904', in R. Tombs (ed.), *Nationhood and Nationalism in France. From Boulangism to the Great War. 1889–1918*, London, Routledge, pp. 147–158.
Joubrel, Albert (1904) *Du droit de réunion*, Rennes, Librairie générale Pilhon et Hommay.
Jouet, Alphonse (1891) *Des clubs*, Paris, A. Giard, Henri Jouve.
Kale, Steven D. (1992) *Legitimism and the Reconstruction of French Society. 1852–1883*, Baton Rouge, Louisiana State University Press.
Karila-Cohen, Pierre (2003) *'L'État des esprits'. L'administration et l'observation de l'opinion départementale en France sous la monarchie constitutionnelle (1814–1848)*, PhD dissertation, Paris I.
Labarthe, Émile (1938) *Gambetta et ses amis*, Paris, Éditions des Presses Modernes.
Lacroix, Bernard (1994) 'La "crise de la démocratie représentative en France". Éléments pour une discussion sociologique du problème', *Scalpel* 1: 6–29.
Lagadec, Yann (2003) 'Quelles élites pour le progrès agricole au XIXe siècle? L'exemple des comices agricoles bretons', in F. Pitou (ed.) *Elites et notables de l'Ouest. XVIe–XXe siècle. Entre conservatisme et modernité*, Rennes, PUR, pp. 105–120.
Lagoueyte, Patrick (1990) *Candidature officielle et pratiques électorales sous le Second Empire (1852–1870)*, PhD dissertation, Paris I.
Laidié, Franck (2005) 'L'insulte en politique saisie par le droit', in T. Bouchet, M. Leggett, J. Vigreux and G. Verdo (eds) *L'insulte (en) politique. Europe et Amérique latine du XIXe siècle à nos jours*, Dijon, Éditions Universitaires de Dijon, pp. 259–268.
Lalouette, Jacqueline (2002) 'Banqueter', in V. Duclert and C. Prochasson (eds) *Dictionnaire critique de la République*, Paris, Flammarion, pp. 988–993.
— (2005) *La séparation des Églises et de l'État. Genèse et développement d'une idée, 1789–1905*, Paris, Le Seuil.
Lalouette, Jacqueline and Machelon, Jean-Pierre (eds) (2002) *Les congrégations hors la loi? Autour de la loi du 1er juillet 1901*, Paris, Letouzey & Ané.
Lambert, Pierre-Arnaud (1995) *La Charbonnerie française, 1821–1823. Du secret en politique*, Lyon, Presses Universitaires de Lyon.
Larousse, Pierre (1865–1878) *Grand dictionnaire universel du XIXe siècle*, Paris, Administration du grand dictionnaire universel.
Lawrence, Jon (2009) *Electing Our Masters. The Hustings in British Politics from Hogarth to Blair*, Oxford, Oxford University Press.
Le Béguec, Gilles (2001) 'Le moment 1901', in C. Andrieu, G. Le Béguec and D. Tartakowsky (eds) *Associations et champ politique. La loi de 1901 à l'épreuve du siècle*, Paris, Publications de la Sorbonne, pp. 67–74.

Le Bon, Gustave (1895) *Psychologie des foules*, Paris, Alcan.
Leca, Jean [1986] (1991) 'Individualisme et citoyenneté', in P. Birnbaum and J. Leca (eds) *Sur l'individualisme. Théories et méthodes*, Paris, Presses de la FNSP, pp. 159–209.
Le Clère, Marcel (1945) *Les réunions, manifestations et attroupements en droit français et comparé*, Paris, Impr. Petites Affiches.
Lecomte, Maxime (1888) *Le boulangisme dans le Nord. Histoire de l'élection du 15 avril*, Paris, À la librairie illustrée.
Lefebvre, Edouard-René (1903) *Le droit de réunion*, Paris, Impr. H. Bouillant.
Lefebvre, Rémi (2001), '"Le conseil des buveurs de bière" de Roubaix (1892–1902). Subversion et apprentissage des règles du jeu institutionnel', *Politix* 14(53): 87–116.
Lehning, James R. (2001) *To Be a Citizen. The Political Culture of the Early French Third Republic*, Ithaca, Cornell University Press.
Leyret, Henry (1895) *En plein faubourg (mœurs ouvrières)*, Paris, G. Charpentier et E. Fasquelle.
Littré, Émile (1863–1869) *Dictionnaire de la langue française*, Paris, Hachette.
Lochak, Danièle (1994) 'Le droit à l'épreuve des bonnes mœurs. Puissance et impuissance de la norme juridique', in *Les bonnes mœurs*, Paris, PUF, pp. 15–53.
Loubat, Guillaume (1895) *Code de la législation contre les anarchistes*, Paris, Chevalier-Marescq.
Lynch, Édouard (2005) 'Le Parti agraire et paysan français entre politique et manifestation', *Histoire et sociétés* 13: 54–66.
Machelon, Jean-Pierre (1976) *La République contre les libertés? Les restrictions aux libertés publiques de 1879 à 1914*, Paris, FNSP.
— (2001) 'La liberté d'association sous la IIIe République. Le temps du refus (1871–1901)', in C. Andrieu, G. Le Béguec and D. Tartakowsky (eds) *Associations et champ politique. La loi de 1901 à l'épreuve du siècle*, Paris, Publications de la Sorbonne, pp. 141–155.
Mac-Nab, Maurice (2002) *Poèmes mobiles. Œuvres complètes*, Paris, L'Atelier des Brisants.
Maitron, Jean (1975) *Le mouvement anarchiste en France*, Paris, Maspero.
Manfredonia, Gaetano (1990) *Études sur le mouvement anarchiste en France (1848–1914)*, PhD dissertation, IEP Paris.
Manin, Bernard (1997) *Principles of Representative Government*, Cambridge, Cambridge University Press.
Mann, Patrice (1991) *L'action collective. Mobilisation et organisation des minorités actives*, Paris, A. Colin.
Marandon, Sylvaine (1982) 'Français et Juifs dans la conscience anglaise', in J. Pirotte (ed.) *Stéréotypes nationaux et préjugés raciaux aux XIXe et XXe siècles. Sources et méthodes pour une approche historique*, Louvain-la-Neuve, Collège Erasme, Leuven, Nauwelaerts, pp. 4–18.
Mariot, Nicolas (1995) '"Propagande par la vue". Souveraineté régalienne et gestion du nombre dans les voyages en province de Carnot (1888–1894)', *Genèses* 20: 24–47.

— (1998) 'Morphologie des comportements et induction de croyances. Quelques remarques à propos de l'exemplaire circularité de la fonction intégratrice des rites', *Hypothèses 1997. Travaux de l'École doctorale d'histoire de l'Université Paris I-Panthéon Sorbonne*, pp. 59–66.

— (1999) *Conquérir unanimement les cœurs. Usages politiques et scientifiques des rites. Le cas du voyage présidentiel en province, 1888–1998*, PhD dissertation, Paris, EHESS.

— (2001) 'Les formes élémentaires de l'effervescence collective, ou l'état d'esprit prêté aux foules', *Revue française de science politique* 51(5): 707–738.

— (2002) '"Nos fleurs et nos cœurs". La visite présidentielle comme évènement institué', *Terrain* 38: 79–96.

— (2006) 'Le frisson fait-il la manifestation?', *Pouvoirs* 116: 87–99.

Marpeau, Benoît (2000) *Gustave Le Bon. Parcours d'un intellectuel. 1841–1931*, Paris, Éditions CNRS.

Martin, Pierre Éric (2002) *Le mouvement anarchiste français et la violence politique. 1892–1894*, M.A. IEP Paris.

Martinez, Gilles (1998) 'Joseph Barthélémy et la crise de la démocratie libérale', *Vingtième Siècle* 59: 28–47.

Masseras, Étienne (1969) *La campagne électorale de 1869*, Paris, A. Lacroix, Verboeckhover et Cie.

Mathieu, Maurice (1984) 'Un enjeu dans les luttes politiques dans la Vienne. Les comices et les sociétés agricoles. Vers 1880, début du XXe siècle', *Bulletin de la Société des antiquaires de l'ouest et des musées de Poitiers* 2: 457–484.

Mayeur, Jean-Marie (2008) *Léon Gambetta. La Patrie et la République*, Paris, Fayard.

McPhee, Peter (1992) *The Politics of Rural Life. Political Mobilization in the French Countryside, 1846–1852*, Oxford, Clarendon Press.

Méadel, Cécile and Proulx, Serge (1998) 'Usagers en chiffres, usagers en actes', in S. Proulx (ed.) *Accusé de réception. Le téléspectateur construit par les sciences sociales*, Québec, Presses Universitaires de Laval, Paris, L'Harmattan, pp. 79–94.

Menanteau, Maurice (1937) *Les nouveaux aspects de la liberté de réunion. Essai sur les caractères juridiques et politiques de la liberté de réunion en France*, Paris, Librairie technique et économique.

Merlet, Jean-François (2001) *Une grande loi de la Troisième République. La loi du 1er juillet 1901*, Paris, LGDJ.

Merriman, John M. (1978) *The Agony of the Republic. The Repression of the Left in Revolutionary France, 1848–1851*, New Haven CT, Yale University Press.

— (1991) *The Margins of City Life. Explorations on the French Urban Frontier, 1815–1851*, New York, Oxford University Press.

Million, René (2000) 'Histoire des banquets politiques', *Cahiers d'histoire sociale* 14: 99–116.

Milza, Pierre (1994) 'L'ultra-droite des années 1930', in M. Winock (ed.) *Histoire de l'extrême droite en France*, Paris, Le Seuil, pp. 157–189.
Miquet-Marty, François (1997) *Aux origines du parti politique moderne. Les groupes sociaux à l'épreuve du formalisme démocratique, France, 1848–1914*, PhD dissertation, EHESS.
Moch, Jules (1976) *Une si longue vie*, Paris, R. Laffont.
Mollenhauer, Daniel (1998) 'À la recherche de la "vraie République". Quelques jalons pour une histoire du radicalisme des débuts de la Troisième République', *Revue Historique* 607: 579–615.
Mollier, Jean-Yves (2004) *Le camelot et la rue. Politique et démocratie au tournant des XIXe et XXe siècles*, Paris, Fayard.
— (2005) 'Quand les camelots se politisent en manient l'insulte…', in T. Bouchet, M. Leggett, J. Vigreux and G. Verdo (eds) *L'insulte (en) politique. Europe et Amérique latine du XIXe siècle à nos jours*, Dijon, Éditions Universitaires de Dijon, pp. 53–61.
Monier, Frédéric (2002) *Le Front Populaire*, Paris, La Découverte.
Monnier, Raymonde (1994) *L'espace public démocratique. Essai sur l'opinion à Paris de la Révolution au Directoire*, Paris, Kimé.
Morange, Jean (2000) *Droits de l'homme et libertés publiques*, Paris, PUF.
Morgand, Léon (1884–1885) *La Loi municipale, commentaire de la loi du 5 avril 1884 sur l'organisation et les attributions des conseils municipaux*, Paris, Berger-Levrault
Moscovici, Serge (1981) *L'âge des foules. Un traité historique de psychologie des masses*, Paris, Fayard.
Mosse, George L. (1990) *Fallen Soldiers. Reshaping the Memory of the World Wars*, New York, Oxford University Press.
Nadaud, Éric (1990) 'Le renouvellement des pratiques militantes à la SFIO au début du Front Populaire (1934–1936)', *Le Mouvement Social* 153: 9–34.
Nicolet, Claude (1982) *L'idée républicaine en France. Essai d'histoire critique*, Paris, Gallimard.
Nord, Philip (1995) *The Republican Moment. Struggles for Democracy in Nineteenth Century France*, Cambridge MA, Harvard University Press.
Nourrisson, Paul (1920) *Histoire de la liberté d'association en France depuis 1789*, vol. 2, Paris, Sirey.
Nucé de Lamothe, Henri (1911) *La liberté de réunion en France. Réunions publiques proprement dites. Réunions publiques cultuelles. Réunions privées*, Toulouse, Impr. Sebille.
Nye, Robert. A. (1975) *The Origins of Crowd Psychology. Gustave Le Bon and the Crisis of Mass Democracy in the Third Republic*, London, Sage.
Offerlé, Michel (1979) *Les socialistes et Paris, 1881–1900, des communards aux conseillers municipaux*, PhD dissertation, Paris I.
— (1984) 'La mobilisation électorale en milieu urbain. L'exemple de la France à la fin du XIXe siècle', 2e Congrès national de l'AFSP, Grenoble.
— (1993) *Un homme, une voix? Histoire du suffrage universel*, Paris, Gallimard.
— (1994) *Sociologie des groupes d'intérêt*, Paris, Montchrestien.

— (1998) 'La nationalisation de la citoyenneté civique en France à la fin du XIXᵉ siècle', in R. Romanelli (ed.) *How Did they Become Voters? The History of Franchise in Modern European Representation*, The Hague, Kluwer Law International, pp. 37–52.

— (1999) 'Professions et profession politique', in M. Offerlé (ed.) *La profession politique. 19ᵉ–20ᵉ siècle*, Paris, Belin, pp. 7–35.

— 'Périmètres du politique et coproduction de la radicalité à la fin du XIXᵉ siècle', in A. Collovald and B. Gaïti (eds) *La démocratie aux extrêmes. Sur la radicalisation politique*, Paris, La Dispute, pp. 247–268.

— (2007) 'Capacités politiques et politisations: faire voter et voter, XIXᵉ–XXᵉ siècles', *Genèses* 67: 131–149, and 68: 145–160.

— (2007) 'De l'histoire électorale à la socio-histoire des électeurs', *Romantisme* 135: 61–69.

— (2008) 'Retour critique sur les répertoires de l'action collective (XVIIIᵉ–XXIᵉ siècles)', *Politix* 81: 181–202.

Ollivier, Émile (1905) *L'Empire libéral. Études, récits, souvenirs*, Paris, Garnier Frères.

Ory, Pascal (1994) *La belle illusion. Culture et politique sous le signe du Front Populaire. 1935–1938*, Paris, Plon.

Palmeira, Moacir and Hérédia, Beatriz (1993) 'Le temps de la politique', *Études rurales* 131–132: 73–87.

Papadopoulos, Yannis (2004) 'Délibération et action publique', *Swiss Political Science Review* 10(4): 147–157.

Papaud, Michel (1987) 'La répression durant le ministère Léon Faucher (janvier-mai 1849)', in Société d'Histoire de la Révolution de 1848 et des Révolutions du XIXᵉ siècle, *Maintien de l'ordre et polices en France et en Europe au XIXᵉ siècle*, Paris, Créaphis, pp. 93–102.

Perreux, Gabriel (1931) *Au temps des sociétés secrètes. La propagande républicaine au début de la Monarchie de Juillet (1830–1835)*, Paris, Hachette.

Perrot, Michelle (1973) *Les ouvriers en grève. France, 1871–1890*, Paris, La Haye, Mouton.

Petit, René (1883) *Du droit de réunion*, Paris, A. Cotillon.

Petit, Vincent (1993) *Légitimisme et catholicisme au début de la Troisième République, 1871–1883. L'exemple du département du Doubs*, M.A., Université de Franche-Comté.

Peyrard, Christine (1994) 'Les débats sur le droit d'association et de réunion sous le Directoire', *Annales historiques de la Révolution française* 3: 463–478.

Phelippeau, Eric (1993) 'La fabrication administrative des opinions politiques. votes, déclarations de candidature et verdict des préfets (1852–1914)', *Revue française de science politique* 43(4): 587–612.

— (1994) 'Conjonctures électorales et conjectures préfectorales. Le vote et la formation d'un savoir politico-administratif', *Scalpel* 1: 52–73.

— (1996) *Le baron de Mackau en politique. Contribution à l'étude de la professionnalisation politique*, PhD dissertation, Paris X.

— (1997) 'Sociogenèse de la profession politique', in A. Garrigou and B. Lacroix (eds) *Norbert Elias, la politique et l'histoire*, Paris, La Découverte, pp. 239–265.
— (2002) *L'invention de la politique moderne. Mackau, l'Orne et la République*, Paris, Belin.
Pichon, Adolphe (1905) *Des caractères distinctifs des associations soumises à la loi du 1er juillet 1901*, Paris, Impr. de H. Jouve.
Pilbeam, Pamela M. (1995) *Republicanism in Nineteenth Century France, 1814–1871*, London, Macmillan.
Pivert, Charles (1950) *Le parti socialiste et ses hommes. Souvenirs d'un militant*, Paris, France-éditions.
Pourcher, Yves (1990) '"Un homme une rose à la main", Meetings en Languedoc de 1985 à 1989', *Terrain* 15: 77–90.
Prendergast, Christopher (1992) *Paris and the Nineteenth Century*, Oxford, Blackwell.
Price, Roger (2001) *The French Second Empire. An Anatomy of Political Power*, Cambridge, Cambridge University Press.
Puibaraud, Louis (1880) *La législation sur le droit de réunion en France. Extrait de la Revue générale d'administration*, Paris, Berger-Levrault et Cie.
Rangeon, François (1986) *L'idéologie de l'intérêt général*, Paris, Economica.
Rawls, John (2001) *Justice as Fairness. A Restatement*, Cambridge MA, Harvard University Press.
Reddy, William M. (2001) *The Navigation of Feeling. A Framework for the History of Emotions*, New York, Cambridge University Press.
Redor, Marie-Joëlle (1992) *De l'État légal à l'État de droit. L'évolution des conceptions de la doctrine publiciste française. 1879–1914*, Aix-en-Provence, Presses Universitaires Aix-Marseille, Economica.
Reinach, Joseph (1918) *La vie politique de Léon Gambetta*, Paris, Alcan.
Reynié, Dominique (1988) 'Théories du nombre', *Hermès* 2: 95–104.
— (1998) *Le triomphe de l'opinion publique. L'espace public français du XVIe au XXe siècle*, Paris, Odile Jacob.
Rials, Stéphane (1987) *Révolution et contre-révolution au XIXe siècle*, Paris, Albatros.
Rivero, Jean and Moutouh, Hugues (2003) *Libertés publiques*, vol. 2, Paris, PUF.
Robert, Adolphe and Cougny, Gaston (1889–1891) *Dictionnaire des parlementaires français de 1789 à 1889*, Paris, Bourloton.
Robert, Vincent (1996) *Les chemins de la manifestation. 1848–1914*, Lyon, Presses Universitaires de Lyon.
— (2005) *Entre Réforme et Révolution. Horizons, rituels, sociabilités et souvenirs dans la France du dix-neuvième siècle*, Paris I, HDR.
Rodriguez, Miguel (1990) 'Le premier mai 1936 entre deux tours et deux époques', *Vingtième Siècle* 27: 55–60.
Roman D'Amat, Jean-Charles. et al. (eds) (1933) *Dictionnaire de biographie française*, Paris, Letouzey & Ané (20 vols.).
Rosanvallon, Pierre (1989) 'Malaise dans la représentation', in F. Furet, J. Julliard and P. Rosanvallon, *La République du centre. La fin de l'exception française*, Paris, Calmann-Lévy, pp. 133–182.

— (1992) *Le sacre du citoyen. Histoire du suffrage universel en France*, Paris, Gallimard.
— (1997) 'Les élites françaises, la démocratie et l'État. Entretien avec Pierre Rosanvallon', *Esprit* 236: 60–72.
— (1998) *Le peuple introuvable. Histoire de la représentation démocratique en France*, Paris, Gallimard.
— (2000) *La démocratie inachevée. Histoire de la souveraineté du peuple en France*, Paris, Gallimard.
— (2002–2003) 'Les corps intermédiaires dans la démocratie', lecture held at the Collège de France, Online. Available http://www.college-de-france.fr/media/his_pol/UPL25235_prosanvallon.pdf (accessed 6 June 2006).
— (2006) *Le modèle politique français. La société civile contre le jacobinisme de 1789 à nos jours*, Paris, Le Seuil.
Rougerie, Jacques (1995) *Paris insurgé. La Commune de 1871*, Paris, Gallimard.
Rousselle, André and Limousin, Charles (1869) *Manuel des réunions publiques non politiques, publiques électorales, électorales privées*, Paris, A. Le Chevalier.
Roussellier, Nicolas (2000) 'Deux formes de représentation politique: le citoyen et l'individu', in M. Sadoun (ed.) *La démocratie en France*, vol. 1, Paris, Gallimard, pp. 247–331.
— (2001) 'La diffusion de l'éloquence en France sous la IIIe République', in F. D'Almeida (ed.) *L'éloquence politique en France et en Italie de 1870 à nos jours*, Rome, École française de Rome, pp. 41–46.
Rutkoff, Peter M. (1974) 'The Ligue des Patriotes. The Nature of the Radical Right and the Dreyfus Affair', *French Historical Studies* 8(4): 585–603.
Sacriste, Guillaume (2002) *Le droit de la République (1870–1914). Légitimation(s) de l'Etat et construction du rôle de professeur de droit constitutionnel au début du siècle*, PhD dissertation, Paris I.
Sanders, Lynn M. (1997) 'Against Deliberation', *Political Theory* 25(3): 347–376.
Sassi, Odile (1999) *Léon Gambetta. Destin et mémoire. 1838–1938*, PhD dissertation, Paris IV.
Saulnier, Fédéric (2004) *Joseph Barthélémy. 1874–1945. La crise du constitutionnalisme libéral sous la IIIe République*, Paris, LGDJ.
Schulkind, Eugene W. (1960) 'The Activity of Popular Organizations during the Paris Commune of 1871', *French Historical Studies* 1(4): 394–415.
Schweitz, Arlette (2001) *Les parlementaires sous la Troisième République. II. Dictionnaire biographique*, Paris, Publications de la Sorbonne.
Sebastián, Javier Fernández (2004) 'L'avènement de l'opinion publique et le problème de la représentation politique (France, Espagne, Royaume-Uni)', in J. F. Sébastián and J. Chassin (eds) *L'avènement de l'opinion publique. Europe et Amérique, XVIIe–XIXe siècles*, Paris, L'Harmattan, pp. 227–251.
Sebastián, Javier Fernández and Chassin, Joëlle (eds) (2004) *L'avènement de l'opinion publique. Europe et Amérique, XVIIe–XIXe siècles*, Paris, L'Harmattan.

Secondy, Philippe (2003) 'Royalisme et innovations partisanes. Les "blancs du Midi" à la fin du XIXe siècle', *Revue française de science politique* 53(1): 73–99.
Shapiro, Ian (2002) 'Optimal Deliberation?', *The Journal of Political Philosophy* 10(2): 196–211.
Simon, Jules (1869) '*Les réunions publiques*', extract from *Journal Officiel*, (10 August 1868) Paris, Degorce-Cadot.
— (1901) *Le soir de ma journée*, Paris, Flammarion.
Sonn, Richard David (1989) *Anarchism and Cultural Politics in Fin de Siècle France*, Lincoln, University of Nebraska Press.
Sorrel, Christian (2003) *La République contre les congrégations. Histoire d'une passion française (1899–1904)*, Paris, Cerf.
Soucy, Robert J. (2004) *Fascismes français? 1933–1939. Mouvements antidémocratiques*, Paris, Autrement.
Spitzer, Alan (1971) *Old Hatred and Young Hopes. The French Carbonari Against the Bourbon Restauration*, Cambridge MA, Harvard University Press.
Stern, Daniel (1850–1855) *Histoire de la Révolution de 1848*, vol. 2, Paris, Sandré.
Sternhell, Zeev [1978] (1997) *La droite révolutionnaire. 1885–1914. Les origines françaises du fascisme*, Paris, Gallimard.
Talpin, Julien (2005) 'Des écoles de démocratie? Formation à la citoyenneté et démocratie participative', http://www.univ-paris8.fr/scpo/talpin.doc.
— (2006) 'Jouer les bons citoyens. Les effets contrastés de l'engagement au sein de dispositifs participatifs', *Politix* 19(75): 13–31.
Tarde, Gabriel (1901) *L'opinion et la foule*, Paris, Alcan.
Tartakowsky, Danielle (1989) 'La manifestation comme mort de la révolte', *Révolte et société*, vol. 2, Paris, Publications de la Sorbonne, pp. 239–248.
— (1997) *Les manifestations de rue en France. 1918–1968*, Paris, Publications de la Sorbonne.
Tartakowsky, Danielle and Corbin, Alain (1998) 'Théâtre et politique', *Revue française d'histoire des idées politiques* 8: 227–400.
Tchernoff, Iouda (1901) *Le parti républicain sous la Monarchie de Juillet. Formation et évolution de la doctrine républicaine*, Paris, A. Pedone.
— (1905) *Associations et sociétés secrètes sous la deuxième République, 1848–1851*, Paris, F. Alcan.
— (1906) *Le Parti républicain au coup d'État et sous le deuxième Empire*, Paris, A. Pedone.
Théry, Irène (1993) 'Le droit et les mœurs, un enjeu politique. La refonte du code civil et le paradoxe de la situation française', *L'Année sociologique* 43: 85–124.
Thiec, Yvon J. and Treanton, Jean-René (1983) 'La foule comme objet de "science"', *Revue française de sociologie* 24(1): 119–136.
Thuot, Jean François (1998) *La fin de la représentation et les formes contemporaines de la démocratie*, Montreal, Nota Bene.
Thurat, Henri (1883) *Gambetta. Sa vie, son œuvre*, Paris, Bibliothèque des Communes.

Tilly, Charles (1984) 'Les origines du répertoire de l'action collective contemporaine en France et en Grande-Bretagne', *Vingtième Siècle* 4(4): 89–108.
Tulard, Jean (1990) *Guide des films*, Paris, R. Laffont.
Van Ginneken, Jaap (1992) *Crowds, Psychology, and Politics, 1871–1899*, Cambridge/New York, Cambridge University Press.
Varias, Alexander (1997) *Paris and the Anarchists. Aesthetes and Subversives at the Fin-de-Siècle*, Basingstoke, Macmillan.
Vigier, Philippe (1991) *Paris pendant la Monarchie de Juillet, 1830–1848*, Paris, Hachette.
Vincent-Buffault, Anne (1986) *Histoire des larmes. XVIIIe–XIXe siècles*, Paris, Rivages.
Vitu, Auguste (1869) *Les réunions publiques à Paris. 1868–1869*, Paris, Éditions Dentu (published anonymously).
Voilliot, Christophe (2005) *La candidature officielle. Une pratique d'État de la Restauration à la Troisième République*, Rennes, PUR.
Wall, Irwin M. (1970) 'French Socialism and the Popular Front', *Journal of Contemporary History* 5(3): 3–20.
Walzer, Michael (1983) *Spheres of Justice. A Defense of Pluralism and Equality*, New York, Basic Books.
Weber, Eugen (1983) *La fin des terroirs. La modernisation de la France rurale. 1870–1914*, Paris, Fayard.
Weill, Georges (1928) *Histoire du parti républicain en France (1814–1870)*, Paris, F. Alcan
Wilson, Stephen (1973) 'The Antisemitic Riots of 1898 in France', *The Historical Journal* 16(4): 789–806.
Winock, Michel (2006) 'Retour sur le fascisme français. La Rocque et les Croix-de-Feu', *Vingtième Siècle* 90: 3–27.
Wolfe, Robert David (1966) *The Origins of the Paris Commune. The Popular Organizations of 1868–1871*, PhD dissertation, Harvard University.
Woloch, Isser (1970) *Jacobin Legacy. The Democratic Movement Under the Directory*, Princeton NJ, Princeton University Press.

Sources

I. Archives

Archives Nationales

AD I / 91 (dos. B) : Sociétés populaires en général (lois, décrets, rapports et débats législatifs) 1789–an VII.
AD XVI / 73 : Jacobins, 1790–1793.
F7 / 3659-1 : Département des Bouches-du-Rhône. Ministère de l'Intérieur. Correspondance et pièces relatives à la mission des commissaires civils (« envoyés pour y apaiser les troubles »). 1790–1791.
F7 / 12431 : Agissements royalistes. Renseignements de toute nature concernant leur activité. 1883–1902.
F7 / 12451 : Ligue des Patriotes. Articles de journaux et notes de police. 1889–1907.
F7 / 12459 : Antisémites. 1890–1907
F7 / 12466 : Affaire Dreyfus. Réunions. Belgique et France. Classement départemental. 1898–1899.
F7 / 12468 : Surveillance des nationalistes dans le département de la Seine. 1899–1907.
F7 / 12481 : Action électorale catholique. 1895–1904.
F7 / 12504 : Agitation anarchique. Tournées de conférences. 1882–1898.
F7 / 12951 à 12961 : Notes « Jean ». 1918–1936.
F7 / 12962 à 12966 : Notes journalières de la Préfecture de Police sur les réunions et manifestations. 1930–1938
F7 / 13079 : Notes politiques générales sur le parti socialiste. 1928–1932.
F7 / 13080 à 13085 : Activité du parti socialiste. Notes, rapports, extraits de presse. Classement départemental. 1926–1932.
F7 / 13092 à 13095 : Circulaires du P.C.F. 1924–1929
F7 / 13096 à 13098 : Activité des cellules communistes. 1924–1926
F7 / 13102 : Notes générales sur l'activité du P.C.F. 1923–1924.
F7 / 13103 : Notes générales sur l'activité du P.C.F. Département de la Seine. 1925–1926.
F7 / 13104 : activité P.C.F. Notes générales. Rhône-Alpes. 1926.
F7 / 13190 : Affiches, tracts, papillons concernant la propagande communiste. 1928–1930.
F7 / 13319 à 13320 : Réunions et manifestations diverses. 1926; 1934–1935

Archives de la Préfecture de Police

Ba / 62 : Comités bonapartistes. 1874–1889.
Ba / 260 : Elections municipales générales. Réunions électorales. 1er et 9 mai 1904.
Ba / 362 : Réunions publiques. Coupures de journaux. 1869.
Ba / 401 à 405 : Menées légitimistes. 1872–1888.
Ba / 510 : Propagande bonapartiste. Paris. 1878.
Ba / 571 à 577 : Elections 1876. Réunions publiques et privées. Paris et banlieue. 1876.
Ba / 614 : Elections de 1885. Réunions. Paris. 1885.
Ba / 617 : Réunion au Palais de la Bourse. Fédération des travailleurs socialistes de France. Parti ouvrier. Possibilistes. 20 septembre 1885.
Ba / 628 : Elections de 1889. Rapports sur la situation électorale. Paris. 1889.
Ba / 631 : Elections législatives des 22 septembre et 6 octobre 1889 (scrutin de ballottage). Réunions électorales. 1889.
Ba / 917 à 924 : Léon Gambetta. Classement chronologique. 1869–1883.
Ba / 1076 et 1077 : Jules Ferry. 1872–1910.
Ba / 1462 : Elections diverses. Réunions. 1889.
Ba / 1502 : Anarchistes. Propagande par la parole. 1882–1892
Ba / 1520 : Réunions. Dossier de principe. Rapport : Observations sur la pratique de la loi du 6 juin 1868, 27 septembre 1875.
Ba / 1522 : Meetings divers. 1884–1885.
Ba / 1527 : Meeting projeté pour 1884. 1883
Ba / 1528 : Meetings divers. 1883–1887.
Ba / 1531 : Meetings divers. 1891–1893.
Ba / 1533 : Meetings divers. 1884–1887.
Ba / 1644 : Meetings communistes. Place de la Réunion et Pré-saint-Gervais. 1922
Ba / 1956 : S.F.I.O. 1937–1938.
Ba / 1939 : Réunions et soirées artistiques. P.C.F. 1924–1928.
Ba / 1964 : Partis politiques, généralités. 1930–1943

Archives départementales

Archives de Paris

D3U9 / Registre 34 : Jugements de la Cour d'Appel de Paris. 1869.
Perotin / 10441 / 64 / 2 / 73 : Cabinet du Préfet. Opposition politique dans les communes. 1920–1933.
Perotin / 10441 / 64 / 2 / 75 : Cabinet du Préfet. Concession de locaux municipaux et scolaires dans les communes du département. 1936–1939.
Perotin / 10441 / 57 / 1 / 33 : Cabinet du Préfet. Mise à disposition des locaux scolaires pour les comptes-rendus de mandat des députés. 1938–1939.

Archives départementales des Bouches-du-Rhône

1 M / 637 : Opinion publique. Partis, mouvements politiques. 1853–1867.
1 M / 792 : Opinion publique. Partis, mouvements politiques. 1870–1873.
1 M / 863 à 870 : Partis et mouvements politiques. Réunions et associations. 1880–1899.
1 M / 876 à 877 : Partis et mouvements politiques. Réunions et associations. 1906–1911.
L 2.026 à 2.031 : Registres des délibérations de la société des « Antipolitiques » d'Aix (variations de l'appellation du club selon les registres). 1790–1794.
L 2.035 : Règlement de la Société des Antipolitiques d'Aix. 1794.
L 2.071 : Société des Amis de la Liberté et de l'Egalité de Marseille, procès-verbaux de délibérations. 1793

Archives départementales de Haute-Savoie

1 M / 114 à 117 : Affiches à caractère politique et général. 1920–1939.
4 M / 117 : Mesures prises lors de réunions, meetings et manifestations publiques. 1911–1937
4 M / 179 : Surveillance des partis politiques. 1870–1940.

Archives départementales de l'Isère

55 M / 3 à 5 : Police générale. Réunions publiques et privées, conférences. 1909–1939
77 M / 1 à 3 : Sûreté générale. Communistes. 1922–1940 (sauf années 1937–1939)

Archives départementales du Rhône

4 M / 261 : Procès-verbaux de réunions de partis politiques. 1926–1939
4M / 268 : Réunions électorales. 1913–1926
4M / 269 : Réunions électorales. 1927–1939

Archives départementales de Seine-Maritime

1 M / 182 : Affaires politiques. Dossiers : réunions publiques, 1878; opposition, républicains, 1872; opposition, banquets bonapartistes, 1875.
1 M / 183 : Affaires politiques. Réunions publiques. Instructions générales. 1871–1935.
4 M / 349 : Réunions. Déclarations et autorisations de réunions et de conférences. 1897–1919.
4 M / 364 : Réunions. Partis politiques. Partis républicains. 1886.

Archives départementales du Vaucluse

6 L / 5 : Société des Amis de la Constitution de Courthézon. Registre des délibérations. 1791–1794.

Bibliothèque Historique de la Ville de Paris

Na / Ms 155 : Réunions publiques à Paris. 1868–1870.

Bibliothèque Municipale de Marseille

Ms 1373 : Procès-verbaux des séances du club des Amis de la Constitution d'Apt (variations de l'appellation du club selon les cahiers). 1791–1794.

Office Universitaire de Recherche Socialiste

Photographies du rassemblement S.F.I.O. au stade vélodrome de Creil le 5 juillet 1936. Déposées par le fils de Jean Biondi, orateur à ce meeting.

Agence Magnum

Photos David Seymour et Robert Capa.

Agence Roger Viollet

Politique française. 1919–1939. EV Partis socialiste et radical-socialiste. Congrès, locaux, journaux.
Politique française. 1919–1939. EV PCF. Défilés, manifestations, meetings.

Espace Albert Kahn

'Paris vu par les opérateurs d'Albert Kahn, 1913–1928': manifestation communiste contre la guerre du Maroc à Clichy, 2 août 1925; manifestation en faveur de Sacco et Vanzetti, 7 août 1927.

Vidéothèque de Paris

Actualités Gaumont, août 1936: commémoration au Vel'd'hiv' du 22ème anniversaire de la mort de Jean Jaurès; grand rassemblement de la paix à Saint-Cloud
La vie est à nous, Jean Renoir, 1936.
Le temps des cerises, Jean-Paul Dreyfus, 1937.

II. Printed Sources

Legislative Debates

Débats au Corps Législatif précédant l'adoption de la loi du 6 juin 1868 sur les réunions publiques, publiés dans *Le Moniteur Universel*.
Débats à la Chambres des députés et au Sénat précédant l'adoption de la loi du 30 juin 1881 sur la liberté de réunion, publiés au *Journal Officiel*.
Proposition de loi « tendant à assurer la liberté des réunions électorales », 1889, annexe no. 339, publiée au *Journal Officiel* (Projets de lois, propositions et rapports).
Proposition de loi « ayant pour objet l'organisation démocratique du suffrage universel », séance du 21 décembre 1906, publiée au *Journal Officiel* (Documents parlementaires. Chambre).
Débats à la Chambres des députés et au Sénat précédant l'adoption de la loi du 29 mars 1907 relative aux réunions publiques, publiés au Journal Officiel.

Journals

For the Second Empire:

Le Charivari (juin 1868–juin 1869)
Le Constitutionnel (juin 1868–juin 1869)
Le Figaro (juin 1868–juin 1869)
La Gazette de France (juin 1868–juin 1869)
Le Journal des Débats (juin 1868–juin 1869)
Le Journal de Paris (juin 1868–juin 1869)
La Lanterne (juin 1868–juin 1869)
Le Monde illustré (juin 1868–juin 1869)
Le Moniteur Universel (janvier–juin 1869. NB: a cessé d'être le *journal officiel* de l'Empire)
Le Peuple (1869)
La Presse (juin 1868–juin 1869)
Le Rappel (mai–juin 1869)
Le Réfractaire (1869)
Le Réveil (juin 1868–juin 1869)
Le Siècle (juin 1868–juin 1869)
La Tribune populaire illustrée (2 numéros, février 1869)
L'Union (juin 1868–juin 1869)

For the Third Republic:

L'Action Française (octobre 1936; mars 1937)
L'Almanach populaire, publication annuelle du parti socialiste (1937–1940).
Bulletin d'information du Parti Communiste (1925–1929)
Les Cahiers du propagandiste, publication mensuelle de documentation socialiste (1935–1939).

La Croix (1889)
Le Figaro (juin 1881–juin 1882; 1889; mars 1937)
L'Humanité (octobre 1936; mars 1937; 1938)
Le Journal des Débats (juin 1881–juin 1882; 1889)
La Justice (juin 1881–juin 1882; 1889)
Le Matin (1889)
L'Oeuvre (octobre 1936)
La Petite République Française (juin 1881–juin 1882)
Le Populaire (octobre 1936; mars 1937; 1938)
Le Rappel (juin 1881–juin 1882)
Le Soleil (juin 1881–juin 1882)
La Vie socialiste (1926–1933)

Others:

L'Illustration (1843–1909; 1932–1939)
La Revue des deux Mondes (1855–1910)
Le Temps (1861–1910; octobre 1936; mars 1937; articles de J. Barthélémy, 1936–1937)

Index

anarchism 52–3, 186–96
  assemblies and 18, 39, 52, 63, 64, 85, 89, 181–2, 189–90, 195–6
    public highway disorder and 63
    republican ideal, compatibility with 189–90
  assembly obstruction and 2, 38, 181–2, 183, 185, 186, 187, 197
  press treatment of 52, 53, 64, 74
  as reaction to republicanism 190–1, 193
  republican view of 63, 77, 190–1
    'bad mores' argument and 178
  violence, incitement/justification of 190–7, 199
    legal reaction to 193–5
    socialist militants, fights with 196–7
anti-semitism 186, 188, 198–200, 208, 211, 212, 262
  see also Dreyfus affair; nationalism
assemblies, political
  banning of 264–76
    administrative power, use of 268–70
    authorisation system and 272
    erroneous definitional substitution and 267–8
    1930s protests and 268–70
  concept/definition of 16–17, 95, 267
    criteria of 17
    Paganon interpretation and 267–8
  costs of 56–8, 129–30
    democratic critique of 57
    meeting-places and 56, 57, 130
  defined place of 7, 56–7, 58–62, 246, 247, 248, 277
    as a covered place 58–61, 247

  interwar period and 250
  electoral *see* electoral assemblies
  organisation of speeches in 29, 83–90
    bureaux, use of 38, 43, 81, 83–5, 189
    chairmen, role of 83, 85–6, 88
  republican view of *see* under republicanism
  1930s crises of 16, 18, 245, 263, 271, 256, 263
    see also demonstrations; under freedom of assembly
  women's participation in 53, 54–7
    see also electoral assemblies; rallies, political
assemblies, private 66–70, 83, 86, 87–8, 102, 122, 124–5, 127, 264
  confusion with public assemblies and 264–5
  debate and 86–7
  definition of 67
  distinguishing criteria and 67–9, 264
  electoral assemblies and 107, 124–6, 127
  political use of 69
associations, political 15, 17, 90–1, 94–7, 98–100
  assembly, confusion with 17, 91, 94, 94–7, 100, 264
    republican distinction and 91, 96, 99–100
  definition of (1901 law) 17, 90–1, 100
  deliberative forms of 98
  fear of 98
  political parties and 100
  republican tolerance of (1880–90) 90–1

as threat to democracy 91
see also freedom of assembly
banquets, political 18, 24–5, 267, 270
  as a form of assembly 24, 124
  1848 banquet campaign and 24
Barthélémy, J. 263, 264, 265, 268, 270, 272, 276
Blanc, L. 38, 41, 45, 46, 47, 98, 128, 131, 137, 140, 153
  absolute freedom of assembly, view of 45, 47, 60, 95, 153
  association as different 95, 98
blanquists 2, 38, 130, 196
Blum, L. 225, 229, 231–5, 254, 261, 262, 271, 274
Bonapartists 18, 85, 129, 165, 170, 171–2
Boulanger, General 129, 134–6, 139, 182, 185, 198
Boulangists 113, 114, 129, 134–6, 179, 192, 197
  assemblies of 18, 129–30, 134–6, 139, 140
  obstructionism and 178, 179, 182–3, 184, 185, 186–7
  violence and 197–8, 201
  republican view of 178, 180, 182
Britain
  Ballot Act 1872 5
  freedom of assembly in 148
    British mores and 148–9, 150
  public assemblies in 82, 83, 150
  public order in 150

citizenship education
  apprenticeship and 4, 9, 10, 147, 150, 151, 152, 154, 177, 279
  assemblies, role in 9, 11, 14, 146, 153, 159, 160, 176, 279
  mores and rights debate 147–50, 152
    British/French comparisons 148–50, 153
  republican notion/ideal of 9–11, 12, 18, 146–8, 163

civic immaturity and 146–7, 148, 151, 152
  emotions and reason in 163, 170–6, 279
  as moral education 148
  models of conduct and 158, 161–2
  mores of freedom, learning of 151–4, 158, 159
  see also under Gambetta, L.
clubs 20–6, 27, 30, 89–96, 98, 159–60, 161
  assemblies known as 20, 30–1, 94, 159
  as associations and 93, 94, 96–7, 160
  as hybrid mix with assemblies 96–7
  as a citizen's right 25, 26
  1848 revolutionary 25–7, 92–3, 94
  Jacobin 20–1, 93, 94
  'red clubs' and 29
  use of term and 26, 97
  see also under Paris Commune
collective action 15–16, 245, 250
  assemblies, place in 16
  political rallies and 244
  in public places 246–8
  collectivists 38, 78, 79
communism 51, 78, 171
  assemblies and 29, 50, 55, 75 n.13, 160, 161, 264
  outside spaces, use of 247, 248–9
  use of spectacle in 235
  Parti Communiste Française (PCF) 18, 217, 227–8
  anti-fascist rallies and 258
  posters and advertising 222–4, 226
  PSF duels and counter-demonstrations 273–6
  rallies of 217, 222, 236, 237, 238, 243, 246, 268–70, 272, 273
  street protest and 248–9, 250–1, 252–3

use of theatre and cinema 236, 237, 238
contradictory assemblies 3, 4, 12, 78, 81–3, 89, 109, 121, 278
  debate, nature of in 83–4, 85, 86, 88
  deliberation, ideal of and 89, 178
  elections, role in 82
  press views of 83
  rallies as replacement of 217
crowds 6–7, 211–14
  as an assembly public 211
  fear of 6, 7, 62
  street demonstrations and 219
  theories of 6
  transition to 'public' 212
  see also demonstrations; public space; rallies, political

deliberation 4, 5, 146, 177–8
  assemblies, republican promotion of 72, 73–4, 77, 83, 145–7, 177–8
    force of reason in 73, 74, 75–6, 277
    political passions, direction 71, 73–4, 147
  1880s–90s resistance to 188
  public opinion formation and 9, 83, 278
  rejection of harmful ideology and 77
  role in public decision making 16, 80–1
deliberative democracy and 4, 72, 74, 76–7, 146
  consensus and 76–7, 79
  ideal speech situation and 74, 76
  as 'school for democracy' 146
demonstrations 16, 17, 245, 246–52, 262–3
  counter-demonstrations and 252–63, 275
    as blackmail to ban assemblies 271, 273
    Clichy riots (1937) and 261–3, 271, 272
    fascist/nationalist/socialist groups and 258, 260
    government credibility, undermining of 262–3
    policing of 261, 261–2
    press reporting of 260–1
  evocation of the multitude and 219
  freedom of assembly, effect on 263–4
    as confusion with association 264
    definition confusion and 267–8
    public/private assemblies distinction and 264
  organisation of 248
  street/public highways use and 245, 246–51, 258
    freedom of assembly, effect on 245
  see also public space; rallies, political
despotism 36, 41, 43, 154
Dreyfus affair 87, 178, 183–4, 188, 196, 198–208

electoral assemblies 28, 29, 30, 101–8, 278
  candidates and
    official candidates, system of 119, 120–2
    presentation/image/eloquence and 112, 117, 126–8
    social origins, change in 117–20
    vote of confidence and 112–14
  claquers and 128, 130
  costs of 128–30
  definitions of 101
  electoral forecasting and 103, 132–43
  organisation of 109–14, 119, 129–33, 278
    candidate support and 125–6
    candidate withdrawal and 114
    electoral committees 130–3
    noise, problem of 125–8, 140–1

see also under violence and
dissent
police role in 133–4, 135, 137–42
opinion, surveillance of 133–4,
135, 136, 137, 140, 142
reports, analysis in 138–42
republican critique of 152–4
speech supervision and 133
public opinion formation and 101,
103, 104, 115
representation, role in 101, 102–3,
114
candidate questioning and 115
as citizen enlightenment 104–5,
106
participant's contributions and 116
universal suffrage, effect on 104,
105, 106, 108, 109
deliberative assemblies and 109

fascism 226, 258, 261–3, 274
Front populaire 249–50, 259–64,
268, 270, 274
Clichy riots (1937) and 259–3,
271, 272, 276
street demonstrations and 249–50
freedom of assembly 17, 18
association, freedom of and 96–98
confusion with and 17, 22, 27,
94, 95–7, 264
congregations, battle against
98–9, 100
law, respect for and 148–9
blurring of public/private distinction
and 264–5
clubs, effect on 93
counter-demonstrations as threat to
259, 262–3
see also demonstrations
as a democratic right 50, 263, 264,
277
free discussion and 71–9
repression of 76, 78–9, 193–4
revolutionary ideas and 73–4, 79
see also deliberation

as a natural right and 45–7
law as protection of 47–8
1930s' crises and legal banning of
263–76
authoritarian reaction to 264–6
Clichy riots (1937) and 260–3,
271, 272
fascist mobilisation and 263,
267, 270, 274, 276
1933 Benjamin judgement and
265–6
1936 Bucard judgement and 267
1937 Bijadoux judgement and
267
Paganon Memorandum interpretation and 267–8, 270
political rallies and 245
public opinion, development of and
35, 95, 277
public order issue and 7–8, 41–5,
48, 149–50
municipal law and 41–5
rights and regulation debate and
46
see also under violence and
dissent
republican discourse of 6, 14, 78,
145, 148, 149–52, 277
mores and rights debate in
147–8, 150, 188
see also civic education
French Revolution 19–22, 90, 92
Constitution 1791 and 19, 20
freedom of assembly, development
of 19–20, 21
control and limitation measures 20
Le Chapelier law (1791) and 20
Jacobin societies and 20–1, 23
right of assembly and 19–20, 21
women's participation in 54

Gambetta, L. 87–8, 94, 105, 124, 136,
148, 153, 163–76
assembly speeches of 87–8, 110,
163–76

use of emotion in 163–4, 165–6, 167, 169, 170–1, 173–6, 279
eloquence of 163, 164, 165–6, 167–70, 173–4, 176
as master of self and passions 164, 168
as republican ideal 164, 174–6
an educator of reason and 173–4

legitimists 17, 18, 122–6, 141, 171, 173
assemblies of 18, 86, 125–6
Legrand, L. 38, 41

Naquet, A. 37–8, 41, 42, 54, 60–1, 62, 103, 105, 169, 180
freedom of assembly, arguments for 37, 45, 46, 47, 73, 96, 153
freedom of association and 96, 97, 98
Opportunism and 37
nationalists 178, 183, 192, 196, 198, 258
assemblies of 18, 186, 187, 188
fascism, synthesis with 258
L'Action française 255, 256, *257*, 258, 260, 261, 262, 270, 273
republican view of 178
see also anti-semitism; Dreyfus affair

obstructionism 165, 180–7, 252–6
counter-demonstrations and 256–63
as government provocation 188
use of police and 186
as premeditated 181
use of singing and 185
see also under anarchism; Boulangists; socialism; violence and dissent

Paris Commune 4, 6, 7, 18, 29, 30–1, 63, 65, 171, 230, 238
club assemblies, role in 30–1, 92–3
parties, political
formation of 100, 218, 264
rallies, role in cohesion of 217
role of the spectacle in 235
use of spectacle in meetings of 235
see also rallies, political
popular sovereignty 2, 36, 37, 38
press, the
assemblies, presentation of 5, 16, 24, 38–9, 41–53, 60, 135
downgrading/exaggeration and 50–1, 52, 53
liberal support for 41, 51–2
right to assemble, support for 51, 52, 46
women, attitudes to 54–6
electoral forecasting and 133, 135
freedom of 36, 41, 48–53, 108
legal prosecution and 52–3
legislation and 48
political rallies and 220–2, 231–2
campaigning and mobilisation by 220–2
description of crowds/multitude 219–21, 230–1
party propaganda and 220, 222
public passion, portrayal of 231–2
public order, threat presentation and 63–4
public opinion 7–9, 35–7
assemblies, role in forming 7–8, 35, 41, 58, 133, 163
opinion evaluation and 117, 133–5
reason, development of and 71, 74, 278
use of meeting rooms and 58
democracy, necessity for 35, 41
consensus and 71–2
elitist/democratic vision and 48–9
see also deliberation
distrust of 36
notions of 8–9
popular opinion, difference with 8

republican promotion of 8, 14, 35, 278
  common good/social harmony and 71, 72
public order 2, 27, 38, 41, 48, 58, 63, 193
  assemblies and 7, 29, 43, 44, 46, 51, 84, 140, 150, 156, 258, 259, 264–6
    banning of 267, 269, 270–3
    group militarisation and 255–6
    outside places, use of 247
    policing and 59–60, 65, 133–4, 136, 137–42, 186, 259
    street spillover and 59–62, 205, 280
    see also obstructionism
  counter-demonstrations and 259–60, 262–3
  mass participation and 7–8, 36, 48
  see also obstructionism; violence and dissent
public space
  assemblies and 7, 12, 47, 66, 246, 248–51, 277
    in covered/closed room and 58–61, 246
    departure of the audience, rules on 259
    loudspeaker use and 125, 181, 248
    processions, organisation of 250–1, 259
    republican view of 62–6, 277
  definition of 6
  emotions/passions, expression of 11, 63, 65
  press freedom and 48
  public thoroughfare, defining of 246–7, 248
  republican notion of 2, 11–12, 57–9
    as masculine 56
  street as place of assembly and 59–62, 66, 246, 258–9
    communist rallies and 246, 248–9

socialists/anarchists, use of 63, 258
see also demonstrations

rallies, political 217–44, 248, 262, 277, 279, 280
  advertising, importance of 218, 226
    cars and loudspeakers, use of 226
    leaflet distribution and 225
    posters, use of 222–5, 227, 254
    slogans, use of 226–7
    speaker announcements and 226–7
  audience size as success 218, 219, 234, 279
    description of the room and 219–20
  police observation reports of 228, 229, 233, 234–5, 237, 242, 251
    descriptive role of 228
    public expressions of support and 229, 244
  press reports of
    collective emotion and 232–4
    partisan presentations and 231–2, 233
    propaganda use and 219–22
    speakers' descriptions and 231–2
  public expressions of support 229–34, 279
    clapping/chants and slogans 229–30, 244
    leader portraits and 242
    partisan songs and 230, 238–9
  streets, use of 246, 248
    announcements and 226
    loudspeakers and 226, 248, 253
    processions and 251
    public order fears and 251
    see also demonstrations
  theatralisation of 234
    banners and decorations 239–40, 241
    cinema and 237–9
    image presentations 242–3

Index | 313

platform boundaries and 243
reaction, provocation of 234–5
speakers, staging of 243–4
spectacle, use of 234, 235–6
symbolism, use of 234, 240–1
see also communism; demonstrations

republicanism
absolute freedom and 38, 45, 46–7, 61, 95, 153, 181, 265
assemblies, participation role of 2, 5, 73–4, 77, 83, 145–7, 278
emotion, role of in 279
ideal model of 7, 8 n.27, 91, 158, 161
political mores, civilisation of 278, 279
see also civic education; deliberation
authoritarianism and 154, 156, 279
police power, critique of 154–7
democracy, notion of and 6, 35, 79
public opinion and 35, 36–7, 45, 71, 79–80
role of assemblies in 2, 13, 35, 71, 79, 146, 154
public order, views of 7–8
public highway use and 63
public space, use of and 59–63, 277
reason, faith in 71, 74, 75–6, 147, 187, 194, 279
anarchist violence, effect on 194–5
consensus/common sense and 71–2, 75, 77, 79, 278

SFIO (*Section Française de l'Internationale Ouvrière*) 18, 217, 235
leaflets and advertising 222–4, 226
press propaganda and 220–1
public expressions of support for 229–30
banners and symbolism 240

partisan songs and 238
rallies of 217, 219, 220, 222, 238–40, 242, 251, 253, 269
PCF obstruction of 253–6
use of theatre and cinema 237–8, 239
Simon, Jules 28, 41, 43, 71, 74, 76, 94, 120, 122, 127, 160, 162, 188, 197
socialism
assemblies and 18, 29, 30, 39, 50, 55, 57, 63, 64, 75 n.13, 77–8, 109, 113–14, 131, 160, 161, 196, 253
deliberation, role of and 79–80
didactic type of 218
public highway disorder and 61, 62, 63
assembly obstruction and 52, 187, 196, 197
PCF and 253–6
violence and 198, 256
party propaganda, role of 218
political rallies and 218, 235, 241, 243, 254
propaganda techniques and 235
see also under SFIO
press attitudes and 52, 53, 63, 181, 197
propaganda rallies of 217
republican view of 63, 76, 77, 79, 136, 178
women's rights and 54, 55
see also Paris Commune

United States
deliberation and 5
public assemblies in 5, 82, 83, 134, 136
opinion surveillance and 136
rallies in 218

violence and dissent 12, 38–9, 65, 133, 153, 154, 156–7, 171, 176, 177–214, 280
anti-semitism and 186, 188,

198–200, 208, 211, 212, 262
counter-demonstrations and 261,
  262, 271
large cities and 188
in political discourse 63–5, 74, 75,
  157–8, 188, 191, 194–5, 196
1880s–90s obstructionism and *see*
  obstructionism
rallies, political and 254–6
republican argument from reason
  and 74, 146, 187, 188–9, 194–5,
  200, 277
police/government promotion of
  156–8, 200
press reactions to 38–9, 63, 65,
  157–8, 186–7, 190, 197
streets, debate on use of 59–63, 65,
  188, 246–7
see also anarchism; Dreyfus affair;
  public order